WATER LAW
IN A NUTSHELL®

FIFTH EDITION

by

DAVID H. GETCHES
Late Dean and Raphael J. Moses Professor of
Natural Resources Law
University of Colorado Law School

SANDRA B. ZELLMER
Robert B. Daugherty Professor of Law
University of Nebraska College of Law

ADELL L. AMOS
Associate Dean for Academic Affairs &
Associate Professor
James O. and Alfred T. Goodwin Senior Fellow
University of Oregon School of Law

WEST
ACADEMIC
PUBLISHING

This book is dedicated to

David Getches

Mentor, Leader, Scholar, and Inspiration
to generations of natural resources lawyers

ACKNOWLEDGMENTS

Sandra Zellmer is deeply grateful to David Getches for his guidance and his monumental contribution to the field of water law. She also thanks the University of Nebraska College of Law for its generous scholarship stipend, the University of Colorado Law School for supporting her as a visiting scholar-in-residence during the preparation of this manuscript, and Nebraska law students Samantha Staley and Katherine Miller for their outstanding research assistance.

Adell Amos also extends her gratitude to David Getches for years of dedication to teaching and advancing the field of water law. She would like to thank the superb research assistants from University of Oregon School of Law Nate Bellinger, James Bunts, Will Carlon, Matt Cline, Elena Domingo, Nate Gurol, Malia Losordo, Jamie McCleod, Wes Knoll, and Victoria Wilder as well as the administrative support of Jill Elizabeth and the Environmental and Natural Resources Law Center, particularly Emily Johnson. She would like to dedicate this version of the Nutshell to her new baby girl, Mildred, born in August of 2014 during the last months of preparing this manuscript.

Both authors are grateful to the Rocky Mountain Mineral Law Foundation for providing a research grant to complete this project.

SANDRA ZELLMER
ADELL AMOS

FOREWORD TO THE FIFTH EDITION

It is somewhat unusual for an area of law to be defined by a particular resource, but water is unique in the diversity and importance of the needs it fills. Water quenches our thirst, gives life to essential food crops, furnishes habitat to fish and wildlife, produces power, and satisfies recreational and aesthetic needs. Although it is one of the most plentiful substances, it is considered precious because there is not always enough fresh water of the right quality in the right place at the right time. There is keen competition among water users. The same stream may be sought by a municipality for domestic use, a farmer for irrigation, a factory for carrying away waste, a power plant for cooling, boaters and fishers for recreation, and conservation interests for preservation of stream flows and the fish and wildlife species that rely on them.

A decision to use water for a particular purpose can have far-reaching impacts. For instance, transporting water from a rural area across a mountain range to a city may provide water to sustain the city's population, but it may also force a decline in agricultural productivity and the farming community built on it, facilitate more rapid growth in the importing city, prevent future development of the exporting rural area, curtail recreational opportunities, make sewage treatment more difficult as streamflows to dilute wastewater discharges are diminished, deprive the exporting area of groundwater recharge, and cause ecological changes in both areas. Balancing these conflicting interests and demands is made ever more complex, challenging, and essential in the face of chronic drought cycles intensified by climate change.

The role of law is particularly important when so many varied needs must be recognized. More and more lawyers will be called upon to recognize and to resolve water rights conflicts. Although law students are the primary audience of this Nutshell, the growing demand for and interest among lawyers addressing water-related legal issues has guided us in preparing this edition.

This book is designed to support water law courses based on any of the major casebooks in the field; thus, nearly every principal case in each of the casebooks is discussed or at least cited. Much of the organizational scheme of the fourth edition has been retained, but we have taken some liberties to clarify, streamline, and highlight important emerging issues, such as the public trust doctrine, environmental interests, non-consumptive uses of water, federal reserved rights, conjunctive use and management of surface and groundwater resources, and interstate and international themes. Throughout the book, we have strived to remain true to the vision of Professor Getches. We are honored—and humbled—by the opportunity to follow in his footsteps, though of course we could never purport to fill his shoes.

SBZ
ALA

Jamestown, Colorado
Eugene, Oregon
June 2015

FOREWORD TO THE FOURTH EDITION

Water law is a growing area of attention for lawyers and policy makers throughout the country. It is more important than ever in the West and now, with population growth and climate change, the East has begun to feel the pressure of limits that were long familiar in less humid regions. It is predictable that more lawyers in more regions of the country will be called upon to recognize and to resolve water rights issues. Although the primary audience of this book is law students, the growing demand for and interest among lawyers addressing water law issues has also guided this revision.

From the early days of western expansion, water law has been a hot topic in the semi-arid regions of the United States. Initially, agriculture and mining and later the settlement of towns and cities demanded water from scarce seasonal supplies. In many areas water users years ago established legal rights to take the full capacity of nearby rivers. Today, the West is the most urbanized region of the country and cities seek to import water from afar and enter into transactions to buy or lease water rights from farmers who hold valuable old water rights. The impacts of chronic drought cycles are now exacerbated by climate change.

Especially important in the eastern states is the demand placed on groundwater, leading to more exacting administration by state officials and more conflicts among users. Municipal groundwater pumping often interferes with small wells. In the last decade one of the most active areas of water law in the West has been conflict over the use of groundwater that depletes surface supplies of water users taking their water directly from rivers.

Another area that continues to increase in importance is the use of water for recreation and fish and wildlife as the economic value of those uses competes with the value of agriculture and other uses that have well-established rights. This is part of a larger effort to allocate water—traditionally considered a public resource—consistent with "the public interest." Water administrators in West and East alike are challenged to determine and to apply public interest criteria in issuing water rights permits. Interstate conflict over shared rivers continues, with major tensions over the Colorado River and several other rivers of the Southeast.

All of these issues are treated in this revision, at least with the brevity suggested by the title of the book and the series of which is a part. The robust activity in the field in recent years has resulted in the addition of citations to more than fifty new cases and many statutory cites, even following a conservative approach to including only the most important or illustrative cases. Because the book is designed to support courses based on any of the three major casebooks in the field, nearly every principal case in each of those books is cited or discussed. This edition retains the organization of earlier editions, which has drawn compliments from students and their professors. Only cursory treatment is given to the related field of water pollution law. That issue is thoroughly treated elsewhere, such as in *Environmental Law in a Nutshell.*

As with earlier editions, the updating of sources has been painstakingly purused by talented research assistants at the University of Colorado. In particular, I am grateful to Amy Steinfeld, Class of 2005, Craig Corona, Class of 2006, Janel Chin, Class of 2007, and Susie Tehlirian, Class of 2008. The continuing attention and assistance of Amy Steinfeld long after graduating from law school and beginning an active water law practice in California has been invaluable and has given continuity, currency, and accuracy to this book. My assistant Douglas Enzor has assisted the effort by carefully reviewing and formatting and the chapters. Mr. Enzor also supervised proofreading, cite-checking and indexing by Matthew Hoppe, Class of 2009, and William Wombacher, Class of 2010. I thank all of these fine professionals for making the book possible.

DHG

Boulder, Colorado
October 2008

FOREWORD TO THE THIRD EDITION

When the first edition of this book appeared in 1984, there was a dearth of current supplemental sources available to students or lawyers to assist them in gaining a basic understanding of water law. That changed with the appearance in 1988 of the treatise by A. Dan Tarlock entitled *Law of Water Rights and Resources* and a thorough revision of the multi-volume work *Water and Water Rights* edited by Robert E. Beck. Because of favorable response from practicing lawyers as well as students, this edition continues to address the fundamentals of water law in a way that will be useful to both sets of readers. Deeper treatment can be provided by the two treatises.

Over one hundred case citations have been added to this edition of the *Nutshell*. It is current through the summer of 1996. As in the previous edition, an effort was made to include virtually every principal case found in the three leading law school casebooks: Tarlock, Corbridge & Getches, *Water Resources Management* (Fourth Edition, 1993), Gould & Grant, *Water Law* (Fifth Edition, 1995), and Sax, Abrams & Thompson, *Legal Control of Water Resources* (Second Edition, 1991).

This third edition of *Water Law in a Nutshell* has been revised to capture the latest developments in this fast-moving field. Competition for water in the western United States has always been keen. Now, shortages and conflicting uses are felt more frequently in the East as a result of urbanization and population growth. The competition for water is compounded as the value of water flowing in streams for recreation and for ecological integrity increases.

State laws reflect the pressures for accommodating diverse and expanding water uses. Courts, agencies, and legislatures are beginning to weigh issues of public interest and environmental considerations in water decisions. To cope with rising demands, states are tightening their administration of water rights, insisting on greater efficiency and conservation, and many are adjudicating all the rights in a river basin to ensure more certainty and to cull out unused and over-stated rights. The law of surface use continues to change in response to recreational demands. States are also turning more to the conjunctive management of groundwater and surface water to get optimum use out of their available water resources. The basic principles of riparian and appropriation law have not changed greatly. Indeed, today they are less often determinative of disputes than regulatory and administrative requirements of permit statutes. One exception is the doctrine of beneficial use in prior appropriation law which is slowly evolving to reflect a changing concept of the kinds of water uses that are "beneficial" to society.

The role of federal law is more pervasive than ever in deciding the extent to which water can be allocated and used for particular purposes. Because states typically have been slow to incorporate environmental and other public concerns in their water laws, federal laws have filled some of the gaps. Not only water quality protection under the Clean Water Act, but provisions that protect wetlands and waterways from being filled in or drained, and laws like the Endangered Species Act, profoundly influence how and where water is used. Meanwhile, the predominant federal role in financing and building water projects through most of this century has faded in relative importance.

I am greatly indebted to my student research assistants at the University of Colorado School of Law for their excellent support. Christopher Wirth (Class of '97) was careful and untiring in searching out new developments in the law and contributed to the organization and editing of the book. Morgan Word (Class of '97) did solid research work and Scott Miller (Class of '98) assisted in the editing.

DHG

Boulder, Colorado
August, 1996

FOREWORD TO THE SECOND EDITION

Water law has been an especially active field since the first edition of *Water Law in a Nutshell*. There have been court decisions in hundreds of cases and statutory changes in several states. In addition, scholarship in the field has been expanding. There are now three water law casebooks in use in law schools and a new treatise entitled *Law of Water Rights and Resources* by Professor A. Dan Tarlock. More law review articles are being written than ever before in water law.

This second edition represents a revision of the first in light of changes in the law through late 1989. Citations appear at relevant places to nearly all of the principal cases appearing in Meyers, Tarlock, Corbridge, and Getches, *Water Resource Management* (Third Edition, 1988), Trelease and Gould, *Water Law* (4th Edition, 1986), Sax and Abrams, *Legal Control of Water Resources* (1986). And a new chapter has been added on surface use of waters in light of the increased importance of public recreational water uses. Throughout this edition, wherever appropriate, information has been expanded on instream flow protection, water quality and public interest concerns in water use and water allocation. This reflects the growing interest in those matters throughout the country. For thorough treatment of water pollution control, however, readers are urged to look to other sources, including *Environmental Law in a Nutshell.*

I am indebted to research assistants from the University of Colorado School of Law for their work in making this edition possible. Ellen Ostheimer Creagar and Michael James Grode spent many hours to ensure the accuracy and currency of this edition and edited the manuscript with care. I am also grateful to Elizabeth Thomas and John S. Hajdik for their assistance earlier in the project.

DHG

Escazu, Costa Rica
April, 1990

FOREWORD TO THE FIRST EDITION

In spite of all its interesting issues and its great practical importance, water law is a field in which there is a dearth of supplemental sources that are useful to students. A few voluminous treatises are available to aid the practitioner in finding answers to difficult questions. But there is no basic source. This book is a modest effort at providing a supple. mental source for the student of water law. It also should serve as an orientation device for lawyers who do not regularly practice in the field and for non-lawyers who need a background in the subject.

The study of water is complicated by the widely differing systems that exist in the several states. No attempt is made here to draw together and explicate the complete law of any particular state. This book states the general rules that apply within major systems of water law and attempts to give examples of special rules applicable in particular states. Generally, the statutory and case law of the states is current through 1982, and relevant United States Supreme Court cases is current through July, 1983.

This book owes its existence to many people. A number of student research assistants at the University of Colorado School of Law worked on its preparation. Mark Cohen, Esq. worked diligently and made an important imprint on Chapters Two and Four. Richard Cauble, Esq. devoted many hours and made a fine, professional contribution to Chapters Five, Six, Eight, and Nine. George Jent, Esq., Stephen Ellis, Esq., Sharon Nelson, Esq. and Dary James all assisted with parts of Chapter Three.

The author is greatly indebted to Ann Amundson, Esq. for her splendid editorial assistance with the manuscript. My colleagues Professor Charles Wilkinson and Professor James Corbridge were kind enough to review portions of the draft manuscript and made important suggestions on how to improve it. I am very grateful to Anne Guthrie who typed and retyped successive drafts of the manuscript. Finally, I thank my wife Ann and my children on whose time this book was written.

DHG

Boulder, Colorado
February, 1984

OUTLINE

TABLE OF CASES

References are to Pages

WATER LAW
IN A NUTSHELL®

FIFTH EDITION

CHAPTER ONE

OVERVIEW AND INTRODUCTION TO WATER LAW

I. THE STUDY OF WATER LAW

The study of water law is, at one level, the study of property concepts, though rights to use water are peculiar. The fact that water is a moving resource necessarily limits the appropriateness of traditional concepts of ownership. Although water laws differ widely, notions of substantial public rights in the resource is a major theme across allocation regimes and throughout history. One result is that lawmakers have superimposed administrative systems in an attempt to regulate private interests in the use of water and to advance the broader public interest. Accordingly, the study of water law in the modern era requires a deep understanding of state and federal administrative law.

The field of water law also includes a study of the legal process. In many areas, the law is well-developed and it changes only slowly and at the periphery, but water law is a comparatively dynamic field. It illustrates how courts, legislatures, and agencies create and alter law according to physical and societal stimuli: one set of conditions drove the initial development of water law in the eastern United States, but different circumstances provoked changes in the West.

Three central questions arise in the study of water law: (1) how do the established legal systems for allocating rights to use water compare; (2) how well do these systems perform in equitably allocating this precious resource; and (3) what are appropriate solutions to the unresolved issues in water law. The law's success—in any field, but especially in water law—has to be evaluated in terms of what society needs from it.

We ask a great deal of water law. Since we depend on water for so much, it touches our deepest values. Besides its pervasive commercial importance, it is at the core of things we care the most about, such as health, sustenance, ecological integrity, and aesthetics. It even can provide community identity and spiritual satisfaction. Is it possible for any legal system to fulfill all these values and to provide stability and fairness? With so much at stake, water law presents unparalleled opportunities for analysis and creativity. It is an evolving field bristling with conflicts among our most cherished values.

II. LEGAL SYSTEMS FOR SURFACE WATER ALLOCATION

American jurisdictions can be grouped roughly into three legal systems governing surface water uses: riparian; prior appropriation; and hybrid states. This book treats the systems separately, so that readers may focus attention on issues within the system of particular interest. The systems, however, overlap and borrow from one another so that it is useful to compare them. Moreover, in operation, nearly all states rely on some sort of permitting system administered by a state agency, some of which share common attributes regardless of the particular doctrine followed in the state.

A. RIPARIAN RIGHTS

Landowners bordering a waterway are considered riparians. Their location gives them certain appurtenant rights under the laws of most states. Historically, a riparian location had special advantages because it enabled the owner to operate water-driven mills, to consume reasonable quantities of water, and to have access to the water's surface for boating, hunting, and fishing. There is generally no right to use water on non-riparian land.

Theoretically, early American decisions subscribed to a "natural flow" rule that gave every riparian owner the right to have water flow past the land undiminished in quantity or quality. In fact, the law as it was developed and enforced overcame the obvious objections to a rule that appeared to bar all consumption. From some of the earliest cases, the courts tempered the doctrine with "reasonable use" principles. Besides making exceptions for domestic uses, the early courts showed concern for existing users. Today, all riparian doctrine states (mostly located in the eastern United States) permit riparians to use water in a way that is "reasonable" relative to all other users. If there is insufficient water to satisfy the reasonable needs of all riparians, all must reduce usage of water in proportion to their rights.

Because riparian rights inhere in land ownership, they need not be exercised to be kept alive. Thus, a landowner may initiate new uses at any time and other users must adjust their uses accordingly.

The riparian doctrine, which is covered in Chapter Two, still applies to some extent in most of the eastern states, and it has some viability in the hybrid states covered in Chapter Four. However, riparian rules have been altered extensively by statute and case law so that no modern riparian state is governed simply by common law. Typically, riparians must obtain permits from a state agency in order to use water. In some states, permits may also be available to non-riparians.

Regardless of the legal doctrine that any particular state has adopted for allocating rights to use water, riparian landowners in all states have special rights to make use of the surface of waters adjoining their property. As Chapter Seven explains, if the waterway is considered navigable, however, riparians must tolerate certain surface uses by members of the public.

B. PRIOR APPROPRIATION

Two factors distinguish the legal system governing the use of surface water in the West. First, the West was settled on lands owned by the federal government; private and state ownership of land arose *after* many uses of water had commenced. Moreover, water is much more scarce throughout the arid lands west of the one-hundredth meridian.

The early miners, notably in California, sought water for their placer mining operations on the public lands. Miners could not assert riparian rights because they did not own the land. So the miners simply followed the same rule they used in resolving disputes over the minerals on the public domain: "first in time, first in right." The earliest miner to put the water to work had a right to continue using it to the exclusion of others.

Early court decisions in the West recognized water rights based on the miners' customs. The system worked satisfactorily for farmers, too, and became entrenched in the laws of virtually every western state. Rights, then, belong to anyone who puts water to a "beneficial use" anywhere (on riparian or non-riparian land), with superiority over anyone who later begins using water. Unlike riparian law, the development of water rights depends on usage and not on land ownership. Once a person puts water to a beneficial use and complies with any statutory requirements, a water right is perfected and remains valid so long as it continues to be used.

Given a choice between riparian and appropriation law, western states realized that riparian law, at least in its theoretical rigidity, did not fit local needs. Mines and farms needing water could not always be located on riparian lands in a region where waterways are few and far between. Development would have been frustrated if the fortunate landowners along streams could monopolize scarce water and hoard it, unused, until they felt like putting it to some use.

The prior appropriation doctrine governs surface water rights in about a dozen western states. As Chapter Three details, all "pure" appropriation states except Colorado require permits to appropriate water. An administrative agency issues permits based on requirements designed to protect other water users. Most state agencies also consider public interest concerns. Permits to transfer or change appropriative water rights will be issued if the ability of others to exercise vested water rights is not impaired.

C. HYBRID SYSTEMS

Several states originally recognized riparian rights, but later converted to a system of appropriation while preserving existing riparian rights. California is the leading hybrid state, but Oklahoma, Texas, and several others maintain aspects of both prior appropriation and riparianism. Hawaii's system is a unique combination of rights established under laws of the ancient Hawaiian Kingdom and recent statutes. Louisiana's water law is unique as well, as it is adapted from the French Civil Code. Hybrid systems are addressed in Chapter Four.

III. SPECIAL TYPES OF WATER

Most surface water available for use is subject to one of the three allocation schemes listed above, but certain waters fall outside those systems.

A. GROUNDWATER

Groundwater law grapples with two dominant concerns: depletion of essentially nonrenewable stores of underground water and conflicts among competing well-owners. In addition, contamination problems are increasingly troubling and give rise to legal issues.

Vast underground resources supply much of the nation's needs. The law was slow to develop systems for the allocation of rights and disputed claims to groundwater. Until recently, the dynamics of groundwater occurrence and movement were considered too uncertain, even too mysterious, to try to regulate. The failure of states to deal comprehensively with groundwater left overlying owners free to extract water from under their lands as they pleased.

Even when water beneath the surface of land was connected with a stream or lake, the law treated groundwater under a separate set of rules or no rules at all. More progressive legal approaches now integrate groundwater and surface water management. For example, when pumping from a well affects the rights of a person using stream water (or vice-versa) most states now administer the groundwater as a part of the surface water system.

Special rules are needed for groundwater management because waters may be withdrawn at a faster rate than they are replenished. Moreover, new wells may endanger existing wells by pumping groundwater from the same portion of the aquifer, even when the aquifer as a whole is not being withdrawn in excess of recharge rates. Some systems for allocating rights in groundwater are analogous to riparian rights (*e.g.,* correlative interests in water underlying neighboring parcels) and prior appropriation (*e.g.,* older wells are protected against depletion by newer pumpers).

Surface water allocation schemes, however, do not fit the physical realities of groundwater because they do not prevent rapid draining of an aquifer or protect the interests of neighboring pumpers. For example, appropriation concepts, if strictly applied, would give such complete protection to the first pumper that almost any new use could cause harm and be subject to legal objections. Consequently, special groundwater rules have been developed to balance competing interests of new and old well users and overlying owners, and to fulfill the state's obligation to prolong the life of the resource while allowing efficient usage. Many jurisdictions base their rules of liability between pumpers, and their criteria for granting permits for new wells, on a reasonable use standard, requiring that the relative utility of uses and equities of the parties be weighed. Groundwater laws are discussed in Chapter Five.

B. DIFFUSED SURFACE WATER

Ordinarily, only waters in natural streams are subject to surface water allocation systems. Besides groundwater, ocean water, water in the process of evaporation or transpiration, and precipitation are excluded from coverage.

Water that is on the surface of land because of rain, melting snow, or floods is called diffused surface water, and it is generally not subject to water allocation rules. Nearly all states allow diffused surface waters to be captured and used by a landowner without state regulation or limitation. However, legal rules concerning diffused surface waters were developed to determine liability between landowners when one attempts to drain such waters away from their property, thereby causing flooding and other problems for neighboring landowners. A majority of states allow landowners to divert or channel floodwaters away from their land if it is reasonable under the circumstances. These matters are covered in Chapter Six.

IV. PUBLIC RIGHTS

Water is legally and historically a public resource. Although private property rights can be perfected in the use of water, it remains essentially public; private rights are always incomplete and subject to the public's common needs. The earliest expression of these needs, still viable, involved navigation. Navigable waters remain subject to public access and use for boating, bathing, fishing, hunting, and, more recently, recreational and aesthetic interests. Private activity affecting the quantity and quality of water cannot lawfully interfere with the overriding public interest.

Chapter Seven deals with the special public rights that exist in the use of the surface of waterways, and the government's power and responsibility to recognize and maintain those rights. Public rights often turn on the definition of navigability, which is also the point of reference for ownership of the beds of waterways. Public rights to use the surface of non-navigable waters have also been recognized based on their capacity to support recreational uses, the public trust doctrine, and various state laws. Access rights to and from the shores of waterbodies where public surface rights exist have also been recognized.

Landowners and holders of water rights may assert claims for compensation under the Fifth Amendment takings clause of the U.S. Constitution when their interests are impacted by public rights. Takings claims are addressed in relevant sections of various chapters throughout this book, including Chapters Three (Prior Appropriation) and Six (Navigable Waters).

V. INTERGOVERNMENTAL PROBLEMS

Although the creation and regulation of rights to use water are primarily state affairs, there are important spheres of federal ownership and control. As noted above, federal navigational projects may affect the way state water laws operate; state and private interests may also be impacted by other exercises of congressional power, ranging from water development projects to environmental laws. In addition, the federal government has an interest in waters for use on public lands that have been reserved for special purposes, like parks, forests, and military bases, as well as lands held for federally recognized Indian reservations. The allocation of interstate water bodies is also governed by federal law.

A. RESERVED RIGHTS

The doctrine of federal reserved rights traces to early litigation over water for Indian reservations. The Supreme Court held that Indian tribes could not be deprived of sufficient water supplies to make the reservation a viable place to live and to farm. To hold otherwise would have defeated the purposes the government and the tribes had in mind in agreeing to move the Indians onto the reservation. The reserved rights doctrine recognized a right to sufficient water to fulfill the purposes of the reservation. The same principle was later applied to federal reservations of public lands.

Reserved water rights, which are covered in Chapter Eight, have a priority as of the date the reservation was established, whether or not water has ever been used. In a system in which water rights are based on prior use, assertions of reserved water rights can cause dislocations among those whose water rights have a priority date later than the establishment of the reservation. To ease the effects of the reserved rights doctrine, the courts have narrowly construed the extent of rights reserved and Congress has allowed reserved rights to be quantified in state courts in general stream adjudications.

B. FEDERAL ACTIONS AFFECTING STATE WATER RIGHTS

The United States is involved in activities that sometimes affect, and because of federal supremacy, preempt state water law. In the first sixty or seventy years of the twentieth century, the federal role in water resources involved giving technical and financial support to states and managing large federal water development projects for navigation, flood control, agriculture, power generation, and other uses. Since the 1970s, the federal government's involvement with water has turned away from development and become more focused on environmental regulation. Today, federal laws that protect endangered species, wetlands, and water quality are at least as important as state water laws in shaping water development and use.

C. INTERSTATE PROBLEMS

Tensions frequently exist among states that share access to rivers, lakes, and groundwater sources. Chapter Nine covers the various methods for resolving these tensions. Allocations among states can be made by compact—a negotiated interstate agreement made with the consent of Congress—or by adjudication in a judicial proceeding. In one instance, Congress passed legislation effectively allocating waters of the Colorado River among the abutting states, demonstrating a third means for interstate allocation.

In attempting to protect their water resources, states may not improperly inhibit interstate commerce by placing limits on exports. Water is considered an article of commerce and, as such, trade in it cannot be restricted by regulations that discriminate against interstate commerce.

VI. WATER INSTITUTIONS

Chapter Ten describes various types of organizations formed to develop and distribute water, ranging from public municipal water systems to private irrigation districts. These organizations come in many different forms and may be established under state or federal law. They are the operating entities that deliver most of the water in the country.

CHAPTER TWO
RIPARIAN RIGHTS

The term "riparian" is based on the Latin word for the bank of a stream (*ripa*). Thus, riparian rights to water exist for those who own land adjacent to a water source. In the eastern United States, primarily east of the one-hundredth meridian (a line running south through the middle of North Dakota into Texas), water rights are established based on principles of riparianism. Other states, primarily those west of or along the one-hundredth meridian, have a hybrid system based on some combination of riparian and prior appropriation doctrines. *See infra* Chapter Four.

Riparian law developed as a common law doctrine. In a riparian jurisdiction, the owner of land bordering a waterbody, (*i.e.*, the riparian owner), may make reasonable use of the water on the riparian land if the use does not interfere with reasonable uses of other riparian owners. Today, many eastern states have codified at least some principles of the common law into various statutory provisions. Some states have adopted more comprehensive statutory provisions and are commonly referred to as "regulated riparian" jurisdictions. Regulated riparian states typically authorize state agencies to play a significant role in allocating and enforcing water rights.

I. HISTORY OF THE RIPARIAN DOCTRINE

A. EUROPEAN PRECEDENTS

Prior to the eighteenth century, most U.S. water cases involved rights of navigation and fishing. Notions of "water rights" were governed by the natural flow doctrine, which entitled each riparian owner to the enjoyment of the watercourse without interference from others. The dawn of the Industrial Revolution, and the consequent increase in water-driven mills, created a need for uniform principles of law that could be applied in the growing number of water disputes concerned with access to the flow of the stream and the quantity of water available for particular uses. The riparian doctrine, with deep origins in the Institutes of Justinian from Roman law as well as English common law and the French civil code, soon emerged in American courts.

The Institutes of Justinian, published in 533–34 A.D., held that running water was a part of the "negative community" of things that could not be owned, similar to the air, seas, and wildlife. At the same time, it was recognized that such things could be used through so-called usufructory rights, a legal principle of water law that survives today. The "usufruct" is the right to use the advantages of the resource without over-exploitation. In modern U.S. law, water rights are referred to as usufructory rights—rights to use without altering the fundamental nature of the resource. The Institutes declared that the right to use water belonged only to those who had access to the water by virtue of their ownership of riparian land. Others could not gain access without committing a trespass, unless the stream was on the public domain. This doctrine was codified in France in 1804 with the promulgation of the Napoleonic Code.

The early English law of water rights resembled the modern prior appropriation system. One who had made use of a stream from time immemorial was entitled to continue, even if the use deprived others of the natural flow of the stream. In the eighteenth century, the English courts modified this doctrine of "ancient use" and substituted a test of "prior use." Under this test, one could not use or divert water if the effect would be to deprive a prior user of water. This principle protected earlier mills from interference with their water supplies by newer mills. *See, e.g.*, Bealey v. Shaw, 102 Eng. Rep. 1266 (Eng. 1805).

The prior use test was short-lived however. In the 1820s, the English courts began to accept a "natural flow" theory, under which every riparian landowner had an equal right to use water in the stream and a duty not to diminish the quantity of water otherwise flowing to proprietors lower on the stream. Wright v. Howard, 1 Sim. St. 190 (Eng. 1823). This remained the law in England for a few decades until English judges, borrowing from the opinions of American Justices Story and Kent, incorporated the "reasonable use" theory, in large part because "natural flow" unduly restricted important new industrial users. Mason v. Hill, 110 E.R. 692 (Eng. 1833). Reasonable use principles modified the natural flow theory by allowing each riparian user to make all reasonable uses of the waters so long as those uses did not interfere with the reasonable uses of other riparian users.

B. DEVELOPMENT IN THE EASTERN UNITED STATES

After the Revolutionary War, each state began developing its own common law with regard to water allocation. The sparse population of European settlers lived mostly on the eastern seaboard, a rainy area with abundant brooks, streams, and rivers. Some states, including Connecticut and Massachusetts, had few restrictions on the use of streams, and allowed diversions of water if the surplus was returned to the stream. Other states, such as New Jersey, adopted a type of natural flow rule that allowed a riparian landowner to make use of the stream in its natural state but prohibited any diversion that might materially reduce the flow to another. Farrell v. Richards, 30 N.J. Eq. 511 (N.J.Ch. 1879); Martin v. Bigelow, 2 Aik. 184 16 Am. Dec. 696 (Vt. 1827).

As America grew in the nineteenth century, large mills required reservoirs for storage, and at the same time irrigation and industry needed to use water away from the stream banks. Consequently, the need to alter streams to maximize water uses rendered the notion of preserving the natural flow of streams for each user unworkable. Against this backdrop, the famous case of Tyler v. Wilkinson, 24 F.Cas. 472 (C.C.R.I. 1827), was decided. The Tylers were riparian proprietors with mills near a small dam used to impound water so that it would flow faster past their mills once it was released. The Wilkinsons constructed an upstream dam and diverted water into a trench that began above the Tylers' mills. The Wilkinsons' water use thus deprived the downstream Tylers of the flow of water they otherwise would have stored behind their dam. Justice Story held that, while the Tylers had a right to the natural flow of the river, any rights to water for the dam and mills would have to be based on "actual appropriation and use." In setting forth the principles of law applicable to watercourses in general, Justice Story stated that all riparian users had an equal right to the use the balance of the water naturally flowing in the stream and, departing from the natural flow doctrine, held that each riparian was entitled to make a reasonable use of the waters.

Many courts in the United States followed suit, and shifted from the natural flow theory to riparianism, as reflected in reasonable use principles, in deciding water allocation disputes. *See* Snow v. Parsons, 28 Vt. 459 (Vt. 1856) (holding that reasonableness should be determined based on the facts of the case and remanding to determine whether an upstream tannery that released so much debris that the downstream mill could not function was a reasonable use); Herminghaus v. Southern California Edison Co., 252 P. 607 (Cal. 1926) (enclosing the reasonable use doctrine). Thus, balancing these reasonable uses became the work of the courts. Riparian law was further developed and enforced through common law cases involving one riparian landowner suing another over the reasonableness of a particular use of water. The common law riparian rights that developed through this case law included a right to make reasonable use of water flowing past one's land, to purity of the water, to fish, to access the waterway, and to protect the banks of a stream from erosion.

Over time, an increase in population, development, and demand for limited resources resulted in an increase in the number and frequency of disputes over water. Ultimately, these conflicts, and the desire to be more proactive in water allocation, led many eastern states to adopt statutory permit systems for some or all water uses. These states are now referred to as regulated riparian jurisdictions. Many of the judicial factors for determining "reasonableness" are now reflected in the permit systems. *See infra* Section V of this chapter.

C. THE ROLE OF RIPARIAN LAW IN THE AMERICAN WEST

The riparian doctrine was thought to be impractical for many regions west of the one-hundredth meridian. As European settlers moved west, they built their livelihood on mining or homesteading, both of which required access to water. The eastern riparian system, which, that limited water rights to the owners of land bordering on a watercourse would have stifled development in a region where so few parcels were riparian.

Further, the federal government owned most western land, so the early miners and homesteaders were often trespassers on the public domain, with no riparian rights. As many of the most promising mineral deposits were far from any stream, many mines could not operate without transporting water being transported to the site.

The arid landscape resulted in the early miners developing their own customary "law" that recognized rights of individuals to divert water to the mines that were not riparian to the watersource. Access to water became an issue of timeliness, rather than location. The developing western customary law allowed anyone to divert water on a "first come-first served" basis, as long as they did not deprive "prior appropriators" of the quantity of water they were already diverting for themselves. *See infra* Chapter Three. While some western states initially adopted riparian rights for their more humid regions, many eventually phased them out. The few "hybrid" states that preserved pre-existing riparian rights still apply riparian law in certain situations. *See infra* Chapter Four.

II.   CONTOURS OF THE RIPARIAN DOCTRINE

Under the riparian doctrine, rights attach to riparian land (*i.e.,* land bordering on a natural stream or lake) by virtue of its location. The riparian landowner does not actually own the water or the watercourse, but does have numerous usufructory rights to it, including: the right to the flow of the stream; the right to make a reasonable use of the waterbody, provided reasonable uses of other riparian users are not injured; the right of access to the waterbody; the right to fish; the right to wharf out; the right to prevent erosion of the banks; the right to purity of the water; the right to claim title to the beds of non-navigable lakes and streams. Many of these rights, however, are limited by principles of public ownership and through state and federal regulation.

The ownership of riparian land not only creates rights, it also creates duties. Each riparian landowner has a duty to refrain from interfering with the rights of fellow riparian users under the reasonable use doctrine. Riparian rights are further limited by public rights to use the surface of certain waterways. At common law, all persons had the right to travel any navigable river and to hunt and fish along the river. Today, public uses include not only navigation but also recreation, and public rights have been extended to non-navigable waters in many states. Public surface use rights are covered in Section D.8 of this Chapter. Use of water in place for instream or non-consumptive uses by the general public has substantial modern importance and may be recognized judicially in pure riparian jurisdictions or by statute in regulated riparian jurisdictions.

A. THE BASIS FOR RIPARIAN RIGHTS—RIPARIAN LAND

In a pure riparian jurisdiction, only the owner of riparian land acquires rights to make use of the adjacent watercourse. This section defines what constitutes riparian land, the types of water bodies to which the owner of adjacent land may hold rights, and how subdividing riparian land impacts water rights. While all parcels of land are part of a watershed and are directly or indirectly connected to surrounding bodies of water, not all land is riparian. The law distinguishes between riparian land and non-riparian land based on the somewhat artificial concept of ownership. Only the owner of a parcel of land touching a watercourse—contiguous with the water's edge—has riparian rights. Restatement (Second) of Torts § 843. Riparian rights to use water attach only to riparian land contiguous to the watercourse, and do not extend to any portion of a parcel that is outside the immediate watershed of the watercourse.

1. Defining Riparian Land

a. *Watershed Limitation*

Riparian rights attach only to an owner's land within the watershed. Gordonsville, Town of v. Zinn, 129 Va. 542, 106 S.E. 508 (Va. 1921). Thus, neither a non-contiguous parcel of land owned by a riparian landowner nor a portion of a riparian tract that is in another watershed qualifies for riparian rights.

Most jurisdictions consider use outside the watershed of origin to be unreasonable per se, though many will not enjoin it unless another riparian is actually harmed. While some jurisdictions bar all use of water outside the watershed, others permit it subject to the reasonable use restriction. *See, e.g.,* Rancho Santa Margarita v. Vail, 81 P.2d 533 (Cal. 1938) (riparian rights only attach to use on the watershed); Pyle v. Gilbert, 245 Ga. 403, 265 S.E.2d 584 (1980) (right to reasonable use on non-riparian land can be acquired by grant) *overruled on other grounds,* Tunison v. Harper, 286 Ga. 687, 690 S.E.2d 819 (2010) (overruled *Pyle*). Long-standing non-watershed use may ripen into a prescriptive right. *See infra* Section IV.B.3.

b. *Divisions of Riparian Land*

A conveyance of riparian land carries with it all of the appurtenant riparian rights unless those rights have been severed. The extent to which these rights can be reserved by a grantor or conveyed to a grantee are discussed in Section II.E of this chapter. Riparian rights attach only to waterfront land; consequently, when a riparian owner conveys a parcel of land that is not on the water, riparian rights no longer attach to the conveyed parcel. If the parcels are reunited under common ownership, the parcel of land that is not on the water may remain without riparian rights, depending on which of the following rules prevails in the jurisdiction.

i. Unity of Title Rule

Under the unity of title rule, an entire tract of land fronting on a waterway held by a single owner is entitled to riparian rights. It does not matter that the land earlier had been divided into several parcels, some of which did not front on the waterway. Thus, all land contiguous to a riparian parcel that is held by the same riparian landowner has riparian rights regardless of when or from whom the contiguous lands were conveyed. For example, Jones severs riparian land, retains the non-riparian lot and conveys the riparian plot to Smith. Only Smith has the riparian rights. Under the unity of title rule, if Smith later re-conveys the non-riparian plot back to Jones, the entire tract (both plots) would again have riparian rights. Most riparian states follow this rule.

ii. Source of Title Rule

Under the source of title rule (also called the smallest tract rule), riparian rights attach only to the smallest subdivision of waterfront land in the chain of title leading to the present owner. Thus, even if the original riparian owner later reacquires the tract, only the smallest parcel with frontage on the waterway has riparian rights; any land ever severed from contact with the waterway by conveyance can never regain riparian rights. Under this rule, the amount of riparian land shrinks as conveyances sever waterfront lands from uplands. For example, Jones conveys a portion of a tract of riparian land—the part bordering the stream—to

Smith. No riparian rights remain with non-riparian tract. Under the source of title rule, if Smith later re-conveys the riparian plot back to Jones, riparian rights will not reattach to the non-riparian plot.

While most riparian states follow the unity of title rule, many western states apply the source of title rule. In these states, the apparent harshness of reducing the amount of land subject to riparian rights is tempered by the fact that water rights may be acquired by appropriation for the severed parcels. The rule furthers the policy, typical in hybrid jurisdictions, of minimizing the reach of riparian rights and building a reliable system based on prior appropriation. Western and hybrid systems are discussed in Chapters Three and Four.

2. Types of Watercourses

To have riparian rights, a landowner must own property adjacent to or abutting a source of water that fits the definition of a "watercourse." The term "watercourse" may include natural streams, lakes, ponds, springs, marshes, so-called underground streams, and other natural waterways, as well as artificial bodies of water made by humans. Each state has its own body of common law that sets forth which waters are included within the definition of a watercourse.

In contrast, diffused surface water, including the runoff from rain or melted snow, flows intermittently over the land, without a defined channel. It is not subject to riparian rights until it enters a watercourse, though courts have discretion in determining whether water is diffuse or part of a watercourse. Borgmann v. Florissant Dev. Co., 515 S.W.2d 189 (Mo. Ct. App. 1974). The rules applicable to diffused surface water are covered in Chapter Six.

a. Streams

A natural stream is a watercourse that flows constantly or recurrently on the surface of the earth in a reasonably definite channel. A stream may originate or flow through a spring, lake, or marsh. An early Maine case described a stream as a water body that "flows in a particular direction; and by a particular channel, having a bed with banks and sides; and (usually) discharging itself into some other body or stream of water. It may sometimes be dry. It need not flow continuously; but it must have a well defined and substantial existence." Morrison v. Bucksport and Bangor R.R. Co., 67 Me. 353, 356 (1877). *See also* People ex rel. T-Mobile USA, Inc. v. Village of Hawthorn Woods, 359 Ill. Dec. 392, 402, 966 N.E.2d 1080, 1090 (2012). However, because streams are so varied in form, a more precise definition is difficult to provide, and the determination of whether flowing water is or is not a stream is often highly fact intensive.

b. Lakes and Ponds

Lakes and ponds are also watercourses subject to riparian rights. A lake is defined as a reasonably permanent body of water substantially at rest in a depression in the surface of the earth, if both the depression and the body of water are of natural origin or part of a watercourse. Libby, McNeil & Libby v. Roberts, 110 So. 2d 82 (Fla. Dist. Ct. App. 1959). Similar, smaller bodies of water are sometimes called ponds, but no legal distinction exists between the two. Also, in some eastern states, bodies of water known as "great ponds" are considerably larger than many lakes. Hollenberg v. Town of Union, 918 A.2d 1214 (Me. 2007). A person who owns land bordering on a lake or pond is sometimes referred to as a "littoral" landowner, but can also be called a "riparian." *See, e.g.,* 2000 Baum Family Trust v. Babel, 793 N.W.2d 633 (Mich. 2010).

c. *Springs and Other Natural Water Bodies*

A spring is a concentrated flow of water naturally occurring at the surface from under the ground. Holliston v. Holliston Water Co., 306 Mass. 17, 27 N.E.2d 194 (1940). Whether the owner of land with a spring on it has riparian rights depends upon the source of the spring. The riparian doctrine usually applies to springs emanating from definite underground watercourses. Landowners are entitled only to make reasonable use of the waters from such springs. However, in the absence of evidence to the contrary, it is presumed that percolating groundwater formed the spring and the law of groundwater treated in Chapter Five applies.

A spring will be treated as diffused surface water if its flow dissipates before reaching a watercourse or before crossing the boundary of the parcel on

which it is located. *See infra* Chapter Six. The owner
of the land owns such springs and may use all the
water from them. However, these determinations
are highly fact-specific, and courts sometimes treat
springs as watercourses even if the water does not
flow off the owner's land in a regular, well-defined
channel. *See* Oklahoma Water Resources Board v.
City of Lawton, 580 P.2d 510 (Okla. 1978) (holding
that spring water was a stream rather than
groundwater or diffused surface water).

d. Underground Watercourses

Some courts have found that the owner of land
above waters flowing underground has all the rights
of a riparian landowner so long as the course and
the channel of the so-called "stream" are definitely
ascertained. *See, e.g.,* Findley v. Teeter Stone, Inc.,
248 A.2d 106, 109 (Md. 1968). Evidence of an
underground "stream" may include soil composition,
the growth of vegetation in dry seasons, and
evaluations of groundwater and surface water
interactions over time. The notion that groundwater
may flow in "streams" is more legal fiction than
physical reality, though, and most states presume
that underground water is groundwater and not
subject to riparian principles. *See infra* Chapter 5.I.

e. Oceans and Bays

Principles of riparian law do not typically apply to
lands associated with oceans or bays. Principles of
navigability and property boundaries govern
questions of access to tidal water by littoral owners.

Boundaries are typically established at high tide, though bays and coves require more intricate treatment. Joyce v. Templeton, 468 A.2d 1369 (Md. Spec. 1984). Most of the thirteen original states established their common law boundaries along shorelines. Cooper v. United States, 779 F. Supp. 833 (E.D.N.C. 1991). In Texas, the property boundaries for land grants established under Spanish or Mexican law is the mean of the higher of the two daily tides. Luttes v. State, 324 S.W.2d 167 (Tex. 1958). However, salt water and brackish water are not typically the subject of state allocation doctrines.

f. Out of Basin (Foreign) Waters

The phrase "foreign waters" describes water transported from one watershed into another by human effort. Use of water outside its watershed is often held to be unreasonable per se. But once water is exported, the exporter may obtain rights to it by prescription. Crane v. Stevinson, 54 P.2d 1100 (Cal. 1936). Ownership of land bordering on a stream or ditch carrying out of basin waters does not usually give the landowner riparian rights to the foreign water. *City of Virginia Beach v. Champion International Corp.*, Civ. 84–10–N. (D. Va. 1984).

g. Artificially Created Watercourses

Sometimes a canal is built, a stream re-channeled, or a lake created through human effort. The new artificial watercourse may be an important source of water for those adjoining it. However, as a general rule, riparian rights attach only to natural watercourses and lakes. Thus, the rights of owners of land riparian to an artificial stream or lake are not controlled by riparian doctrine. However, artificial watercourses that are maintained long enough, however, may be treated as natural watercourses. In Bollinger v. Henry, 375 S.W.2d 161 (Mo. 1964), the court treated a century-old millrace (a channel conveying taking water to power a mill) as if it were a natural watercourse. Similarly, in Iowa, artificial watercourses only give rise to riparian rights if they have been in place for a long time. Gannon v. Rumbaugh, 772 N.W.2d 258 (Iowa 2009). By contrast, other riparian states have been reluctant to qualify man-made features as watercourses for the purpose of establishing riparian water rights.

If a reservoir is created by construction of a dam, the property owners adjacent to the reservoir may acquire certain rights over time. In the classic case of Kray v. Muggli, 86 N.W. 882 (Minn. 1901), where a dam owner wanted to remove the dam after forty years, the court held that the upland property owners had acquired a prescriptive right to have the artificial lake maintained, and the dam owner had acquired a reciprocal prescriptive duty to maintain the artificial water level. *Id. See also* Greisinger v. Klinhardt, 9 S.W 2d 978 (Mo. 1928) (holding that riparian landowners were entitled to maintain the lake level based on substantial improvements they made in reliance on the lake being permanent). Some courts, however, have been less willing to find a prescriptive easement for property owners adjacent to an artificial lake. *See* Green v. City of Williamstown, 848 F. Supp. 102 (E.D. Ky. 1994) (neighboring landowners did not have a right to compel dam owner to maintain a consistent water level in an artificial lake, despite having made improvements on their property based on the presence of the lake); Alderson v. Fatlan, 898 N.E.2d 595 (Ill. 2008) (riparian landowners were not entitled to surface rights to a water-filled quarry because they had not used it without dispute for a lengthy period of time).

B. MEASURE OF RIPARIAN RIGHTS— REASONABLE USE

All riparian states follow some variant of the reasonable use doctrine, which allows riparian landowners to use adjacent waters if the use does not interfere with the reasonable uses of other riparian users. Thus, reasonable use is determined by comparing the uses of all riparians, a very fact intensive process. Mason v. Hoyle, 14 A. 786 (Conn. 1888); Red River Roller Mills v. Wright, 15 N.W. 167 (Minn. 1883); Botton v. State, 420 P.2d 352 (Wash. 1966). Some riparian states have adopted rules and/or statutory provisions to address specific problems; others have adopted more comprehensive water codes known as regulated riparian law. *See infra* Section III of this chapter.

In those states without comprehensive water codes or specific statutory provisions, courts determine the reasonableness of uses when disputes arise between riparian users. The Restatement

(Second) of Torts incorporates the common law notion that reasonableness is relative. It contains two sections applicable to riparian disputes that provide an analytical framework often used by the courts:

§ 850. Harm by One Riparian Proprietor to Another

A riparian proprietor is subject to liability for making an unreasonable use of the water of a watercourse or lake that causes harm to another riparian proprietor's reasonable use of the water or his land.

§ 850A. Reasonableness of the Use of Water

The determination of the reasonableness of a use of water depends upon a consideration of the interests of the riparian proprietor making the use, of any riparian proprietor harmed by it and of society as a whole. Factors that affect the determination include the following:

(a) the purpose of the use,

(b) the suitability of the use to the watercourse or lake,

(c) the economic value of the use,

(d) the social value of the use,

(e) the extent and amount of the harm it causes,

(f)   the practicality of avoiding the harm by adjusting the use or method of use of one proprietor or the other,

(g)   the practicality of adjusting the quantity of water used by each proprietor,

(h)   the protection of existing values of water uses, land, investments and enterprises, and

(i)   the justice of requiring the user causing harm to bear the loss.

In suits between riparian landowners, the reasonableness of both riparian landowners' uses is at issue. To prove that rights have been infringed, the plaintiff's own use of the water must be shown to be reasonable. This usually calls for the application of factors (a)–(d). A dispute often involves riparian users who are each putting the water to good use by suitable means, and producing socially and economically desirable results. Because the uses are inconsistent, however, the court must consider additional factors (e)–(i). Factor (e) requires in effect that insubstantial, or *de minimis*, harms be borne by the complaining party. Factors (f) and (g) require the court to determine if the dispute can be settled by making adjustments to the uses. For instance, a court might require that the parties use the stream at different times. Factors (h) and (i) generally are applied if the defendant's reasonable use causes serious harm that cannot be avoided by adjustments. Factor (h) recognizes that, other things being equal, it is usually unreasonable for a new use to destroy an existing use. Factor (i) allows courts to address situations where the defendant's use is of greater utility, but nevertheless, fairness requires that the defendant pay for the harm he has caused.

Courts applied the § 850A factors to determine reasonableness of competing uses include Ripka v. Wansing, 589 S.W.2d 333 (Mo. Ct. App. 1979) (determining the reasonable use of competing agricultural uses), and Bollinger v. Henry, 375 S.W.2d 161 (Mo. 1964) (applying common law reasonableness factors to a dispute regarding millrace water). In Harris v. Brooks, 283 S.W.2d 129 (Ark. 1955), the Supreme Court of Arkansas applied the Restatement factors to find that a farmer should be enjoined from withdrawing water from a lake for irrigation when the water fell below the "normal" level, as the farmer was unreasonably interfering with the use of the lake for commercial boating, a non-consumptive use of the water. The Michigan Court of Appeals established a case-specific "reasonable use balancing test" that emphasized three principles: 1) fair participation in the use of water for the greatest number of users; 2) protection of a reasonable use; and 3) redress limited to unreasonable harms. Mich. Citizens for Water Conservation v. Nestle Waters N. Am., Inc., 269 Mich. App. 25, 709 N.W.2d 174 (2005), *rev'd on other grounds*, 479 Mich. 280, 737 N.W.2d 447 (2007). The court issued a partial injunction against a bottling company's excessive pumping of groundwater. While other aspects of the case were challenged, the reasonable use balancing test was not overturned.

As these representative cases demonstrate, state courts vary considerably in their application of the Restatement factors.

C. LIMITS ON RIPARIAN RIGHTS

1. Unreasonable Use

In a riparian system, each riparian user has equal rights as against every other riparian user. The "reasonableness" or "unreasonableness" of a particular use represents the limitation that any riparian water rights holder faces. If a new riparian use emerges, an existing right can be lost or diminished because it is deemed unreasonable with respect to the other riparian rights in the system. 1 Water and Water Rights § 7.02(d)(1) (Amy L. Kelley, ed., 3rd ed. 2014). To determine whether a use should be curtailed because it is unreasonable, courts often consider whether the use substantially harms other riparian rights. *See* Harris v. Brooks, 225 Ark. 436, 447, 283 S.W.2d 129, 135–36 (1955) (holding that one riparian use must be limited because it unreasonably interfered with another riparian use). Often, resolving conflicts between two competing riparian uses, courts have turned to the principle of sharing shortage, frequently called "just proportion," to determine which existing riparian use should be diminished. Evans v. Merriweather, 4 Ill.492, 495 (1842); Cf: Jones v. Oz-Ark-Val Poultry Co., 228 Ark. 76, 306 S.W.2d 111 (1957); Cozy Lake v. Nyoda Girls' Camp, 99 N.J. Eq. 384, 131 A. 892 (1926).

2. Prohibition of Use on Non-Riparian Lands and Its Exceptions

Common law rules restricted use of water to "riparian land." As explained in Section II.A, *supra,* riparian lands are only the portions of parcels that are adjacent to a watercourse and within the same watershed. Many pure riparian jurisdictions continue to hold that any non-riparian use that interferes in any way with a riparian use is *per se* unreasonable. Stratton v. Mount Hermon Boys' School, 216 Mass. 83, 85–87, 103 N.E. 87, 88 (1913); Michigan Citizens for Water Conserv. v. Nestle Waters N. Am., Inc., 269 Mich. App. 25, 57–58, 71–73, 709 N.W.2d 174, 196, 204 (2005), *rev'd on other grounds*, 479 Mich. 280, 737 N.W.2d 447 (2007). Strict application of the watershed limitation has been the subject of much criticism and was rejected in the Restatement (Second) of Torts § 855. 1 Waters and Water Rights § 7.02(d)(1). The Restatement provides that reasonableness of a water use by a riparian proprietor is not controlled by classification of the use as riparian or non-riparian. Thus, use on unconnected land or land outside the watershed may be reasonable. Expansion of the reasonable use approach to non-riparian uses recognizes that the best economic use of water may be for agriculture, mining, manufacturing, or other purposes on land apart from the watercourse. A number of riparian states have followed the Restatement rule and have evaluated the reasonableness of a non-riparian use against a riparian use. *See, e.g.,* Pyle v. Gilbert, 245

Ga. 403, 265 S.E.2d 584 (1980); Baumler v. Town of Newstead, 247 A.D.2d 861, 669 N.Y.S.2d 814 (1998).

The harshness of the watershed limitation is tempered by states with permit systems, known as regulated riparianism, and in hybrid states, where the law combines riparian and prior appropriation rights. In regulated riparian states, permits may be issued for water use outside the watershed of origin, such that the permittee need not be a riparian landowner. In hybrid states, water rights for non-riparian lands may be established by appropriation if sufficient water is available and can be put to a beneficial use without waste.

D. SCOPE OF RIPARIAN USES

1. Preference for "Natural" Uses

Riparian law distinguishes between "natural" uses and "artificial" uses. Natural uses include those that meet the domestic needs of the riparian landowner, such as drinking, washing, and watering small gardens or a few livestock. Historically, under the natural flow rule, a riparian user could use water for natural (*i.e.,* domestic) purposes even if it diminished the flow to the harm of lower riparian users.

The modern reasonable use doctrine also reflects a preference for natural uses and typically prioritizes domestic uses before all other uses. *See, e.g.,* Prather v. Hoberg, 150 P.2d 405 (Cal. 1944); Harris v. Brooks, 225 Ark. 436, 283 S.W.2d 129 (1955); Tunison v. Harper, 690 S.E.2d 819 (Ga.

2010). In most jurisdictions today, any riparian user can make natural uses of the water in the adjacent stream regardless of consequences to lower riparian users, while artificial uses such as for irrigation and industrial purposes are subject to reasonableness restrictions. There are practical reasons for the preference for natural or domestic uses. First, such uses are unlikely to consume enough water to injure lower riparian users. Second, enforcement of any restriction on domestic uses is difficult. Finally, uses that are necessary to sustain life are bound to be "reasonable" as against uses that are not directly related to survival.

2. Irrigation, Industrial, and Mining Uses

Historically, at common law, any significant irrigation was an "artificial" use of water. Theoretically, under this principle, no irrigation was allowed except for small household gardens. However, most common law riparian jurisdictions now recognize irrigation uses as reasonable. Some riparian states have even enacted laws that prefer agricultural uses. In Kentucky, for example, agricultural uses do not require the permits needed for other riparian uses. Louisville v. Tway, 180 S.W.2d 278 (Ky. 1944). Other states single out specific crops for preferential treatment. *See e.g.,* State v. Zawistowski, 95 Wis. 2d 250, 290 N.W.2d 303 (1980) (construing Wisconsin's cranberry preference). Agriculture also may get preferential treatment through statutes exempting farm ponds from regulations governing construction of dams.

Manufacturing and industrial uses of water, like agricultural uses, are artificial uses. Today, those uses are subject to the reasonable use rule. *See, e.g.,* Michigan Citizens for Water Conserv. v. Nestlé Waters N. Am., Inc., 269 Mich. App. 25, 54–56, 71–72, 709 N.W.2d 174, 194–95, 204 (2005), *rev'd on other grounds,* 479 Mich. 280, 737 N.W.2d 447 (2007) (recognizing the industrial use of water as an artificial use subject to the reasonable use rule).

Mining often requires substantial amounts of water and is also considered an artificial use. Some states require a finding that a particular mining operation is in the public interest before a permit will be issued. *See, e.g.,* Minn. Stat. Ann. § 103G.297 Subd. 3(3). Other states have statutes giving miners a right of access to waterways, implying that they have a right to use those waters. *See, e.g.,* Ga. Code Ann. § 44–9–70; N.C. Gen. Stat. Ann. § 74–25.

Agricultural, industrial, and mining uses may come into conflict with the rights of downstream riparian users right to pure water. The reasonable use rule requires a balancing test that may allow some pollution, similar to the approach used in actions for private nuisance or public nuisance cases. Reasonableness may also be measured by state and federal water pollution standards (*e.g.,* federal Clean Water Act). In regulated riparian states, pollution is often an express factor to be weighed in issuing permits for water use.

3. Municipal Uses

When the United States was predominantly rural, local streams or individual wells provided most of the water needed for domestic uses. With urbanization came the growth of municipal water systems to supply domestic needs, to fight fires, and to water public parks. Since the 1990s, jurisdictions following riparian law have been required to confront the tension between requiring riparian land ownership and securing adequate public supplies for water. Courts have split on the question of whether municipal water systems qualify as riparian users. In some cases, cities move water many miles from distant watersheds to satisfy their growing populations. *See, e.g.,* Catskill Mountains Chapter of Trout Unlimited, Inc. v. City of New York, 451 F.3d 77 (2d Cir. 2006); North Carolina v. Hudson, 731 F. Supp. 1261 (E.D.N.C. 1990).

Courts have split on the question of whether municipal water systems qualify as riparian users. The more prevalent, and historic, view is that a public water system is only a riparian user with regard to parcels it owns along the watercourse. *See* Pernell v. Henderson, 220 N.C. 79, 16 S.E.2d 449 (1941) (holding that providing water to municipal customers is an impermissible non-riparian use); Harrell v. City of Conway, 224 Ark. 100, 271 S.W2d 924 (1954). Other states treat municipalities as riparian users. *See* City of Canton v. Shock, 66 Ohio St. 19, 63 N.W. 600 (1902); Hackensack Water Co. v. Village of Nyack, 289 F. Supp. 671 (S.D.N.Y. 1968).

Often, this tension, found in the case law, has been resolved through legislative means. The charters incorporating most cities gave them powers to procure water supplies for such purposes as firefighting, watering public parks, supplying public buildings, and for meeting the domestic needs of their residents. States have also passed special legislative acts giving such powers to particular cities. Some states have even chartered water corporations with the power to condemn water for public and domestic supply. *See, Adams v. Greenwich Water Co.*, 83 A.2d 177 (Conn. 1951). Today states often grant such powers in general statutes applicable to all municipalities.

4. Storage Rights

Under the reasonable use rule, a riparian user can impound water so long as the reasonable uses of others are not impaired. Portage Cty. Bd. of Commrs. v. Akron, 109 Ohio St. 3d 106, 846 N.E.2d 478, 494 (2006); Cent. Delta Water Agency v. State Water Res. Control Bd., 124 Cal. App. 4th 245, 20 Cal. Rptr. 3d 898 (2004); Heise v. Schulz, 204 P.2d 706 (Kan. 1949). Accordingly, a riparian user may not unreasonably alter the flow when releasing water from a storage facility. In addition, some riparian states give environmental agencies discretion to issue permits for water diversion and storage facilities upon consideration of the public necessity, instream flows, and other factors. *See, e.g.,* Hudson River Fisherman's Ass'n v. Williams, 531 N.Y.S.2d 379 (App. Div. 1988).

5. Waterpower

Harnessing the flow of a stream to generate power is one of the oldest uses of water. Waterpower uses range from the earliest waterwheels to large, modern hydroelectric dams.

a. Waterwheels and Mills

Early in the nation's history, small waterwheels and mills adorned numerous streams, providing a cheap and accessible source of power. Eventually, larger mills were needed for manufacturing. As bigger waterwheels were needed, dams were often constructed upstream from the mills to create storage pools from which releases could be made to provide a stronger current. This could cause deepen the channel and slow the flow elsewhere in the watercourse, thereby interfering with other uses. Thus, some state legislatures enacted so-called "mill dam" acts to allow storage dams, provided they did not injure existing mills. This built an element of priority into the riparian system by assuring protection to the earliest uses that relied on the flow of the stream.

b. Hydroelectric Generation

From the Industrial Revolution and through modern times, the generation of electrical power has represented an important riparian use of water. Under the reasonable use rule, operators of a hydroelectric dam may not unreasonably store or release water to the detriment of other riparian users. Factors weighed to determine the reasonableness of dam operators' storage and release methods include the stream size, the state of technology, and uses of the stream by other riparian users. Otwell v. Ala. Power Co., 944 F. Supp. 2d 1134 (N.D. Ala. 2013), *aff'd,* 747 F.3d 1275 (2014); Hazard Powder Co. v. Somersville Mfg. Co., 61 A. 519 (Conn. 1905). Although the riparian doctrine generally limits water use to riparian land, electricity generated from hydroelectric dams may be transmitted to and used by owners of non-riparian land.

Hydroelectric dams may also raise public concern because such structures can interfere with use of the surface of navigable rivers. Exercising its power under the commerce clause, Congress has dictated in the Federal Power Act that no hydroelectric dam may be built on any navigable river unless first licensed by the Federal Energy Regulatory Commission (formerly the Federal Power Commission). Before it issues a license, the Commission must find that the proposed "project be best adapted to a comprehensive plan for improving or developing the waterway." *See infra* Chapter 8.IV.

6. Recovery of Gravel

Some jurisdictions treat the removal of sand and gravel from a watercourse like any other riparian use and evaluate its reasonableness against other riparian uses on a case-by-case basis. Other jurisdictions treat the removal of sand and gravel as a lesser riparian use. In Joslin v. Marin Mun. Water

Dist., 429 P.2d 889 (Cal. 1967), the Supreme Court of California put sand and gravel use on lower footing than an upstream storage dam for a water district. The Court concluded that the dam, which interfered with gravel transport to a downstream sand and gravel business, was reasonable and served the public interest; while the operation of the sand and gravel business did not provide any comparable benefit to the public. Still other jurisdictions seem to favor sand and gravel removal. In Arkansas, for example, a the court held that while a statute only referenced the White River in permitting the removal of sand and gravel, the court could extend the permitting authority to all navigable streams in the state based on subsequent legislative intent. White River Sand & Gravel Removal Com. v. Hayes Bros. Land & Timber Co., 532 S.W.2d 191 (Ark. 1976).

7. Discharge of Waste and the Protection of Water Quality

Historically, the riparian doctrine required landowners along the watercourse to prevent any deterioration in water quality. Over time, this requirement gave way to reasonable use principles. Almost every use of water alters the chemistry or temperature of a watercourse, either because it discharges some waste back into the stream or because the removal of water makes the stream less capable of diluting other contaminants. Consequently, whether the degree of change in water quality renders a water use unreasonable is a question of fact. *See* Borough of Westville v.

Whitney Home Builders, Inc., 122 A.2d 233 (N.J. Super. Div. 1956) (balancing the uses of water and their harms); Snow v. Parsons, 28 Vt. 459 (1856) (remanded to determine if a tannery's discharge of waste into stream was a reasonable use).

A riparian user may also have a tort remedy for water pollution. Causes of action exist in trespass (for negligent or intentional interference with the possession of land to which riparian rights are appurtenant) and in nuisance (for interference with the use and enjoyment of land). To find nuisance under Restatement (Second) of Torts § 826, a court uses a balancing test to decide if the defendant's conduct was unreasonable by asking whether: "(a) the gravity of the harm outweighs the utility of the actor's conduct, or (b) the harm caused by the conduct is serious and the financial burden of compensating . . . would not make continuation of the conduct not feasible."

Today, state and federal statutes, most notably the Clean Water Act (CWA), govern nearly all discharges from point sources into waterways. Section 301 of the CWA prohibits discharges to waters of the U.S. except with a permit. 33 U.S.C. § 1311(a). *See infra* Chapter 8.VI. However, there are many non-point sources of pollution, including runoff from agricultural irrigation, that are exempt from the Clean Water Act's permit system. 33 U.S.C. § 1342(1); 40 C.F.R. § 122.3. Despite these statutory schemes, state common law retains its relevance. *See, e.g.,* Anglers of AuSable v. Dept. of Env. Quality, 283 Mich.App. 115, 770 N.W.2d 359

(2009), *vacated on other grounds,* 489 Mich. 884, 796 N.W.2d 240 (2011).

8. Reciprocal Rights Among Riparian Users to Use the Entire Surface

The rights of riparian users whose lands border navigable waters are limited to the extent that public rights exist in such waters. The English common law rule allowed any person to navigate on navigable waters and to make uses incident to navigation such as hunting and fishing. This rule has been universally accepted in the United States, although the definition of "navigable waters" varies. *See infra* Chapter 8.I.

Some states recognize public rights in waterways even where the watercourse is determined non-navigable and title to the bed has passed to the upland owner. In Wisconsin, all riparian owners own the bed unless their ownership is limited by deed. Mayer v. Grueber, 29 Wis. 2d 168, 138 N.W.2d 197 (1965). However, a riparian's ownership of navigable beds remains subject to the public right to use the surface. Muench v. Public Service Comm., 261 Wis. 492, 53 N.W.2d 514 (Wis. 1952). A Minnesota statute declares certain waters that are managed or accessible for public purposes to be public waters. Minn. Stat. § 103G.201. Since colonial times in areas within Maine, Massachusetts, and New Hampshire, the common law has recognized that large, freshwater lakes known as "great ponds" (having surface area over ten acres), though non-navigable, are subject to

public use with limited rights of public access across
private lands to reach the ponds.

Issues involving the use of the surface of a
waterbody also arise in the context of multiple
riparian owners. States are divided on whether a
riparian owner has a right to make reasonable use
of an entire lake surface. Two disparate rules have
emerged. Some states follow the "common law" rule,
which supports a property owner's right to exclude
others from the water surface overlying their
property. *See, e.g.,* Orr v. Mortvedt, 735 N.W.2d 610,
618 (Iowa 2007); Wehby v. Turpin, 710 So.2d 1243,
1249 (Ala. 1998); Ace Equip. Sales, Inc. v. Buccino,
273 Conn. 217, 869 A.2d 626, 635 (2005); Lanier v.
Ocean Pond Fishing Club, Inc., 253 Ga. 549, 322
S.E.2d 494, 496 (1984); Duval v. Thomas, 114 So.2d
791, 795 (Fla. 1959). Other states follow the "civil"
rule, which supports the right of every riparian to
use the entire water surface for recreational
purposes. *See, e.g.,* Duval v. Thomas, 114 So.2d 791,
795 (Fla. 1959); Beacham v. Lake Zurich Prop.
Owners Ass'n, 123 Ill.2d 227, 122 Ill.Dec. 14, 526
N.E.2d 154, 157 (1988). Under the civil rule, the
rights of riparian users in waters overlying their
privately owned beds are qualified by the common
right of other riparian owners to use the entire
water surface for transportation, fishing, swimming,
hunting, and other purposes. But multiple owners of
the bed of a private, non-navigable lake can only use
the surface water if they do not unduly interfere
with the reasonable use of the waters by other
owners and their licensees. *See, e.g.,* Beacham v.
Lake Zurich Property Owners Ass'n, 526 N.E.2d 154

(Ill. 1988). *See also* Johnson v. Seifert, 257 Minn. 159, 100 N.W.2d 689 (1960) (adopting a free access rule, but noting it would not apply to "[a] minor body of water which by its nature and character reasonably has no overall utility common to two or more abutting owners").

Waterbodies that are developed by private parties to promote recreational use present unique issues. In Anderson v. Bell, 433 So.2d 1202, 1204 (Fla. 1983), the court held that an owner of property that lies adjacent to a manmade, non-navigable reservoir is not entitled to use the surface of the entire water body by sole virtue of the fact that he owns contiguous land. In Thompson v. Enz, 379 Mich. 667, 154 N.W.2d 473 (1967), a court found that users dredging a canal from a lake to subdivided parcels did not grant riparian rights to parcels not adjacent to the canal. Additionally, whether owners of land abutting the canal had right-of-way access to the lake depended on a reasonableness test.

9. Right to Wharf Out

The right to "wharf out" allows a riparian to build a wharf or dock for private use if the structure does not impede navigation, although any obstruction that is a purpresture (an enclosure of what belongs to the public) is not allowed at common law. Williams v. Guthrie, 102 Fla. 1047, 137 So. 682, 685 (1931). Also, if the public right to navigation is injured, the obstruction can be removed as a nuisance. Weems Steamboat Co. v. People's Steamboat Co., 214 U.S. 345, 355 (1909); Engs v.

Peckham, 11 R.I. 210, 223–24 (1875). However, some courts have recognized that riparian landowners have a right to erect and maintain wharves and piers cannot be taken or damaged for public use without just compensation. 627 Smith St. Corp. v. Bureau of Waste Disposal, 289 A.D.2d 472, 473 (N.Y. App. Div. 2001).

Although most Eastern and Midwestern states recognize a right to wharf out, Pacific Coast states generally do not, except by statute. *See, e.g.,* Port of Seattle v. Oregon & W. R. Co., 255 U.S. 56, 69 (1921) (applying Washington law). In Alaska, the Department of Natural Resources has the authority to require a commercial property owner to enter into a lease with the state before constructing wharves into adjacent navigable waters. State v. Alaska Riverways, Inc., 232 P.3d 1203 (Ak. 2010).

In order to protect the states' interest in the beds of navigable waters and the rights of other riparian owners, many states have adopted regulatory provisions and permitting requirements that limit a riparian owner's right to wharf out. For example, in Wisconsin, a pier permit may be conditioned upon compliance with a town's pier placement ordinance. Borsellino v. Wisconsin Dept. of Natural Resources, 606 N.W.2d 255, 260 (Wis. 1999).

10. Right to Maintain Water Levels

Dam installation or removal alters the elevation of the reservoir and the receiving stream. A riparian property owner's right to have water levels maintained may depend on whether there is an express or negative easement, how long a dam has been in place, and whether it is a private or publically owned dam.

Absent an easement or other enforceable agreement, an owner of land beneath or contiguous to an artificial lake has no right to use the entire lake based solely by virtue of land ownership; as a result, the landowner would have no right to prevent the developer of the lake from draining it. Anderson v. Bell, 433 So. 2d 1202, 1207 (Fla. 1983) (citing Taylor v. Tampa Coal Co., 46 So.2d 392, 394 (Fla. 1950)). *See* Lake Williams Beach Ass'n v. Gilman Bros. Co., 197 Conn. 134, 496 A.2d 182 (1985) (rejecting claims by lakefront owners against dam owners following reduction in water levels in accordance with engineering recommendations for dam safety); Green v. City of Williamstown, 848 F. Supp. 102 (E.D. Ky. 1994) (owners of property adjacent to a lake created by a municipal dam did not have rights to a consistent water level even if they had improved their property in reliance on the lake).

Many states have adopted dam safety requirements and environmental provisions related to dam construction and operation. For example, Wisconsin law gives the Department of Natural Resources power to regulate water levels "to promote safety and protect life, health and property. . . ." Wis. Stat. Ann. § 31.02(1). In Michigan, the Supreme Court affirmed the authority of a watershed management organization to manage the water level of a lake by use of a dam, but it ordered the adoption of the riparian owners' proposed management plan to protect downstream recreational and environmental interests. Glen Lake-Crystal River Watershed Riparians v. Glen Lake Ass'n, 695 N.W.2d 508, 544 (Mich. 2004). The Michigan Court of Appeals has also upheld a partial injunction to protect riparian rights when excessive groundwater pumping resulted in a drop in the water level of a stream. Mich. Citizens for Water Conservation v. Nestle Waters N. Am., Inc., 269 Mich. App. 25, 709 N.W.2d 174 (2005), *rev'd on other grounds*, 479 Mich. 280, 737 N.W.2d 447 (2007).

11. Scenic Rights

Some courts have begun to recognize a riparian's right to enjoy the scenic beauty of an adjoining waterway. In Collens v. New Canaan Water Co., 234 A.2d 825, 829–30 (Conn. 1967), plaintiffs were awarded compensatory damages and injunctive relief because defendant's pumping of river water for municipal purposes had an adverse effect upon "the recreational and scenic advantages of the plaintiffs' [river-front] properties." Moreover, the loss of scenic amenities may warrant compensation in an eminent domain action. In an action to condemn the rights of riparian owners surrounding Mono Lake so that the lake's tributaries could be drawn down for Los Angeles's water supply, the court awarded "substantial" damages based on injuries to scenic and recreational values. City of Los Angeles v. Aitken, 52 P.2d 585, 588 (Cal. App. 1935).

With some degree of variation, courts in Florida, Mississippi, Georgia, and New Jersey recognize a riparian right to an unobstructed view of the water. In Florida, for example, riparian owners were compensated because the construction of a bridge by the county interfered with 80% of their view of a channel. Lee County v. Kiesel, 705 So. 2d 1013 (Fla. 1998). By contrast, an Indiana court declined to find that a riparian landowner had rights to an unobstructed view when the city installed a pedestrian bridge to connect a city park to an island. The court reasoned that the scope of a landowner's view was a policy decision "best left to the legislative branch generally and the local zoning authorities specifically." Ctr. Townhouse Corp. v. City of Mishaw, 882 N.E.2d 762, 772 (Ind. App. 2008).

E. TRANSFERS OF RIPARIAN RIGHTS

1. Granting Riparian Rights

Because riparian rights attach to those who own riparian land, riparian rights are often thought of as being a part of land ownership. Because parties generally intend to transfer water rights along with the land, courts have held that a conveyance of riparian land carries with it all of the riparian rights appurtenant to that land even if not expressly conveyed by the deed. *See* 1 Waters and Water Rights § 7.04(a)(1), footnotes 532, 533 (providing an inventory of state cases following this principle). However, the presumption that a conveyance of riparian land conveys the appurtenant riparian rights is rebuttable. To avoid disputes, parties should express their intent in the deed.

2. Reserving Riparian Rights

Although riparian rights attach only to riparian land, the right to use the water may be expressly reserved by a riparian landowner when conveying part of a riparian parcel to another. Such reservations of water rights are typically binding only as between the parties. Reservations typically arise in two settings.

In the first, a landowner divides a riparian parcel, and assuming the divided parcel remains riparian, the landowner expressly reserves the water rights that had attached to the parcel. The grantor may later convey to some other person the retained portion of the riparian parcel, granting along with it the riparian rights expressly reserved from the first conveyance. Any such reservation is only effective if recorded. 1 Waters and Water Rights § 7.04(a)(2). As a practical matter, the grantor who reserves water rights in such a situation will usually allow the grantee at least sufficient water to satisfy the grantee's domestic needs. *See* Steuart Transportation Co. v. Ashe, 269 Md. 74, 304 A.2d 788 (1973); Legendary, Inc. v. Destin Yacht Club Owners Assoc., Inc., 724 So. 2d 623 (Fla. App. 1998).

In the second, a riparian landowner retains a portion of the original riparian tract that does not border on the waterbody and conveys the abutting riparian potion to another, reserving some or all riparian rights. These cases are handled similar to situations where a riparian owner grants an easement that allows non-riparian owners use of the water. Because non-riparian use is disfavored, easement holders typically face a high burden to establish that the easement exists. *See* Little v. Kin, 664 N.W.2d 749 (Mich. 2003) (recognizing that courts will look first to the language of the easement, considering extrinsic evidence only if the text is ambiguous). *See also* Burkhart v. City of Fort Lauderdale, 168 So. 2d 65 (Fla. 1964); J-T Assoc. v. Hudson River-Black River Regulating Dist., 175 A.D.2d 438, 572 N.Y.S.2d 122 (1991); Cooper v. Kolberg, 247 Va. 341, 442 S.E.2d 639 (1994). For a more comprehensive look at riparian transfer cases, *see* 1 Waters and Water Rights § 7.04 (a)(1)–(3).

3. Acquiring Riparian Rights by Prescription

Riparian rights can be obtained by prescription. 1 Water and Water Rights § 7.04(c) (inventorying state cases recognizing riparian rights established through prescription). Typical adverse possession laws provide that the open and notorious, hostile, exclusive, actual, and continuous possession of property for a prescribed number of years vests title in the adverse possessor. A prescriptive riparian right can be established through adverse possession. Obtaining a prescriptive right turns on two factors: whether the person against whom the prescriptive right is sought is (1) a riparian or a non-riparian owner, and (2) upstream or downstream from the riparian plaintiff. Moreover, riparian states now incorporate some form of the reasonable use rule when considering whether a prescriptive right has been established.

When a prescription conflict is between two riparian owners—an upstream defendant and a downstream plaintiff—the rule is that an upper riparian owner's use is not adverse unless it unreasonably interferes with the rights of lower riparian owner's. Pabst v. Finmand, 211 P. 11 (Cal. 1922). *Cf.* Kirby v. Hook, 347 Md. 380, 395, 701 A.2d 397, 405 (1997) (landowners' use of water from spring on neighbors' property through an underground pipeline without written permission was "adverse" for purposes of establishing an easement by prescription).

Downstream users (riparian or non-riparian) generally cannot acquire prescriptive rights against upstream riparian users. The rule is sometimes stated as "prescription does not run upstream." Since it is difficult for a downstream use to adversely affect an upstream riparian use, the downstream use is not adverse and cannot be the basis of a prescriptive right. *See* 1 Waters and Water Rights § 7.04. For two interesting exceptions, see Dontanello v. Gust, 150 P. 420 (Wash. 1915) (lower riparian acquired prescriptive right by building a diversion mechanism on upper riparian's land), and Sandford v. Town of Wolfeboro, 740 A.2d 1019 (N.H. 1999) (trespassory flowage established prescriptive right).

Generally, the rules governing prescription in riparian states also apply in the hybrid states, at least as between riparian landowners. As between a riparian and a non-riparian owner, the rules may differ because, under most hybrid systems, new (non-riparian) uses must be acquired by making an appropriation pursuant to statutory requirements. Prescription in hybrid states is discussed in *infra* Chapter 4.III.C.

F. LOSS OF RIPARIAN RIGHTS

The general rule, in contrast with prior appropriation jurisdictions, is that riparian rights cannot be lost by non-use. Riparian rights may be extinguished, however, by prescription, avulsion, under permit systems, or through the exercise of eminent domain by a city or other governmental unit to secure water supply. Additionally, in most states with hybrid systems, statutes limit the right of a riparian owner to initiate new uses and may even declare vested riparian rights to be forfeited by non-use over a statutorily prescribed period. Thus, regulated riparian jurisdictions often require a riparian owner to obtain a permit before initiating new uses, effectively limiting common law riparian rights.

1. Effect of Non-Use

Ordinarily, riparian rights are not lost by non-use. Because riparian rights attach only to riparian land, it follows that the owner of a riparian parcel also has riparian rights in the adjacent watercourse whether those rights are exercised or not. As one court put it, "[u]se does not create the right, and disuse cannot destroy or suspend it." Lux v. Haggin,

69 Cal. 255, 391, 10 P. 674, 753 (1886). *See* 1 Waters
and Water Rights § 7.04(d). In prior appropriation
states, the rule is quite different: because the
appropriative right is based on putting a certain
quantity of water to a beneficial use, the failure to
continue using it is evidence of intent to abandon it.

The rule that non-use (even for a long period of
time) will not destroy riparian rights has often been
criticized, particularly in the arid hybrid states
where uses of appropriators are at risk of being
disrupted by uses initiated by riparian owners.
Almost all hybrid states now have forfeiture
statutes that limit the ability of riparian
landowners to initiate new riparian uses after a
certain date, although in most, vested riparian
rights still cannot be lost simply by non-use.

2. Accretion, Reliction, Erosion, and Avulsion

Accretion and reliction occur when a stream
changes course over a period of many years.
Accretion is the gradual addition of sediment to one
bank along the waterline. Reliction occurs when
water gradually withdraws from one side of the
stream. Erosion is a term used to describe the
gradual wearing away of land and is sometimes
used interchangeably with accretion and reliction as
a more general term. If accretion, reliction, or
erosion occur, the property boundary line shifts with
the waterline so that a riparian owner adjacent to
added land will gain title to the new land, keeping
riparian rights. 1 Waters and Water Rights
§ 6.03(b)(2). A riparian owner whose land is carried

away loses title to that land but retains appurtenant riparian rights so long as the stream remains adjacent to the land. *See* Burkart v. City of Fort Lauderdale, 168 So.2d 65 (Fla. 1964); Strom v. Sheldon, 527 P.2d 1382 (Wash. App. 1974); *see also* Fly Fish Vt., Inc. v. Chapin Hill Estates, Inc., 996 A.2d 1167, 1171 (Vt. 2010).

In contrast, courts treat avulsion—which occurs when a stream suddenly changes its channel—quite differently. If avulsion moves a stream away from a landowner's property, the property boundary line remains where it was before the stream left its channel. *See* Cox v. F-S Prestress, Inc., 797 So.2d 839, 844 (Miss. 2001); City of Long Branch v. Jui Yung Liu, 203 N.J. 464, 477–78, 4 A.3d 542, 550–551 (2010). Avulsion can effectively transform riparian land into non-riparian, thereby depriving the unfortunate owner of riparian rights. Although the distinction between avulsion and accretion is murky, a change in stream course generally constitutes avulsion if it is considerable, violent, and abrupt. Courts consider the circumstances of the shift in channel and the consequences to the parties in deciding which rule to apply. *See, e.g.,* Fly Fish Vt., Inc. v. Chapin Hill Estates, Inc., 996 A.2d 1167, 1171 (Vt. 2010). Thus, in one case, a court applied the accretion rule to a sudden shift in channel caused by the defendant's dredging that would have cut off the plaintiff entirely from stream access if the avulsion rule were applied. Strom v. Sheldon, 527 P.2d 1382 (Wash. App. 1974).

3. Legislation—Moving from a Common Law to Statutory Law System

Conversion to statutory permit systems or to hybrid systems was intended in part to remedy the uncertainty and insecurity of the riparian system. A riparian owner's ability to commence any reasonable uses in the future, as well as to continue existing uses, allows great and unanticipated increases in water use. Forfeiture statutes are designed to limit riparian rights that have not been exercised within a certain period of time in an attempt to diminish this uncertainty. In the hybrid states of Kansas and Washington, even vested riparian rights—those the riparian has historically exercised—can be lost by a period of non-use under statutory forfeiture provisions. In addition, as discussed in Section III below, the movement from common law to regulated riparian systems also attempts to address this uncertainty by requiring permits for riparian uses and by creating time limited permits in some cases.

III. PERMIT SYSTEMS—
REGULATED RIPARIANISM

For many years, the common law system of reconciling water use conflicts through courts applying a reasonable use standard was an effective and efficient way to manage water resources in the eastern United States. In the last several decades, however, eastern states have seen more frequent water shortages, increased demand from urban and industrial growth, and excessive pollution. This dynamic has led many riparian states to adopt statutory provisions, including permit requirements, to address competing water uses. These states are known as "regulated riparian" states. 1 Waters and Water Rights § 9.

"Regulated riparianism" is a relatively new term in water law. It is meant to capture the wide array of statutory provisions adopted in the various eastern states that have moved away from judicially determined standards of reasonableness toward legislatively-enacted permit systems. Statutory schemes can range from relatively simple registration systems to comprehensive water codes. In an attempt to create a set of general provisions, the American Society of Civil Engineers developed the Regulated Riparian Model Water Code in 2003. This Model Code serves as a useful tool for looking broadly at the basic structure and function of comprehensive regulated riparian codes, but each state has tailored its statutory provisions to its own particular needs.

About half of the eastern states (19 out of 31 states) have developed regulatory permit systems to allocate rights to divert water. These states include Alabama, Arkansas, Connecticut, Delaware, Florida, Georgia, Iowa, Kentucky, Maryland, Massachusetts, Michigan, Minnesota, Mississippi, New Jersey, New York, North Carolina, South Carolina, Virginia, and Wisconsin. *See* 1 Waters and Water Rights § 9.01, footnote 37 (providing cites to state code provisions). Several also require permits for use of groundwater (*e.g.*, Illinois, Maryland,

Kentucky, South Carolina). Thus, common-law riparianism for the most part has been replaced with varying degrees of "regulated riparianism." Iowa and Florida have implemented very detailed permit systems, while other states have adopted less comprehensive systems of regulation. Many other eastern states have adopted some sort of administrative system to address water management for at least some portion of the water supply. *See* A Summary Digest of State Water Law 17–23 (Richard Dewsnup & Dallin Jensen eds. 1973). States without permitting systems often require, at a minimum, that surface water users report the amount of water used to a central agency. *See* Me. Rev. Stat. §§ 470–A to 470–H (requiring a report of water withdrawals in Maine).

Statutory provisions vary by state but share some common themes and characteristics. First, states with comprehensive systems require a permit to divert water. Permits are granted based on riparian principles, and the reasonableness standard is the primary method for determining if a use is appropriate. Second, water use is often expressly allowed on non-riparian land. This represents one of the more dramatic substantive departures from the common law. Third, in many states, the permits are time limited. Fourth, regulated riparianism often expressly recognizes public values, and in some instances, treats water as a form of public property that cannot be fully privatized by any individual. These code provisions are typically designed to protect the public's interest in sustaining a reliable supply of water, maintaining stream flows, and allowing states to make decisions about water uses and their impacts. Finally, competing uses are resolved through an administrative process rather than through the courts. *See, e.g.,* Fla. Stat. § 373.245; Green v. City of Williamstown, 848 F. Supp. 102, 104 (E.D. Ky. 1994). When disputes arise, they often present as state administrative law cases rather than the typically private disputes that give rise to court cases in pure riparian jurisdictions.

A. REQUIRING A PERMIT TO DIVERT WATER

Among the most significant differences between pure riparian law and regulated riparianism is the requirement that a water user obtain a permit to divert water. States vary considerably with regard to when a permit is required though, and sometimes, significant consumers of water are not required to obtain a permit. Several states exempt withdrawals up to a certain amount from the permit requirement. Ala. Code § 9–10B–20(c); Conn. Gen. Stat. § 22a–377(a)(2); Del. Code Ann. Tit.7, § 6029(2); Mich. Comp. Laws § 324.32723; Wis. Stat. Ann. §§ 30.18(2)(b), 281.35(4)(b). Other states exempt domestic uses from permit requirements. Fla. Stat. §§ 373.019(6), 373.219(1); Ky. Rev. Stat. Ann. §§ 151.140, 151.210(1); Md. Code Ann., Envir. § 5–502(b)(1); Minn. Stat. §§ 103G.271(1)(b)(1); Miss. Code Ann. §§ 51–3–3(c), 51–3–7(1). Agricultural irrigation is also exempt from the permit requirement in certain states. Ky. Rev. Stat. Ann. § 151.140; N.J. Stat. Ann. § 58: 1A–1–17; Tenn. Code Ann. §§ 69–7–301–309; Wis. Stat.

§ 30.18. All state permit requirements include some special exemptions and preferences can be found for activities like oil and gas recovery, fire emergencies, water for steam power plants, which are the result of political compromises made when the legislation was enacted. 1 Water and Water Rights § 9.03.

In general, regulated riparian permits specify the location, volume, and rate of diversion, and the location and nature of the permitted use. Permit holders are often required to monitor and report on their diversions. Many state statutes authorize various enforcement mechanisms, such as injunctions and civil and criminal penalties. Some states charge water users a set fee to obtain a permit or charge a fee based on the amount of water used.

B. ALLOWING WATER USE ON NON-RIPARIAN LAND

Theoretically, under the Regulated Riparian Model Water Code, regulated riparian jurisdictions can depart from pure riparian law and issue permits for water use on non-riparian lands. *See* American Soc'y of Civil Eng'rs, Regulated Riparian Model Water Code § 2R–2–02. Despite the Model Code's allowance for water use on non-riparian lands, many regulated riparian states have not expressly adopted this provision. In some states, however, water use can be permitted even on non-riparian lands that are outside the watershed of origin. *See* N.C. Gen. State § 143–215.221 (giving the Department of Water Resources authority to approve transfers outside the watershed or origin); Fla. Stat. Ann. § 373.223(2) (providing for permits to divert water outside the watershed from which it is taken). Other regulated riparian states allow for use on non-riparian lands when there is "excess" or "surplus" water. *See, e.g.,* Ark. Stat. Ann. § 15–22–304; Minn. Stat. § 103G.265; Wis. Stat. § 30.18(5)(a)(2).

C. ISSUING TIME LIMITED PERMITS

In both riparian and prior appropriation jurisdictions, water rights are essentially permanent. In riparian states, one must retain ownership of the riparian lands to preserve a water right. In a prior appropriation state one must put the water to beneficial use to maintain a water right. As long as these conditions are met, the water right never expires or is forfeited. Both riparian law and prior appropriation law have been critiqued for protecting early uses without a mechanism to re-evaluate as new needs for water arise. Regulated riparian law attempts to address this concern by limiting the duration of a water rights permit.

Of the regulated riparian states that have permit systems in place, very few allow a water use permit to be issued in perpetuity. N.Y. Envtl. Conserv. Law §§ 15–1501, 15–1503; Md. Code Ann., Envir. § 5–511. The majority of regulated riparian states with a permit system grant the water right for a fixed term of years. The term of the permit varies from state to state. *See, e.g.,* Fla. Stat. § 373.236 (20 year permits for private entities, 50 year permits for public entities); Ga. Code Ann. § 12–5–97(a) (50 year permits); Miss. Code Ann. § 51–3–9(1) (10 year permits with unspecified longer period for public entities); Md. Code Ann., Envir. § 5–511 (3 year review of most permits). At the time the right expires, the state agency can re-evaluate the reasonableness of the water use as against other, potentially new, uses for the water. Renewal of fixed term permits is not automatic, though in some states renewal applications are favored. Fla. Stat. § 373.239(3) (renewal not favored); Iowa Code § 455B.265 (renewal favored).

D. PROTECTING THE PUBLIC INTEREST IN A REGULATED RIPARIAN JURISDICTION

While both riparian law and prior appropriation law have mechanisms to protect the public's interest in water, each doctrine has limitations. In pure riparian jurisdictions, water rights are essentially an interest associated with land ownership. Often the "public" does not qualify as a landowner that can assert the reasonableness of their use in the typical riparian case. In the modern era, all prior appropriation jurisdictions have provisions that allow water rights to be established for non-consumptive uses and have requirements that water rights applications be evaluated against public interest standards. However, given the first-in-time, first-in-right nature of appropriative rights, the public's interest in the water is often established later in time in the priority system. Regulated riparian law seeks to remedy some of these challenges.

Regulated riparian statutes typically provide that water is a form of public property. 1 Waters and Water Rights § 9.01. The recognition of water as public property distinguishes regulated riparianism from pure riparian law, where water rights are essentially a form of common property, and prior appropriation law, where water rights are often characterized as private property. Regulated riparian codes also set forth criteria for evaluating water use and/or preferences for water use that specifically recognize the public's interest in the water. These often include particular reference to conserving water, protecting the public interest, establishing minimum stream flows, and protecting public water supplies, among others. *See, e.g.,* Ala. Code § 9–10B–2; Ark. Code Ann. § 15–22–201; Conn. Gen. Stat. § 22a–380; Del. Code Ann. tit. 7, § 6001(c); Fla. Stat.§ 373.016(3); Haw. Rev. Stat. § 174C–2; Iowa Code § 455B.262; Ky. Rev. Stat. Ann. § 151.110(1); Md. Code Ann., Envir. § 5–501; Mass. Gen. Laws ch. 21G, § 3; Mich. Comp. Laws § 324.32702(1); Minn. Stat. § 103G.101; Miss. Code Ann. § 51–3–1; N.Y. Envtl. Conserv. Law § 15–0105; N.C. Gen. Stat. § 143–215; Va. Code Ann. § 62.1–11. Georgia, Iowa, and Kentucky provide that permits may be modified to deal with shortages or otherwise to accommodate the public interest or property rights of others. Ga. Code Ann. § 12–5–31(e), (f) (1982); Iowa Code Ann. § 455A.28(3) (West 1971); Ky. Rev. Stat. Ann. § 151.200(l) (1980). Some states, such as Florida, Georgia, Maryland, North Carolina, and South Carolina, may revoke or cancel a permit if contrary to public interest. Ga. Code Ann. § 12–5–

96(c)(4) (Supp. 1982); Md. Code Ann., Nat. Res. § 8–807(a) (LexisNexis 1974); N.C. Gen. Stat. § 143–215.21(5) (1978); S.C. Code Ann. § 49–5–40(a), 60(c) (1976).

Despite the movement toward protecting non-consumptive uses and the public's interest in water, regulated riparian jurisdictions, like pure riparian and prior appropriative states, have complex dynamics regarding preferences and priorities for certain private uses of waters. Typically, states recognize human consumption as the highest use. After human consumption, an array of private uses may be preferred over recreational, aesthetic, or other non-consumptive uses, including agriculture, municipal, industrial, commercial, and hydropower, among others. *See, e.g.,* Ark. Code Ann. § 15–22–217; Minn. Stat. § 103G.261(a); Iowa Code § 455B.266; Md. Code Ann., Envir. § 5–502(d); Ala. Code § 9–10B–2(7).

E. ALLOCATING WATER THROUGH AN ADMINISTRATIVE AGENCY

In most regulated riparian states, the state legislature has given an administrative agency the power to confer water rights. 1 Waters and Water Rights § 9.03. Florida and Arkansas represent exceptions to this general trend by delegating the permitting authority to regional conservation and water districts. Ark. Code Ann. §§ 15–22–202(4); 15–22–221; Fla. Stat. §§ 373.069 to 373.083. Administrative officials charged with issuing permits must evaluate competing uses using factors that closely resemble the common law reasonableness factors set forth in pure riparian states. 1 Waters and Water Rights § 9.03(5)(A). Thus, the difference between pure riparian states and regulated riparian states does not lie in the substantive decisions of which rights are reasonable and which are not. Rather, the differences are found in the decision maker and the timing of the decision. In terms of the decision maker, a court determines the reasonableness of a water use as against another water use in pure riparian jurisdictions. In a regulated riparian jurisdiction, an administrative agency determines the reasonableness of competing uses. In terms of timing, for a pure riparian jurisdiction, competing uses are not reconciled against one another unless there is a conflict that makes its way to court. In a regulated riparian jurisdiction, competing uses are reconciled during the permitting process in advance of the use commencing.

In the process of determining the reasonableness of a water use, in a regulated riparian jurisdiction, the administrative agency determines the quantity one may divert and sets the terms and conditions. The administrative process typically provides for public hearings and notice to those impacted by a permit decision. Once the agency has issued the permit, the agency decision is subject to judicial review pursuant to state administrative law mechanisms. *See, e.g.,* Marion County v. Greene, 5 So.3d 775 (Fla. Dist. Ct. App. 2009) (Judicial review of St. Johns Water Management District's decision to adopt an Administrative Law Judge's order approving a consumptive use permit). In the end, commentators have noted that regulated riparian law, in theory, transfers the decision-making power from private litigants in courts to executive branch agencies with expertise in water management. Joseph W. Dellapenna, *The Importance of Getting Names Right: The Myth of Markets for Water*, 25 Wm. & Mary Envtl. L. & Pol'y 317 (2000); Eric Freyfogle, *Water Rights and the Common Wealth*, 26 Envtl. L. 27 (1996).

CHAPTER THREE
PRIOR APPROPRIATION

I.   INTRODUCTION TO PRIOR APPROPRIATION

The prior appropriation doctrine was developed to serve the practical demands of nineteenth century water users in the western United States. It originated in the customs of miners on the federal public lands who recognized superior rights of those who first used water. Later, ranchers, farmers, and other users began diverting water for use on public and private lands.

Where the doctrine applies, water rights are granted based on the time when a person applies a particular quantity of water to a beneficial use. Those rights continue so long as the beneficial use is maintained. The basic elements of a valid appropriation are:

- *Intent* to apply water to a beneficial use;

- An actual *diversion* of water from a natural source of surface water;

- Application of the water to a *beneficial use* within a reasonable time.

The date of the appropriation determines the user's priority to use water, with the earliest user having the superior right. If water is insufficient to meet all needs, those earliest in time of appropriation (senior appropriators) will typically obtain all of their allotted water; those who appropriated later (junior appropriators) may receive only some, or none, of the water to which they have rights, depending on the amount available. This "first in time, first in right" concept contrasts sharply with the riparian tradition of prorating the entitlement to water among all users during times of scarcity. However, a few states, most notably California, have "hybrid" systems that employ elements of the riparian doctrine as well as the appropriation doctrine.

A beneficial use that will support an appropriation must have a specific, stated purpose such as irrigation, domestic, industrial, firefighting, or livestock watering. The property where water is applied does not have to be adjacent to the source and does not even need to be within the same watershed. Most states allow the transfer of water away from the property to which the rights first attached if the rights of other appropriators are not harmed.

In general, water may be appropriated for any use the state deems beneficial. More economically or socially useful purposes that commenced later in time ordinarily will not be preferred over older, less valuable ones. Although some state statutes or constitutions express preferences for domestic and other critical uses, they do not alter the basic principle of priority based on first use.

Because the measure of an appropriative right is the quantity of water that is put to a beneficial use, an appropriator has no right to waste water.

Diverting more water than is reasonably necessary is wasteful, deprives other users of water, and is not considered a beneficial use. If a determination of waste is made, the appropriator may lose that portion of the water right. Moreover, long term failure to use appropriated water can result in the loss of the right. If disuse is intentional, it may be construed as abandonment; unintended disuse results in forfeiture in some states.

Although the early reasons for creating private rights to use public waters—like mining on the public lands—were short-lived, and today's uses are far more diverse, the appropriation doctrine remains intact. It has, however, been tempered and modified. Although the underlying rights to most surface water in the West were established by prior appropriation, in most western states today, their use is governed, and new rights must be established, according to complex statutory schemes. Most require water users to have permits. In addition, in most states, statutes charge administrative agencies with assuring that new, transferred, or changed appropriations are in the public interest. The public interest test varies among states, but it may necessitate choices among competing appropriators based on whether the public interest will be served and in some cases it requires denials or conditions upon new appropriations, changes of use, or transfers. Some courts have held that states have a "public trust" obligation to examine appropriations to ensure that they are consistent with public purposes.

II. DEVELOPMENT OF PRIOR APPROPRIATION DOCTRINE

The doctrine of prior appropriation can be traced to local customs developed during the nation's rapid western expansion, particularly after the discovery of gold in California in 1848. Available water sources were limited, and mining (especially placer mining) demanded large quantities of water and it often took place on federal public lands, which meant that riparian reasonable use rules did not work well. Agriculture to support a growing population also required water to irrigate crops on arid lands, sometimes far away from the water body.

Rules were developed in the mining camps to allocate the available water peaceably. The rules were similar to those adopted for the establishment and protection of mining claims on public lands: first in time, first in right. Essentially, the first user of water from a specific source held a right that would be protected against the claims of others who came later. The same system was applied to agricultural lands as homesteaders moved west. It prevented the farmers who took up land along the streams from monopolizing water that could be productively used on lands not touching any water source. This made sense in an arid region where much of the land and a majority of homesteads hybrid were far from a stream.

The United States acquired western territory from foreign nations and Indian nations, and then disposed of its lands through a variety of public land laws, including the General Preemption Act of 1841, the Homestead Act of 1862, the Mining Act of 1866, the Desert Land Act of 1877, and the Stock-Raising Homestead Act of 1916. The government could have decided to convey the land and (riparian) water rights together. Instead, it acquiesced in the establishment of private water rights on public lands under local customs, including rights to divert water across public land to distant mining claims and irrigated tracts. Lands were then patented (granted by the government) separately from these water rights, but were subject to any rights that were previously established by others. For a more detailed treatment of federal public lands history, *see* SANDRA ZELLMER AND JAN LAITOS, PRINCIPLES OF NATURAL RESOURCES LAW Ch. 4 (West 2014).

A. FEDERAL STATUTES

1. 1866 and 1870 Mining Acts

Shortly after the Civil War, proposals were made in Congress to withdraw mines from the public domain and operate or sell them to pay war debts. When western legislators from states with extensive private mineral development opposed this suggestion, Congress enacted the 1866 Mining Act. The Act reads in relevant part:

Whenever, by priority of possession, rights to the use of water for mining, agricultural, manufacturing, or other purposes have vested and accrued, and the same are recognized and acknowledged by the local customs, laws and decisions of courts, the possessors and owners of such vested rights shall be maintained and protected in the same.

30 U.S.C. § 51. The Act expressly confirmed the rights of miners and appropriators of water. It formally sanctioned appropriations of water on the public lands made before or after passage of the Act, as well as rights of way for transporting the water across public lands. The Act failed to define any method of acquiring water rights from the federal government, thus deferring to established local customs, state or territorial laws, and judicial rulings. Broder v. Natoma Water Co., 101 U.S. 274, 276 (1879).

Even after the 1866 Act, it was not clear whether riparian landowners who obtained grants of land from the United States held riparian water rights or were instead subject to claims of prior appropriators. The 1870 amendment to the Mining Act clarified that issue in favor of prior appropriators. It stipulated that anyone who acquired title to public lands through federal patents, homestead rights, or rights of preemption took title subject to any water rights, easements for water rights, or rights of way acquired by others while lands were in public ownership. 30 U.S.C. § 52; 43 U.S.C. § 661. These rights are good against both the United States and its grantees.

2. 1877 Desert Land Act

The Desert Land Act provided that water from non-navigable sources on the public lands was available for appropriation for irrigation, mining, and manufacturing purposes subject to existing rights. 43 U.S.C. § 321. It applied specifically to arid lands within Arizona, California, Idaho, Montana, Nevada, New Mexico, North Dakota, Oregon, South Dakota, Utah, Washington, and Wyoming. 43 U.S.C. § 323. Colorado was added by amendment in 1891.

For several decades, western states were divided concerning whether the Desert Land Act applied only to desert lands. The Supreme Court ultimately decided that the Act's acceptance of the appropriation doctrine applied to all public domain in the named states and territories. California Oregon Power Co. v. Beaver Portland Cement Co., 295 U.S. 142 (1935). The Court also found that the Desert Land Act severed the water from public lands, so that only water rights established under local law passed with a patent. *Id.* at 162. The Act states:

> [T]he right to the use of water by the person so conducting the same on or to any tract of desert land of 640 acres shall depend upon bona fide prior appropriation, and such right shall not exceed the amount of water actually appropriated and necessarily used for the purpose of irrigation and reclamation; *and all surplus water over and above such actual appropriation and use, together with the water of all lakes, rivers, and other sources of water supply on the public lands and not navigable, shall remain and be held free for the appropriation and use of the public for*

irrigation, mining, and manufacturing purposes, subject to existing rights.

43 U.S.C. § 321 (emphasis added). Thus, all unappropriated waters of non-navigable sources remained open to appropriation and use according to state law.

B. DEVELOPMENT OF MODERN SYSTEMS

The appropriation system was an expedient means to encourage development of the arid West, where much of the arable land is distant from streams and water is limited. It rewarded those who first risked their effort and money with security for their investments.

The eight most arid states (Arizona, Colorado, Idaho, Montana, Nevada, New Mexico, Utah, and Wyoming) constitutionally or statutorily repudiated riparian rights very early and adopted prior appropriation as the sole method of acquiring rights to the use of water for beneficial purposes. *See, e.g.,* Ariz. Const. Art. 17 § 1 ("The common law doctrine of riparian water rights shall not obtain or be of any force or effect in the state"); Colo. Const. Art.16 § 6 ("Priority of appropriation shall give the better right as between those using the water for the same purpose"). In these states, statutory systems have evolved to provide for initiation of appropriations, establishment and enforcement of priorities, and water distribution.

Early in Alaska's development, some riparian uses for mining purposes were allowed, but in 1966, its legislature enacted the Water Use Act, converting all riparian rights into appropriative water rights. Alaska Stat. § 46.15.040. This conversion was more ambitious than the approach taken by several other western states, where existing riparian rights were preserved to some extent after adoption of the appropriation doctrine. *See, e.g.,* Mont. Const. Art. 9 § 3(1).

Some degree of riparian common law continues to exist side-by-side with the statutory provisions of prior appropriation in California, Kansas, Nebraska, North Dakota, Oklahoma, Oregon, South Dakota, Texas, and Washington. These states generally recognized riparian rights but limited their expansion and recognized new rights only by prior appropriation. *See e.g.,* Cal. Water Code § 101. Hybrid systems are discussed in Chapter Four of this book.

III. ELEMENTS OF APPROPRIATION

Although the definitions and details of water rights by appropriation vary from state to state, a valid appropriation generally turns on water being *diverted* with *intent* to *apply* it for *beneficial use.*

At first, the appropriation system was encumbered by few procedures and legal requirements. One who needed water had only to begin using it. But in order to perfect a legal right in the water, the user had to show that the use amounted to an appropriation. The three elements—diversion, intent, application to beneficial use—were designed to prevent fraud and to provide some order in an otherwise unstructured system. Additionally, states have a special interest in assuring that water, as a public resource, is devoted to beneficial uses consistent with the public good.

Historically, it was necessary for an appropriator to be able to prove that all three elements were satisfied. Since these elements have become incorporated into modern state water allocation statutes, their importance is largely theoretical. Permit systems and administrative agencies that review the sufficiency of applications for water rights impose a variety of requirements designed to achieve the purposes of the common law elements of appropriation.

A. INTENT

An appropriation is not valid unless the appropriator intends to divert water and apply it to a beneficial use. Thus, one who diverts water away from its normal flow pattern in order to prevent flood damage is not an appropriator. But such a diverter who later finds a beneficial use for the water as channeled may become an appropriator as of the time the requisite intent is manifested.

Issues regarding intent arise most frequently when one seeks to secure a priority that predates the diversion. The "relation back" doctrine allows an appropriator to perfect a water right with a priority date as of the time an intent to appropriate was first formed. "[T]he appropriation is not deemed complete until the actual diversion or use of the water, still if such work be prosecuted with reasonable diligence, the right relates to the time when the first step was taken to secure it." Ophir Silver Min. Co. v. Carpenter, 4 Nev. 534 (1869). Evidence must be presented to prove that one had such intent and that work was proceeding toward an actual diversion of water (not just speculation) as of the priority date.

In states where a permit is required for a valid appropriation, application for a permit is objective evidence of intent. However, one may not apply for a water right and then seek a place to use it, as that would constitute speculation. Lemmon v. Hardy, 519 P.2d 1168 (Idaho 1974). Early statutory systems gave appropriators the option of diverting or applying for a permit to secure water rights. A person could choose to divert without a permit and still relate back the priority to the time that work on the diversion facilities began. Sand Point Water & Light Co. v. Panhandle Dev. Co., 83 P. 347 (Idaho 1905).

Where permits are not required for a valid appropriation, as in Colorado, proof of intent retains some importance. To establish the priority of an appropriation, an applicant must make a clear decision to use water and an "open, physical demonstration of that intent." Harvey Land & Cattle Co. v. Southeastern Colo. Water Conservancy Dist., 631 P.2d 1111, 1113 (Colo. 1981). This requirement is a means of giving notice to others that one intends to appropriate water, though the actual diversion will be in the future. City of

Thornton v. Bijou Irrigation Co., 926 P.2d 1 (Colo. 1996).

Courts may examine other relevant evidence besides the first open physical act to determine whether the requisite intent was present. A survey that is not accompanied by a clear decision to undertake the project may not be sufficient. Colorado River Water Conservation Dist. v. Rocky Mountain Power Co., 486 P.2d 438 (Colo. 1971). *Rocky Mountain Power* shows that it is possible for intent to be formed after the physical act, in which case priority is based on the later of the two events. In Harvey Land & Cattle Co. v. Southeastern Colo. Water Conservancy Dist., 631 P.2d 1111 (Colo. 1981), the court found that drilling wells with capacity greater than old right constituted a "physical act" necessary to perfect a new water right; however, the priority date related back only to the time, years after the wells were drilled, when the intent to use the wells for larger quantities was formed.

Colorado law provides for conditional decrees that recognize rights to a particular quantity of water for a specific future use. In order to get a conditional decree, one must demonstrate a present, non-speculative intent to put the water to a beneficial use and then must proceed with due diligence to divert the water. Colo. Rev. Stat. §§ 37–92–103(6), 37–92–305(1). *See* Pagosa Area Water and Sanitation Dist. v. Trout Unlimited, 219 P.3d 774 (2009) (holding that a public water supply agency can get a conditional decree for future use only for the amount of water that is reasonably necessary for substantiated population projections for a reasonable planning period). The applicant must describe with particularity the amount of water to be appropriated and the construction plans. Colo. Rev. Stat. § 37–92–302. Those opposing the proposed conditional decree can file objections, and the application is adjudicated with respect to the rights of all parties in the stream system.

A conditional decree may be lost if a city loses a contractual agreement to use a necessary diversion facility. City of Lafayette v. New Anderson Ditch Co., 962 P.2d 955 (Colo. 1998). The applicant must establish that there is a substantial probability that the facilities necessary for the appropriation "can and will" be completed and the water put to a beneficial use within a reasonable time. Colo. Rev. Stat. § 37–92–305. In determining whether water is available for the conditional decree, the court considers absolute decrees and conditional decrees under which diversions have taken place, but can disregard conditional decrees for which no diversions have been made. Board of County Commissioners of the County of Arapahoe v. United States, 891 P.2d 952 (Colo. 1995). Environmental factors need not be considered in issuing the conditional decree (and hence in granting water rights) in Colorado. *Id.* at 971. However, if an instream flow right has been recognized, it will be superior to subsequent appropriators. Colorado Water Conservation Bd. v. City of Cent., 125 P.3d 424, 439 (Colo. 2005). *See infra* Section III.D.3.

B. DIVERSION

Historically, water had to be physically diverted from a surface water body in order to obtain a valid appropriation. The diversion requirement provided notice to present and prospective appropriators that water had been appropriated. Moreover, the capacity of the diversion works could be used to define the quantity of water appropriated. Many western states now consider various uses that do not depend on structures or human acts to be valid appropriations, despite the lack of a diversion.

1. Types of Diversions

A diversion is an alteration of part or all of a stream's flow away from its natural course. A common method of diversion is to build a dam in or across a stream, directing water into a canal or ditch. Water may be channeled farther into smaller ditches, each with a "headgate" that controls when and how much water is used in each of several parcels of land, often by several appropriators. Other methods of diverting water include reservoirs, flumes, pipes, pumps, and water wheels.

Traditionally, a diversion had to be a human-made method of physically removing water from the stream, but courts have forged numerous exceptions for various kinds of uses, as discussed below in Section III.B.3. States that continue to insist on physical diversions have sometimes approved of the creative use of low control structures that divert the stream back to its historic channel to maintain recreational or aesthetic stream qualities. City of

Thornton By and Through Utilities Bd. v. City of Fort Collins, 830 P.2d 915 (Colo. 1992).

2. Due Diligence Requirement and Conditional Rights

In states that require a permit to appropriate water, the priority date may relate back to the date the application was filed. In order to keep that priority date and to perfect a water right, the appropriator must complete construction with due diligence and actually use the water within the time specified in the permit or statute.

Some state statutes set maximum time periods for construction of facilities and application of water to beneficial use, often five years, subject to extension for good cause (*e.g.,* Arizona, Idaho, Nevada, Oregon, Wyoming, and New Mexico allow four additional years after construction to use the water). A few require actual construction to begin within a certain time, ranging from six months to two years after approval of the application. Some states readily allow time extensions upon a showing that the applicant has proceeded with due diligence; others grant extensions only in narrowly defined or extraordinary circumstances. Idaho, for example, allows extensions after its five-year limit only if the applicant is prevented from continuing by delays in receiving necessary federal approvals or the completion of litigation, or if the project is extremely large. Idaho Code Ann. § 42–222(3) (2004).

In Colorado, which does not have a permit system, an appropriator's priority date is generally the date of an application for a conditional right. Colo. Rev. Stat § 37–92–306.1 (1981); City and County of Denver v. Sheriff, 96 P.2d 836 (Colo. 1939). The priority date, however, will relate back only to the point when the "first step" was taken to appropriate water from a specific stream and not the first step taken to commence a project involving several streams, unless the appropriator can demonstrate that the diversions are for "one over-all integral plan" from "tributaries of one stream and one water basin in one water district." Metro. Suburban Water Users Ass'n v. Colo. River Water Conservation Dist., 365 P.2d 273, 283 (Colo. 1961). Also, a conditional priority date will be lost unless the prospective appropriator completes construction with due diligence within a reasonable time. Purgatoire River Water Conservancy Dist. v. Witte, 859 P.2d 825, 832 (Colo. 1993); City of Thornton v. Bijou Irrigation Co., 926 P.2d 1 (Colo. 1996).

Colorado's procedure for obtaining a conditional decree is discussed in the preceding subsection. If a conditional decree is granted, the prospective user must proceed with due diligence in constructing the waterworks or risk forfeiture of the conditional right. Colo. Rev. Stat. § 37–92–301 (2013). The decree holder must obtain a finding of due diligence by a water court referee every six years. Colo. Rev. Stat § 37–92–301(4)(a)(1) (2013). Failure to do so will result in cancellation of the conditionally decreed right. Town of De Beque v. Enewold, 606 P.2d 48 (Colo. 1980). However, a conditional right cannot be cancelled absent adequate notice of cancellation. Double RL Co. v. Telluray Ranch

Props., 54 P.3d 908 (Colo. 2002). Once the diversion takes place, an absolute decree can be obtained that is senior to all appropriators who commenced their appropriations after the initiation of the conditional decree.

3. Exceptions to the Diversion Requirement

Several states no longer require an actual, physical diversion from the stream. *See e.g.,* Phelps Dodge Corp. v. Arizona Dep't of Water Resources, 118 P.3d 1110 (Ariz.App. 2005). A diversion may not be required if intent to appropriate to a beneficial use, notice to others, and application to a beneficial use are clearly established. In Montana, for example, a physical diversion is not required unless the beneficial use depends on it. In re Adjudication of Existing Rights to the Use of All the Water, 55 P.3d 396, 402 (Mont. 2002). In dicta, one court even hinted that mist from a waterfall that nourishes vegetation might constitute a valid appropriation. Empire Water & Power Co. v. Cascade Town Co., 205 F. 123 (8th Cir. 1913). If farmland can be irrigated naturally with the help of existing channels and depressions, it may be considered a waste of resources to require the appropriator to construct a system of artificial ditches.

California, Colorado, Idaho, and Nevada consider it to be a diversion when ranchers allow livestock to drink water from ponds, marshes, or directly from a stream. Joyce Livestock Co. v. U.S., 156 P.3d 502, 512 (Idaho 2007). However, the New Mexico Supreme Court rejected a rancher's claim that grazing his cattle on grass that was watered annually by intermittent runoff evidenced his intention to appropriate water and thus entitled him to water rights. State ex rel. Reynolds v. Miranda, 493 P.2d 409 (N.M. 1972). The court held that a man-made diversion was necessary for a valid appropriation, and found that the rancher had made no attempt to actually divert any of the water into the area. *Id.* at 411.

Several states have embraced a trend allowing instream (*in situ*) appropriations of water. *See* In re Application A-16642, 463 N.W.2d 591 (Neb. 1990) (upholding instream appropriations for a naturally occurring trout fishery despite the lack of a diversion). Alaska, California, Colorado, Hawaii, Idaho, Kansas, Montana, Nebraska, Oklahoma, Oregon, Utah, Washington, and Wyoming have enacted legislation allowing instream uses of water. An instream appropriation generally requires that a certain amount of water be allowed to flow through a stretch of stream in order to protect fish and wildlife, scenic beauty, or water-borne recreation. *See* State, Dept. of Parks v. Idaho Dept. of Water Administration, 530 P.2d 924 (Idaho 1974) (upholding a statute declaring preservation of water in Malad Canyon for scenic and recreational purposes to be a beneficial use).

In most states, instream flows may be appropriated only by a state agency, although the agency may be able to act upon requests of private individuals, other state and local agencies, or the federal government. Colorado allows instream flows to be appropriated exclusively by the state Water Conservation Board upon a finding that it will "preserve the natural environment to a reasonable degree." Colo. Rev. Stat. § 37–92–102(3) (2013). Rights also may be purchased or accepted by gift and converted to instream flow rights. *Id.* Cities, nevertheless, were successful in getting the state supreme court to uphold their rights to an appropriation of flowing water for recreational uses by constructing facilities such as boat chutes and fish ladders to ostensibly control the stream without actually removing water. City of Thornton v. City of Fort Collins, 830 P.2d 915 (Colo. 1992). This type of so-called diversion was later regulated by legislation that allows water courts to adjudicate rights for "recreational in-channel diversions" upon findings related to promoting full development of the state's water and the appropriateness of the use for the particular stream in question. Colo. Rev. Stat. § 37–92–102(5)–(6)(c) (2013).

Arizona, Nevada, and South Dakota have recognized instream appropriations without enabling legislation; instead they allow instream appropriations as part of their general appropriation procedures. The New Mexico Attorney General determined that a traditional water right can be changed to an instream use under certain circumstances and that the state constitution does not require an actual diversion. Op.Atty.Gen.No. 98–01 (March 27, 1998). The New Mexico legislature has also authorized its interstate stream commission to purchase or lease water to create a "strategic water reserve" in order to achieve compliance with the Endangered Species Act and to meet water delivery requirements under various interstate compacts. N.M. Stat. Ann. § 72–14–3.3.

C. BENEFICIAL USE

The last and most important step in perfecting an appropriation is application of the water to beneficial use. "Beneficial use" is "the use of such water as may be necessary for some useful and beneficial purpose in connection with the land from which it is taken ... require[ing] actual use for some purpose that is socially accepted as beneficial." State ex rel. Office of State Eng'r v. United States, 296 P.3d 1217, 1222 (N.M. App. 2012), *cert. denied,* 299 P.3d 862 (2013).

All prior appropriation states consider domestic, municipal, agricultural, and industrial uses to be beneficial. Recognized types of beneficial uses may be defined more elaborately by statute or case law (see Table A). Just because a use is among the types listed, however, does not mean it will be deemed "beneficial" under the circumstances or for all time. Yesterday's beneficial use may be unreasonable or wasteful, and thus impermissible, today.

David H. Getches 2008

BENEFICIAL USES SPECIFIED BY STATE LAW

Use:	Domestic	Municipal	Irrigation or agricultural	Industrial	Stock-watering	Power	Mining	Recreation	Fish & wildlife	Other
Alaska	X	X	X	X		X	X	X	X	manufacturing, navigation, transportation, water quality
Arizona	X	X	X		X	X	X	X	X	groundwater recharge
California	X	X	X	X	X	X	X	X	X	water quality
Colorado	X	X	X	X				X	X	
Idaho*										
Kansas	X	X	X	X		X		X		
Montana	X	X	X	X		X	X	X		
Nebraska*					X	X			X	
Nevada*			X				X	X	X	state conservation purposes
New Mexico**					X					
North Dakota	X	X	X	X				X	X	
Oklahoma*	X	X	X	X				X	X	not limited to these
Oregon	X	X	X	X		X	X	X	X	pollution abatement
South Dakota***						X	X			
Texas	X	X	X	X	X	X	X	X	X	parks, aquifer recharge, "any other beneficial use"
Utah*			X		X					
Washington	X		X	X	X	X	X	X		
Wyoming*	X	X	X			X		X	X	frost protection

* No comprehensive definition furnished by statute or case law.

** Case law defines beneficial use as "the use of such water as may be necessary for some useful and beneficial purpose in connection with the land from which it is taken." Erickson v. McLean, 62 N.M. 264, 308 P.2d 983 (1957).

*** Statute defines beneficial use as "any use of water within or outside of the state, that is reasonable and useful and beneficial to the appropriator, and at the same time is consistent with the interests of the public...." S.D.Cod.Laws § 46-1-6 (3).

Domestic use generally includes household uses such as cooking, drinking, laundering, washing, and watering a small garden. In rural areas, domestic use may also include water for raising animals on a small scale, such as keeping a few dairy cows or chickens. Municipal use includes domestic use by residents, water used in operating public buildings, and even irrigation of city parks.

Initially, the range of beneficial uses was very limited. In Empire Water & Power Co. v. Cascade Town Co., 205 F. 123 (8th Cir. 1913), a federal appeals court refused to consider recreation a beneficial use. The court would not allow a resort town to assert a right to keep the town's major attraction, a waterfall, flowing merely to retain its scenic beauty. *Id.* at 129. However, the court seemed willing to allow the waterfall to continue flowing if the town could assert an agricultural use, such as misting the vegetation growing on the banks of Cascade Falls. *Id.* Most states now have accepted recreation as a beneficial use. *See, e.g.,* Or. Rev. Stat. § 536.300(1) (2005); Mont. Code Ann. § 85–2–102(4)(a). Some statutory provisions specify that scenic or aesthetic uses are also beneficial. *See, e.g.,* Wash. Rev. Code § 90.54.020(3)(a); Hawaii Rev. Stat. § 174C–71(1)(C).

Once an appropriator puts water to a use considered beneficial by state law, the right is perfected. The right becomes absolute and its priority in times of shortage will not be defeated even by more socially important, more economically valuable, or more efficient uses by a junior appropriator. Thus, a senior user applying vast quantities of water to the unprofitable production of rice in the desert might prevent a city with a junior right from receiving desperately needed water for domestic purposes, or a highly profitable industry from taking the water that it requires. Janet C. Neuman, *Beneficial Use, Waste, and Forfeiture: The Inefficient Search for Efficiency in Western Water Use,* 28 Envtl. L. 919, 970 (1998). To temper the effects of this rule, some jurisdictions have enacted preference statutes that allow junior appropriators with certain preferred uses, such as domestic and agricultural uses, to condemn senior rights that are being put to a beneficial use in a lower preference category, such as industry. *See infra* Section IV.D.

D. WATERS SUBJECT TO APPROPRIATION

Private rights to use water cannot be acquired in all types of water. A state's constitution or statutes may define waters subject to state jurisdiction and control in a way that excludes certain waters from the allocation of private rights. Such provisions may describe waters of a "natural stream" as being "public property" or subject to appropriation, or they may exclude certain types of waters (such as runoff or seasonal floods) from the reach of private water rights. State law may also recognize greater or lesser private rights in various types of water (*e.g.,* groundwater) and define the extent to which such waters are subject to public use.

1. Watercourses

Once water joins a watercourse, it becomes subject to state control. In appropriation states, it becomes available for private uses according to state law.

Watercourses could be defined to include not only rivers and lakes, but every tiny brook flowing into them, all the gullies through which water flows to the brooks, the snow pack and rainfall that feed them, and the evaporating or transpiring water in the process of forming clouds. But it would be an immense challenge to regulate these sources. Legal definitions are intended to delineate a point beyond which a state does not regulate water use. Usually that point is when water is not in a "natural stream." *See* Cal. Const., art. X, § 2 ("The right to water . . . in or from any natural stream or water course in this State is and shall be limited to such water as shall be reasonably required for the beneficial use"); Chatfield East Well Co., Ltd. v. Chatfield East Property Owners Ass'n, 956 P.2d 1260, 1268 (Colo. 1998) (holding that waters of a natural stream, including tributary ground water, belong to the public and are subject to use under Colorado's constitution and implementing statutes).

Courts often define a stream or watercourse as a body of water flowing in a defined channel with a bed and banks. Generally, the waterbody must have some permanence. Montana, for instance, defines a watercourse as "any naturally occurring stream or river from which water is diverted for beneficial uses." Mont. Code Ann. § 85–2–102(30). The definition excludes "ditches, culverts, or other constructed waterways." *Id.*

In contrast to defined watercourses, diffused surface water ordinarily may be freely taken and used by landowners without state regulation. Drainage Dist. No. 1 of Lincoln Cnty. v. Suburban Irr. Dist., 139 Neb. 460, 298 N.W. 131, 132 (1941); State v. Hiber, 44 P.2d 1005, 1008 (Wyo. 1935). However, Alaska, Montana, Nevada, Oregon, Texas, and Utah claim broader control over various kinds of waters, and Utah and Colorado construe the state's authority as extending well beyond natural watercourses to virtually all surface water and even some groundwater, *see* Utah Code Ann. § 73–1–1(1); Colo. Const, Art. 16 § 5. For details on diffused surface water, *see* Chapter Six, *infra.*

a. Streams

Although western states typically apply the prior appropriation doctrine to watercourses with a definite bed, bank, and channel, these requirements rarely resolve hard cases. For example, freshets (flows due to runoff from rainfall or melting snow) may appear to be streams at least part of the year, cutting draws or ravines as water flows toward rivers and their tributaries, but a court may require, in addition, that there be a continuous flow to be covered as a natural stream. Yet some indisputable "watercourses" flow only intermittently and are made up solely of snowmelt and rainwater. This is especially true in the high mountains of the West where streams dry up in summer. Further, some genuine streams simply do not run in great enough volume or speed to carve out banks or scour a bed. In flat areas, a river may spread out and avoid cutting a defined channel, or it may meander through different routes each season.

Besides considering the geographic characteristics discussed above, some courts resort to a functional test. In Texas, the courts have asked whether the volume and regularity make it practicable to use the stream for irrigation. Hoefs v. Short, 273 S.W. 785 (Tex. 1925). Other courts have rested their decisions on factual determinations that escape easy classification. In State v. Hiber, 44 P.2d 1005 (Wyo. 1935), the state sought to enjoin the defendant from impounding waters that flowed down a swale or draw behind a small dam because the impoundment allegedly interfered with the flow of a natural stream. The court reviewed decisions in various states that distinguished between watercourses and diffused surface water, and found some attributes of a watercourse present, but some lacking. Id. at 1009–10. Concluding that it was not a watercourse, the court leaned heavily on the peculiar characteristics of the flow in question, stating "[j]udging from the testimony, no one would instantaneously perceive that it is a watercourse." Id. at 1011.

This perception test ("I know a stream when I see it") may seem unworkable, but in difficult cases that determine the appropriate limits of state authority, the outcome may be dictated by the practicality and utility of state regulation of the water. Presumably, the more arid the area, the more important a small flow will be and the greater the likelihood it will be found to be a watercourse in a close case.

b. Lakes and Ponds

The water of natural lakes and ponds ordinarily is subject to appropriation by state law. The right to appropriate water from such sources may be qualified by rights to use the surface (as distinguished from rights to consume water) that are appurtenant to riparian land and are recognized in littoral (lakeshore) landowners, even in prior appropriation states. *See supra* Chapter 2.II.D. For instance, an appropriator may be precluded from drawing water from a lake if it would substantially lower water levels and interfere with littoral owners' rights to access the lake for fishing, recreation, or other lawful purposes. In re Martha Lake Water Co. No. 1, 277 P. 382 (Wash. 1929).

c. Springs

The treatment of spring water varies by state, and also by the type of spring. Some states consider a spring subject to appropriation only if its flow forms a stream; otherwise, spring water is treated as groundwater. Okla. Water Res. Bd. v. City of Lawton, 580 P.2d 510, 513 (Okla. 1977). Others subject spring water to appropriation. Parker v. McIntyre, 56 P.2d 1337, 1340 (Ariz. 1936); Dalton v. Wadley, 355 P.2d 69, 88 (Utah 1960). Colorado treats springs and seeps as surface waters subject to appropriation if they are "tributary" (closely connected, hydrologically) to a creek. SRJ I Venture v. Smith Cattle, Inc., 820 P.2d 341, 345 (Colo. 1991) (citing Colo. Rev. Stat. § 37–82–102).

2. Waters Made Available by Human Effort

Sometimes water ends up in a natural stream at times and places and in quantities other than that which would normally occur in nature. This may be because irrigation return flows delay the seasonal decline in natural streamflow, or it may be the result of massive diversions from one watershed to another. The general rule is that water that would never be available in the stream except for human efforts can be used without restriction by the person responsible for its being there, and it is not subject to appropriation until that person abandons it. Ariz. Pub. Serv. Co. v. Long, 773 P.2d 988, 995 (Ariz. 1989). Courts draw distinctions, however, between foreign and developed water and salvage water.

a. Foreign and Developed Water

Foreign or developed water is characterized as water that would not have been in a stream without human effort. It includes imported water brought to the stream from another watershed by tunnels, canals, pumps, and other facilities. It also includes groundwater pumped from an aquifer not hydrologically connected with the stream, as well as trapped water recovered from a mine. The rainfall from artificially induced precipitation, *i.e.,* "rain-making" by seeding clouds, is considered developed water in some states but not others. It may be sound policy to reward such private efforts, though it is virtually impossible to differentiate natural precipitation from the results of cloud seeding.

Imported or foreign water, *e.g.*, from transbasin diversions, is not part of the stream and thus not subject to appropriation. City and County of Denver v. Fulton Irrigating Ditch Co., 506 P.2d 144 (Colo. 1972). Foreign water, unlike water subject to appropriation, is also not subject to restrictions on recapture and reuse. Water Supply and Storage Co. v. Curtis, 733 P.2d 680 (Colo. 1987); *see infra* Section V.C. Similarly, such water is not subject to the change of use restrictions discussed in Section VII.D.

Western irrigation practices involve repeated diversions, applications, and return flows of waters as they move downstream. Consequently, successive irrigators, often relying on return flows from upstream irrigators, depend on waters being used in essentially the same manner year after year. If water is not naturally in the stream, the downstream irrigators may be cut off, despite their reliance on continued flows. City of Thornton v. Bijou Irr. Co., 926 P.2d 1 (Colo. 1996).

Thanks to importers, appropriators may have supplies available to them at times when they otherwise would have insufficient water. For instance, in a year of low natural flow, juniors below the point in a stream where a large importer ceases using water may, in effect, be using almost entirely return flows of imported water. Although such users may benefit incidentally, they can gain no appropriative right in the imported water. *Id.* at 69.

Just as an importer can stop importing water at any time, the importer can decide to reuse the water, remove it from the stream at a different location, or sell it to others, without legal restraint. Thayer v. City of Rawlins, 594 P.2d 951, 956 (Wyo. 1979); Arizona Public Service Co. v. Long, 773 P.2d 988 (Ariz. 1989). Typically, imported water has been obtained from another watershed pursuant to a water right in that watershed. The right is, as to the original watershed, 100% consumptive. Streams in the new watershed are used only to transport the water and so it never becomes a part of the "natural stream." An exception arises if both the importing and exporting watersheds are part of the same larger watershed. In that case, the water remaining in the stream below the confluence of the two sub-watersheds would belong to the stream and again be subject to appropriation.

Once an importer ceases using imported water, the water is similar to abandoned personalty and can be taken and used by others. Elgin v. Weatherstone, 212 P. 562 (Wash. 1923); Dodge v. Ellensburg Water Co., 729 P.2d 631 (Wash. App. 1986).

b. Salvaged Water

In contrast to foreign or developed water, which would not naturally be in a stream but for human effort, salvaged water is recovered from existing uses or losses within the original watershed. City of

Santa Maria v. Adam, 19 Cal.Rptr. 491, 522 (2012). For instance, if seepage or evaporative losses are prevented by human effort, fuller use could be made of the water. But it is not "new" to the stream in the same sense that imported water is. Thus, salvaged water is considered subject to appropriation. It can be recaptured and reused according to rules discussed in Section V.C of this chapter, but it is subject to the priority system.

In Southeastern Colorado Water Conservancy Dist. v. Shelton Farms, Inc., 529 P.2d 1321, 1326 (Colo. 1974), the court denied water rights free of all calls to applicants who had increased flow by removing water-consuming plants (phreatophytes). The water that had been freed from the plants was subject to the priority system and was therefore made available to other appropriators whose appropriations had not been fulfilled in the past. The court reached a similar result when an applicant proposed to lower the water table by pumping water out of an aquifer, which would reduce the number of plants in the area and ultimately result in lower evapotranspiration rates. City of Aurora v. Simpson (In re Water Rights of Park County Sportsmen's Ranch), 105 P.3d 595 (Colo. 2005).

3. Withdrawals from Appropriation

Water in natural watercourses can be removed from availability for some or all forms of appropriation by state action or federal law for instream flows or to preserve it for some future public use.

a. Maintenance of Instream Flows

Protection of streamflows or lake levels for fish and wildlife, recreation, water quality, and scenic beauty is accomplished in two ways. The waters can be "appropriated" for instream uses or they can be withdrawn from appropriation to preserve flows from depletion by private appropriators. The first approach initially conflicted with the fundamental requirements of the appropriation doctrine that water be diverted and put to a beneficial use. Most states have expressly relaxed their diversion requirements, and most consider recreation and wildlife protection to be beneficial uses. *See supra* Section III.B.3.

Withdrawing water from appropriation was one of the earliest methods pursued for avoiding the obstacles that prevented appropriations for instream flows. Statutes that remove waters from appropriation usually preserve all pre-existing, perfected appropriations as the date of enactment. Oregon and Idaho enacted statutes that removed certain rivers and lakes from appropriation and protected them from damage by state or private projects. The state engineer of North Dakota has power to reserve water for aquatic life, recreation, or other future beneficial uses. Other states, such as Alaska, Oklahoma, and California, identify particular rivers to be protected as "recreation rivers," "scenic river areas," "wild rivers," or "free-flowing rivers."

Utah allows its state engineer to deny appropriations if they would be detrimental to recreation or the natural stream environment. In Washington, the Department of Ecology has required maintenance of instream flows to protect endangered fish as a condition to a Clean Water Act water quality certification. PUD No. 1 of Pend Oreille v. Washington, 51 P.3d 744 (Wash. 2002); PUD No. 1 of Jefferson Cnty. v. Washington, 511 U.S. 700 (1994). Washington also allows administrative withdrawal of certain amounts of water from critical rivers or lakes, but only if withdrawal is in the public interest. Wash. Rev. Code. § 90.54.020(3)(a) (2007). Montana enacted the most sweeping law of this type when it gave state, municipal, and federal agencies the authority to apply for the reservation of waters for instream flows for fish and wildlife, recreation, and water quality. Such reservations may not exceed 50% of the average annual flow. Mont. Code Ann. §§ 85–2–316 (2007), 85–2–331 (2007). Montana law also allows reservations of water for future uses, as discussed in the next subsection.

Instream flows may receive some protection under the federal Wild and Scenic Rivers Act, 16 U.S.C. §§ 1271–87. *See infra* Chapter 8.III.E. Congress, or state legislatures with the Secretary of Interior's approval, may designate certain river segments that contain "remarkable scenic, recreational, geologic, fish and wildlife, historic, cultural or other similar values." 16 U.S.C. § 1271. Once a river is designated, hydropower facilities and some other types of water development projects that affect its flow are restricted. 16 U.S.C. § 1278. If the United States wants to protect the flow from existing users, it may purchase water rights or exercise its power of eminent domain to acquire the rights of appropriators upon payment of compensation. 16 U.S.C. § 1284(b).

The doctrine of federal reserved water rights (*see infra* Chapter Eight) may also be applied to preserve instream flows on federal public lands or Indian lands. If the federal government reserves public land for particular uses that require maintenance of instream flows (*e.g.*, enough water to sustain aquatic life in a wildlife refuge, natural conditions in a park, or a fishery on an Indian reservation), the courts have recognized impliedly reserved rights to sufficient water to fulfill that purpose. Cappaert v. U.S., 426 U.S. 128, 138 (1976). Each reservation must be examined to determine whether reserved instream flows were essential to its purposes. *See* United States v. New Mexico, 438 U.S. 696 (1978) (water was not reserved for instream flows in a national forest because fish and wildlife maintenance was not among the primary purposes of the reservation).

b. Reservations for Future Uses

Many states provide by statute (Arizona, California, Idaho, Nevada, North Dakota, Oklahoma, Oregon, Washington) or by judicial decision (Wyoming), or both (Colorado), that municipalities can appropriate water for reasonably anticipated future needs. The Montana Water Use Act allows all levels of government to apply for water to be reserved for any future beneficial use (including municipal or irrigation). Mont. Code Ann. §§ 85–2–316, 85–2–102(4). In most states, the water need not be diverted and applied to a beneficial use in the meantime. Colorado and California require that a beneficial use be made, but this can be satisfied by leasing the water for other purposes.

IV. PRIORITY AND PREFERENCES

A. PRIORITY

Priority is the bedrock feature of prior appropriation. A person whose appropriation is first in time has the highest priority and hence a right to make beneficial use of water superior to all others. An appropriator with an earlier priority date is known as the senior, as compared to a later appropriator, who is the junior. All water rights holders are ranked according to the dates of their appropriations. When there is not enough water for all appropriators, the doctrine of priority allows the full senior right to be exercised before the junior can use any water. The first user to be limited is the most junior on the list of priorities; juniors must abate their use until everyone senior to them has been served.

The priority date may relate back to an earlier date when one first formulated the intent to appropriate or received a permit or decree for a planned future use. Thus, the doctrine protects priorities of early appropriators, providing an incentive for water users to invest in expensive diversion works by assuring them of legal protection for their water supply as against juniors. But the doctrine as applied may have adverse economic consequences. First, appropriators may build diversion works prematurely or unnecessarily in order to protect their early priority. Second, the doctrine often frustrates transfers of water to higher economic uses. For example, a senior may hold a reliable water right to irrigate crops of comparatively low value. If a municipal or industrial user wishes to use that water in a higher-value use, it may "buy out" the senior's water right. In practice, however, the transfer of water rights may be legally prohibited or at least inhibited by transaction costs and the "no harm" rule. *See infra* Section VII.

B. QUALIFICATIONS OF THE SENIOR'S RIGHT

No appropriator, including those with senior rights, has a right to waste water. Water in a stream belongs to the public, and private rights are allowed only to the extent that appropriators can use water beneficially. Nebraska, Neb.Art. XV, § 5. As a practical matter, however, one who holds a right to a specific quantity of water is rarely restricted from diverting the full quantity recognized in the permit, although states are beginning to be more rigorous in imposing restrictions on wasteful or inefficient uses. *See infra* Section V.B.

A senior cannot change an established use to the detriment of a junior. Seniors may be obligated to ensure juniors the same stream conditions that existed at the time the juniors began using water. Farmers Highline Canal & Reservoir Co. v. City of Golden, 272 P.2d 629 (Colo. 1954); Okanogan Wilderness League, Inc. v. Town of Twisp, 947 P.2d 732 (Wash. 1997). For example, a senior cannot change the place water is taken out of the stream ("point of diversion") if it adversely affects a junior. *Farmers Highline,* 272 P.2d at 632. The same rule applies to a change of purpose or time of use. If an appropriator has only used water during a particular growing season, a transferee's use of the right ordinarily will be limited to that season. Farmers Reservoir & Irrigation Co. v. City of Golden, 44 P.3d 241 (Colo. 2002). *See infra* Section VII.D.

C. ENFORCEMENT OF PRIORITIES

Juniors may not deprive seniors of water in quantities, at times, at places, or of a quality necessary to support the seniors' use. A senior appropriator seeking to enforce rights as against a junior "calls the river." It is usually the job of the state engineer or some other official to ensure that appropriators do not take water out of priority. If shutting down the junior will not actually result in water being delivered to the senior, however, the senior is said to have made a "futile call" and the state official will not enforce it.

Strict enforcement of priorities can cause waste, as illustrated by State ex rel. Cary v. Cochran, 292 N.W. 239 (Neb. 1940). In *Cary*, senior appropriators downstream on the Platte River sued to compel the state engineer to prevent upstream juniors from interfering with their rights. Because of seepage and evaporation losses along the lengthy stretch of river between the juniors and seniors, the juniors had to let 700 c.f.s. of water pass by in order for the 162 c.f.s. needed to satisfy the seniors' rights to reach them. The court enforced the seniors' right to shut off the juniors, but only so long as usable quantities would reach the seniors. *Id.* at 247. Requiring some water to be deliverable before the seniors' call would be heeded prevented a futile call. Yet the juniors were prevented from taking a substantial amount of water to allow small usable quantities to pass to the seniors.

D. PREFERENCES

Many states have statutes or constitutional provisions that express a preference for certain types of water use over others. Typically, they rank uses according to the view of the relative importance of various uses that prevailed at the time the preferences were established. Almost all place the highest preference on domestic or municipal purposes. Although there are many variations, most put agricultural use second and industrial and mining third. *See, e.g.* Colo. Const. art. 16 § 6; Neb. Const. art. 15 § 6.

Some state statutes or constitutional provisions require condemnation and compensation as the means of effectuating preferred uses, thereby requiring the preferred users to condemn the rights of senior users with lower preferences. *See, e.g.,* Neb. Rev. Stat. §§ 70–669, 76–711; In re 2007 Administration of Appropriations of the Niobrara River, 278 Neb. 137, 768 N.W.2d 420 (2009). A few preference laws are interpreted as mandates for agencies to give preference to applicants for higher water uses over those whose applications for less preferred uses are simultaneously pending. *See, e.g.,* East Bay Municipal Utility Dist. v. Dept. of Public Works, 35 P.2d 1027 (Cal. 1934).

V. EXTENT OF THE APPROPRIATIVE RIGHT

The quantity of water to which one is entitled under the prior appropriation doctrine is the amount continuously taken and beneficially used. The quantities stated in many old permits or decrees, however, are much larger than the amounts actually diverted or needed for the appropriator's purposes. This is because old paper rights often were based only on declarations of the appropriators or the capacity of the diversion works. Overstating rights is less widespread today, largely because state appropriation systems are administered by professional engineers who verify claims before rights are granted.

All modern appropriation systems provide that persons may object to the granting or recognition of a new right by an administrative agency or court on the ground that the right is excessive for the purposes claimed. In addition, junior appropriators may challenge water rights of a senior, claiming that some portion of the rights has been abandoned by non-use. East Twin Lakes Ditches and Water Works, Inc. v. Bd. of County Com'rs of Lake County, 76 P.3d 918 (Colo. 2003).

Appropriative rights also entail a sufficient quality of water to allow a continuation of beneficial uses. However, this principle has been invoked only rarely to prevent another appropriator from polluting. Early cases prevented upstream miners from polluting water to the detriment of downstream seniors. Arizona Copper Co. v. Gillespie, 100 P. 465 (Ariz. Terr. 1909). Most states now have dual systems under which one agency or a court deals with water allocation and a separate agency deals with water pollution. In Colorado, a Water Quality Control Commission regulates water quality and is prohibited by statute from interfering with the exercise of water rights. Colo. Rev. Stat. § 25–8–205 (2013). The water court deals exclusively with water rights, but when approving an exchange (*i.e.,* when water is substituted into the stream to satisfy the rights of another appropriator), it considers whether the water is of comparable quality. In re Application for Plan for Augmentation of City and County of Denver ex rel. Bd. of Water Com'rs, 44 P.3d 1019, 1032 (2002).

A depletion in flow that results in stricter limitations on a discharger's effluent does not constitute a legally cognizable injury to a party under the prior appropriation doctrine as long as the party is still able to divert the full amount of the water right. City of Thornton v. Bijou Irr. Co., 926 P.2d 1 (Colo. 1996). To hold otherwise would effectively create a private instream flow right for the purpose of waste dilution or assimilation, which is not allowed. *Id.* at 93.

A. MEASURE OF THE RIGHT: BENEFICIAL USE

Beneficial use is said to be the basis, the measure, and the limit of an appropriator's right to use water. Before development of modern administrative systems, the primary limit on an appropriator's right to use a certain quantity of water was the capacity of the diversion facilities. *See, e.g.,* Fort Morgan Land & Canal Co. v. South Platte Ditch Co., 30 P. 1032 (Colo. 1892). This was based on the assumption that one would not go to the expense of building ditches with a capacity far greater than was necessary, but in fact most appropriators built oversized ditches to be certain they had sufficient capacity. Further, they did not use the ditches continuously during every irrigation season, though they sometimes claimed rights to do so.

Challenges to an appropriator's' claims were rare, and the aggregate claims on a stream sometimes amounted to many times its total flow. Only in extreme cases did a court find that an appropriator's right exceeded beneficial use. *See, e.g.,* State ex rel. Erickson v. McLean, 308 P.2d 983 (N.M. 1957). Some courts are now taking a stricter view of beneficial use, even under old rights. For example, in State ex rel. Martinez v. City of Las Vegas, 89 P.3d 47 (N.M. 2004), the court found that the pueblo water rights doctrine, which allows the pueblos to use as much water as is necessary, including expansion of the right to meet future needs, was inconsistent with the requirement that water be put to a beneficial use.

The statutory systems of all western states include administrative mechanisms for verifying amounts of water that are to be put to a beneficial use before rights are embodied in a permit or decree. In addition, adjudications of all existing rights throughout large watersheds have been undertaken in many states, including Arizona, California, Idaho, Montana, and Washington. *See* Section VI.B. Such adjudications typically require holders of existing rights to prove that their existing uses are beneficial. Competing users may object to appropriations of excessive quantities of water.

A water right, once manifested in a permit or decree, is rarely disturbed. Change of place, purpose of use, or point of diversion requires permission by an agency or court. No change may be made if it results in harm to other appropriators.

In assessing harm, the agency or court may deny the application if the change will result in an increase in the amount of water that has historically been put to a beneficial use. Historical use may be limited to the amount of water actually required for optimum beneficial uses of the kind made. Thus, the quantity that can be applied to the changed use may be reduced to less than the amount of the original appropriation. The same process is followed when one appropriator seeks to transfer a water right to another.

The historical use approach may be equally useful in showing that one has abandoned the unused portion of a water right. Washington, for example, requires partial relinquishment of rights after five years of using less than the full permitted amount. Wash. Rev. Code § 90.14.140 (2012); Dept. of Ecology v. Acquavella, 935 P.2d 595 (Wash. 1997). However, it is rare to find partial abandonment, even in states like Washington.

B. BENEFICIAL USE AS A LIMIT

Appropriative rights extend only to beneficial use, and therefore there is no right to use water wastefully. State laws and court decisions interpret "beneficial use" as requiring that water use be "reasonable" or "reasonably efficient." *See, e.g.,* McNaughton v. Eaton, 242 P.2d 570, 575 (Utah 1952). Standards for reasonableness or efficiency change as the demand for scarce resources grows and conservation technology improves, leading to stricter regulation.

Because there is no vested right to waste water, state regulation of water use can restrict the amount of water used to amounts less than a permit or decree provides and to means of diversion and manner of application other than were used historically. As described below, administrators and courts may consider the "duty of water" in determining whether waste is occurring. They may also consider whether the amount being used is "unreasonable." When the California Water Resources Control Board found that hundreds of thousands of acre-feet of water were being lost by inefficient delivery and distribution systems in the Imperial Irrigation District, it required major conservation efforts, substantially changing the district's use of water. Imperial Irr. Dist. v. State Water Resources Control Board, 275 Cal.Rptr. 250 (Ct. App. 1990).

In addition, basin-wide general stream adjudications represent an opportunity for examining the quantity and manner of water use. Besides providing evidence that they have actually diverted a quantity of water, existing users must prove that their uses continue to be beneficial, *i.e.,* consistent with actual necessities under the circumstances. *See* Washington Dept. of Ecology v. Grimes, 852 P.2d 1044 (Wash. 1993) (reducing the an appropriation to half of the amount historically diverted because the delivery system was highly inefficient).

1. "Duty of Water" Limitations

Irrigation uses account for around 90% of all water withdrawals in the West. Water is sometimes applied to land far in excess of what crops can use. One means of limiting waste is to limit the volume or rate of water use based on a presumption of the maximum quantity required in the area. This limit is called the "duty of water." Water duties are indicative of whether the water is being beneficially used, and such duties may be presented as evidence of partial forfeiture through waste. Delta Canal Co. v. Frank Vincent Family Ranch, 2013 UT 69, 2013 WL 8476817, *9 (2013).

Rates or volumes are determined according to informed judgments of the maximum amounts of water needed for agriculture in the area and the maximum rate at which it could be applied without waste, considering soil conditions, climate, crops, and other relevant factors. State engineers and courts consider the duty of water when they review applications for new appropriations, changes in use, and transfers.

In South Dakota, Wyoming, and Nebraska, appropriators may apply water at a rate of no more than one cubic foot per second (c.f.s.) for every seventy acres irrigated. In addition, Nebraska law specifies that no more than three acre-feet of water may be used per year per acre of land. Neb. Rev. St. § 46–231. South Dakota allows no more than two acre-feet of water to be used per year for each acre of land and California allows no more than two and one half acre-feet per acre on uncultivated areas. S.D. Codified Laws § 46–5–6; Cal. Water Code § 1004. In Kansas, "reasonable quantities" of water for irrigation range from one acre-foot to two acre-feet per acre of land, depending on the geography of the area. Kan. Admin. Regs. § 5–3–19 (2014). New

Mexico, by contrast, requires the amount of water appropriated for irrigation to be consistent with "good agricultural practices." N.M. Stat. Ann. § 72–5–18(A).

Some states authorize exceptions from the water duty if irrigation methods, time constraints on diversions, or types of soil so require. *See, e.g.,* S.D. Codified Laws § 46–5–6. Moreover, if a water duty unreasonably limits the ability of the appropriator to make the beneficial use that is the basis of the right, the law may constitute an impermissible interference with vested water rights. In Enterprise Irrigation Dist. v. Willis, 284 N.W. 326 (Neb. 1939), the Nebraska Supreme Court enjoined enforcement of a provision limiting appropriations to three acre-feet per acre per year against an irrigator who had perfected greater rights (3.5 acre-feet per acre) before passage of the act. Although the opinion broadly disapproved of applying a statutory limitation enacted after a water right had been perfected, it can be read as limited to the facts of the case because there was evidence that the crops required more water than the duty of water allowed. *Id.* at 329–30. Other courts have found that reductions of appropriators' usage based on statutory requirements for "reasonable use" were necessary to prevent waste and were not unconstitutional takings. *See, e.g.,* Washington Dept. of Ecology v. Grimes, 852 P.2d 1044, 1055 (Wash. 1993); Imperial Irr. Dist. v. Water Resources Control Board, 275 Cal.Rptr. 250, 265 (Ct. App. 1990).

2. Reasonably Efficient Means of Diversion

Some of the earliest cases invoking the beneficial use doctrine to prevent waste involved inefficient diversion and conveyance facilities. Facilities for diversion and transportation of water must be reasonably efficient to avoid waste. In an early case, the Supreme Court refused relief to a party whose waterwheel, used to remove water from the Snake River to irrigate 429 acres, was inundated by the defendant's downstream dam, which was part of a project to irrigate some 300,000 acres. Schodde v. Twin Falls Land & Water Co., 224 U.S. 107 (1912). One of the Court's alternate holdings was that an unreasonable and inefficient means of diversion (the waterwheel) could not interfere with the reasonable use of water by others. *Id.* at 125. Similarly, where 5/6ths of the water diverted by an appropriator was lost to evaporation and seepage in a two and one half mile open ditch, a California court found impermissible waste. Erickson v. Queen Valley Ranch Co., 99 Cal.Rptr. 446, 449–50 (Ct. App. 1971). Although the *Erickson* court found excessive waste, it refused to order the senior appropriator to line his ditch, imposing a "physical solution" instead where juniors could pay to line it if they wished. *Id.* at 450–51. Senior appropriators are rarely ordered to line marginally leaky ditches. *See, e.g.,* United States v. Gila Valley Irrigation Dist., 31 F.3d 1428 (9th Cir. 1994); Middelkamp v. Bessemer Irrigating Ditch Co., 46 Colo. 102, 103 P. 280 (1909).

Whether a senior appropriator has a reasonably efficient means of diversion is typically judged by standards applicable when the diversion works were built. In State ex rel. Crowley v. District Court, 88 P.2d 23 (Mont. 1939), the court upheld the right of a downstream senior to insist that upstream juniors leave sufficient water in the stream to reach the senior's rudimentary, turn-of-the-century wing dam. Streamflows would have been adequate for all users if the senior had modified its diversion dam, but the court refused to require modifications. *Id.* at 24.

On a related note, appropriators' arguments that they were entitled to a certain silt content in their water were rejected in A-B Cattle Co. v. United States, 589 P.2d 57 (Colo. 1978). The presence of silt in the water served to seal unlined earthen ditches and prevented seepage losses. When the federal government constructed a dam on the river, the silt settled out. The clear water released from the dam seeped from the ditches more readily, resulting in less water being delivered to the appropriators. But the court found that they had no right to maintain earthen ditches; their right was solely to divert a quantity of water. Citing the principle of maximum utilization of water, it suggested that, "while the time may not yet have arrived when all ditches can be required to be lined or placed in pipes," the notion of beneficial use may eventually require such measures. *Id.* at 61. *See also* In re Willow Creek, 144 P. 505, 647 (Or. 1914) (suggesting that diversion facilities efficient enough to support a water right at the time they were built may have to be made more efficient as conditions and technology change).

Economic theory indicates that water use will become efficient whether the burden of efficiency is placed on the senior or junior. Under both *Crowley*, in Montana, and *Erickson,* in California, if greater efficiency by the senior would benefit the junior appropriators, the juniors would pay the senior to make the needed improvements or buy out the senior's rights. If instead the Oregon *Willow Creek* rule applied and the senior had to bear the burden of upgrading the diversion facilities to modern standards, the senior would either make the expenditure or buy out the juniors. If it were not to the senior's advantage to do so, the senior would sell to the juniors. In practice, transaction costs and other factors, such as devotion to a lifestyle or a location, disparity in size of use, and relative wealth of the parties, may be barriers to moving water to efficient use. Thus, legislatures and courts may seek to impose rules that maximize efficiency. In Alamosa-La Jara Water Users Protection Ass'n v. Gould, 674 P.2d 914 (Colo. 1983), the Colorado court indicated that the state engineer should require optimum utilization of water pursuant to regulations requiring consideration of "all significant factors, including environmental and economic concerns." The court held that seniors could be required to construct wells to divert stream water for themselves rather than preventing juniors from taking water from the stream to protect the seniors' diversions. *Id.* at 935. Similarly, the Idaho court upheld rules requiring senior surface water users to employ reasonable diversion and conveyance efficiency and conservation practices before calling a junior well owner who was allegedly interfering with the senior's use. American Falls Reservoir Dist. No. 2 v. Idaho Dept. of Water Resources, 154 P.3d 433 (Idaho 2007).

3. The Evolving Concept of Beneficial Use and the Public Trust Doctrine

Water is a public resource, but rights to use it may be appropriated by private parties so long as the use is "beneficial." The public now recognizes a wider array of non-economic uses (beauty and spiritual fulfillment) and economic uses (recreation) of water. The beneficial use doctrine can provide a means to account for changing values. In addition, greater understanding of the physical environment and the value of functioning ecosystems may influence decisions about water allocation and uses.

Some modern cases recognize the dynamic nature of beneficial use. As water supplies become more scarce and as demands increase, the negative consequences of allowing less socially valuable uses of water come into question, and what once may have been deemed beneficial may no longer be seen as such. In Environmental Defense Fund, Inc. v. East Bay Municipal Utility Dist., 125 Cal.Rptr. 601 (Ct. App. 1975), *vacated*, 605 P.2d 1 (Cal. 1980), an environmental group successfully argued that the applicant failed to make reasonable and beneficial use of water because the applicant was not reclaiming its *existing* water supply. *Id.* at 195.

The public trust doctrine has developed alongside the water allocation systems in each state. Although allocation systems seek to establish reliable rights to use water and in some contexts recognize such rights as "vested property interests," the law in most states also maintains that water is a public and common resource that may not be capable of full privatization.

Because the public trust doctrine is "a matter of state law," PPL Montana, LLC v. Montana, 132 S. Ct. 1215 (2012), the reach of the doctrine varies considerably. In some jurisdictions, it has been interpreted very narrowly. *See, e.g.,* Idaho Code §§ 58–1201 to 58–1203 (declaring that as a matter of state law the public trust doctrine shall not apply to the appropriation or use of water). Other states have taken a more expansive view, and in some cases the concept of "beneficial use" has been qualified by the public trust doctrine. A few of these states have begun to recognize the public trust doctrine as a limitation on private appropriations. *See, e.g.,* National Audubon Society v. Superior Court (Mono Lake), 33 Cal.3d 419, 658 P.2d 709 (1983); In re Water Use Permit Applications, 93 P.3d 643, 650, 657 (Haw. 2004).

With its now-famous *Mono Lake* decision, the California Supreme Court limited private appropriative rights in a non-navigable tributary to Mono Lake in order to protect the public's interest in maintaining water levels in the lake. *National Audubon Society (Mono Lake),* 33 Cal.3d at 448. In applying the public trust doctrine to the water, the court noted the potential conflict with the appropriative rights system, but acknowledged that the doctrine reflects the state's power as a sovereign to exercise continuous supervision and control over the waters of the state. The court described the public trust as "an affirmation of the duty of the state to protect the people's common heritage of streams, lakes, marshlands, and tidelands, surrendering that right of protection only in rare cases when the abandonment of that right is consistent with the purposes of the trust." *Id.* at 441.

There may be limited circumstances in which a state can extinguish the public's rights under the public trust doctrine, *i.e.,* where extinguishing the trust furthers a value within the scope of the trust or where developing trust lands or waters does not substantially impair public use. *See* Illinois Central R.R. v. Illinois, 146 U.S. 387, 452 (1892) (observing that the state could sell small parcels of public trust land to promote the public interest so long as it could be done without impairing the public interest in the remaining submerged land and water); Phillips Petroleum Co. v. Mississippi, 484 U.S. 469, 475 (1988) (stating that states are empowered to "define the limits of the lands held in public trust and to recognize private rights in such lands as they see fit."). However, in San Carlos Apache Tribe v. Superior Court ex rel. Cnty. of Maricopa, 193 Ariz. 195, 972 P.2d 179, 215 (1999), the Arizona Supreme Court held that a state statute ordering courts to make the public trust doctrine inapplicable in water rights adjudications violated separation of powers and a constitutional limit on legislative authority to give away trust resources. *See infra* Chapter 7.II.C (navigability and the public trust).

C. RECAPTURE AND REUSE

Water is "reused" multiple times. Agricultural water is diverted, spread on fields, and then some is returned through tail ditches or by seepage to a stream. Municipal water is usually returned as treated (or untreated) sewage to a waterway, where others may divert and use it. These return flows become supplies for other water users. Maximizing the number and extent of uses promotes efficiency and is an important conservation goal. A legal question arises, however, when an appropriator seeks to recapture and reuse water without initiating a new appropriation.

Waters originating within the watershed generally can be recaptured and reused by an appropriator if: (1) the total used does not exceed rights under a permit or decree; and (2) the recapture and reuse occur within the land for which the appropriation was made. No such limits are imposed on reuse of foreign waters imported by an appropriator. Stevens v. Oakdale Irrig. Dist., 90 P.2d 58 (Cal. 1939); Water Supply and Storage Co. v. Curtis, 733 P.2d 680 (Colo. 1987).

Recapture and reuse of water encourages conservation and maximum utilization of water. Much of the water diverted for irrigation is not actually consumed by crops. Most unconsumed water seeps into the ground or goes back to the stream as return flow and is appropriated and put to use by others. Such water is not truly "wasted" in the sense that it cannot be used by anyone. Still, significant amounts of water used in irrigation become unusable by becoming "trapped" in marshy areas or as unrecoverable groundwater or by flowing away from the stream. Much is lost by evaporation from open canals or transpiration through unwanted (non-crop) plants that draw water out of the earth. Because millions of acre-feet of water are "lost" annually, states are seeking ways to encourage greater efficiency through reuse and other methods.

1. Total Use Must Not Exceed Water Right

Typically, one uses only a portion of the total water diverted and returns the rest to the stream. Water rights are usually expressed as a maximum amount or rate of flow that may be diverted for a certain time period and use on specific land. A right may also be limited by the amount that may be consumed. Within these limits, consumption may be increased by reuse so long as there is no "change of use"—a change in the place, purpose, or time of use, or the means or point of diversion. Thus, an appropriator ordinarily may "recycle" irrigation return flows or capture seepage and use it within limits imposed by state law.

The upstream appropriator's increased efficiency or reuse of water on the original land can potentially reduce the downstream appropriator's supply. Downstream appropriators often are dependent on the upstream appropriator's "waste" as a source of supply. If the increased consumption came about by a change in use, it would not be allowed to harm other appropriators. But when it is the result of recapture and reuse or conservation measures on the same land, it will be permitted without regard to harm caused to others so long as the amount diverted (and the amount consumed, if it has been quantified) does not exceed one's "paper right" (*i.e.*, the amount specified in a permit or court decree). The applicable principle is that a junior appropriator who depends on a senior's waste as a source of supply is subject to the waste being curtailed. Montana v. Wyoming, 131 S. Ct. 1765 (2011); Thayer v. City of Rawlins, 594 P.2d 951 (Wyo. 1979). *See* Binning v. Miller, 102 P.2d 54 (1940) (noting that "[t]he lower landowner using such water merely takes his chances as to future supplies"). This rule also applies to groundwater that is discharged into a stream; the discharge may be stopped even to the detriment of the downstream user as long as the upstream user can identify the water that is not subject to appropriation. Arizona Public Service Co. v. Long, 773 P.2d 988 (Ariz. 1989). The Arizona court also ruled that cities may sell sewage effluent to the detriment of water users downstream of the former sewage return. *Id.* at 998.

In contrast to recapturing return flows for reuse, one may not enlarge a decreed right by means of water salvage techniques. In Southeastern Colorado Water Conservancy Dist. v. Shelton Farms, Inc., 529 P.2d 1321 (Colo. 1974), a landowner removed streamside phreatophytes (plants that consume large amounts of water) and filled in marshy areas.

The growth of phreatophytes over the years had gradually deprived many junior users of the water to which they were entitled. Since the saved water was originally in the stream and had been appropriated by juniors, the court held that it was error to create a new and senior right in it. *Id.* at 1327. Similarly, in R.J.A., Inc. v. Water Users Ass'n of Dist. No. 6, 690 P.2d 823 (Colo. 1984), the court denied an expansion of a senior water right to include water saved by draining a 3000 year-old peat bog. The water belonged to the stream and could not be used to enlarge an existing right, because to hold otherwise would encourage "altercations of long existing physical characteristics of the land" with potentially adverse effects. *Id.* at 828. Presumably the court would have recognized rights to the water in each case if its original source had been the senior's diversion (not from natural circumstances which trapped water on the seniors' land) and the total amount of the senior's right was not enlarged beyond the decree. The senior also could have applied for a junior appropriation of the salvaged water added to the stream.

2. Reuse Limited to Original Land

The general rule is that one may recapture and reuse seepage and "waste-water" so long as it is within the original land and for the original purpose of the right. Cleaver v. Judd, 393 P.2d 193 (Or. 1964) (citing Stevens v. Oakdale Irr. Dist., 90 P.2d 58 (Cal. 1939)); Estate of Steed v. New Escalante Irrig. Co., 846 P.2d 1223 (Utah 1992). Recaptured water may be used on the same land to increase yield. However, it cannot be reused on an adjoining parcel. Salt River Valley Water Users' Ass'n v. Kovacovich, 411 P.2d 201 (Ariz.App. 1966). Of course, if the diversion point, means of diversion, or place, time, or purpose of use is changed, a reuse will be allowed only if no harm occurs to other appropriators. *See infra* Section VII.

Once the water leaves the appropriator's land and is destined for or has reached a natural stream, it may be subject to appropriation by others. Fuss v. Franks, 610 P.2d 17 (Wyo. 1980). Some states qualify this rule, requiring that the appropriator must have intended to recapture the water when it was appropriated and must actually recapture it within a reasonable time or else the water will be considered abandoned to the stream. Jones v. Warmsprings Irr. Dist., 91 P.2d 542 (Or. 1939). Other states hold that after water is commingled, appropriators who attempt to recapture the water must be able to identify their portion. Arizona Public Service Co. v. Long, 773 P.2d 988 (Ariz. 1989). A minority of jurisdictions hold that water that enters a stream or seeps into the ground, even while on the original land, is not subject to recapture and reuse. *See* Fort Morgan Reservoir & Irr. Co. v. McCune, 206 P. 393 (Colo. 1922) (seepage from dam on owner's land was destined for stream and could not be recaptured).

The rule allowing recapture and reuse of reclaimed water on the original land can result in more efficiency, but it can also result in more water being consumed. For instance, if a water user is consuming less than the permitted amount of water and plants a more water-intensive crop or puts in a more efficient irrigation system, most or all of the water that had previously been returned to the stream might be consumed. This can deprive other appropriators of water on which they depend, but it is allowed since it is technically within the terms of the original appropriation. Montana v. Wyoming, 131 S. Ct. 1765, 1774 (2011). Being able to recapture and reuse water on the land benefited by the original use provides a substantial advantage for irrigation districts or federal water projects having extensive geographic scope. *See id.;* Dept. of Ecology v. U.S. Bureau of Reclamation, 827 P.2d 275 (Wash. 1992) (federal reclamation project irrigating lands in Columbia River basin retained right to recapture waste, seepage, and return flow throughout project area). To encourage more efficient water use, a few states (*e.g.,* California, Montana, New Mexico, and Oregon) have passed laws facilitating the use of reclaimed and even salvaged water on other land or for new purposes.

Any person, including the original appropriator, who intercepts seepage water that has left the land is considered a junior appropriator subject to the rights of all prior appropriators. An appropriator of seepage water remains at the mercy of the person whose activity makes the seepage available. The original appropriator may cause the seepage to stop by making more efficient use of it, by lining, relocating, or abandoning a canal or reservoir, or by ceasing the appropriation, without liability to the seepage appropriator. Bower v. Big Horn Canal Ass'n, 307 P.2d 593 (Wyo. 1957).

VI. PROCEDURES FOR PERFECTING AND ADMINISTERING RIGHTS

Appropriation of water began several years before statehood in most western states. Miners developed relatively uniform customs for water appropriations, and these were incorporated into the common law of water rights by the early territorial and state court systems. A miner's right to get water depended upon two acts: posting notice at the point of diversion and diverting the water to apply it to a beneficial use.

The quaint system of appropriation that spread throughout the West reflected the independent-minded miners who conceived it. There was no administration required, no central authority, and no records. But there were conflicts. Courts were called upon to resolve disputes between appropriators competing for priority to water and between appropriators and riparian landowners. *See* Power v. People, 28 P. 1121 (Colo. 1892) (rejecting a justifiable homicide defense raised by a riparian who shot an appropriator). Litigation, however, was reactive, rather than proactive, and was determinative only of the rights of the parties, not of all users of the same water sources.

In 1873, California became the first state to enact a statutory appropriation procedure. Since then, all western states have followed suit, primarily with administrative permit systems.

A. PERMIT SYSTEMS

1. Purpose

All western states have statutory systems to allocate and administer rights to use water. In addition, every state but Colorado has vested authority in an administrative agency. Colorado has a judicial system whose function is similar to agencies in other states. It is split into seven water divisions, with a designated "water judge" in each county district court to hear disputes and adjudicate water rights. Colo.Rev.Stat.Ann. § 37–92–201 (West 2009); Colo.Rev.Stat.Ann. § 37–92–203 (West 1985).

The chief purpose of administrative procedures is to provide an orderly method for appropriating water and regulating established water rights. Some states allow appropriators the option of applying for a permit or perfecting a common law appropriation by posting notice and diverting water. More typically, state law requires a permit as the exclusive means of making a valid appropriation. Wyoming Hereford Ranch v. Hammond Packing Co., 236 P. 764 (Wyo. 1925).

2. Constitutionality

The authority to adopt and enforce permit systems to govern the use of water flows from the broad police power of the state. Ormsby County v. Kearney, 142 P. 803, 806 (Nev. 1914). Water is subject to public control by state statutes or constitutions. *See, e.g.,* Cal. Const. Art. 10, § 5; Neb. Const. Art. XV § 5. Although the state's interest may be expressed in property-like terms, it is not one of ownership but of sovereignty. Sporhase v. Nebraska ex rel. Douglas, 458 U.S. 941, 956 (1982).

Most state systems for the administration of water rights include an adjudication process that casts an administrative body or official in a quasi-judicial role. Water users have challenged the mixed executive (regulatory) and judicial role of agencies. However, courts have upheld the delegation of administrative powers to an agency, official, or board. Farm Investment Co. v. Carpenter, 61 P. 258, 267 (Wyo. 1900); Crawford Co. v. Hathaway, 93 N.W. 781 (Neb. 1903). Oregon, for example, has a mixed judicial and administrative system in which permit determinations are made by the state engineer and filed in a court that that presides over appeals, makes further modifications, and grants final approvals. The Oregon Supreme Court found the duties of the engineer to be "quasi-judicial in their character," and the findings only *"prima facie* final and binding." In re Willow Creek, 144 P. 505 (Or. 1914). The U.S. Supreme Court agreed "that the state, consistently with due process of law, may thus commit the preliminary proceedings to the board and the final hearing and adjudication to the court." Pacific Live Stock Co. v. Lewis, 241 U.S. 440 (1916). *See* United States v. Oregon, 44 F.3d 758 (9th Cir. 1994).

The Texas Supreme Court invalidated a 1917 water rights statute, though it was similar to Wyoming's, pointing out that the Wyoming constitution provided ample authority for such a system but that Texas had no similar constitutional provision. Board of Water Engineers v. McKnight, 229 S.W. 301 (Tex. 1921). Texas later amended its constitution and adopted a system similar to Oregon's, Tex. Const. art. XVI, § 59; Tex. Water Code Ann. §§ 11.301, 11.320–11.321 (West 1977), and the court found that it did not violate separation of powers or constitute a taking. In re Adjudication of Water Rights of Upper Guadalupe Segment of Guadalupe River Basin, 642 S.W.2d 438 (Tex. 1982).

3. Permitting Procedures

All appropriation states except Colorado have statutes requiring permits to appropriate water. The first permit system was adopted by Wyoming in 1890. It divided the state into four water divisions and established the office of state engineer to collect stream records, make surveys, and provide staff support to the Board of Control, which adjudicates all claims and administers the permit system. *See* Wyo. Const. art. 8 § 2; Wyo. Stat. Ann. § 41–3–501.

Under most statutory permit systems, a permit will be approved if an applicant follows prescribed procedures and if the state engineer finds that there is unappropriated water and that the appropriation is not detrimental to the public welfare.

a. Filing

In all permit states, a formal written application for a permit to take unappropriated water must be made to the state engineer or an administrative body such as the Department of Natural Resources or Water Resources Control Board. This is almost always the exclusive way to obtain a water right, and must be done before any physical act such as digging a diversion ditch. The time of filing generally becomes the priority date if all later requirements are met.

Montana's water law is typical. Data that must be included under the Montana law include the name of claimant and watercourse, quantity of water, time of use, legal description of point of diversion, purpose of use, date of application to beneficial use, and any applicable support such as a map, plat, or aerial photograph. Mont. Code Ann. § 85–2–361.

b. Notice

Applications for new appropriation permits must give notice of the application. The notice must be published and efforts must be made to contact all affected appropriators. *See, e.g.*, Mont. Code Ann. § 85–2–307–308; Western Water, LLC v. Olds, 184 P.3d 578, 585 (Utah 2008); Pete's Mountain Homeowners Ass'n v. Oregon Water Resources Dept., 238 P.3d 395, 399 (2010). In Colorado, a monthly resume of all applications is compiled from pertinent information provided by the applicants, and the water clerk must then publish the resume in local newspapers of general circulation and mail it to potentially affected parties. Colo. Rev. Stat. § 37–92–302(3); SL Group LLC v. Go West Industries, 42 P.3d 637, 641 (Colo. 2002). However, personal service is not required. S. Ute Indian Tribe

v. King Consol. Ditch Co., 250 P.3d 1226, 1236 (Colo. 2011). Absent sufficient notice, new appropriations may not be perfected. *Id.*; City of Thornton v. Bijou Irr. Co., 926 P.2d 1, 24 (Colo. 1996).

c. Hearing

Opponents to a permit application have a fixed time in which to file objections, but most states recognize exceptions for cause. *See* In re Adjudication of the Existing Rights to the Use of All the Water, 55 P.3d 396, 398 (Mont. 2002) (allowing an objection by the Department of Fish, Wildlife, and Parks outside of the 10-day objection period). Objections are typically based on allegations that the statutory criteria for permit issuance are lacking, either legally or factually. Water right holders who may be adversely affected by a new permit generally have standing to object. *See, e.g.,* Idaho Code § 42–203A ("any person, firm, association or corporation concerned in . . . such application" may object); Wash. Rev. Code § 90.03.200 ("any interested party" may object). Whether non-appropriators have standing to object to a new permit varies from state to state. *Compare* Texas Rivers Protection Ass'n v. Texas Natural Resource Conservation Com'n, 910 S.W.2d 147, 151–52 (Tex. App. 1995), *writ denied* (Apr. 12, 1996) (riparians have standing to challenge an application on the ground that it may damage aesthetic, recreational, and business interests), *and* Montana Trout Unlimited v. Beaverhead Water Co., 255 P.3d 179, 184 (Mont. 2011) (conservation organization had sufficient ownership interest in water or its use to demonstrate "good cause" to compel a hearing on its objections), *with* Middle Niobrara Natural Res. Dist. v. Dept. of Nat. Res., 281 Neb. 634, 799 N.W.2d 305, 314–16 (2011) (natural resource districts were "interested persons" and therefore had standing to object and appeal a permit decision, but a property owner did not).

The administrative agency holds a public hearing on properly filed objections, serving notice of the hearing on the applicant and objector. *See, e.g.,* Mont. Code Ann. § 85–2–309. The state engineer or equivalent official investigates factual data upon which the agency relies and reports to the agency on whether the statutory criteria were satisfied. The agency then approves, disapproves, or approves with modification the permit application. The applicant has a right to present any pertinent evidence. The agency's findings may then be appealed to the courts. *See, e.g., id.* § 85–2–235.

d. Issuance of Permit

The next stage of the process is issuance of a permit. A permit is not a water right but will ripen into one if all conditions of the permit are met. During a stipulated time period, the permittee is required to construct diversion works, make a diversion, and apply water to a beneficial use. The water right vests upon application of the water to a beneficial use. If the permittee exercised "due diligence" throughout the process, priority will relate back to the date of filing.

Most administrative agencies impose permit conditions that dictate how the water right is to be exercised. California, for instance, authorizes the State Water Resources Control Board to permit the appropriation for beneficial purposes under "such terms and conditions as in its judgment will best develop, conserve, and utilize in the public interest, the water sought to be appropriated." Cal. Water Code § 1253 (West 1957). The Board may not delegate authority to issue permits or to decide the merits of an application. Central Delta Water Agency v. State Water Resources Control Board, 20 Cal.Rptr.3d 898 (Ct.App. 2004). But the Board has considerable discretion to fashion conditions, which will be set aside only if a court finds them to be unreasonable or not based on substantial evidence. East Bay Mun. Utility Dist. v. Dept. of Public Works, 35 P.2d 1027 (Cal. 1934). In Bank of America National Trust & Savings Ass'n v. State Water Resources Control Bd., 116 Cal.Rptr. 770, 780 (Ct. App. 1974), a condition requiring the applicant to keep a proposed reservoir open to the public for recreational uses was rejected because the record lacked substantial evidence of the need for such a condition.

In addition to regular permits, temporary and seasonal permits are issued by some states. In California, such permits create no vested rights and may be issued if there is unappropriated water available, and no harm to downstream users or unreasonable harm to the environment will occur. Cal. Water Code §§ 1425, 1430.

In most states, the final document issued in the permit process is called a "license," "certificate," "certificate of appropriation," or "water right certificate." The certificate may be recorded like a deed to real property.

4. Statutory Criteria

The permit procedures discussed above are to determine whether the criteria set forth in the statute have been satisfied. In most states, this requires evidence of:

a. a beneficial use;

b. availability of unappropriated water at the time and period of use;

c. no harm to prior appropriators;

d. adequate diversion facilities; and

e. possessory interest in the property where water is to be put to beneficial use.

See, e.g., Mont. Code Ann. § 85–2–311 (2013). Montana also requires that there be no interference with reservations of water for future use or other planned uses.

The requirement that there be available unappropriated water has become a significant obstacle in recent years. On many streams, the "paper rights" to divert water far exceed the quantity of water actually flowing in the stream. This is a result of two phenomena: (a) many users may depend on the same water, as downstream

users divert water that has already been diverted
and returned by upstream users; and (b) the most
junior rights may be exercisable only in years of
heavy flow or low senior usage. Thus, many streams
in the West are "overappropriated."

5. Public Interest Considerations and the Public Trust

The laws of most states authorize the agency to
reject or condition applications that are not
consistent with the public interest or public welfare.
In Young & Norton v. Hinderlider, 110 P. 1045,
1050 (N.M. 1910), the New Mexico state engineer
rejected an application for a proposed irrigation
project that seemed too large for the available water
supply and thus might result in high costs and
uncertain supplies for those who bought land and
accompanying water rights. The Supreme Court of
the Territory of New Mexico upheld the engineer's
use of these broad policy concerns, and rejected the
applicant's contention that "public welfare" concerns
should only include matters that are a "menace to
public health and safety."

A Utah statute requires the state engineer to
determine whether proposed appropriations would
interfere with a "more beneficial use" or "prove
detrimental to the public welfare." Utah Code Ann.
§ 100–3–8, now codified at Utah Code Ann. § 73–3–8
(2007). The Utah Supreme Court upheld rejection of
an early application in favor of a later one because
the interests of the public would be better served by
the later appropriation (a federal water project)

than by the earlier one (a private power plant). Tanner v. Bacon, 136 P.2d 957 (Utah 1943).

In Washington, public interest considerations have been held to include environmental factors. Stempel v. Department of Water Resources, 508 P.2d 166, 171 (Wash. 1973). In Swinomish Indian Tribal Cmty. v. Washington State Dep't of Ecology, 178 Wash. 2d 571, 311 P.3d 6 (2013) (en banc), the Washington Supreme Court invalidated the Department's attempt to reserve water for future year-round out-of-stream uses that would impair minimum instream flows necessary for fish, wildlife, scenic, and aesthetic values as against the state's public interest test. The court noted that the statutory exception for overriding considerations of the public interest was a narrow one, not a device for reweighing or reallocating water for possible future economic uses.

Alaska has enacted one of the most detailed state statutes related to public interest considerations. It delineates an array of public interest factors, including: (1) benefit to applicant; (2) effect of resulting economic activity; (3) effect on fish and game and recreation; (4) public health effects; (5) loss of future alternative uses; (6) harm to others; (7) intent and ability of applicant; (8) effect on access to navigable or public waters. Alaska Stat. Ann. § 46.15.080.

In states with less explicit public interest provisions, courts have directed water administrators to consider a wide variety of factors. Idaho's statute says only that the Director of Water

Resources is to reject or modify a permit application if the appropriation "will conflict with the local public interest." Idaho Code Ann. § 42–203A. Local public interest is defined as "the interests that the people in the area directly affected by a proposed water use have in the effects of such use on the public water resource." *Id.* § 42–202B. The statute further provides that the director must consider whether the proposed use "will adversely affect the local economy of the watershed or local area within which the source of water for the proposed use originates, in the case where the place of use is outside of the watershed or local area where the source of water originates." *Id.* § 42–203A. The Idaho Supreme Court held that public interest elements also include those reflected in Idaho laws dealing with instream flows, water quality, water waste, and conservation. Shokal v. Dunn, 707 P.2d 441 (Idaho 1985). In addition, the court found that the factors specified in Alaska and other state statutes made "common sense" when evaluating the public interest. *Id.* at 449. In contrast, the Nevada Supreme Court upheld the state engineer's administrative definition of the public interest based on reference to Nevada water statutes, but found that the laws of other states could not be considered. Pyramid Lake Paiute Tribe of Indians v. Washoe County, 918 P.2d 697 (Nev. 1996).

Opponents to appropriation permits have argued that the state agency not only has the authority, but has an affirmative duty, to reject applications for permits that may be contrary to the public interest. One court has applied the public trust doctrine to require "at a minimum, a determination of the potential effect of the allocation of water [to major energy projects] on the present water supply and future water needs of this State." United Plainsmen Ass'n v. North Dakota State Water Conservation Comm'n, 247 N.W.2d 457, 462 (N.D. 1976). The ruling requires comprehensive planning or some other method of weighing the effects of allocating substantial quantities of water to appropriators.

National Audubon Soc'y v. Superior Court (Mono Lake), 33 Cal.3d 419, 658 P.2d 709 (1983), represents the most extensive application of the public trust doctrine to limit a state's authority over appropriation permits. There, the court found that Los Angeles' 1940 permit to use water from tributaries to Mono Lake had been granted without consideration of public trust factors including fish, wildlife, and recreation, and that such factors provided grounds for later permit challenges. Thus, the city's established appropriations may be qualified by subsequent restrictions to protect the public trust uses dependent on an inflow of fresh water to the lake. The decision is remarkable in that it effectively impresses every permit with a condition that allows it to be reviewed and modified if public uses were not adequately considered when the permit was issued.

A later case held that the California State Water Resources Control Board, which has authority over surface water allocation and water quality in the state, has a public trust duty to exercise its authority to condition water permits to accomplish water quality goals. United States v. State Water Resources Control Bd., 227 Cal.Rptr. 161 (Ct. App. 1986). The Board may also regulate another agency's actions if the actions affect the quality of water resources. Pacific Lumber Co. v. State Water Resources Control Board, 126 P.3d 1040 (Cal. 2006).

California applies the public trust doctrine to all tidelands and navigable lakes and streams. Santa Teresa Citizen Action Group v. City of San Jose, 7 Cal.Rptr.3d 868 (Ct.App. 2003). A district court in California also extended the doctrine to hydrologically connected groundwater "if extraction of groundwater adversely impacts a navigable waterway to which the public trust doctrine does apply." Environmental Law Fnd. v. State Water Res. Control Bd., Case No. 34–2010–80000583 (Sup. Ct. Cal. Sacramento Cty. July 15, 2014), available at http://www.envirolaw.org/documents/ScottOrder onCrossMotions.pdf (appeal pending). Hawaii applies the doctrine to all water resources, including groundwater. In re Water Use Permit Applications, 9 P.2d 409, 453 (Haw. 2000). Other states vary as to the geographic scope of the doctrine.

In Idaho, the public trust applies to all water rights, although the doctrine may not be considered by the court in a general stream adjudication absent specific legislative direction. Idaho Conservation League, Inc. v. State of Idaho, 911 P.2d 748 (Idaho 1995). Although the Colorado Supreme Court has rejected public trust concerns as a basis for reviewing water rights filings, Board of County Commissioners of Arapahoe County v. United

States, 891 P.2d 952, 972 (Co
that "[m]aximum utilization c
every ounce of Colorado's natu
ought to be appropriated; optim.
achieved only through proper re
significant factors, including environ.
economic concerns." Pagosa Area Water and
Sanitation Dist. v. Trout Unlimited, 170 ι ˌod 307,
314 (Colo. 2007).

B. ADJUDICATION

There are three general types of judicial
procedures affecting water rights: general stream
adjudications; appeals of agency permit decisions;
and resolution of conflicts among individual
appropriators.

1. General Stream Adjudications (GSAs)

Many states have adopted procedures for
adjudicating the competing rights of all water users
in a particular stream system. All persons claiming
water rights in the system typically must be joined
as parties. In some states, judicial proceedings may
be initiated by the users, in others by a state
agency, and in others by either users or an agency.

State-initiated adjudications proceed according to
rules set by legislatures. They typically require all
water rights claimants to state and prove their
water rights relative to all other appropriators.
Legislatures have been motivated to pass GSA laws
not only to achieve a greater degree of certainty in
quantifying and setting the relative priorities of

existing water rights throughout major watersheds, but also to take advantage of the McCarran Amendment, a statute that requires the United States to participate in adjudication of its water rights if it is joined in a GSA. 43 U.S.C. § 666. In recent years, GSAs have been undertaken pursuant to legislation in Arizona (Ariz. Rev. Stat. Ann. § 45–252 (1992)) (Gila River), Idaho (Idaho Code Ann. § 42–1405 (1994)) (Snake River), Oregon (Or. Rev. Stat. § 539.005 (1989)) (Klamath River Basin), Utah (Utah Code Ann. § 73–4–1 (2013)) (Great Salt Lake and Colorado River Basins), and Washington (Wash. Rev. Code § 90.03.105 (1997)) (Yakima River Basin) (*see also* Act of May 5, 2009, ch. 332, 2009 Wash. Sess. Laws 1663, codified at Wash. Rev. Code ch. 90.03). Montana authorized a statewide GSA process in 1979 pursuant to Mont. Code Ann. §§ 85–2–212–228, and it is in the process of adjudicating over 200,000 claims. *See, e.g.,* Rights to the Use of All the Water, 55 P.3d 396 (Mont. 2002).

In a GSA, a state agency or special master often serves as a fact-finder, gathering information, conducting surveys, and compiling claims. The initial hearings and decisions are typically made by an administrative body. The administrative determination of rights is filed in a court, which will embody the determination in a final decree, except to the extent findings may be altered in response to appeals from interested parties. The GSA legislation or decree may provide a process for integrating new permits that are issued after a GSA is commenced.

2. Review of Agency Permit Decisions

Once an official or agency makes a determination on an appropriation permit, it is final unless someone appeals. Appeals may go to another administrative level before proceeding to court. In some states, the court engages in a trial de novo, but most appeals are based on the administrative record, and administrative decisions will only be overturned if they are arbitrary and capricious or lack substantial evidence. Revert v. Ray, 95 Nev. 782, 603 P.2d 262 (1979). However, on questions of law, including the meaning of statutes, reviewing courts will reach their own conclusions independent of the administrative body's legal conclusions. In re 2007 Admin. of Appropriations of Waters of Niobrara River, 288 Neb. 497, 501, 851 N.W.2d 640, 645 (2014).

Courts may overturn an administrative decision to approve an application for a water right if the official failed to consider the "public interest" or other statutory criteria. In re: Howard Sleeper, No. RA 84–53(C). However, on appeal of *In re: Howard Sleeper*, the New Mexico Court of Appeals reversed the decision of the district court, holding that the engineer need not consider public interest impacts for transfers or changes of water rights when the statute required such considerations only for new applications. In re: Application of Sleeper, 760 P.2d 787 (N.M. App. 1988).

3. Conflicts Among Water Users

One or more water users can sue other water users who allegedly violate their water rights. The court's decision generally binds only those who are parties. In some states, administrative bodies may have authority to resolve conflicts between individual water users. Decisions of an administrative body are subject to judicial review either on appeal or as a required step in the permitting process.

C. REGULATION OF WATER DISTRIBUTION

An administrative agency usually enforces established rights based on the relative priorities of appropriators. Wyoming's system is illustrative. The state engineer has overall supervision, with division superintendents located in each of four water divisions. Wyo. Stat. Ann. § 41–3–501 (West 1977). Each superintendent oversees several water commissioners who regulate physical distribution of the water. *Id.* § 41–3–503. The commissioner's job, under the guidance of a superintendent and the state engineer, is to make sure the water of each stream is distributed in proper quantities at the right times to those who are authorized to receive it. *Id.* § 41–3–603.

The commissioner opens, closes, adjusts, and locks headgates in accordance with a list of all appropriators in order of their priority in time, and is a streamside policeman with power to make arrests if necessary. *Id.* § 41–3–605. As streamflow wanes in late summer, the commissioner closes headgates starting with the lowest priority (*i.e.,* latest in time) to ensure that the senior appropriators have access to the quantity of water to which they are entitled from available supplies. *Id.* § 41–3–604. If streamflow increases, the commissioner can open gates and give juniors the benefit of the increase. Regulation of headgates requires no notice or hearing because it is purely a ministerial duty of the water commissioner. Hamp v. State, 118 P. 653 (Wyo. 1911). Commissioners report streamflow measurements and water usage to the division superintendents. *Id.* § 41–3–608. Appeals from decisions of a water commissioner are taken first to the division superintendent, then to the state engineer, and finally to the district court of the county where the controversy is located. *Id.* § 41–3–603.

D. THE COLORADO SYSTEM

Unlike the other western states, Colorado did not create an agency with permitting and regulation authority. Instead, it retained a judicial system and charged it with administrative functions.

The Water Rights Determination and Administration Act of 1969, C.R.S. §§ 37–92–101 through 37–92–602, divided the state into seven water divisions that correspond to the seven major drainages. Colo. Rev. Stat. Ann. § 37–92–201 (West 2009). A division engineer is appointed for each division. *Id.* § 37–92–202. "Water judges" with jurisdiction over water rights determinations are selected from among district court judges in each division. *Id.* § 27–92–203.

Applications for determinations of water rights are made to the clerk of the water court. *Id.* § 37–92–302. The clerk prepares monthly resumes of applications that are sent to any potential party and published in local newspapers and other media. After an opportunity for statements of opposition to be filed by those objecting to the application, a referee conducts fact-finding. The state engineer and subordinate officials provide the clerk with a list of decreed and conditional water rights. The referee then approves, disapproves, or approves in part the application. *Id.* § 37–92–303. In some difficult cases, the referee refers the matter back to the water judge.

Interested parties then have an opportunity to protest the ruling to the water judge. *Id.* § 37–92–302. Rulings not protested are confirmed unless the water judge finds them to be contrary to law. Protested rulings may be confirmed, modified, reversed, or reversed and remanded. Once confirmed, the water right has a priority as of the date of filing the application. *Id.* § 37–92–306.1. Appellate review from the decree of the water judge is available in the supreme court. *Id.* § 37–304.

The state and division engineers regulate the distribution of water according to priorities and quantities decreed by the courts. *Id.* § 37–92–501. Division engineers compile and maintain tabulations of all water rights in a division. 2014 Colo. Legis. Serv. Ch. 4 (S.B. 14–026) (West). The tabulations are available to the public and are subject to protests, which are resolved by the water judge. Colo. Rev. Stat. Ann. § 37–92–401.

The functions of Colorado's water courts are similar to the permitting agencies of other states. One key distinction in the Colorado system is that appropriators may begin using water before asking the court for a water right. This reflects Colorado's interpretation of a state's constitutional provision declaring that "the right to divert the unappropriated waters of any natural stream to beneficial uses shall never be denied." Colo. Const. Art. 16, § 6. In fact, the ability to exercise a constitutional right to divert water has little importance because it is always subordinate to, and subject to the call of, all senior users with adjudicated rights. Kobobel v. State, 249 P.3d 1127, 1134 (Colo. 2011).

VII. TRANSFERS AND CHANGES OF WATER RIGHTS

The increasing urbanization of the West has created a demand for water to be transferred from agriculture to uses that return higher economic benefits. Agriculture requires vastly larger quantities of water than municipal and industrial uses, so the acquisition of irrigation water rights can yield plentiful water for such uses. The early priority of irrigation rights makes them especially desirable.

Transfer of a water right along with land is a routine matter. Water rights in most states pass with the land upon its conveyance unless otherwise provided in the deed. When land is divided, a pro rata portion of water rights may accompany each parcel. Stephens v. Burton, 546 P.2d 240 (Utah 1976).

Water rights may also be granted separately from the land, or by a reservation of the water right by the grantor upon conveyance of the land. Transfers for uses in different locations, for different purposes, at different times, or involving changes in the points of diversion or return are more complicated, as the rights of other appropriators must be protected under the "no harm" rule.

A. TRANSFERS GENERALLY

Water rights may be transferred by sale, lease, or exchange. However, applications for water rights are not assignable as they are not vested rights until approved. In re Application of Catherland Reclamation District, 433 N.W.2d 161 (Neb. 1988).

A transfer may not exceed the quantity of rights held by the transferor. Rocky Ford Irr. Co. v. Kents Lake Reservoir Co., 135 P.2d 108, 114 (Utah 1943). A transfer may or may not be accompanied by a change of use (*e.g.,* a different place or purpose of use). If land is conveyed along with appurtenant water rights and there is no change in the purpose, time, or place of use, or in the point of diversion or return, state permission may not be required.

When water rights are conveyed separately or where a different use is contemplated, any or all of the above use characteristics may change, thus affecting the rights of other stream appropriators. This triggers procedures for determining whether harm to other appropriators would result, as described below.

B. RESTRICTIONS ON TRANSFERS APART FROM THE LAND

Some states have historically restricted transfers for uses away from the land (*e.g.,* Montana, Oklahoma, Nebraska, Nevada, South Dakota, Wyoming). A likely motive was to prevent appropriators from making speculative claims to water in amounts well beyond the quantity that could be used beneficially on their lands and then selling the early priority water right to others for use elsewhere.

Some remnants of the historic restrictions remain on the books. Wyoming's 1909 "no-change" statute provides that no severance of water rights from land may be made without loss of priority, Wyo. Stat. Ann. § 41–3–101, but this rule is riddled with exceptions for domestic uses, transportation, steam power, industry, and other activities. Wyo. Stat. Ann. §§ 41–3–104–112. Nebraska's Irrigation District Act of 1895 makes irrigation water rights appurtenant to land. Neb. Rev. Stat. § 46–122(1); State ex rel. Blome v. Bridgeport Irr. Dist., 286 N.W.2d 426, 432 (1979). Because the statute applies prospectively, however, pre-1895 rights (very desirable because of their seniority) can be sold, and modern statutory amendments allow a variety of other transfers. Similarly, in Idaho, the fact that a water right has been decreed for the irrigation of appurtenant lands does not prevent a substitution or exchange of water. Board of Directors of Wilder Irr. Dist. v. Jorgensen, 136 P.2d 461 (Idaho 1943).

In Nevada, Oklahoma, and South Dakota, water rights are ordinarily appurtenant, but may be severed if their use on the originally benefited land becomes economically infeasible. Nev. Rev. Stat. § 533.040; Okla. Stat. tit. 82, § 105.22; S.D. Codified Laws §§ 46–5–33, –34. The Nevada statute limits only the transfer of irrigation rights; others are freely transferable. However, the state engineer may allow water rights to be transferred even if the original land can be irrigated. U.S. v. Alpine Land and Reservoir Co., 878 F.2d 1217 (9th Cir. 1989). In Arizona, transfers of irrigation rights apart from the land are subject to approval of the Director of Water Resources; transfers outside the boundaries of irrigation districts also require the consent of the district. Ariz. Rev. Stat. Ann. § 45–172.

In addition to statutory restrictions, some mutual ditch companies and irrigation districts impose restrictions on private stock transfers. *See infra* Chapter Ten. These restrictions may appear on the face of stock or may be included in the company's by-laws or articles of incorporation.

C. TRANSBASIN DIVERSIONS

Removing water from one watershed for use in another, known as transbasin diversions or interbasin transfers, is generally permitted under the prior appropriation doctrine. The seminal case of Coffin v. Left Hand Ditch Co., 6 Colo. 443 (1882), involved a diversion of water out of the basin of its origin. The court recognized that the appropriation doctrine is fundamentally different from the doctrine of riparian rights in that it allows such diversions. *Id.* at 449.

Transbasin diversions are sought when population growth and economic expansion arise in areas where water supplies are inadequate. Great investments in diversion facilities are made in order to bring the water to the watershed where it is demanded. Southern California and Colorado's eastern slope have been able to flourish because of imported water. If rights are purchased from appropriators in the area of origin, the no harm rule applicable to changes in use provides some protection for existing appropriators. But the no harm rule does not consider harm to the economy, ecology, lifestyle, and potential for future growth of the area where the water originates. Because these effects tend to be severe and lasting when there are massive exports of water out of a watershed, some states have enacted restrictions to protect the interests of areas of origin.

Area of origin legislation often attempts to safeguard present conditions, including established water rights and streamflows for fish and wildlife. Some laws attempt to provide for future development in the area of origin, but in practice it is difficult to quantify future needs. California allows transbasin diversions subject to the right of the area of origin to appropriate the water when it is needed, with an absolute priority over the exporter. California also protects the county of origin's ability to develop water that may be necessary in the future. *See, e.g.,* Watershed Protection Act, Water Code §§ 11460–11465; County of Origin Protection Act, Water Code § 10505; Delta Protection Act, Water Code §§ 12201–12205; and Protected Area Act, Water Code §§ 1215–1222.

The largest transbasin diversions in Colorado are from the Colorado River basin west of the continental divide to Denver and other heavily populated areas in the east. The legislature enacted a statute to protect the western slope's "present appropriations of water and, in addition thereto, prospective uses of water for irrigation and other beneficial consumptive use purposes." Colo. Rev. Stat. Ann. § 37–45–118(1)(b)(II). Those who divert water from the western slope must show that future water supplies for the western slope "will not be impaired nor increased in cost." *Id.* This can be satisfied by providing "compensatory storage" to help meet future needs in the area of origin. Colorado River Water Conservation Dist. v. Municipal Subdistrict, N. Colorado Water Conservancy Dist., 610 P.2d 81 (Colo. 1979).

Texas law allows interbasin transfers if the water diverted is surplus to the reasonably foreseeable needs of the basin of origin for the next fifty years. Tex. Water Code Ann. § 11.085. Oklahoma requires that sufficient reserves be established to meet present and future needs. Okla. Stat. tit. 82, § 1085.20.

A Nebraska provision that allowed interbasin transfers of 75% of the flow of major rivers in the state was interpreted to authorize the denial of transfers that are "contrary to the public interest." Little Blue Natural Resources Dist. v. Lower Platte N. Natural Resources Dist., 294 N.W.2d 598 (Neb. 1980). Subsequently, the statute was amended to set out specific factors to be considered by the Director of Natural Resources in deciding whether an interbasin transfer is in the public interest. Neb. Rev. Stat. § 46–289.

D. CHANGES IN USE

1. No Harm Rule

Whenever one seeks to change the point of diversion, or the place, purpose, or time of using a water right, special protections against harm to other appropriators apply. An appropriator who seeks to change a use or to transfer a right to another for a changed use must apply to the appropriate administrative body or court for approval.

Changes in use may affect stream conditions upon which other appropriators depend for their beneficial uses. Of course a junior appropriator may not impair a senior appropriator's prior rights to water, but juniors are also protected from changes made by seniors. The prior appropriation doctrine recognizes a right of junior appropriators "in the

continuation of stream conditions as they existed at
the time of their respective appropriations."
Farmers Highline Canal & Reservoir Co. v. City of
Golden, 272 P.2d 629 (Colo. 1954). *See* Okanogan
Wilderness League, Inc. v. Town of Twisp, 947 P.2d
732 (Wash. 1997).

Irrigation practices typically result in about half,
often more, of all water that is diverted returning to
the stream. Only a portion is actually consumed by
evaporation or by being taken up by plants to be
retained or transpired into the atmosphere. The rest
either flows or seeps back to the stream from ditches
or fields or is caught in sumps, ponds, groundwater
aquifers, and the like. The amount that does return
to the stream—"return flow"—becomes available at
certain times and places for others to divert.
Changes in the point of diversion, or the place, time,
or purpose of use must not cause material harm to
the uses of other appropriators.

Not all actions that injure juniors are subject to
the no harm rule. Reuse or more intensive
consumptive use of the water on the same land for
the same general purposes (*e.g.,* irrigation), changes
in use of imported water, and, in some jurisdictions,
certain changes in the point of return are not
covered. Moreover, a change in the use of relatively
small quantities of water may be allowed where the
change meets certain minimal criteria. *See* Mont.
Code. Ann. § 85–2–402 (imposing more stringent
requirements on changes over 5.5 c.f.s. or 4,000 acre
feet per year).

2. Procedures

An appropriator who seeks to change the use or to transfer a water right to another who will use the right differently must seek permission. In permit jurisdictions, the decision whether a change in use will be allowed rests with a state agency or state engineer. Such administrative decisions are subject to review by state courts. In Colorado, a change of use is approved through a statutorily established court proceeding and evidenced by a court decree. Colo. Rev. Stat. §§ 37–92–302—37–92–505; Santa Fe Trail Ranches Prop. Owners Ass'n. v. Simpson, 990 P.2d 46, 53 (Colo. 1999). In either type of jurisdiction, the main substantive issue in the change of use proceeding is whether the change violates the no harm rule.

In most states, the person seeking the new use has the burden of proving that no harm will result. *See* Matter of Application for Change of Appropriation Water Rights, 816 P.2d 1054 (Mont. 1991) (seniors seeking increase of appropriation and switch to sprinkler irrigation failed to prove that their increased use would not harm downstream juniors). Once a prima facie case has been made, the burden is on objectors to refute the evidence and prove harm.

Some states authorize additional requirements. Under Wyoming's change in use statute, the Board of Control may consider economic loss to the locality and the state. Wyo. Stat. Ann. § 41–3–104. Nevada allows the state engineer to consider the economic consequences to the state of changes to uses "involving the industrial purpose of generating electricity to be exported." Nev. Rev. Stat. § 533.372.

Changes may also be denied on "public interest" grounds. A Utah statute specifically required the state engineer to apply public welfare criteria to applications for new appropriations; however, the Utah Supreme Court held that it would be unreasonable to allow the state's interest in protecting public recreation, natural environment, or public welfare at the time of an appropriation to be defeated on a change of use. Bonham v. Morgan, 788 P.2d 497 (Utah 1989). In one New Mexico case, a change of water rights from agricultural to a proposed resort was found contrary to the public welfare. In re: Application of Sleeper, 760 P.2d 787 (N.M. App. 1988). The decision was reversed on appeal because, at the time, the public welfare statute did not apply to changes, only new appropriations. *Id.* at 791. The statute was subsequently extended to transfers of water rights. N.M. Stat. Ann. § 72–5–23.

3. Types of Changes

A change in use may take several forms. Changes may be made in the point of diversion or point of return; in the place of use or place of storage; in the purpose of use (*e.g.,* irrigation or municipal); or in the time of use (*e.g.,* seasonal, intermittent, or continuous). Harm may occur either from depriving an appropriator of the quantity or quality of water that was available before the change or by increasing an appropriator's obligations to seniors.

a. Change in Point of Diversion

One of the most common types of change in use is a change in the point of diversion. An irrigator may want to divert through a new ditch or use a surface diversion instead of a well drawing on the same water source. The change may not harm other appropriators. Langenegger v. Carlsbad Irr. Dist., 82 N.M. 416, 483 P.2d 297 (1971). In addition, a decree permitting a change in point of diversion cannot enlarge the right of the recipient; the right is limited to the amount of water historically used even if that amount was less than the full amount of the decreed right. Orr v. Arapahoe Water and Sanitation District, 753 P.2d 1217 (Colo. 1988).

b. Change in Place of Use

Changes in place of use often change the place or timing of return flows from irrigation. A change in place of use must not increase consumptive use even if the amount diverted remains the same. Enlarged Southside Irrigation Ditch Co. v. John's Flood Ditch Co., 210 P.2d 982 (Colo. 1949). Changing to out-of-basin uses, in particular, yield no return flows, making the new use 100% consumptive.

A change in the place of storage, such as an alternative reservoir site, is a type of change in the place of use. Increased seepage and evaporation loss could harm juniors, but a change may be permitted, for instance, if the new reservoir is at a higher elevation with lower losses than the original site. Lindsey v. McClure, 136 F.2d 65 (10th Cir. 1943). Uses that involve a change from direct use to storage may affect both the timing of usage and amount of consumptive use.

Exchange statutes in several western states (including Utah, Colorado, and Idaho) authorize agreements between water users to furnish water at one point in the stream and withdraw at another. Utah Code Ann. § 73–3–3 (2013); Colo. Rev. Stat. § 37–83–101 (2013); Idaho Code Ann. § 42–240 (2003). Exchanges are subject to the no harm rule. Almo Water Co. v. Darrington, 501 P.2d 700 (Idaho 1972).

c. Change in Purpose of Use

A change in purpose of use typically involves a change from irrigation use to municipal or industrial use. Municipal uses are usually more consumptive than agricultural uses because returns (usually sewage effluent) are a small percentage of the quantity diverted, while irrigation return flows are more substantial. By contrast, hydroelectric power generation and cooling are less consumptive than irrigation. Thus, changes from irrigation to municipal use (Farmers Reservoir & Irrigation Co. v. City of Golden, 44 P.3d 241 (Colo. 2002); City of Westminster v. Church, 445 P.2d 52 (Colo. 1968)) or from power generation to irrigation use (Hutchinson v. Stricklin, 28 P.2d 225 (Or. 1933), *overruled on other grounds*, Rencken v. Young, 711 P.2d 954 (1985)), may be limited to prevent increased consumption.

Planting crops that consume more water or using different facilities to irrigate (*e.g.,* sprinklers instead of flood irrigation) are not usually considered changes in purpose though the manner of use is different and others may be harmed by a reduction in seepage or elimination of return flows resulting from reduced application or increased consumption. Montana v. Wyoming, 131 S. Ct. 1765 (2011). This apparent loophole in the no harm rule is built on traditional assumptions of water users, especially irrigators, that they should be able to plant whatever they want and irrigate as necessary so long as the amount of water used does not exceed the amount allowed by a permit or decree. The prevailing rule remains: changes in the purpose of use that necessitate permission of an administrative agency or court and invocation of the no harm rule occur only when water is put to a different type of beneficial use.

d. Change in Time of Use

A change in the timing of use can harm others. For example, irrigation rights are seasonal (used only during the growing season), while municipal and industrial uses are typically year-around. Similarly, a storage right may permit constant diversion into the reservoir although actual uses from the reservoir are intermittent, but a direct flow right is occasional, occurring only when there are present uses. A change in the timing of return flows is also a possible source of harm. The slow-moving character of seepage returning to the stream provides a form of "transient storage" that may furnish late-season return flows to juniors, thus extending their irrigation season.

e. Change in Point of Return

A change in the point of return of water also can cause harm to others. Ordinarily such a change accompanies other changes in use. Although cases involving only a change in point of return are rare, one would expect the no harm rule to apply. But in Metropolitan Denver Sewage Disposal Dist. No. 1 v. Farmers Reservoir & Irrigation Co., 499 P.2d 1190 (Colo. 1972), the court held that irrigators who depended on discharges of Denver's sewage effluent suffered no legal harm from Denver's change in the point of return when a new sewage plant was constructed. The *Metro Denver* decision may be limited to the facts. The contest was over who should pay to pump the treated effluent back upstream to where the farmers could use it, and perhaps the court did not want to interfere with the investment that the city had made in the new plant. Alternatively, the court might have decided that, as a municipal supplier, Denver had a right to consume (or reuse) 100% of the water it diverted and therefore downstream users could establish no rights in waters that might return to the stream. *See* Arizona Public Service Co. v. Long, 773 P.2d 988 (Ariz. 1989) (allowing city to market sewage effluent).

In a later case, the Colorado Supreme Court in dicta reiterated the proposition that a change in the point of return is not subject to the no harm rule. City of Boulder v. Boulder & Left Hand Ditch Co., 557 P.2d 1182 (Colo. 1976). The case was distinguishable from *Metro Denver* because a change in place of use was also involved. However, the court moderated the *Metro Denver* rule, saying it only applies to "waste water." Thus, there is no protectable right to the continued flow of "waste water" (water returning to a stream in surface ditches), but there is a right to protection against changes in "return flow" (water seeping back to the stream), at least when triggered by a change in the place of use.

4. Limits on Changed Use

A change in use will not be denied if conditions can be imposed that are sufficient to protect junior appropriators from harm. For example, a seasonally used direct-flow irrigation right may be transferred to a continuous storage use provided diversions are restricted to the irrigation season, Brighton Ditch Co. v. City of Englewood, 237 P.2d 116 (Colo. 1951), and are made under the same conditions as the original direct-flow diversions, Colorado Milling & Elevator Co. v. Larimer & Weld Irrigation Co., 56 P. 185 (Colo. 1899).

The amount diverted to accomplish the changed use can never exceed the diversion right stated in the permit or decree. Schuh v. State Dept. of Ecology, 667 P.2d 64, 68 (Wash. 1983); Santa Fe Trail Ranches Property Owners Ass'n v. Simpson, 990 P.2d 46 (Colo. 1999). If the historical consumptive use of a decreed right of 200 c.f.s. was 100 c.f.s. (50% consumptive), the new user is entitled to consume 100 c.f.s. If the new use is only 40% efficient, however, the new user would have to divert 250 c.f.s. in order to consume 100 c.f.s. Since the changed use or transferred right is also limited to the original decreed diversion right of 200 c.f.s., the new user will, in fact, only be able to use 80 c.f.s. (200 c.f.s. x 40% consumption).

A common restriction on changes in use is that the new use be limited to reasonably necessary historical consumptive use. Neb. Rev. St. § 46–294(1)(e); Okanogan Wilderness League, Inc. v. Town of Twisp, 133 Wash. 2d 769, 947 P.2d 732 (1997). Actual historical use can be shown by records of the amount of water diverted and the amount of water returned. Expert testimony is usually necessary, however. First, records may not exist, and they are rarely adequate to demonstrate the amount of water that has been diverted and returned. Further, actual usage may exceed the amount of water reasonably necessary to make beneficial use of the water for the purpose of the appropriation. Thus, historical use may depend on evidence of the amount of water that would have been reasonably required for the purposes to which it was devoted. Evidence includes soil conditions, proximity to the stream, crop water requirements minus average rainfall, and efficiency of irrigation. Green v. Chaffee Ditch Co., 371 P.2d 775 (Colo. 1962). *See* CF & I Steel Corp. v. Rooks, 495 P.2d 1134 (Colo. 1972) (objectors lost for failure to refute applicant's expert testimony).

Statutes, case law, and regulations restricting transfers to historical consumptive use are intended to prevent harm to others. The rules have been applied to restrict a change even if the impact on the stream from the new use would be lower. For instance, in one case water had been taken to another watershed where it was used for irrigation, so the old use was 100% consumptive as to the watershed of origin. The new use, however, was entirely within the watershed of origin. One might have expected the change to be approved for the full amount "used" historically—all the water diverted. But the court limited the right transferred to the quantity of water that was consumed in the destination watershed (diversion less returns), although none of the returns had actually reached the basin of origin. Basin Electric Power Coop. v. State Board of Control, 578 P.2d 557 (Wyo. 1978). The decision may be explained by the fact the court was upholding a determination within the administrative discretion of the Board of Control.

Changes may also be denied or restricted if they diminish the quality of water supplied to other appropriators. *See* Heine v. Reynolds, 367 P.2d 708 (N.M. 1962) (denying an application for a change where stream salinity would be increased). An increasingly common condition requires bypasses or releases of water necessary to maintain streamflows or quality. *See* City of Thornton v. City & County of Denver ex rel. Bd. of Water Commissioners, 44 P.3d 1019 (Colo. 2002) (finding that the water court had jurisdiction to decide whether decreased water quality made it unsuitable for city's use). Other water quality-related barriers to changes of use exist, such as federal and state environmental pollution laws, minimum and maximum streamflow requirements, and land use restrictions.

VIII. LOSS OF WATER RIGHTS

Water rights acquired by prior appropriation may be lost if they are not used. Nonuse for a long time, coupled with intent to relinquish, constitutes abandonment. Statutory forfeiture for nonuse may occur despite the appropriator's contrary intent. However, a water user cannot generally gain an appropriative water right by prescription because any water not used by appropriators in priority belongs to the stream, to be used for the satisfaction of rights of existing appropriators and for new appropriation permits.

A. ABANDONMENT

Rights to use water established by prior appropriation will be abandoned and lost if they are not used for an extended time. Mere nonuse is not enough, however. One must intend to abandon the rights. Beaver Park Water, Inc. v. City of Victor, 649 P.2d 300 (Colo. 1982). The burden of proving intent to abandon is on the person attempting to establish abandonment, but an unreasonable period of nonuse may create a rebuttable presumption of intent to abandon. Haystack Ranch, LLC v. Fazzio, 997 P.2d 548, 553 (Colo. 2000).

The period giving rise to the presumption is found in statute or case law. In Colorado, the state engineer publishes a list of abandoned water rights based on the statutory presumption arising from ten years of nonuse. Colo. Rev. Stat. § 37–92–401(4).

Once a presumption of abandonment arises, the rights holder may rebut it by showing facts or conditions justifying the nonuse; however, broad, general reasons unsupported by evidence are not sufficient to overcome the presumption. Musselshell River Drainage Area, 840 P.2d 577 (Mont. 1992); Beaver Park Water, Inc. v. City of Victor, 649 P.2d 300, 302 (Colo. 1982). Natural disasters and economic, financial, or legal obstacles that frustrated attempts to use water may negate intent to abandon. *See* Hallenbeck v. Granby Ditch & Reservoir Co., 420 P.2d 419 (Colo. 1966) ("financial difficulties ... during the depression prevented Granby's ability to keep reservoirs in peak operating condition"). Economic infeasibility of the project, however, is not enough to overcome the presumption. CF & I Steel Corp. v. Purgatoire River Water Conservancy Dist., 515 P.2d 456 (Colo. 1973). The distinction seems to be that in the former case water use was impeded by genuine economic impediments and in the latter it was delayed based on strategic business reasons. However, the Colorado court has allowed an appropriator to negate its intent to abandon with evidence that it was trying to sell the water right for which it apparently had no use. People ex rel. Danielson v. City of Thornton, 775 P.2d 11 (Colo. 1989).

B. FORFEITURE

Forfeiture, unlike abandonment, does not require proof that the appropriator intended to abandon water rights by nonuse. Involuntary loss of all or a portion of one's water rights is triggered simply by nonuse for a period set by statute. The burden of proving nonuse is on the state (or other party) asserting forfeiture. Rencken v. Young, 711 P.2d 954 (Or. 1985).

Some statutes authorize a court to declare a right "forfeited" where evidence is inadequate to prove intent to abandon. Jenkins v. State, Dept. of Water Resources, 647 P.2d 1256 (Idaho 1982). Forfeiture statutes may provide for notice by a state agency or official that rights will be forfeited if nonuse is not cured within a statutorily specified grace period. New Mexico provided for automatic forfeiture after four years of nonuse, State ex rel. Reynolds v. South Springs Co., 452 P.2d 478 (N.M. 1969). The statute was subsequently amended to allow a one-year period during which use can be recommenced or a showing made as to why it was impossible to put the water to a beneficial use at that time. N.M. Stat. Ann. § 72–12–8. By contrast, the Idaho Supreme Court held that resumption of use as a defense to forfeiture is ineffective if a junior appropriator used the water for a beneficial use *after* non-use reached the statutory period. Sagewillow, Inc. v. Idaho Dept. of Water Resources, 70 P.3d 669 (Idaho 2003); Millview County Water Dist. v. State Water Resources Control Bd., 229 Ca. App. 4th 879 (Cal.

App. 1st Dist., 2014) (following the resumption of use doctrine established in *Sagewillow*).

Some courts have held that once the right is lost, it cannot be revived. *See* Baugh v. Criddle, 431 P.2d 790 (Utah 1967) (following a fire that destroyed a mill, the party who failed to provide notice that the use had been resumed lost his right to use water). In other states, however, the right continues to exist until there has been a declaration of forfeiture. *See* Sturgeon v. Brooks, 281 P.2d 675 (Wyo. 1955) (allowing additional time for using the right or for proving an excuse for nonuse). In Oregon, forfeiture is not automatic because the Water Resources Division has to initiate proceedings within the statute of limitation and follow the correct procedures. Or. Rev. Stat. § 555.100.

To encourage efficient use of water, some states have provided that a right is not subject to forfeiture when appropriators use less water to carry out the same beneficial use so long as they still are capable of using the entire amount. Or. Rev. Stat. § 540.610(3). California protects water rights against abandonment of those whose reduction in use is due to conservation efforts. Cal. Water. Code. § 1011(1).

C. ADVERSE POSSESSION AND PRESCRIPTIVE RIGHTS

One may obtain another's rights in real property by taking actual, open, notorious, continuous, and hostile exclusive possession of the property. A few courts have ruled that in certain circumstances a junior appropriator could adversely possess a senior's right. *See, e.g.,* Sears v. Berryman, 101 Idaho 843 (1984); Head v. Merrick, 203 P.2d 608 (Idaho 1949). Although Utah was once among these states, Smith v. North Canyon Water Co., 52 P. 283, 286 (Utah 1898), the Utah legislature has abolished prescriptive rights to water. Utah Code Ann. § 73–3–1 (West 2010).

In the majority of states, rights held by prior appropriation cannot be lost to others by adverse possession. First, private individuals can obtain water rights only by compliance with statutory procedures. Montana's statute explicitly provides that a right to appropriate water cannot be acquired by any method that is not statutorily provided, including by adverse possession, estoppel, or prescription. Mont. Code Ann. § 85–2–301(3). Second, one's use of water cannot be adverse to others because everyone has a right to assume that any water use occurred within the priority system. Coryell v. Robinson, 194 P.2d 342 (Colo. 1948). This is especially true if the would-be adverse possessor holds some rights on the watercourse. Third, some courts have reasoned that rights to use a public resource, like water, cannot be adversely possessed. *See* Mountain Meadow Ditch & Irrigation Co. v. Park Ditch & Reservoir Co., 277 P.2d 527 (Colo. 1954) (unappropriated water in stream was property of the public and could not be adversely possessed). Although People v. Shirokow, 605 P.2d 859 (Cal. 1980), held that claims to prescriptive rights are not valid against the state, California recognizes prescriptive water rights between private parties. Brewer v. Murphy, 74 Cal.Rptr.3d 436 (Ct. App. 2008).

IX. PHYSICAL ACCESS TO SOURCE AND TRANSPORTATION OF WATER

Irrigated land, particularly in the western United States, does not often border a stream. Therefore, rights-of-way for ditches, canals, and pipelines are critically important to water users. Water users often need to build facilities on the land of one or more intervening property owners in order to bring water to their tract of land. Even when land is adjacent to a stream, use of another's land may be necessary in order to use a gravity flow pipe or ditch that follows contours of the terrain. To address these various access issues, federal and state laws govern acquisition of rights-of-way by water rights holders across public and private lands.

A. ACROSS FEDERAL PUBLIC LANDS

As water law began to develop during the western expansion of the United States, much of the land in the West was public, owned and controlled by the federal government. Congress provided for ditch and canal rights-of-way across public lands in the 1866 Mining Act. In addition to recognizing the right of trespassers to establish water rights by prior appropriation on federal lands, the Act stated, "the right of way for the construction of ditches and canals for the purposes herein specified is acknowledged and confirmed." 30 U.S.C. § 51. The 1870 amendment to the Mining Act made all patents of public lands and all homesteads "subject to any vested and accrued water rights, or rights to ditches and reservoirs used in connection with such water rights." 43 U.S.C. § 661. These laws opened the way for construction of all necessary facilities without fear of later dispossession or interruption by the government or its patentees. *See supra* Section II.A of this chapter.

Today, rights-of-way across public land are obtained by special permission from the federal agency that manages the area. For BLM and Forest Service lands, the Federal Land Policy and Management Act of 1976 (FLPMA), 43 U.S.C. § 1761, authorizes the Secretary of the Interior (and the Secretary of Agriculture) to grant or renew rights-of-way across public lands for water storage and distribution facilities (e.g., ditches, pipelines, and tunnels). Securing rights-of-way requires application to the Secretary of Interior (or the Secretary of Agriculture in the case of National Forest lands). Permits are granted for a fixed term and subject to annual rentals and conditions on use deemed necessary to comply with mandates in public land laws, such as requirements for protecting fish and wildlife, recreational uses, biodiversity, and other environmental values. 43 U.S.C. § 1765; 43 C.F.R. § 2805.12. For rights-of-way across lands managed by agencies other than the Forest Service or the Bureau of Land Management, water rights holders must secure a permit from the relevant agency. *See, e.g.,* 43 U.S.C. § 959, 36 C.F.R. pt. 14 (National Park Service

Permits); 16 U.S.C. §§ 668dd(d), 50 C.F.R. pt. 29 (National Wildlife Refuge Permits).

In 1890, Congress created a right of way for ditches and canals constructed by the authority of the United States, on all public lands patented to private ownership west of the 100th meridian. 43 U.S.C. § 945. A 1964 amendment to this act required the government to pay compensation for any such lands that were actually used for rights-of-way for accessing water. 43 U.S.C. § 945a. Thus, many lands in the West are impressed with rights-of-way for private uses. New appropriators whose water uses began after the land was privately patented, even if formerly part of the public domain, generally seek their rights-of-way under state law from private landowners. In some instances, if the federal government denies access that was formerly available across federal land, the land owners may be able to seek compensation under the Takings Clause of the Fifth Amendment. *See* Estate of Hage v. United States, 687 F.3d 1281, 1290 (Fed. Cir. 2012) (holding that USFS could reasonably regulate the use of ditches but could not deny access to vested water rights without providing compensation). The law remains somewhat unresolved in terms of determining what will trigger a compensation claim for these rights under the Fifth Amendment in these circumstances. *See, e.g.,* Walker v. United States, 142 N.M. 45, 162 P.3d 882 (2007); Joyce Livestock Co. v. United States (In re SRBA Case No. 39576), 144 Idaho 1, 156 P.3d 502 (2007).

B. ACROSS PRIVATE LANDS
UNDER STATE LAW

1. Status of Trespassing Appropriators

Under the prior appropriation doctrine, use (not land ownership along the watercourse) is the basis of a water right. Mettler v. Ames Realty Co., 61 Mont. 152, 162, 201 P. 702 (Mont. 1921). Therefore, appropriators often take water by accessing a watercourse adjacent to lands owned by another private party. State laws govern rights-of-way across private land. As indicated above, federal legislation validated the appropriative rights and use of lands for ditch rights-of-way by "trespassers" on the public lands. Lands conveyed to private parties were patented subject to rights of those who already had perfected water rights and use the land for ditch rights-of-way.

A number of state laws and cases address whether appropriators may transport water across lands of others. Some state courts (*e.g.,* Idaho and Oregon) have invalidated the appropriation of one who trespasses on the land of another to make a diversion. Allen v. Magill, 96 Or. 610, 619 189 P. 986, 989 (1920). The right to contest these appropriations may be limited to the non-consenting landowner. More typically, trespassing appropriators may be subject to a trespass claim, but this does not void their water right. For instance, in Colorado, trespass cannot be asserted to prevent perfection of a water right, but the trespasser must compensate the owner for the fair market value of using the lands and for any resulting damage to the residue. Bubb v. Christensen, 610 P.2d 1343, 1346 (Colo. 1980). This is tantamount to a right of private condemnation, although the owner, if aware of the intrusion when it begins, could probably control the choice of a route across the land.

While appropriators who transport surface water across the land of another may be subject to a trespass claim, storing or transporting water in an aquifer under another party's property does not constitute a trespass. Board of County Comm'rs v. Park County Sportsmen's Ranch, LLP, 45 P.3d 693, 713–14 (Colo. 2002); South West Sand & Gravel, Inc. v. Cent. Ariz. Water Conservation Dist., 221 Ariz. 309, 318, 212 P.3d 1, 10 (Ariz. 2008), *as amended* (Mar. 9, 2009). Moreover, the state's approval of an application for recognition of an incidental aquifer storage right was not an unconstitutional taking of private property. In re Application U-2, 226 Neb. 594, 606, 413 N.W.2d 290, 299 (1987).

If a trespasser enters the land of another and constructs pipelines, ditches, or other facilities without the landowner's permission, and the facilities remain for a long enough time period, the use could ripen into a prescriptive right for the water. Pabst v. Finmand, 190 Cal. 124, 211 P.11 (Cal. 1922); Pedersen v. Dep't of Transp., 43 Wash. App. 413, 717 P.2d 773 (Wash. Ct. App. 1986); Graveley Simmental Ranch Co. v. Quigley, 314 Mont. 226, 65 P.3d 225 (Mont. 2003).

2. Purchase of Rights-of-Way

The most common way to obtain a right-of-way to convey water across private land is by purchase. Often the water delivery facilities can also serve the property owner, and the parties can reach a mutually beneficial arrangement. The right-of-way for a canal, ditch, or pipeline typically includes a secondary easement for necessary maintenance and repairs. Ass'n of Apt. Owners of Wailea Elua v. Wailea Resort Co., 100 Haw. 97, 115, 58 P.3d 608, 626 (2002); Newmyer v. Roush, 21 Idaho 106, 120 P. 464 (1912).

Grants of easements or rights-of-way, like other interests in land, usually must be in writing and conform to other property conveyance formalities. *See, e.g.,* Or. Rev. Stat. § 93.020. Yet in some states courts have held that a landowner's oral permission or informal letter to construct a ditch is valid as a license. The landowner is then estopped from contesting that license. Shaw v. Proffitt, 57 Or. 192, 109 P. 584 (1910). In order to become irrevocable and transferable, courts require licensees to show reliance through a substantial amount of money and labor invested in the project. In McReynolds v. Harrigfeld, 26 Idaho 26, 140 P. 1096 (1914), the court refused to quiet title to an irrigation ditch because the ditch builder could not show that he made an investment dependent upon landowner's permission. When a water user can prove substantial investment, these licenses are essentially treated as easements. However, not all courts treat licenses the same. For example, the

Washington court in Rhoades v. Barnes, 54 Wash. 145, 102 P. 884 (1909), stated that the licensor may revoke the license at any time, regardless of the acts performed under the license or the amount of money spent in reliance on the license.

3. Condemnation of Rights-of-Way

Some western states enacted statutes authorizing appropriators to condemn rights-of-way to transport water across private lands. *See, e.g.,* Wash. Rev. Code § 90.03.040. Water rights holders can use these statutes, where they exist, to gain access to water when the owner is unwilling or unavailable to grant permission. In New Mexico, for example, an irrigation company was granted the right to enter onto private property for the purpose of installing a canal to divert surplus water from the Rio Grande River. Albuquerque Land & Irrigation Co. v. Gutierrez, 10 N.M. 177, 61 P. 357 (1900).

Challenges to these private condemnation statutes argue they do not further a public use. The U.S. Supreme Court upheld Utah's grant of eminent domain power against a challenge that the law offended the due process clause of the fourteenth amendment. The Court recognized the great importance of water development under conditions prevailing in the West. Clark v. Nash, 198 U.S. 361 (1905). *See* O'Neill v. Leamer, 239 U.S. 244, 36 S. Ct. 54 (1915); California Oregon Power Co. v. Beaver Portland Cement Co., 295 U.S. 142, 55 S. Ct. 725 (1935). Western state courts have upheld similar statutes. In Kaiser Steel Corp. v. W.S.

Ranch Co., 81 N.M. 414, 420, 467 P.2d 986, 992 (1970), the Supreme Court of New Mexico held that any beneficial use pursuant to state law (coal mining in that case) would suffice to support a valid "public use." Further, the New Mexico court found that a landowner's only remedy against an appropriator who enters without permission is an inverse condemnation action. *Id.* at 421, 993.

C. APPURTENANCY OF DITCH RIGHTS TO WATER RIGHTS

The right-of-way for a ditch and a water right are usually considered appurtenant to one another—conveyance of one carries the other with it; unless reserved in the conveyance, the right-of-way passes by the deed. Ruhnke v. Aubert, 113 P. 38 (Or. 1911). This does not prevent one from being sold apart from the other if the parties express that intention. Fitzstephens v. Watson, 218 Or. 185, 344 P.2d 221 (Or. 1959).

X. STORAGE

In nearly all areas of the western United States, storage rights are an essential piece of the water allocation system. Water can be stored underground in an aquifer or above ground in a reservoir, tank, or channel. Without storage, beneficial use of water would be limited to short runoff periods and the maximum use of scarce water resources would be defeated. Storage water rights function differently than direct appropriations because they do not require the immediate diversion and use of water.

On-channel storage means the facility is physically part of the appropriated stream. Most dams, which often function to retain natural flow during peak periods, are examples of on-channel storage. This on-channel storage allows water not needed for senior downstream appropriators to be stored for later use. Off-channel storage requires diversion and transportation works to get water to a storage location away from the stream channel. As a legal matter, there is no distinction between off-stream and on-stream storage rights. In general, for purposes of the diversion requirement, retention of water in the streambed by artificial means constitutes a "diversion" for purposes of perfecting a water right. A&B Irrigation Dist. v. State (In re SRBA), 336 P. 3d 792, 796 (Idaho 2014); City of Lafayette v. New Anderson Ditch Co., 962 P.2d 955 (Colo. 1998). Many states recognize an exception to the diversion and storage requirements for the protection of established minimum instream flows. *See, e.g.*, Swinomish Indian Tribal Cmty. v. Dep't of Ecology, 178 Wash.2d 571, 311 P.3d 6 (Wash. 2012); California v. Federal Power Com., 345 F.2d 917 (9th Cir. 1965).

A. ACQUISITION OF STORAGE RIGHTS

State and federal law treat permission to divert and store water as distinct from permission to construct and maintain the physical works. In order to maintain a storage reservoir, a person or organization must secure a storage water right under state law and also secure the relevant permits and permission to construct and maintain the dam facilities either under state or federal law depending on the size and location of that facility.

1. Storage Water Rights

The same general principles of appropriation for immediate use, "direct flow water rights," govern appropriations for subsequent uses, "storage water rights," though some states make a statutory distinction between the two. Users obtain a permit or decree for a storage water right from the same agency or court that determines direct flow water rights. Storage rights are usually only valid if the stored water will eventually go to satisfy a recognized beneficial use; storage itself is not deemed a beneficial use. People ex. rel. Simpson v. Highland Irrigation Co., 917 P.2d 1242, 1251 (1996). A Washington court held that in order for a water right permit to vest, actual application of the water to a beneficial use must be made before the right is perfected. Lummi Indian Nation v. State, 170 Wn.2d 247, 241 P.3d 1220 (2010). A storage appropriation should not be granted if it would injure any prior appropriator on the stream. Whitcomb v. Helena Water Works Co., 151 Mont. 443, 444 P.2d 301, 303 (Mont. 1968); Colo. Rev. Stat. §37–87–101 ("No water storage facility may be operated in such a manner as to cause material injury to the senior appropriative rights of others.")

A right to use water directly from the stream does not entitle the user to store any water and a right to store water does not mean that water can be used directly from the stream. Handy Ditch Co. v.

Greeley & Loveland Irrigation Co., 86 Colo. 197, 280 P. 481 (1929). In other words, the right to extract and use water does not create a concomitant right to store water. Central and West Basin Water Replenishment Dist. v. Southern Calif. Water Co., 109 Cal. App. 4th 891, 917, 135 Cal. Rptr. 2d 486, 505 (2003).

Some states require separate permits for storage and for application to a beneficial use, *e.g.*, Ariz. Rev. Stat. § 45–161; Nev. Rev. Stat. Ann. § 533.440; Wyo. Stat. Ann. § 41–3–302; Neb. Rev. St. § 46–242. This approach recognizes that often the entity diverting and holding the water (*e.g.*, a reservoir company) is different from the entity or persons using the water (*e.g.*, irrigators). Some states consider the two to be joint appropriators. Others require the ultimate user to obtain an appropriation permit by showing a valid agreement with the owner of the reservoir. *See, e.g.*, Wyo. Stat. Ann. § 41–3–302.

2. Permission to Construct Storage Facilities

Besides perfecting a right to store water, one seeking to impound it in a reservoir must have permission to build the facility. Federal law applies if the facility is to be built on a navigable waterway and generates a sufficient level of hydropower as defined in the Federal Power Act (FPA). 16 U.S.C. § 817. The FPA is administered by the Federal Energy Regulatory Commission and the process of licensing and re-licensing dams within defined waters represents a significant amount of regulation

under federal law. In addition, the federal
government may own and operate its own dams as
part of flood control or irrigation projects that are
directly authorized by Congress. *See infra* Water
Organizations Chapter Ten. Federal law provides
for the construction of these facilities, but often the
authorizing legislation requires the federal agency
to secure water rights under state law. *See* 16
U.S.C. § 802(a)(2).

Outside of these federal authorizations to
construct facilities, state law applies to facilities on
non-navigable waterways, with some exceptions. *See
e.g.,* Or. Rev. Stat. §§ 537.00–409; Wash. Admin.
Code § 173–175–100. In most states, the same
agency that determines water rights, approves
plans for the construction of dams and reservoirs.
Often the agency or official may consider factors
related to the public interest such as safety, impacts
on fish and wildlife, and aesthetics. For example,
the Oregon Water Resources Department approves
engineering plans and specifications before
construction of a storage project begins and can
consider various environmental factors. Or. Rev.
Stat. §§ 540.330, 540.340, 540.350; Or. Admin. R.
§ 690–020–0025. The party proposing to use the
stored water must also file an application for a
permit to apply the water to a beneficial use, known
as a secondary permit. Or. Rev. Stat. § 537.145.
Arizona only requires a single permit when the
same person is going to construct the reservoir and
put the water to beneficial use. Ariz. Rev. Stat.
§ 45–161(D).

Most states exempt small storage facilities like stock watering ponds from permit requirements. For example, in Washington, the building of any dam that is capable of storing at least 10 acre-feet is required to have a permit to construct and maintain the dam, but those under 10-acre feet do not require a permit. Wash. Admin. Code § 173–175–020.

B. USE OF STORAGE RIGHTS

The holder of a storage water right can use stored water for any beneficial purpose. Basey v. Gallagher, 87 U.S. 670 (1874); California Oregon Power Co. v. Beaver Portland Cement Co., 295 U.S. 142 (1935). Appropriative rights on a stream, whether for storage or direct flow, are governed by the same rules of priority. Donich v. Johnson, 77 Mont. 229, 250 P. 963 (1926). Storage and direct flow water rights are integrated in that neither is given preference over the other. People ex. rel. Park Reservoir Co. v. Hinderlider, 98 Colo. 505, 516, 57 P.2d 894, 899 (1936).

Some states allow exchanges between appropriators. For instance, water stored downstream may be exchanged for direct flow diversions upstream. Exchanges among rights holders maximize the beneficial use of water, allowing junior appropriators (with storage rights and available capacity) to share storage with senior appropriators (with no storage rights) that have rights to direct flow in excess of their need. The seniors' water is stored in the juniors' reservoir and its use later shared. In Colorado, an appropriator can devise a plan for augmentation that provides for such an exchange, which is approved so long as others are not harmed. Colorado Water Conservancy Dist. v. Fort Lyon Canal Co., 720 P.2d 133, 145 (Colo. 1986). Exchanges are permitted in most states upon compliance with conditions imposed by an administrative agency. Moreover, stored water may also be used under a contract, lease, or other arrangement. Kearney Lake, Land & Reservoir Co. v. Lake DeSmet Reservoir Co., 475 P.2d 548 (Wyo. 1970).

C. LIMITS ON STORAGE

A widely applied limitation on holders of storage water rights is the "one-fill rule." The rule allows an appropriator to fill a reservoir only once annually and the appropriator cannot use their priority storage right over the course of a year to store a cumulative quantity greater than the reservoir's full capacity. City of Grand Junction v. City & County of Denver by & Through Board of Water Commissioners, 960 P.2d 675 (Colo. 1998); Burlington Ditch Reservoir & Land Co. v. Metro Wastewater Reclamation District, 256 P.3d 645 (Colo. 2011); Wheatland Irrigation Dist. v. Pioneer Canal Co., 464 P.2d 533 (Wyo. 1970).

The purpose of the one-fill limitation was the ease of regulation, but its application can be complex. A series of several fillings and drawdowns may be necessary to even out flows throughout the year. A small regulating dam can release many times its capacity during a year, but this pattern of fill and release is prohibited whenever the one-fill rule is strictly applied. Moreover, if the purpose of the dam is hydropower generation as opposed to irrigation storage, the application of the one-fill rule greatly reduces the dam's utility. In fact, most of the case law concerns irrigation storage reservoirs. *See, e.g.,* Burlington Ditch Reservoir & Land Co. v. Metro Wastewater Reclamation Dist., 256 P.3d 645 (Colo. 2011).

Water diverted to a reservoir but not immediately used may be retained for future use by the appropriator. *See e.g.,* American Falls Reservoir Dist. No. 2 v. Idaho Dept. of Water Resources, 143 Idaho 862, 154 P.3d 433 (2007). This is known as "carryover storage," and has developed as a practice to help reservoir operators balance water supply over wet and dry years. *See* Pagosa Area Water & Sanitation District v. Trout Unlimited, 219 P.3d 774 (Colo. 2009) (carryover storage may be necessary to meet reasonably anticipated water needs). Some states do not allow the appropriator to use the amount of carryover storage plus the reservoir's full capacity of new water the following year; the limit of one filling still applies, with the amount carried over debited against the single filling. *See, e.g.,* Wyo. Stat. Ann. § 41–3–325; Lake De Smet Reservoir Co. v. Kaufmann, 75 Wyo. 87, 101, 292 P.2d 482, 487 (1956).

CHAPTER FOUR
HYBRID SYSTEMS AND OTHER VARIATIONS

Not all states fit neatly within the two categories of prior appropriation or riparian law, though principles or riparian and appropriative rights form the foundation even in states where different systems have emerged. Ten states employ a mixture of riparian and appropriation doctrine in their water laws. They include the four West Coast states (California, Oregon, Washington, and Alaska) and the six states that straddle the 100th meridian—the dividing line between the arid West and the relatively wet East (Texas, Oklahoma, Kansas, Nebraska, South Dakota, and North Dakota). These states flank a cluster of eight states, often referred to as the "Intermountain West," that embrace the pure appropriation doctrine. Mississippi also has a hybrid system based on riparian law, but later modified it by a statutory code that closely resembles prior appropriation.

Hybrid states are sometimes said to follow the "California doctrine" because California addressed the relationship between the two systems from the time that the appropriative code was adopted. Other states adopted their appropriative codes and then, later addressed riparian rights, often creating a system to phase riparian rights out. Oregon was the first state to adopt a process for simultaneously addressing vested riparian rights and extinguishing new riparian rights in an approach known as the

"Oregon doctrine." In practice, each hybrid state has its own approach for reconciling early riparian rights with appropriative rights established under an adopted code. Today, California, Nebraska, and Oklahoma represent special circumstances because riparians can still originate new uses superior to prior appropriators in these states.

The states that abolished all prior riparian rights upon the adoption of their appropriative codes are often referred to as "Colorado doctrine" states because Colorado was the first state to adopt this approach. In addition to Colorado, the Colorado Doctrine states include Arizona, Utah, Nevada, Idaho, Wyoming, New Mexico, and Montana. In these states, riparian law is not relevant to the allocation of water rights because all riparian rights were abolished either at the time that state's comprehensive water code was enacted or relatively soon after through common law. The only mechanism for securing a water right in Colorado Doctrine states is through the prior appropriation system.

This chapter also considers several special water allocation schemes existing in the United States, including the unique features of Louisiana's and Hawaii's water law as well as Pueblo water rights as recognized by California and New Mexico.

I. DEVELOPMENT OF HYBRID SYSTEMS

The historical roots of hybrid systems vary among jurisdictions. All of the hybrid states, however, share a common ancestry—they each recognized riparian rights from the start but also adopted the prior appropriation system because it was believed to be more suitable for allocating rights to use water. For states on the West Coast and in central states that lie between higher elevation arid land and lower land with greater rainfall, neither the riparian system nor the appropriation system was entirely fitting. Instead, they continued to recognize rights under both riparian and appropriative law—a "hybrid" system of water law. Hybrid states differ in the ways they have adapted to accommodate and reconcile uses of water under the two inconsistent systems of allocation.

A. CALIFORNIA'S EARLY RECOGNITION OF BOTH RIPARIAN RIGHTS AND APPROPRIATIVE RIGHTS

In Irwin v. Phillips, 5 Cal. 140 (1855), the Supreme Court of California rejected an argument by junior miners with claims on land that were riparian to the stream that they held the better water right. The court's rationale turned on the fact that the subsequent miners were not riparian *landowners* (as they were operating on federal public land) and so they could not assert riparian rights to prevent the earlier miner from interfering with their use. The court concluded that, among trespassers on the public domain, the rule of prior appropriation, that was a custom among the early miners, had become so firmly fixed as to be "looked upon as having the force and effect of res judicata." *Id.* at 145. In reaching this conclusion, the court noted that the state legislature had recognized canals for mining purposes as property subject to taxation, thereby implicitly approving the use of water by prior appropriation. *Id.* at 146. *See* Maynard v. Watkins, 173 P. 551 (1918) (holding that a completed ditch and application of water to a beneficial use constituted a valid appropriation).

Shortly after the decision in *Irwin*, the California Supreme Court acknowledged the continuing viability of the riparian doctrine as between bona fide settlers and appropriators subsequent to settlement. In Crandall v. Woods, 8 Cal. 136 (1857), as in *Irwin*, the parties were all on the public domain. The defendant, however, had settled on a tract contiguous to a stream under the public land laws so was not a trespasser on public land. The defendant did not start using water until after the plaintiff had put water to use downstream to supply a nearby town. When the defendant later started diverting water, the downstream user sued, claiming it had a valid prior appropriation. The court held that the defendant had settled under federal laws and was the absolute owner as against all but the United States. Thus the defendant was entitled to riparian rights subject only to the rights of appropriators who diverted water prior to the time he claimed his land. From these two cases, the rule for California emerged—between appropriators on the public land, the prior appropriator acquires the superior right, but a settler (with legal rights to land) who has not yet taken water could not be defeated by an appropriator whose water use began after the settler claimed the land.

The California Supreme Court later affirmed the common law of riparian rights as between riparian landowners. Lux v. Haggin, 10 P. 674 (Cal. 1886). The court, however, suggested in dictum that the rights of riparians whose land was patented (conveyed) to them by the United States after Congress passed the Mining Act of July 26, 1866 and an 1870 amendment (declaring that prior appropriation would determine water rights on the public lands) might be defeated by appropriations made after the Act.

B. FEDERAL RECOGNITION OF APPROPRIATIVE RIGHTS

As discussed above, the California courts assumed that water on federal land belonged to the federal government and passed with the land to settlers. However, courts in Colorado and other appropriation states—the Colorado Doctrine states—held that water law was entirely a state matter and that a federal patent carried with it no riparian rights. Coffin v. Left Hand Ditch Co., 6 Colo. 443 (1882). These two distinct approaches created a question of whether Colorado doctrine states were depriving landowners of riparian rights the federal government intended to convey with the underlying land patent. A few federal land statutes helped to clarify the situation.

The 1866 Mining Act, codified at 30 U.S.C. § 51 and 43 U.S.C. § 661, reads in relevant part:

Whenever, by priority of possession, rights to the use of water for mining, agricultural,

manufacturing, or other purposes have vested
and accrued, and the same are recognized and
acknowledged by the local customs, laws and
decisions of courts, the possessors and owners
of such vested rights shall be maintained and
protected in the same.

By the Act, Congress recognized the validity of
rights established under the appropriation doctrine
that many western states were applying on the
public domain. The statute should have made clear
that a patentee of riparian land could not defeat the
rights of an appropriator on the public domain. To
eliminate any doubt, the Placer Act of 1870
(amending the 1866 Act) said that future patentees
of riparian land would take subject to the vested
rights of appropriators.

In addition to the mining act, the Desert Land Act
of 1877, 43 U.S.C. § 329, intended as an incentive
program in which the federal government gave
desert lands to persons who would establish
agriculture, provided that:

[T]he right to the use of water by the person so
conducting the same on or to any tract of desert
land of 640 acres shall depend upon bona fide
prior appropriation, and such right shall not
exceed the amount of water actually
appropriated and necessarily used for the
purpose of irrigation and reclamation; *and all
surplus water over and above such actual
appropriation and use, together with the water
of all lakes, rivers, and other sources of water
supply on the public lands and not navigable,*

shall remain and be held free for the appropriation and use of the public for irrigation, mining, and manufacturing purposes, subject to existing rights. [Emphasis added]

The italicized portion of the Act was probably intended only to limit the amount of water an appropriator could claim. States have differed on the impact of this language on existing riparian rights. *See* Hough v. Porter, 95 P. 732 (Or. 1908) (holding that the Desert Lands Act removed all riparian rights from federal land patents); Cook v. Evans, 185 N.W. 262 (S.D. 1921) (following the rule established in Oregon); *cf.* Still v. Palouse Irrigation & Power Co., 117 P. 466 (Wash. 1911) (interpreting the Desert Lands Act as removing riparian rights on the narrow set of lands patented under that particular provision, but not other federal lands patented under other federal statutes); San Joaquin and Kings River Canal & Irrigation Co. v. Worswick, 203 P. 999 (Cal. 1922) (holding that riparian land patents (as opposed to desert land patents) had riparian rights that trumped the rights of prior appropriators).

The issue of whether the Desert Lands Act extinguished all riparian rights on federal lands patented after March 3, 1877 was before the U.S. Supreme Court in California Oregon Power Co. v. Beaver Portland Cement Co., 295 U.S. 142 (1935). An Oregon landowner, whose property bordered on a stream, claimed riparian rights based on an 1885 patent, predating Oregon's statute subjecting all

water in the state to appropriation. The Court
upheld Oregon's interpretation of the Desert Land
Act in Hough v. Porter, 95 P. 732 (Or. 1908), which
abrogated riparian rights on lands patented after
1877, but left other states free to define water rights
as they pleased. The Court in *Beaver Portland
Cement* said that federal land laws recognize that
each state has "the right . . . to determine for itself
to what extent the rule of appropriation or the
common law rule in respect to riparian rights
should obtain." 295 U.S. at 164. The Court
announced that Congress "effected a severance of all
waters upon the public domain . . . from the land
itself," but that state law could establish water
rights for these lands. *Id.* at 158. Notably, the
Supreme Court recognized two specific situations
where the federal government retained an interest
in water. First, the federal government retains an
interest in the water on public domain lands where
water is needed to carry out purposes on federal
land. *See infra* Chapter Eight (Federal Reserved
Rights). Second, the federal government retains an
interest in water to satisfy navigational interests.
See infra Chapter Seven (Navigable Waters).

II. MODIFICATIONS OF RIPARIAN
RIGHTS IN HYBRID SYSTEMS

All hybrid states limited the extent to which
present riparian rights could be exercised and
future riparian rights asserted. The ability of
riparians to insist on the continued flow of a
watercourse and to begin and cease using water as

they pleased was incompatible with successful operation of an appropriation system.

A. REASONABLE USE LIMITATIONS

In an early case, the California Supreme Court upheld the right of riparians to enjoin diversions by subsequent appropriators even in the absence of actual harm. Lux v. Haggin, 10 P. 674 (Cal. 1886). The practical inefficiency of the rule was that riparians could lock up water and prevent other beneficial uses. *See* Herminghaus v. Southern California Edison Co., 252 P. 607 (Cal. 1926) (riparians on the San Joaquin River, who relied on heavy spring flows to flood their lands, successfully enjoined construction of an upstream hydroelectric plant that would have deprived them of natural irrigation). As a result, all hybrid states now follow some form of the reasonable use rule. Thus, a riparian cannot defeat an appropriation unless undue interference with the riparian's reasonable use of the water is proved. *See, e.g.,* Tulare Irr. Dist. v. Lindsay-Strathmore Irrigation Dist., 45 P.2d 972 (Cal. 1935); City of Barstow v. Mojave Water Agency, 5 P.3d 853 (Cal. 2000); Brown v. Chase, 217 P. 23 (Wash. 1923).

B. EXTINGUISHMENT OF UNUSED RIPARIAN RIGHTS

Riparian and appropriation systems conflict at an essential level, namely riparian rights—being appurtenant to riparian land—do not depend on use. Appropriation rights are based on putting the water to beneficial use. In prior appropriation states where riparian rights were not abolished, the so-called California doctrine states, appropriators had no assurance that their rights would not be defeated by formerly inactive riparians who suddenly decided to exercise their rights. This uncertainty provided little incentive for appropriators to undertake expensive water projects. As a result, all of the hybrid states have attempted to curtail unused riparian rights by statute.

In Colorado doctrine states, previous riparian rights were simply abolished. However, in California doctrine states, the state legislatures have adopted provisions for recognizing early or "vested" riparian rights. These statutory provisions typically created a time period in which all those who claimed a prior riparian right must have asserted that right for it to be recognized in the appropriative system, and some required the riparian landowner to establish the amount of water they actually put to use. *See, e.g.,* Or. Rev. Stat. § 539.010 (effective Feb. 24, 1909); Wash. Rev. Code § 90.03.010 (effective 1917, although fifteen years of "reasonable notice" allowed under In re Deadman Creek, 694 P.2d 1071 (1985)); Okla. Stat. tit. 82, § 105.2 (effective June 10, 1963); Kan. Stat. Ann. § 82a–703 (effective June 28, 1945); Neb. Rev. Stat. § 46–204 (effective April 4, 1895); S.D. Codified Laws § 46–1–9(1) (1987) (effective March 2, 1955); N.D. Cent. Code § 61–04–01.2 (effective July 1, 1963, *Id.* at § 61–04–22).

C. CONSTITUTIONAL CHALLENGES

Legislation limiting or extinguishing riparian rights has been upheld when challenged as a taking of property without just compensation in all but three California doctrine states. As a result, riparian rights are only still at issue today in California, Nebraska, and Oklahoma where efforts to extinguish unexercised riparian rights have been blocked by the courts. Tulare Irr. Dist. v. Lindsay-Strathmore Irrigation District, 45 P.2d 972 (Cal. 1935); Franco-American Charolaise v. Oklahoma Water Resources Board, 855 P.2d 568 (Okla. 1990); Wasserburger v. Coffee, 141 N.W.2d 738 (Neb. 1966).

By contrast, the states of Oregon, Washington, Alaska, Texas, Kansas, South Dakota, and North Dakota have all taken action to address prior riparian rights. Each state has approached it a bit differently, and several examples are provided below.

Kansas adopted a statute stating that: "[s]ubject to vested rights, all waters within the state may be appropriated for beneficial use as herein provided. . . ." Kan. Stat. Ann. § 82a–703 (2013). The statute also required riparians to obtain permits to preserve their vested rights, which were limited to water applied to a beneficial use at or within three years of the law's 1945 enactment. The constitutionality of the statutory scheme was tested when the United States refused to proceed with a major irrigation project that depended on appropriative rights unless the law was found constitutional. The Kansas Supreme Court upheld the legislation. State ex rel. Emery v. Knapp, 207 P.2d 440 (Kan. 1949). The Kansas scheme is typical of others that limited "vested rights" to those applied to a beneficial use some time prior to passage of the statute or, in the case of works under construction at the time of enactment, within a reasonable time afterwards. Such laws have generally been upheld and compensation denied for extinguishment of unused rights. *See, e.g.,* Hough v. Porter, 95 P. 732 (Or. 1908).

A few state courts had difficulties with laws limiting riparian rights in favor of a new appropriation system. In 1913, South Dakota's 1907 appropriation law was declared to be an unconstitutional taking of riparian property without just compensation. St. Germain Irr. Co. v. Hawthorne Ditch Co., 143 N.W. 124 (S.D. 1913). A subsequently enacted system of appropriation in South Dakota was upheld in light of several intervening U.S. Supreme Court decisions distinguishing police power regulation from takings. Knight v. Grimes, 127 N.W.2d 708 (S.D. 1964). More recently, the South Dakota Supreme Court reiterated that legislative control of water rights— even where it divests formerly vested rights—is a legitimate exercise of the state's police power. Parks v. Cooper, 676 N.W.2d 823 (S.D. 2004).

Although California still nominally recognizes unused riparian rights, a 1979 decision held that a legislatively authorized adjudication of the water rights of all users in an entire river system can limit riparian users to the amount of water currently being applied to a beneficial use, plus a quantified future right. In re Waters of Long Valley Creek Stream System, 599 P.2d 656 (Cal. 1979).

Language in the Nebraska Constitution resembles language construed in other states to cut off future riparian claims, but the Nebraska courts have declared that riparian rights on lands patented before the 1895 Act have not been abolished and that riparian uses can still be claimed for these lands. Wasserburger v. Coffee, 141 N.W.2d 738 (Neb. 1966). Riparians are limited to a quantity reasonable for their purposes relative to the purposes of uses by appropriators.

The Oklahoma Supreme Court followed a similar path in holding that a thirty-year-old law adopting the appropriation system was unconstitutional insofar as it purported to extinguish unexercised riparian rights. In Franco-American Charolaise, Ltd. v. Oklahoma Water Resources Board, 855 P.2d 568 (Okla. 1990), it held that a riparian owner has a vested property right to initiate or change reasonable uses of water at any time. Since the statute failed to protect those rights (except for future domestic uses), it violated the takings clause of the Oklahoma Constitution. Thus, the rights of riparians to make future uses continues, limited only by the requirement of reasonableness. The legislature immediately acted to clarify its intent to extinguish future riparian claims, an effort that overcame the portion of Franco-American that said rights could not be extinguished by implication. But it could not overcome the portion of the decision that said such an extinguishment was subject to a takings claim. A trial court held that the 1993 Act is either unconstitutional or does not apply to pre-1993 riparian claims. Thus, Oklahoma was effectively converted back to the hybrid system the legislature tried to curtail in 1963.

III. ADMINISTRATION OF HYBRID SYSTEMS

Because of the substantial differences between riparian and appropriation systems, courts have struggled to give effect to rights under both systems of water law existing in a single jurisdiction. This issue arises in all the California doctrine states because even where unused riparian rights have been extinguished, there may be exercised riparian rights that have been recognized. Most significantly, issues arise in times of shortage where riparians must all share the shortage based on reasonableness, but appropriative rights holders exercise the full measure of their right based on priority.

A. RESOLVING DISPUTES AMONG WATER USERS

In states where permits for riparian rights specify a quantity, these rights can be treated as part of the hierarchy of appropriative water rights. If no fixed quantity is set, it may be necessary to quantify unused riparian rights (discussed in the next subsection). The priority date of riparian rights ordinarily is ahead of many appropriators since appropriative rights were created in most states pursuant to a statutory scheme adopted to replace a riparian system.

California limits the circumstances in which an appropriator on public land can defeat a riparian. Thus, in California, a riparian will prevail over an appropriator except in cases in which water rights were appropriated *after* the 1866 Act and *before* the riparian's patent. Lux v. Haggin, 10 P. 674 (Cal. 1886).

In Oklahoma and Nebraska, the courts have allowed competing rights of riparians and appropriators to be determined based on their relative reasonableness. The issue arises in Nebraska only as to riparian lands patented before the 1895 Nebraska Irrigation Act; prior appropriation prevails as to later patented lands. Wasserburger v. Coffee, 141 N.W.2d 738 (Neb. 1966).

In Alaska, the legislature has contemplated phasing out riparian rights under a 1966 Act. Alaska Stat. § 46.15.060. The statutory language suggests that both used and unused riparian rights are converted to an appropriative rights if the riparian's water right has been put to a beneficial use or establishes a beneficial use within five years of the statute's effective date. Thus, Alaska created an exclusive appropriative rights-based system.

B. ADJUDICATION OF UNUSED RIPARIAN RIGHTS

Most hybrid states have procedures for adjudicating water rights among users. In hybrid states, riparians must be made parties to general adjudications to have their rights reflected in a final determination of all rights on a stream system. Riparian rights may be specifically quantified based on past usage and unused rights may be extinguished.

Some hybrid states have extinguished unused riparian rights, but created exceptions allowing riparians to claim water rights for future "domestic" purposes that are superior to all appropriative rights. Tex. Water Code § 11.303 (2013); Kan. Stat. Ann. § 42–311 (2013); S.D. Codified Laws § 46–1–5 (2014). In Oklahoma, riparians can claim water for other "de minimis" exceptions for general household purposes such as lawn-watering. Okla. Stat. tit. 82, § 1020.1(2) (2013); Heldermon v. Wright, 152 P.3d 855 (Okla. 2006); Franco-American Charolaise, Ltd. v. Okla. Water Res. Bd., 855 P.2d 568 (Okla. 1990). The quantities involved are small so the uncertainties about unquantified, unused rights are minimal.

Although California nominally allows the future exercise of unused riparian rights, the right can be substantially limited by administrative decisions. The California Supreme Court has held that when a riparian uses only a small fraction of its available water, the riparian's right could be limited in "scope, nature and priority" to assure that uses were reasonable and beneficial (in accordance with the 1928 constitutional amendment). *See* In re Waters of Long Valley Creek Stream System, 599 P.2d 656 (Cal. 1979) (riparian owned several thousand acres, but was irrigating only eighty-nine). Thus, unused riparian rights may be put to any reasonable, beneficial use in the future, but may be presently quantified by the Board and granted a priority lower than all appropriations prior to the time riparian uses actually commence.

C. PRESCRIPTION

Appropriation is the sole method of acquiring water rights in prior appropriation states; acquisition of a water right by adverse possession is generally not allowed. *See supra* Chapter 3.VIII. In riparian states, upper riparians can gain prescriptive rights as against lower riparians if the lower owner is aware of the upper owner's prescriptive claim or suffers harm. The opposite is not true because a lower riparian using any amount of water left unused by the upper riparian cannot be adverse; the upper riparian could physically divert the water at any time. An upstream non-riparian may also gain a prescriptive right as against a downstream riparian since any use by one without riparian rights is adverse. *See supra* Chapter 2.VII.C; *see also* Pabst v. Finmand, 211 P. 11 (Cal. 1922) (recognizing the prescriptive right of a non-riparian against lower riparians by virtue of diversions for the statutory period of five years though the riparians had not suffered actual harm).

IV. OTHER WATER LAW VARIATIONS

Some water law systems are not easily characterized as prior appropriation, riparian, or as a hybrid of the two. They include Hawaii's ancient system, remnants of civil law in Louisiana, and pueblo rights applicable in some parts of the southwestern United States.

A. WATER LAW IN LOUISIANA

Although Louisiana is often listed as a riparian state, its system of water law is based on a civil code with French and Spanish origins; it is the only state in the Union that has a civil code system. The relevant rules for settling water disputes are found within the code, which specifies a scheme of regulation. The courts are not bound by the principle of *stare decisis*, but may refer to common law precedents if they are on point.

The code sets forth rudiments similar to a riparian system, such as:

Article 657: The owner of an estate bordering on running water may use it as it runs for the purpose of watering his estate or for other purposes.

Article 658: The owner of an estate through which water runs, whether it originates there or passes from lands above, may make use of it while it runs over his lands. He cannot stop it or give it another direction and is bound to return it to its ordinary channel where it leaves his estate.

Article 657 is a nearly verbatim adoption of the French Civil Code, implemented by Napoleon. It is not clear whether the provision expresses the natural flow rule or the reasonable use rule. The early case of Long v. Louisiana Creosoting Co., 69 So. 281 (La. 1915) applied a reasonable use rule in a water pollution context:

[W]hether a use that pollutes a water course is a reasonable or an unreasonable use is for the judge or jury to determine from all of the circumstances of a case, including the nature of the water course, its adaptability for particular purposes, the extent of injury caused to the riparian owner, etc.

By statute, Louisiana has various types of water districts that supply customers with water for purposes such as domestic use, municipal use, industrial use, and irrigation. Municipalities also have statutory authority to maintain their own waterworks systems.

Until recently, groundwater in Louisiana was almost totally unregulated. The Civil Code states:

Article 490: Unless otherwise provided by law, the ownership of a tract of land carries with it the ownership of everything that is directly above or under it. The owner may make works on, above or below the land as he pleases, and draw all the advantages that accrue from them, unless he is restrained by law or by rights of others.

Adams v. Grigsby, 152 So.2d 619 (La. App. 1963), held that water under a person's land is not owned until it is reduced to possession by pumping. The *Adams* decision was criticized for not providing incentives to conserve water. A 1972 act responded by authorizing the Department of Public Works to regulate wells producing in excess of 50,000 gallons per day. Smaller wells still appear to be governed by the *Adams* rule.

B. HAWAIIAN WATER LAW

Water law in Hawaii is defined more fundamentally than in other states by the notion that water, in its natural state, is part of the state's public trust. Hawaiian water law has its roots in an ancient system of land tenure. During Hawaii's territorial period court decisions dealt with water as an individual property right but state courts later revived Hawaii's ancient notions of water as a public resource. Modern Hawaii follows a State Water Code, which is limited in scope by public trust provisions in the state's constitution. Hawaii Constitution, Article XI, Section 1 and 7.

Historically, water was commonly used by islanders to cultivate taro, a dietary stable, and for this purpose was accepted as a concomitant part of land. *Konohiki* (chiefs of land divisions including fishing and often water rights) acted as trustees and dictated the quantity and location of water used among commoners. The *konohiki* in charge of each subdivision of land allocated any surplus waters remaining after basic needs were satisfied. Water distribution was based on recognition of the mutual dependence of the *konohiki* and those who produced the crops. Judicial decisions under Hawaii's various governments (the Kingdom of Hawaii became a republic, then a United States territory, and eventually a state) announced principles of water law that now apply to creation of individual, privately held water rights. The decisions dealt with "appurtenant" and "surplus" waters.

Appurtenant rights are based on the amount of water used for taro cultivation. Early cases responded to the water demands of sugar plantations and allowed transfers of appurtenant rights, but only upon a showing by the party seeking the transfer that the change would not harm others in the exercise of their water rights or in their means of diversion. Kahookiekie v. Keanini, 8 Haw. 310 (1891). Thus, courts scrutinized changes in place of use, Peck v. Bailey, 8 Haw. 658 (1867), and type of use or point of diversion, Carter v. Territory, 24 Haw. 47 (1917). Appurtenant rights also could be obtained by prescription if there was adverse use for the statutory period. Lonoaea v. Wailuku Sugar Co., 9 Haw. 651 (1895).

"Surplus" waters generally include all waters not needed to satisfy appurtenant water rights. Early courts disagreed about whether the rights to surplus waters belonged to the proprietor ("*konohiki*" or a successor in interest) of the land subdivision (or "*ahupua'a*," typically triangularly shaped with apex at mountains and widening towards the sea) where the water originated or to the *konohikis* of all the

ahupua'as through which the water passed. In 1973,
the Hawaii Supreme Court applied riparian
principles to hold that surplus water rights could
not be used or transferred on any land except the
riparian parcel and that appurtenant rights, by
their nature, could not be used on other lands. The
court also held that appurtenant rights could not be
obtained by prescription. The court accepted the
"natural flow" doctrine of riparian law in that it best
fit the language of an 1895 statute vesting rights to
free-flowing streams in "the people." McBryde Sugar
Co. v. Robinson, 504 P.2d 1330, *on rehearing,* 517
P.2d 26 (Haw. 1973), *cert. denied,* 417 U.S. 976
(1974). A short time later, the court changed its
view, holding that the modern reasonable use test
and requirement of actual harm to the plaintiff
applied to riparian rights. Hawaii. Reppun v. Board
of Water Supply, 656 P.2d 57 (Haw. 1982).

The *McBryde* court also held that an 1850 statute
could not allow uses of surplus water away from the
original land because the water did not belong to the
landowner. Rather, it had been "reserved for the
people of Hawaii for their common good in all of the
land grants." Prescriptive rights were defeated
because prescription is void against the state, which
holds the water in trust for all the people. 504 P.2d
at 1338.

The *McBryde* decision led to vigorous challenges
as the decision's effect was to prohibit parties who
had acquired extensive rights from exercising water
rights on their lands outside the watershed. After
nearly twenty years of litigation, the Ninth Circuit

decided ownership of surplus water was a "settled question in Hawaii law" under *McBryde's* announcement of riparian principles. Robinson v. Ariyoshi, 753 F.2d 1468 (9th Cir. 1985), *vacated on other grounds,* 887 F.2d 215 (9th Cir. 1989). Instead of adhering to the kind of riparianism that exists in other states, the *Robinson* court specially characterized Hawaiian law as rooted in ancient Hawaiian custom giving the state, as trustee for the public, much greater authority to allocate Hawaiian riparian rights than exists in other states.

The court explained that, as successor to the monarchs and chiefs who formerly held all the lands, the state is obligated to assure a fair distribution of waters among all the people who put it to productive use. *Id.* at 675. At the *Mahele*, lands had passed to private parties subject to a reservation of rights in the monarch (now the state) to allocate water among all those needing it. The waters are held in a public trust for common usage of the citizenry, including diversion and use. This is analogous to the public trust doctrine, which obligates states to protect waterways for public uses such as navigation, recreation, wildlife, and fish— which was further clarified by In re Water Use Permit Applications for the Waiāhole Ditch, 9 P.3d 409 (2000), to apply surplus water as instream flow for ecosystem restoration. The Hawaii Supreme Court has also stated that Hawaiian rights are more akin to federally reserved water rights for Indian reservations (see *infra* Chapter Eight) than to true riparian rights. Reppun v. Board of Water Supply, 656 P.2d 57 (Haw. 1982).

During pendency of this litigation, the state constitution was amended to recognize the state's trust obligation to assure water resource use for the public benefit and to require establishment of a water resources agency to regulate resource use and conservation. In 1987, Hawaii adopted its State Water Code providing for a comprehensive state water plan, the designation of water management areas, and the protection of instream uses. While the State Water Code allows for water to be used outside of its original watershed, the public trust provisions of the Hawaiian constitution require greater scrutiny to do so. Existing and new water rights must have permits and the common law is largely supplanted once an area is designated as a water management area triggering the requirements.

The public trust nature of Hawaiian water rights puts affirmative burdens on the state agency charged with water allocation and has been applied to require water users to release water to a stream to provide for more natural conditions on the stream. In addition, the "reasonable-beneficial use" standard together with the requirement that water be used "consistent with the public interest" require that state examine uses—proposed and established—relative to other public and private uses of water from the same source. In re Water Use Permit Applications, 9 P.3d 409, 472–74 (Haw. 2000) (citing HRS § 174C–49(a)). As a result, out-of-stream diversions may be curtailed to protect instream uses.

C. PUEBLO WATER RIGHTS

In a few places in the Southwest, pueblo water rights may be claimed under theories tracing to land grants and principles that were applied by predecessor Spanish or Mexican governments. Similar to the ancient Hawaiian system, pueblo law characterizes water as communal property. Pueblos employ a waterseer to protect water rights. In California, the waterseer is called a zanjero and typically appointed by a government official. In New Mexico, the position is called a majordomo and is typically elected.

Spain ruled portions of the Southwest prior to 1821 and then, the Republic of Mexico governed the area until 1848. In that year, the territory was ceded to the United States by the Treaty of Guadalupe Hidalgo. The treaty confirmed property rights then existing under Mexican law, including pueblo rights. Under Spanish law, municipalities held water rights as common property for their inhabitants. Grants of pueblo lands were intended to encourage settlement by facilitating growth of villages and agricultural production. In the case of the pueblos in New Mexico, the grants seem to have had the dual purposes of evidencing respect for the tribes' aboriginal rights and for defining the areas outside their territory available for settlement by others.

Generally, these rights recognized that municipalities could use all the naturally occurring ground and surface water within their boundaries that was needed for their residents. Residents could use water in common with neighboring pueblos. The quantity of water available under a pueblo water right could increase with population growth, the annexation of new land, or new uses. Existence of pueblo water rights has been acknowledged in cases arising in California (Vernon Irrigation Co. v. City of Los Angeles, 39 P. 762 (Cal. 1895) (overruled in part)) and New Mexico (Cartwright v. Public Service Co., 343 P.2d 654 (N.M. 1958) (overruled in part)). They also have been the subject of claims in other states where such rights had originally existed (*e.g.*, Arizona, Texas, and Colorado). Today, however, their importance is small, having little recognition outside California. They pertain mainly to the rights of cities in California and of Indian tribes (pueblos) in New Mexico.

The pueblo right has special importance to some California cities. Under pueblo law, actual use of the water is not required to keep a city's right alive; a successor city may displace long-established uses even if it has not historically used the water. Thus Los Angeles, as the successor to a pueblo right, was able to assert rights to groundwater supplies as a matter of law to satisfy its municipal needs and those of its inhabitants. City of Los Angeles v. Pomeroy, 57 P. 585 (Cal. 1899). The California Supreme Court also held that the city's rights were superior to established rights of other appropriators (including other cities). City of Los Angeles v. City of San Fernando, 537 P.2d 1250 (Cal. 1975), *overruled in part*, City of Barstow v. Mojave Water Agency, 5 P.3d 853 (Cal. 2000). *City of Barstow* limited the reach of pueblo rights under *City of Los Angeles* and held that the court must not disregard overlying landowner's vested water rights priorities when allocating water in a basin. The policy reason behind California's pueblo right is to limit "waste by leaving water accessible to others until such time as the city needs it." City of Los Angeles v. City of Glendale, 142 P.2d 289, 293 (Cal. 1943).

In New Mexico, the rights of Indian pueblos were central to a decades-long general stream adjudication. New Mexico v. Aamodt, 537 F.2d 1102 (10th Cir. 1976). Unlike the federal reserved rights on public domain lands discussed in Chapter 8.A, pueblos are grant lands with established laws predating the authority of the federal government. The *Aamodt* court confirmed the tribes' pueblo water rights in holding that the pueblos have rights superior to all whose land titles were later than a federal law. This doctrine looks at "historically irrigable acreage," which is based on a pueblo's irrigation practices between the 1848 Treaty of Guadalupe Hidalgo and the 1924 Pueblo Lands Act.

For the New Mexico tribes, the pueblo right is similar to Indian reserved water rights discussed in Chapter 8.B. However, the extent of pueblo rights has been restricted in that it does not allow a pueblo to utilize as much water as is needed for its inhabitants. This limitation on future uses is not what one would expect under either the reserved rights doctrine or pueblo water rights. In 2004, New Mexico departed even further from the California decisions by stating that pueblo water rights are antithetical to the prior appropriation doctrine's

requirement of beneficial use, and by requiring
pueblo rights to be based on actual beneficial use.
New Mexico v. City of Las Vegas, 89 P.3d 47 (N.M.
2004) (overruling Cartwright v. Public Service Co.,
343 P.2d 654 (N.M. 1958)).

CHAPTER FIVE
GROUNDWATER

Though unseen on the surface of Earth, groundwater is a crucial water source, whether it be found in small local sources or vast, multistate systems, such as the Ogallala (High Plains) and Floridan Aquifers. An estimated 30% of the world's freshwater is groundwater (compared to surface water, which only makes up 1.2% of the world's freshwater—the remainder is found in glaciers and ice caps). U.S.G.S., *The World's Water* (2014), *available at* http://water.usgs.gov/edu/earthwhere water.html. In the United States, groundwater is heavily relied upon for agriculture, drinking water, and mining. The resource is especially critical in areas where surface water is scarce, notably in the Southwest. Groundwater is largely governed by a combination of land ownership rights and prior appropriation systems. Conservation and pollution control statutes also impact groundwater use.

The first section of this chapter focuses on basic hydrology of groundwater formations. The second section turns to the mechanisms for allocating groundwater. The third focuses on groundwater that is hydrologically connected and used conjunctively with surface water sources. The final two sections concern groundwater storage and mechanisms for controlling contamination.

I. BASIC HYDROLOGY

A. HOW GROUNDWATER OCCURS

1. Permeability of Rock Formations

Geological conditions and the laws of physics govern the occurrence and movement of groundwater. Although it can occur in relatively defined underground formations, most groundwater is *percolating* water stored in the pores, or interstices, of rock formations. The size of these interstices varies with the size of the rock particles; a bed of gravel has interstices visible to the naked eye, but clay has minute particles and interstices. Interstices are formed either by geological processes at the time the rock was formed or created later by cracking or erosion.

Porosity is the measure of the amount of open space within rock. It is defined as the percentage of the rock's total volume occupied by pore space. Other factors being equal, the greater the porosity, the more freely water can move through the rock and the more water that can be stored within.

The force of gravity can cause water to move "downhill" through rock formations. Slowing this movement are the forces of *molecular attraction*. Molecular attraction is inversely proportional to the surface area of the rock particles, which increases as their size decreases. To illustrate, compare the movement of water through gravel to its movement through sand. The gravel is made up of large particles, so the surface area of all the particles is cumulatively smaller than the surface area of all the particles of sand. Thus, molecular attraction slows the movement of water through minute interstices found in substances such as sand. The porosity of a volume of sand may equal that of gravel, but the *permeability* of the sand (its ability to transmit water) is lower.

Although permeability varies across a spectrum, rock formations are grouped into broad categories, described as "permeable" or "impermeable." Whether water percolates through rock, and the speed at which it does so, are functions of the force of gravity and the permeability of the formation. Groundwater is often in permeable formations that are bounded and contained by impermeable (confined) formations, as depicted in Figure 1, below.

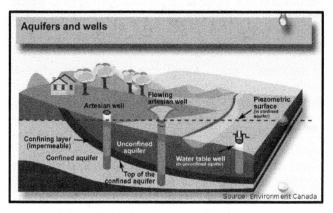

Figure 1: Water Movement in Aquifers,
from U.S.G.S., Aquifers (2014),
http://water.usgs.gov/edu/earthgwaquifer.html.

2. Zones of Groundwater Occurrence

Almost all usable groundwater occurs within two miles of the earth's surface and is commonly within a half mile. Groundwater is found in strata that may be defined as the *zone of aeration* and the *zone of saturation*. In the zone of aeration, which is nearest the surface, moisture is present in the soil and accessible to the root systems of plants. Because it is held by molecular attraction, however, it cannot be captured readily by pumping.

Below the zone of aeration is the *piezometric surface*, or *water table*. Underneath the piezometric surface is the zone of saturation, in which groundwater saturates the interstices completely. In this zone, water flows in response to gravity and can be withdrawn by pumping. Underlying the zone of saturation is a layer of impermeable *bedrock*, which has a very low porosity.

3. Aquifers

Aquifers are sometimes thought of as underground reservoirs. They are permeable rock formations that yield water in significant quantities. Aquifers may be confined or unconfined. Most are *unconfined*, where the water exists under normal atmospheric pressure. Unconfined aquifers must be pumped to withdraw the water. *Confined* or *artesian aquifers*, by contrast, are under a pressure greater than that of the atmosphere. This pressure is generated when the aquifer is squeezed between overlying and underlying impermeable strata. If the pressure between the strata is great enough, the water in a well may rise to the surface without pumping, but any pressure sufficient to raise the water above the water table can make the aquifer artesian. *See* Figure 1. This often occurs when a portion of the aquifer lies above the point where the well (or spring) is located, in which case the pressure is caused by gravity.

A *perched aquifer* is an unconfined aquifer underlain by an impermeable stratum that is perched above another aquifer. Perched aquifers are often hydrologically unaffected by withdrawals from the zone of saturation. Where perched aquifers outcrop on hillsides, springs may result. The term *spring*, however, applies to any concentrated discharge of groundwater that appears on the surface as flowing water.

Aquifers are initially filled with water either by geological processes occurring when the rock was created or by subsequent sources such as rainfall. Typically, an aquifer is recharged by precipitation falling or flowing where the aquifer outcrops on the surface; it may also be recharged by hydrologically connected streams. The rate of recharge, like the rate of water movement, varies greatly and is a function of geologic conditions. Some aquifers get no recharge; others recharge so slowly that it takes millions of years to fill them.

Geologists call the amount of water an aquifer will yield without becoming depleted the "*safe yield*." City of Los Angeles v. City of San Fernando, 537 P.2d 1250, 1263 (Cal. 1975). The term has also been used by economists, courts, and legislatures to describe rates of depletion that may be in excess of recharge, but which considered reasonable in light of current demands for the water. When withdrawals from any aquifer exceed its recharge, an overdraft or *mining* condition is said to exist. Some harmful effects of sustained overdraft are discussed in the next section.

Aquifers may be isolated from other aquifers and from surface streams. If aquifers are hydraulically interconnected, however, the term *groundwater basin* is used to describe the physiographic unit usually consisting of a large aquifer and one or more smaller aquifers.

If an aquifer is hydraulically connected to a stream so that groundwater withdrawals affect the stream flow, the groundwater may be considered *tributary* to the stream. *See* Simpson v. Bijou Irr. Co., 69 P.3d 50, 59 n. 7 (Colo. 2003) (en banc). Whether groundwater is tributary may have important legal consequences; sound management dictates that the tributary groundwater and the stream be managed as a single system. Thus, a court in a prior appropriation state may enjoin pumping from a tributary aquifer to prevent injury to senior appropriators on the stream. Integration of groundwater and surface water uses are discussed in Section III of this chapter.

4. Underground Streams Distinguished

Courts and legislatures have occasionally characterized waters that flow underground within "reasonably ascertainable boundaries" and as "a constant stream in a known and well-defined natural channel" as underground streams. Hayes v. Adams, 218 P. 933, 935 (Or. 1923). An underground stream, like percolating waters, is in fact groundwater, but some states subject it to the law of surface streams rather than groundwater law. *See, e.g.,* Riordan v. Westwood, 203 P.2d 922 (Utah 1949). *See also* N. Gualala Water Co. v. State Water Res. Control Bd., 43 Cal. Rptr. 3d 821, 831 (Cal. Ct. App.), *as modified on denial of reh'g* (2006) (noting that "classification disputes in this field quickly take on an Alice-in-Wonderland quality because the legal categories . . . are drawn from antiquated case law and bear little or no relationship to hydrological realities"). In determining whether groundwater is stream-like or percolating, courts may consider circumstantial evidence, such as vegetation growing on the surface, indicating the course of the alleged stream. *Riordan,* 203 P.2d at 928–29. Drilling and hydrologic modeling are also used.

B. HOW WELLS WORK

1. Drilling and Pumping

As drilling and pumping technologies developed and grew more sophisticated, the character of groundwater use changed. The invention and use of the windmill hastened the spread of irrigated agriculture, especially in the Great Plains and the western United States. Confronted with unreliable surface flows and scant precipitation, irrigators tapped into shallow aquifers. The centrifugal pump and the delivery of electricity to rural America ushered in a new era of intensive groundwater use by making deeper aquifers accessible. WILLIAM ASHWORTH, OGALLALA BLUE: WATER AND LIFE ON THE HIGH PLAINS 140–41 (W.W. Norton 2006). In some cases, junior appropriators with deeper wells and more powerful pumps drew down water tables beyond the reach of the seniors pumping from the same aquifer, causing them substantially increased pumping costs. *See, e.g.,* Prather v. Eisenmann, 261 N.W.2d 766 (Neb. 1978).

2. Effects of Well Use

a. Cone of Influence

Once a well begins operating, water from the surrounding aquifer begins percolating through the formation to replace the water being withdrawn. As shown in Figure 2 below, this creates a *cone of influence*, a cone-shaped depression in the water table from which water has temporarily been removed. The cone is inverted—its tip is at the point of withdrawal and its base is the surface of the water table. As the cone of influence broadens, it may affect the wells of neighboring users, forcing them to deepen or move their wells to avoid losing their supply.

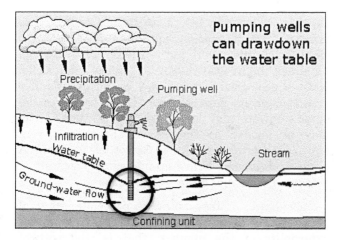

Figure 2. Effects of pumping. Note the cone of influence formed at the source of the well as water is withdrawn. Source: USGS, Aquifers (Mar. 2014), http://water.usgs.gov/edu/earthgwaquifer.html.

b. Effects of Depletion

In addition to the localized cone of influence effect, the rate and extent of pumping also may affect the quality of the groundwater and the aquifer's capacity to produce water. Salt water can contaminate groundwater when water from the ocean or underground deposits intrudes to replace the water withdrawn from an aquifer. Depletion of a finite supply of groundwater may also cause *subsidence*, where the surface of the land overlying an aquifer sinks. Subsidence occurs when certain formations (*e.g.*, compressible, low-permeability clays) are unable to support the weight of overlying strata unless they are saturated with water. As the support provided by *hydrostatic pressure* is removed, the formation collapses. The resultant sinking of the overlying surface may damage buildings, highways, railroads, ditches, and wells. Natural geological features may be harmed, aquifer storage capacity may be reduced, and cracks in the earth's surface may lead to erosion. Coastal areas may be flooded as they sink. The most severe subsidence within the United States has occurred in areas experiencing heavy groundwater overdraft in Arizona, California, Florida, and Texas.

Subsidence, like other consequences of groundwater overdraft, tends to be an economic externality of the pumper; that is, the cost of damage to others is not assessed to the individual pumper. Some jurisdictions provide legal remedies to help internalize the costs of subsidence. Theories of liability include negligence, nuisance, and the obligation for subjacent support. Alabama has applied nuisance law where no liability would have attached under the state's common law of groundwater, which allows landowners to make any use of underlying water for which there is a "reasonable need." Henderson v. Wade Sand & Gravel Co., Inc., 388 So.2d 900 (Ala. 1980). Texas has imposed liability for negligent pumping. Friendswood Dev. Co. v. Smith-Southwest Indus., Inc., 576 S.W.2d 21 (Tex. 1978). Texas also confers power to control subsidence on groundwater conservation districts. Tex. Water Code Ann. § 36.101. Arizona's Groundwater Code authorizes establishment of Active Management Areas in regions affected by overdraft. Ariz. Rev. Stat. Ann. § 45–412.

3. Optimum Yield

A declining water table imposes significant economic burdens on pumpers. Groundwater, a common-pool resource, is available to a number of individual users. A person who owns the land overlying an entire aquifer might want to reduce current consumption to save part of the groundwater for future uses, obtaining the maximum economic benefit over time. If other users have access, however, little incentive exists to conserve for the future. The individual who forgoes present uses takes the risk that others will consume any water saved; each individual is induced to pump as much water from the common pool as can be used for any purpose, even a wasteful or marginal use, before other pumpers use up the supply. This disincentive to conserve results in a "race for the bottom" of the aquifer, preventing optimal economic utilization of the resource. Noh v. Stoner, 26 P.2d 1112, 1114 (Idaho 1933). Garrett Hardin called the phenomenon the "tragedy of the commons."

As water tables fall, progressively deeper wells are required, resulting in increased drilling and pumping costs. Entities such as municipalities and large farms may enjoy economies of scale, enabling them to pump from great depths. In contrast, small irrigators are caught between high pumping costs and comparatively low economic return per unit of water applied. For an irrigator, the cost of pumping an acre-foot of water may be close to the benefit from an acre-foot of water applied to crops. Slight increases in cost can render further pumping uneconomical.

The state's groundwater law determines the obligation of the new pumper to the existing well owner. Depending on which legal system is followed (*see infra* Section II), the newcomer may have to cease pumping, or may be required to pay the well-deepening and increased pumping costs of the senior or furnish the senior with water from the junior's well.

II. ALLOCATING RIGHTS IN GROUNDWATER

A. NATURE OF RIGHTS

Legal rights and obligations pertaining to the use of groundwater may be based on overlying land ownership, established uses, or the notion that water is a shared public resource. However, rules adopted by a state's common law and legislation usually reflect more than a single theory of rights in groundwater. Jurisdictions that claim to follow one theory invariably incorporate elements of others. Thus, a state may proclaim to recognize "ownership" of groundwater by an overlying landowner but limit the owner to reasonable uses, provide protection for earlier users against subsequent pumpers, and protect the public interest by prohibiting contamination of aquifers.

States with relatively plentiful water resources paid relatively little attention to the allocation of legal rights in groundwater in the past, but pollution problems have caused even those areas to focus on groundwater rights. Generally, one having a right to extract groundwater has a right to protect it from pollution by others and to seek remedies when pollution occurs. *See, e.g.,* In re Methyl Tertiary Butyl Ether (MTBE) Products, 457 F. Supp. 2d 455 (S.D.N.Y. 2006); Exxon Corp. v. Yarema, 516 A.2d 990 (Md. Ct. Spec. App. 1986). Although an integrated approach may be desirable, statutory protections and administrative agencies dealing with pollution problems are usually separate from the mechanisms for allocating rights to use groundwater.

1. Rights Based on Land Ownership

a. *Absolute Ownership Doctrine*

Under the absolute ownership doctrine, landowners have an unlimited right to withdraw any water found beneath their land. Also known as the "English Rule," the doctrine was set forth in Acton v. Blundell, 152 E.R. 1223 (Eng. 1843). The *Acton* court viewed groundwater as part of the soil and based its holding upon the ancient right of a landowner to the airspace above and the soil beneath the land. Another reason for the holding, however, seems to have been the mysterious character of groundwater. The primitive state of hydrology at the time made it difficult to establish a causal connection between withdrawals by a

defendant and harm to a plaintiff. *See, e.g.,* Roath v.
Driscoll, 20 Conn. 533, 543 (1850); Frazier v. Brown,
12 Ohio St. 294, 311 (1861).

The absolute ownership doctrine was widely
adopted in the United States during the 1850s. It is
still said to be the law in Indiana, Louisiana, Maine,
Rhode Island, and Texas.

As scientific understanding of groundwater
hydrology improved, legal doctrines evolved. The
absolute ownership doctrine was rejected in a series
of American cases beginning with Bassett v.
Salisbury Mfg. Co., 43 N.H. 569 (1862). Courts
found it harsh and impractical to recognize
"absolute ownership" in groundwater because it
leads to premature depletion of the resource and
leaves groundwater users at the mercy of nearby
high-capacity pumpers. Even malicious withdrawal
of water for the purpose of injuring a neighbor was
not actionable under strict application of the
absolute ownership rule. Friendswood Dev. Co. v.
Smith-Southwest Indus., Inc., 576 S.W.2d 21, 25
(Tex. 1978). Today, even states following the
absolute ownership doctrine allow remedies for
willful injury, and some impose liability for land
subsidence caused by negligent pumping and/or
subject groundwater use to regulation under some of
the rules discussed below.

The reasonable use "American Rule" doctrine is
similar to the absolute ownership rule, but restricts
landowners by requiring them to use the
groundwater on the overlying land. *See infra*
Section II.B.3.

b. Correlative Rights

Under the correlative rights doctrine, rights to groundwater are determined by land ownership. However, owners of land overlying a single aquifer are each limited to a reasonable share of the total supply of groundwater. The correlative rights doctrine was applied in Katz v. Walkinshaw, 74 P. 766, 772 (Cal. 1903), where the court ruled that, in times of shortage, each overlying owner must limit withdrawals to a "fair and just proportion" of the supply—a proportion based on the ratio of each landowner's acreage overlying the aquifer.

California allows surplus groundwater (*i.e.,* groundwater available in excess of a landowner's needs) to be used on lands that do not overlie the aquifer. Santa Maria v. Adam, 149 Cal. Rptr. 3d 491, 502 (Cal. Ct. App. 2012). Rights to export water are based on prior appropriation. As between two exporters, the doctrine of prior appropriation applies. In conflicts between overlying owners and exporters, an overlying owner is entitled to a reasonable share regardless of priority relative to the exporter, but any surplus is allocated according to priority. *Katz*, 74 P. at 772. Other jurisdictions adopting correlative rights have not embraced this aspect of the *Katz* allocation scheme, but have accepted the generalized notion of pro rata reductions based on land ownership or other factors.

California has introduced another appropriation concept, as well as incorporating a measure of public interest, into the law of correlative rights. In a case involving a basin subject to serious overdrafts caused by pumping for both overlying and export uses, the court held that all pumpers had used water contrary to the rights of one another. Consequently, the continuous adverse uses had resulted in "mutual prescription," and the users' rights were allocated in proportion to their actual historical use. City of Pasadena v. City of Alhambra, 207 P.2d 17, 30 (Cal. 1949). The mutual prescription approach was developed to avoid the hardship of completely cutting off some users such as municipalities and public utilities. But it provoked a scramble to pump large amounts of groundwater in order to establish or prevent loss of prescriptive rights.

The mutual prescription doctrine was significantly qualified in City of Los Angeles v. City of San Fernando, 537 P.2d 1250 (Cal. 1975). There, the court held that municipalities were exempt from prescription and required that owners be put on notice of the adversity caused by commencement of the overdraft. The court also altered the correlative rights allocation formula. Under the new formula, prescriptive rights against private owners are determined and a correlative rights allocation made; prescriptive rights are then subtracted from each private owner's allocation. Any remaining surplus is allocated by priority of appropriation. *Id.* at 1280–81.

While *City of Los Angeles* limited the doctrine of mutual prescription, it left open the possibility that equitable apportionment methods could be used in future groundwater adjudications. However, the

California Supreme Court subsequently held that any equitable solutions must respect the existing rights and priorities of overlying landowners. City of Barstow v. Mojave Water Agency, 5 P.3d 853, 868 (Cal. 2000).

2. Rights by Prior Appropriation

Under the prior appropriation doctrine, the person who first begins using water has the best legal rights. This doctrine protects investments in wells, irrigation equipment, land, and businesses that are based on an expectation of a water supply. Farmers Inv. Co. v. Bettwy, 558 P.2d 14, 21 (Ariz. 1976). *See* Guitar Holding Co., L.P. v. Hudspeth Cnty. Underground Water Conservation Dist. No. 1, 263 S.W.3d 910, 916–17 (Tex. 2008) (groundwater conservation district could protect "historic or existing uses" to the maximum extent practicable consistent with its comprehensive management plan).

Allocation of rights in groundwater strictly based on prior use is not practical; a senior groundwater appropriator theoretically could demand that no pumping be allowed because virtually any new pumping causes some effect on existing wells. The appropriation doctrine also ignores the equities of individual uses. It may be unfair to deny rights in groundwater to a junior pumper who owns overlying land and has no other readily available source. Thus, appropriation states must determine the extent to which new uses will be allowed to interfere with established uses. Appropriators also may be limited in the uses they may make of groundwater in order to prevent an aquifer from being overused. This may mean that no more than the average annual recharge can be pumped. Where there is little or no natural recharge, the state must decide whether the resource can be "mined" and, if so, at what rate and for what purposes. *See infra* Section II.D.2 of this chapter.

Laws allowing the first users to monopolize rights in groundwater also run contrary to the public interest, and the state's obligation to protect and regulate use of a limited or nonrenewable public resource. In short, a strict application of prior appropriation could deprive other users—and society—of the ability to make full beneficial use of the resource. A number of appropriation states have adopted statutes that modify the doctrine in order to set reasonable pumping levels for all or parts of the state (*e.g.,* Alaska, Colorado, Idaho, Kansas, Montana, Nevada, New Mexico, North Dakota, Oregon, South Dakota, Utah, Washington, and Wyoming). The objective is to balance the interests in protecting senior users, optimizing new economic uses, and assuring a sustained supply.

3. Groundwater as a Public Resource

Most states consider groundwater to be subject to management as public property. *See, e.g.,* Cal. Water Code § 102; Kan. Stat. Ann. § 82a–702; Ariz. Rev. Stat. § 45–401(B). Rights to use groundwater are typically created under permits granted by the state, usually with some recognition for the interests of overlying owners and established uses. Rights are allocated by an administrative agency or official. The Colorado Supreme Court held that nontributary groundwater is neither subject to the constitutional right of all citizens to appropriate water nor owned by the overlying owner. Thus the legislature is free to decide how to manage the resource. State Dep't of Natural Res. v. Sw. Colorado Water Conservation Dist., 671 P.2d 1294 (Colo. 1983) (en banc).

States may exercise their police power in order to protect competing users and allocate the groundwater resource in the public interest. The police power is extensive enough to justify permit systems and strict regulatory schemes so long as vested property rights are respected. Williams v. City of Wichita, 374 P.2d 578, 595 (Kan. 1962). Changes in the law ordinarily do not result in a taking if they deprive landowners or former users of the right to use a portion of the groundwater. Town of Chino Valley v. City of Prescott, 638 P.2d 1324 (Ariz. 1981); Bamford v. Upper Republican Natural Res. Dist., 512 N.W.2d 642 (Neb. 1994). However, courts have reached varying results when pumping by a governmental unit causes private wells to go dry. *Compare* Bingham v. Roosevelt City Corp., 235 P.3d 730 (Utah 2010) (rejecting a takings claim because land ownership did not create private property interests in water in the soil), *with* McNamara v. Rittman, 838 N.E.2d 640 (Ohio 2005) (finding that landowners have a sufficient property interest in groundwater to support a takings claim when a city interferes with that interest). For more on takings, *see infra* Section II.D.4.

B. RULES OF LIABILITY

Most groundwater disputes arise when an existing user alleges that new or increased pumping by another is causing harm. The principal rules of liability are influenced by, and in turn reflect, the various property law theories defining the source of rights in the particular jurisdiction, detailed above in the preceding subsection.

1. No Liability Rule

Absolute ownership states and other states that recognize property rights to groundwater in overlying landowners often allow pumping without liability to other users. Theoretically, every landowner has a right to take whatever water may be pumped from the land by paying only those costs directly incurred (*e.g.*, drilling, equipment, and electricity); no obligation is incurred for harm or expenses caused to others. *See, e.g.*, Sipriano v. Great Spring Waters of America, Inc., 1 S.W.3d 75 (Tex. 1999).

2. Prior Appropriation—"Junior-Liable" Rule

States that adhere to the prior appropriation doctrine impose liability on new pumpers for harm caused to existing pumpers with vested senior rights. *See, e.g.*, Utah in Current Creek Irr. Co. v. Andrews, 344 P.2d 528 (Utah 1959). Some states have statutorily modified appropriation law to limit protection of seniors to reasonable pumping levels. To the extent such a limit does not apply to certain wells (*e.g.*, domestic), prior appropriation law may hold juniors liable for all harm caused to seniors. Parker v. Wallentine, 650 P.2d 648 (Idaho 1982). However, seniors may be required to show that they have taken reasonable steps to maximize their usage through reasonable methods of diversion and application. A & B Irr. Dist. v. Idaho Dep't of Water Res., 284 P.3d 225, 240 (Idaho 2012).

3. Reasonable Use Doctrine

The reasonable use doctrine has been adopted by so many American jurisdictions that it has become known as the "American Rule." Adams v. Lang, 553 So.2d 89 (Ala. 1989). The doctrine prefers users on overlying land. Traditionally, any beneficial use on the overlying land (short of actual waste) was considered reasonable and any use off the land was considered unreasonable. *See, e.g.,* Brady v. Abbot Laboratories, 433 F.3d 679 (9th Cir. 2005) (applying Arizona law); Martin v. City of Linden, 667 So.2d 732 (Ala. 1995); Higday v. Nickolaus, 469 S.W.2d 859 (Mo. Ct. App. 1971); Finley v. Teeter Stone, Inc., 248 A.2d 106 (Md. 1968); Willis v. City of Perry, 60 N.W. 727, 730 (Iowa 1894). In this sense, the American Rule is another form of the rule of capture, with the limitation that the water must be used on the overlying land.

Some states have modified the American Rule by adding a layer of correlative rights, in recognition that, absent some constraints, a well owner's use of water on overlying land could deplete an aquifer to the point that uses by others become difficult or impossible. The correlative rights doctrine accommodates all overlying owners when the water supply is insufficient to meet the reasonable needs of all. All users must ratably reduce their use of water so that each landowner gets a fair and just proportion of the supply; pumpers making excessive use of the groundwater may be held liable to those who are harmed. *See* Olson v. City of Wahoo, 248 N.W. 304, 308 (Neb. 1933) (adding a "correlative" twist to the American "reasonable use" rule such that, in the event of insufficient supply, each overlying user is entitled to a reasonable proportion).

4. Restatement (Second) of Torts § 858

The Restatement (Second) of Torts Section 858 attempts to balance equities and hardships among competing users. It imposes liability only for withdrawals that unreasonably affect other users. The Restatement approach differs from the American Rule by inquiring into the nature of the competing uses and the relative burdens imposed upon each user. It is distinct from the correlative rights approach in that it attaches no special significance to use of the water on overlying land.

Section 858 is phrased as a rule of non-liability. It states that a well owner is not liable for withdrawal of groundwater unless the withdrawal:

a. unreasonably causes harm to a neighbor by lowering the water table or reducing artesian pressure;

b. exceeds the owner's reasonable share of the total annual supply or total store of groundwater; or

c. has a direct and substantial effect on a watercourse or lake and unreasonably causes harm to a person entitled to the use of its water.

The first limitation uses a balancing test to determine "unreasonableness." It seems to require that a plaintiff's well be reasonably efficient in light of the type of use. A court may inquire into such issues as relative wealth of the parties (*e.g.*, municipalities vs. small farmers), relative ability to obtain financing, and relative value of the uses. The second limitation in § 858 incorporates a "correlative rights" notion as an additional basis of liability. The last limitation contemplates administration of groundwater use in conjunction with surface appropriation systems.

Although most courts in reasonable use jurisdictions apply some of the Restatement considerations, only a few specifically purport to follow it. In Prather v. Eisenmann, 261 N.W.2d 766 (Neb. 1978), the court looked to the nature of the use in determining reasonableness, and held a high-capacity irrigation user liable for lowering the artesian pressure of a domestic well. The court invoked the state preference statute (rather than the Restatement) to say that causing harm to preferred domestic users may be *per se* "unreasonable." *Id.* at 770. A subsequent Nebraska decision, Spear T Ranch v. Knaub, 691 N.W.2d 116 (Neb. 2005), applied § 858 in a case where groundwater pumping interfered with surface water uses. In *Spear T*, a senior surface water irrigator sued junior groundwater irrigators pumping from hundreds of wells that had reduced streamflow. The court found that § 858(c) applied, but denied the claim because *Spear T* had failed to show that the pumpers had "unreasonably caused harm." *Id.* at 132.

Courts in several Great Lakes states have also followed the Restatement approach. Maerz v. United States Steel Corp., 323 N.W.2d 524 (Mich. Ct. App. 1982); Cline v. American Aggregates Corp., 474 N.E.2d 324 (Ohio 1984); State v. Michels Pipeline Constr., Inc., 217 N.W.2d 339, 345 (Wis. 1974) (adopting Tentative Draft No. 17, § 858 (1971)). But *see* Michigan Citizens for Water Conservation v. Nestlé Waters North America, Inc., 709 N.W.2d 174, 200–202 (Mich. Ct. App. 2005) (applying a reasonable use balancing test rather than § 858 to a dispute between riparians and groundwater users), *reversed in part on other grounds,* 737 N.W.2d 447 (Mich. 2007). By contrast, Indiana has specifically rejected Restatement § 858. Wiggins v. Brazil Coal & Clay, 452 N.E.2d 958 (Ind. 1983). Maine has rejected it as well. Maddocks v. Giles, 728 A.2d 150 (Me. 1999).

5. "Economic Reach" Rule

The economic reach approach is somewhat similar to the Restatement in attempting to strike a balance between junior and senior rights. The leading case exemplifying this approach is City of Colorado Springs v. Bender, 366 P.2d 552 (Colo. 1961) (en banc). Colorado applies prior appropriation to hydrologically connected "tributary" groundwater. In *Bender*, a senior groundwater user sought to enjoin a junior pumper who interfered with the senior's shallow well. The court looked to the law of surface streams, which does not protect a senior's means of surface diversion against diversions by juniors unless it is reasonably adequate (a suggestion made by the Supreme Court in Schodde v. Twin Falls Land & Water Co., 224 U.S. 107 (1912)). *Bender* held that a senior well must be reasonably adequate in light of economics and historical use. This implies that an established domestic well need not be as deep as an irrigation well.

The *Bender* rule, like the Restatement, invites inquiry into issues such as the relative wealth of parties and values of competing uses. The court observed that, while seniors "cannot reasonably command the whole source of supply merely to facilitate the taking by them of the fraction," they "cannot be required to improve their extraction facilities beyond their economic reach, upon a consideration of all the factors involved." *Id.* at 556. This rule has been followed in Baker v. Ore-Ida Foods, Inc., 513 P.2d 627 (Idaho 1973), and Wayman

v. Murray City Corp., 458 P.2d 861 (Utah 1969). It reflects a policy compromise concerning the extent to which seniors should be protected against loss of pumping ability.

C. PERMITS

Many states have enacted groundwater permit systems in an attempt to replace piecemeal litigation between water users with a unified administrative scheme that establishes and protects rights to use groundwater consistent with other state goals. Most permit requirements include criteria designed to prevent overdraft and protect existing wells. Rights embodied in permits can be based to some degree on land ownership, prior use, and the public interest. Thus, permit systems largely supplant use of common law and tort remedies. The central objective of permit systems is to regulate development and use of groundwater so that it is used beneficially for society. Such systems also provide for public involvement and community control of pumping activity.

Although the permit systems adopted by a few states, in particular, Florida and Minnesota, are quite comprehensive, most states apply separate requirements to different types of groundwater and different types or quantities of use. Many distinguish groundwater connected with (*i.e.,* "tributary" to) surface streams and lakes. For example, California requires permits only for withdrawals from underground streams or the underflow of surface streams (although special restrictions apply in areas such as municipal water districts and where there are adjudicated rights in a groundwater basin). Cal. Water Code § 1200. Most western states require a permit for all groundwater withdrawals, but exempt small domestic and stock watering wells. Texas requires no permits for groundwater withdrawals (except from the Edwards Aquifer), but provides for voluntary formation of local management districts by landowner petition. Tex. Water Code Ann. § 36.013. Many other states have designated "critical areas" where permit requirements and other regulations apply.

There are two types of permits: well permits and permits evidencing a water right. Both may be required.

1. Well Permits

Permits are often a prerequisite to well drilling. Applications for well permits typically must specify the type of use and amount of water to be withdrawn, legal descriptions of well location and land on which the water is to be used, type of well, and description of geologic strata through which it is to be drilled.

Most states have laws specifying requirements for well construction, and some also govern proximity of wells to one another. Construction provisions may require that all wells be cased or sealed as they pass through other water-bearing formations to prevent migration of pollutants into or from another aquifer and accidental tapping of other aquifers. Well drillers must also be licensed and report information on geological structures, locations, and depths of aquifers for all wells drilled.

2. Permits Evidencing a Water Right

In addition to a well-drilling permit, a separate permit may be required to use groundwater. Permit statutes often require public notice and provide procedures for interested parties to file objections. Many authorize administrative appeals and judicial review of decisions to grant or deny permits.

In evaluating applications for groundwater rights, administrators are primarily concerned with whether the granting of additional permits will impair existing pumpers' rights. Determination of "impairment" is based in part upon hydrologic data on aquifer recharge and on the extent of existing uses. In some states, administrators also make value judgments as to the permissible rate of aquifer depletion, usually guided by statutory criteria. Such criteria reflect policy choices made by the legislature in reconciling priority of use rights with rights of overlying owners, economic efficiency, and other social goals. See A. Dan Tarlock, L. of Water Rights and Resources § 6:15 (noting that Colorado, New Mexico, and Arizona control the rate of groundwater mining).

In states that incorporate appropriation concepts into their permit systems, the user must proceed with reasonable diligence to drill the well and apply the water to a beneficial use once the well and water use permits are issued. The right vests when the water is put to use, and a certificate is usually issued evidencing the right. Permits are subject to loss by abandonment, forfeiture, or violation of conditions.

D. STATUTORY LIMITS ON PUMPING

Typically, state statutes provide some protection for existing uses. Many states also statutorily limit the rate or volume of groundwater pumping to allow for future as well as existing uses. Several states have enacted laws to deal with areas having special groundwater pumping problems.

1. Protection of Existing Rights

States that have replaced common law rights based on appropriation or land ownership with statutory permit systems sometimes "grandfather" pre-existing wells to exclude them in whole or in part from the permit requirements. New wells must receive a permit from a state administrative body and comply with state statutory criteria for allocating groundwater. Harloff v. City of Sarasota, 575 So.2d 1324 (Fla. Dist. Ct. App. 1991).

Most statutory groundwater systems include some measures to protect existing wells. The goal is not absolute protection, because any new well potentially interferes with existing wells in the same aquifer, but rather to prevent "unreasonable" interference.

Prior appropriation states have taken additional steps to protect senior groundwater users. The 1965 Colorado Groundwater Management Act seeks to reconcile protection of vested appropriative rights with full economic utilization of groundwater. The statute employs a "modified" appropriation doctrine to govern administration of designated basins. In contrast to the pure appropriation doctrine under which a new use would be denied if any harm resulted to seniors, the statute requires refusal of a permit only if unreasonable harm to senior rights or unreasonable waste would result. Unreasonable harm is defined as "the unreasonable lowering of the water level, or the unreasonable deterioration of water quality, beyond reasonable economic limits of withdrawal or use." Colo. Rev. Stat. § 37–90–107(5). Criteria for determining unreasonable harm or waste include geologic conditions, average annual yield and recharge rate of the supply, priority and quantity of existing claims to the water, proposed method of use, and other appropriate factors. *Id.* The Colorado Groundwater Commission has adopted complex regulations to implement this rather vague statutory mandate. *See* Fundingsland v. Colorado Ground Water Comm'n, 468 P.2d 835 (Colo. 1970) (en banc) (upholding rule denying new permits that would result in 40% depletion of aquifer by all wells within 3-mile radius in 25 years).

In New Mexico, if a proposed new use will not impair existing water rights, the state engineer is authorized to grant a permit so long as the new use is not contrary to water conservation objectives and is not detrimental to the public welfare. N.M. Stat. Ann. § 72–12–3 (West). In Mathers v. Texaco, Inc., 421 P.2d 771 (N.M. 1966), the court rejected the argument that any pumping whatsoever by juniors in a closed basin constitutes *per se* impairment just because pumping would lower the water table. However, according to the court, "it does not follow that the lowering of the water table may never in itself constitute an impairment of existing rights." City of Roswell v. Reynolds, 522 P.2d 796, 800 (N.M. 1974). A determination of impairment to existing water rights depends on the facts of each case. *See id.* (upholding conditions imposed by the state engineer to protect seniors).

2. Legislative Schedules for Groundwater Mining

Several states have provided for controlled mining of aquifers so that depletion occurs over a predictable number of years. The term "safe yield," in its strictest sense, means a level of withdrawals that does not exceed recharge. In the case of aquifers that are not rechargeable or that take many years to recharge appreciably, the concept has been modified so that "safe yield" refers to a level of withdrawals that will allow depletion of an aquifer over a period thought to be socially optimal.

The choice of time period is a policy judgment. A long depletion period preserves groundwater for future uses, but requires greater limitations on present withdrawals; thus, it imposes a hardship on well owners who must invest large sums in well drilling and irrigation equipment. By contrast, a shorter period allows larger withdrawals for the benefit of current users, but may allow depletion to occur so rapidly that an established irrigation economy can fail suddenly as pumping costs exceed economic returns from the water. Usually, a compromise is reached under which investors have time to recover their equipment costs and aquifer life is also prolonged. Oklahoma's Groundwater Management Act allows a comparatively rapid 100% depletion within 20 years. Okla. Stat. tit. 82, § 1020.5(b). Pumping in non-tributary aquifers outside designated basins in Colorado must provide for a 100-year aquifer life. Colo. Rev. Stat. § 37–90–137(4)(b)(I). The Nebraska legislature has expressed a state-wide goal of extending aquifer life "to the greatest extent practicable consistent with reasonable and beneficial use of the ground water and best management practices." Neb. Rev. Stat. § 46–702. However, Nebraska law authorizes local districts to establish their own depletion timetables unless the basin in question is designated as fully or over-appropriated, at which point an integrated management plan must be adopted in order "to achieve and sustain a balance between water uses and water supplies for the long term." Neb. Rev. Stat. § 46–715(1).

3. Critical Area Legislation

Even where there are no statewide problems of groundwater overdraft, there may be localized overdrafts that demand strict management. Many western states statutorily provide for identification and management of "critical areas" in which new well drilling and pumping may be severely curtailed or prohibited. These states include Arizona,

California, Colorado, Hawaii, Idaho, Kansas, Nebraska, Montana, Nevada, New Mexico, Oklahoma, Oregon, Texas, Washington, and Wyoming. Critical areas are commonly regulated by the state engineer's office or an equivalent administrative body and tend to be geographically defined by the boundaries of an aquifer or basin.

Requirements for critical area status vary. In Montana and Oregon, for example, a critical area may be designated if withdrawals from the basin exceed recharge (the definition of "overdraft"). Mont. Code. Ann. § 85–2–506(5)(a); Or. Rev. Stat. Ann. § 537.730(e). In Wyoming, a "control area" may be designated as soon as withdrawals approach the recharge rate. Wyo. Stat. Ann. § 41–3–912(a)(i). In Colorado, an overdraft condition need not be shown to establish an area as a "designated groundwater basin" if the basin is non-tributary or located in an area where groundwater has been the principal water source for fifteen years prior to the application for designation. Colo. Rev. Stat. § 37–90–106.

Critical area legislation also varies in the remedy applied to correct the overdraft. Under the Idaho Groundwater Management Act, Idaho Code Ann. § 42–226 *et seq.*, groundwater permits will be denied where further withdrawals would affect present or future use of any groundwater right, or cause overall withdrawals to exceed recharge. This provision has been construed to prohibit junior pumping if it would cause groundwater mining to the detriment of seniors. Baker v. Ore-Ida Foods,

Inc., 513 P.2d 627, 636 (Idaho 1973). Senior
pumpers are not absolutely protected in either their
historic water levels or their historic means of
diversion; rather, seniors may have to accept some
modifications of their rights in order to achieve the
state's goal of full economic development of water
resources. If the senior users are maintaining
reasonable pumping levels, however, the
Department of Water Resources may place a call
upon juniors to protect the seniors. Clear Springs
Foods, Inc. v. Spackman, 252 P.3d 71, 84 (Idaho
2011).

Colorado, Nevada, and Washington statutes also
provide for pumping reductions, but reductions are
made on the basis of priority; senior appropriators
may continue to pump while juniors are shut down.
Colo. Rev. Stat. § 37–92–102(2)(d); Nev. Rev. Stat.
§ 534.110(7)(b); Wash. Rev. Code § 90.44.130.

In Arizona, years of unregulated pumping led to
severe overdrafts, particularly in the metropolitan
areas of Phoenix and Tucson. Accordingly, Arizona's
1980 Groundwater Management Act contains some
of the strictest controls of any state statute. It
provides for establishing "active management areas"
that now encompass eighty percent of the state's
population, but only thirteen percent of the land
mass. Ariz. Rev. Stat. Ann. § 45–411. These areas
may be designated if overdraft exists, withdrawals
threaten to create subsidence, or groundwater
quality is threatened by saltwater intrusion. *Id.*
§ 45–412. The management goal for critical areas is
to achieve safe yield (withdrawals not in excess of

recharge) by 2025. *Id.* § 45–562. To reach this goal, the state director of water resources is required to formulate a management plan that includes mandatory conservation by "reasonable reductions" in per capita use by municipalities and individuals, pump taxes with revenues earmarked for expenses of administration and augmentation plans, retirement of irrigated lands, and a requirement that new subdivisions demonstrate an assured water supply for 100 years or have a contract for Central Arizona Project (Colorado River) water. *Id.* §§ 45–564 through 45–568.

Kansas authorizes local residents to petition for the formation of groundwater districts to manage scarce resources. Management plans are subject to approval by the Chief Engineer of the Department of Water Resources. Each local district has permitting authority, and may apply its own standards for safe yield. Kan. Stat. Ann. § 82a–1022; F. Arthur Stone & Sons v. Gibson, 630 P.2d 1164 (Kan. 1981). Nebraska has created 23 natural resource districts with the authority to establish groundwater "management" or "control" areas. The state requires the districts, in coordination with the state department of natural resources, to adopt integrated management plans that "balance" long-term demands and supplies in fully and over-appropriated basins. Neb. Rev. Stat. §§ 46–702 through 45–705; Christina Hoffman & Sandra Zellmer, *Assessing Institutional Ability to Support Adaptive, Integrated Water Resources Management,* 91 Neb. L. Rev. 805, 817–21 (2013).

4. Takings

In some states, groundwater regulations or restrictions may amount to a constitutional taking for which the landowners must be compensated. Actions by a city or other government body that destroy water quality or cause shortages for overlying landowners may also constitute a taking. *See, e.g.,* McNamera v. Rittman, 838 N.E.2d 640 (Ohio 2005).

The Texas Supreme Court found that, under the absolute ownership doctrine, landowners possessed separate, distinct, and exclusive ownership of groundwater found on their land. Edwards Aquifer Authority v. Day, 369 S.W.3d 814, 832 (Tex. 2012). Applying rules that had originated with doctrines concerning the ownership of oil and gas, the court found that the interest in groundwater required compensation when regulatory restrictions prevented pumping. *Id.* at 838. A year later, in Edwards Aquifer Authority v. Bragg, 421 S.W.3d 118, 146 (Tex. App. 2013), the Texas Court of Appeals found that the Aquifer Authority's decision to deny a permit application amounted to a taking of two pecan orchards owned by the plaintiff. However, in City of Lubbock v. Coyote Lake Ranch, LLC, 440 S.W.3d 267 (Tex. App. 2014), the court refused to extend the holding in *Day*, and allowed Lubbock, which owned a severable groundwater estate underlying the plaintiff's surface estate, to proceed with its plan to extract groundwater.

III. CONJUNCTIVE USE AND MANAGEMENT

The term "conjunctive use" refers to the joint use of hydrologically connected groundwater and surface water sources. The term can also refer to the use of two unconnected sources to maximize available supplies. Although "conjunctive management" of connected sources is the only logical way to deal with what is in fact a single resource, most states manage water use from wells and streams separately. In recent years, however, more states are working toward integrated management of interconnected groundwater and surface resources. One promising approach is to create an agency with powers over conjunctive use, but there is often political resistance to giving agencies substantial new powers to tax, incur bonded indebtedness, take legal action, and exercise broad administrative powers over water management.

A. REGULATION OF GROUNDWATER CONNECTED WITH SURFACE SOURCES

1. Interaction of Groundwater and Surface Water

Groundwater is often hydrologically connected to surface streams. For example, seepage from a stream may charge an underlying aquifer. The surface flow of a stream may "ride piggyback" upon the groundwater contained in the aquifer beneath the stream. Or, as noted in Section I.A of this chapter, a stream may be fed by seepage from aquifers. In these situations, stream use may diminish water in the aquifer and, in turn, groundwater withdrawals may diminish surface flow.

Although the scientific community has long recognized the interconnection of groundwater and surface water, the law has been slow to catch up. Although a few early cases enforced rights based on this truth, *see, e.g.*, Smith v. City of Brooklyn, 54 N.E. 787 (N.Y. 1899) (riparian entitled to prevent interference with streamflow from use of groundwater), the laws of many states are still founded on the misconception that the two types of water exist in isolation from one another; thus, they apply separate regulatory systems for groundwater and surface water. *See Spear T Ranch*, 691 N.W.2d at 126, *supra* Section II.B.4.

To varying degrees, several states, including California, Colorado, New Mexico, Utah, and Washington, administer groundwater sources affected by or affecting surface flow as part of the surface appropriation system. Cal. Water Code § 1200; Colo. Rev. Stat § 37–92–102(1)(a); Templeton v. Pecos Val. Artesian Conservancy Dist., 332 P.2d 465 (N.M. 1958); Utah Code Ann. § 73–3–1; Wash. Rev. Code § 90.03.010. *See also* Environmental Law Foundation v. State Water Res. Control Bd., Case No. 34–2010–80000583 (Cal. Super. Ct., July 15, 2014) (imposing California's public trust doctrine on hydrologically connected groundwater); Justesen v. Olsen, 40 P.2d 802, 809 (Utah 1935) ("An appropriation when made follows the water to its original source whether through surface or subterranean streams or through percolation"). The 1973 Report of the National Water Commission and the 1998 Report of the Western Water Policy Review Advisory Commission recommended wider adoption of this approach.

Some states do not treat tributary groundwater as part of the surface system *per se*, but empower regulatory agencies to impose special conditions on groundwater withdrawals that interfere with surface rights. *See, e.g.,* Oregon, Or. Rev. Stat. § 537–525. The Arizona Supreme Court, however, has ruled that tributary groundwater should be treated as part of the groundwater system unless it is "subflow," the extraction of which will "diminish appreciably and directly the flow of the surface stream." Maricopa Cnty. Municipal Water Conservation Dist. No. 1 v. Sw. Cotton Co., 4 P.2d 369 (Ariz. 1931). It defined subflow as "waters which slowly find their way through the sand and gravel constituting the bed of the stream, or the lands under or immediately adjacent to the stream, and are themselves a part of the surface stream." *Id*. at 380. If groundwater is not subflow, it is subject only to reasonable use limitations and is not treated as part of the surface water regime. Arizona has since adopted an administrative test limiting subflow to the saturated floodplain of the stream. In re General Adjudication of All Rights to Use Water in the Gila River System and Source, 9 P.3d 1069 (Ariz. 2000).

Because groundwater may percolate very slowly through aquifers, there is often a delay between groundwater withdrawals from a connected aquifer and their effect on the surface stream. In addition, the effect on the stream may be less in amount than the groundwater withdrawal. The timing and magnitude of the effect of well pumping on streamflows are expressed by the U.S. Geological Survey as the "stream depletion factor," defined as a percentage of the streamflow (not of the amount withdrawn). For example, a thirty-day, five percent stream depletion factor means that pumping will diminish the streamflow by five percent within thirty days. Computer models, stream depletion contour maps, and hydrological data are used to calculate the stream depletion factor.

The length of the delayed effect of well pumping on streamflow helps define which waters have a sufficient hydrologic connection to be conjunctively managed. In addition, in states that do engage in conjunctive management, the length of delay determines when junior well-owners must be shut down to protect senior surface rights holders. It also determines when juniors will be allowed to pump despite the fact that a senior surface user may be deprived of water under the "futile call" doctrine (see *supra* Chapter 3.V).

2. Definition of Hydrologically Connected ("Tributary") Groundwater

The word "tributary" refers to groundwater that has a hydrologic connection with a surface stream that is sufficiently direct to warrant legal attention. Proving that groundwater is tributary to a stream can be difficult and expensive, but it has important legal consequences.

To simplify fact-finding, Colorado courts have adopted a "presumption of tributariness." Safranek v. Limon, 228 P.2d 975 (Colo. 1951) (en banc). *See* Kobobel v. State, Dep't of Natural Res., 249 P.3d 1127, 1136 (Colo. 2011) (well owners pumping tributary groundwater were subject to the presumption that pumping caused material injury to senior appropriators). Where pumping would affect a stream within 40 years, the water is presumed to be tributary; conversely, where pumping would not affect a stream for more than 100 years, courts have ruled that the water is non-tributary. Dist. 10 Water Users Ass'n v. Barnett, 599 P.2d 894 (Colo. 1979) (en banc). A Colorado statute now defines non-tributary water as water, "the withdrawal of which will not, within one hundred years, deplete the flow of any natural stream at an annual rate greater than one-tenth of one percent of the annual rate of withdrawal." Colo. Rev. Stat. § 37–90–103. As a practical matter, the presumption operates in favor of stream appropriators since the burden of proof is borne by proposed junior groundwater users.

3. Conjunctive Use Management

Interrelation of ground and surface supplies gives flexibility to users with access to both. Conjunctive use can take advantage of the delayed stream effects of pumping that may allow months between the time of withdrawals and the time a surface user

feels the effects. In states with flexible
administrative policies, the junior may continue to
pump so long as the senior is provided with
sufficient supplemental water to prevent harm to
appropriative rights.

Stream effects not only may be delayed, but the
magnitude of the measurable stream effects may be
less than the amount withdrawn from the tributary
aquifer. For example, if the withdrawal of five acre-
feet from an aquifer underlying a stream reduces
streamflow by only two acre-feet, other sources of
water can make up the difference, at least in the
short-run or in the immediate vicinity. In this
situation, a pumper may furnish seniors on the
surface stream with a substitute supply of sufficient
quantity and quality, thereby making a much larger
supply of groundwater available. In the example
given, the pumper might withdraw five acre-feet
while bypassing two acre-feet directly into the
stream to avoid stream depletion effects on surface
water users—a technique known as "bypass
pumping." Its effectiveness is limited by the
physical recharge to the aquifer and by possible
effects on adjacent wells. Stored or imported surface
water may also be used to satisfy surface priorities,
thus allowing greater amounts of groundwater to be
pumped without adverse effects on senior rights in
the connected stream.

States have taken varying approaches to
conjunctive use management. In New Mexico, a
senior stream appropriator may be able to "follow
the source" to get a more reliable supply by sinking

a well to tap water flowing under the stream. In Templeton v. Pecos Valley Artesian Conservancy Dist., 332 P.2d 465 (N.M. 1958), a senior water right holder who was unable to divert sufficient surface water because groundwater pumping had diminished surface flows sought to drill a well in the alluvial aquifer supporting the stream. The court held that the supplemental well used the same water from a deeper source, so it had the original surface priority rather than a more recent priority as of the time the well was drilled. *Id.* at 471. Later, the "follow-the-source" rule was held to allow surface appropriators to tap a deep aquifer that partially fed a shallower aquifer connected with the river. Langenegger v. Carlsbad Irrigation Dist., 483 P.2d 297 (N.M. 1971). The factual question is whether the same, hydrologically continuous aquifer that feeds base flow to the source of the senior's surface appropriation provides water to the juniors' wells. Herrington v. State of New Mexico, ex rel. Office of State Engineer, 133 P.3d 258 (N.M. 2006). Remarkably, New Mexico law allows the senior and the junior to pump their full rights, even in times of shortage. However, the state engineer may deny a groundwater permit if pumping would interfere with vested surface rights. City of Albuquerque v. Reynolds, 379 P.2d 73, 81 (N.M. 1962).

In Idaho, when confrontations between established surface users and more recent groundwater pumpers arise, the priority system applies and administrative officials have a duty to enforce those priorities. Musser v. Higginson, 871 P.2d 809 (Idaho 1994). However, by regulation, before allowing a senior surface water user to "call" a junior well owner, the Director of Water Resources must consider whether the senior user's "water right could be met with the user's existing facilities and water supplies by employment of reasonable diversion and conveyance efficiency and conservation practices." American Falls Reservoir Dist. No. 2 v. Idaho Dep't of Water Res., 154 P.3d 433 (Idaho 2007).

The Colorado 1969 Water Rights Determination & Administration Act provides for conjunctive use management by means of "augmentation plans" in order to encourage "maximum beneficial utilization of the waters of the state." Colo. Rev. Stat. § 37–92–501.5. Junior appropriators may satisfy senior rights by use of a comprehensive plan that protects senior priorities. These plans commonly provide for replacement of the seniors' water with groundwater. Other augmentation methods include development of new diversion and storage facilities, alternative points of diversion, water exchange projects, substitute supplies, and development of new sources of water. The plans are subject to terms and conditions designed to protect senior appropriators and must be approved by the State Engineer. Typically, augmentation plans are entered into and costs shared among groups of junior appropriators threatened with curtailment if priorities were strictly enforced. Some augmentation plans are administered by a central water manager, who relies on hydrologic studies and computer models to formulate a basin-wide water budget. Although there is some risk to seniors that their rights will not be satisfied because hydrologic data may be in error or the plan will fail for other reasons, the validity of augmentation plans was upheld in Cache LaPoudre Water Users Ass'n v. Glacier View Meadows, 550 P.2d 288 (Colo. 1976) (en banc).

In addition, Colorado law allows wells as alternate points of diversion for hydrologically connected surface sources. Colo. Rev. Stat. § 37–92–301(c)(3). Colorado law even requires seniors who have wells and surface diversions from the same source to use their wells as alternate points of diversion before they "call the river" (require upstream juniors to shut down). It is not clear how much expense courts will require seniors to bear in operating or deepening a well as an alternate point of diversion. It is likely that the Colorado courts will follow the same approach they use in well interference cases: require the senior's well to have a reasonable economic reach before a junior will be shut down. *See supra* Section II.B.5.

4. Regulation of Tributary Groundwater: The Colorado Example

As noted above in Section III.A.2, the Colorado State Engineer administers tributary groundwater as part of the system of surface priorities. Junior well owners are subject to shutdowns in the event of a senior call, but the Colorado Supreme Court has mandated that the State Engineer's power to protect senior rights be used judiciously in order to maximize economic use of water. In Fellhauer v. People, 447 P.2d 986 (Colo. 1968) (en banc), the court set aside an order shutting down junior wells because it was not shown that seniors would benefit. This is the tributary groundwater equivalent of the "futile call" doctrine (Chapter 3.IV, *supra*). For example, if a junior's pumping does not affect streamflow within twenty days, and if a senior's use would end within the twenty days (*e.g.*, at the end of the irrigation season), the junior is allowed to continue pumping. *Fellhauer*, 447 P.2d at 994.

Fellhauer's mandate of maximum use and acceptance of the futile call doctrine for groundwater was reaffirmed by the Colorado Legislature in the 1969 Water Rights Determination and Administration Act. The Act recognized vested water rights of well owners, but effectively required appropriators to have a reasonably efficient means of diversion. Colo. Rev. Stat. § 37–92–102(2). No one is permitted "to command the whole flow of the stream merely to facilitate his taking of a fraction." City of Colorado Springs v. Bender, 366 P.2d 552, 555 (Colo. 1961) (en banc).

5. Applying the Public Trust Doctrine to Interrelated Sources

In at least one state, groundwater permits are subject to the public trust doctrine. The Supreme Court of Hawaii has held that the state's public trust doctrine "applies to all water resources without exception or distinction." In re Water Use Permit Applications, 9 P.3d 409, 445 (Haw. 2000). The court reasoned that all water is vital to the public welfare, whether it is found below or above ground, and that the public trust should be extended to groundwater because the doctrine "does not remain fixed for all time, but must conform to changing needs and circumstances." *Id.* at 447. Accordingly, groundwater permit decisions must "embod[y] a dual mandate of protection and maximum reasonable and beneficial use." *Id.* at 451. In a subsequent case, the court clarified the sweep of the doctrine, stating that, just as private trustees are judicially accountable to their beneficiaries for dispositions of the res, the legislative and executive branches are also accountable for dispositions of the public trust. In re Waiola O Molokai, Inc., 83 P.3d 664 (Haw. 2004). Although courts cannot supplant their judgment for that of the legislature or agency, courts must take a "close look" to determine if the decision in question complies with the public trust doctrine. *Id.* at 685. The court remanded the agency's determination that a private ranch's proposed water use would not interfere with public trust purposes for further fact finding.

Other states have applied the doctrine when the groundwater in question is hydrologically connected to navigable waters. In Environmental Law Fnd. v. State Water Res. Control Bd., Case No. 34–2010–80000583 (Sup. Ct. Cal. Sacramento Cty. July 15, 2014), available at http://www.envirolaw.org/documents/ScottOrderonCrossMotions.pdf, the court held that, while the state does not have an absolute obligation to protect the public trust, it must take the public trust into consideration when granting groundwater permits. *Id.* at 6 (*citing* National Audubon Society v. Superior Court, 658

P.2d 709, 728 (1983)). Within the last twenty years, Scott River, a major tributary to the Klamath River, had experienced phases of "dewatering" due to increased groundwater pumping, most commonly during the summer months. Dewatering had reduced the river to a series of pools, negatively impacting both fish populations and recreation. The court concluded that the public trust doctrine "protects navigable waters from harms caused by the extraction of groundwater, where the groundwater is so connected to the navigable water that its extraction adversely affects public trust uses." *Id.* at 8. Effectively, hydrologically connected groundwater is protected by the public trust "if extraction of groundwater adversely impacts a navigable waterway to which the public trust doctrine does apply." *Id.* at 9. At time of publication, the case was on appeal to the California Court of Appeals. Meanwhile, the state enacted a new law requiring local governments in areas with groundwater overdraft problems to implement "sustainable groundwater management plans" that limit groundwater pumping. Cal. Stats. 2014, c. 346 (S.B.1168), § 3, eff. Jan. 1, 2015.

B. IMPORTED SUPPLIES AND INTENSIVE MANAGEMENT: THE CALIFORNIA EXAMPLE

Southern California's rapid population growth long ago created demands exceeding the capacity of water supplies. Persistent droughts are not uncommon in this semi-arid region, and 2013 was the driest calendar year on record, with only 30% of average statewide precipitation. Public Policy Inst.

of California, *Just the Facts: California's Latest Drought* (Feb. 2014). Large aquifers have been overdrafted and threatened with saltwater intrusion and subsidence. Meanwhile, building new aboveground storage reservoirs has become increasingly impractical due to excessive costs and environmental impacts. Local water users responded by implementing a unique system to increase the physical supply through actively recharged groundwater banking and management for conjunctive use.

The Metropolitan Water District (MWD) was formed by an act of the state legislature in 1969 to meet the supplemental needs of its public agency members—several southern California municipalities and municipal water districts. Metropolitan Water District Act, Cal. Water Code Ann. §§ 109–1 through 109–551. MWD imports water from northern California and the Colorado River and wholesales it to MWD members, who then distribute it to local users and water companies. Some imported water is used to recharge aquifers, through spreading basins or injection wells, and it is later withdrawn from storage by pumping. *See infra* Section IV (Groundwater Recharge and Storage).

To manage and distribute imported water and to integrate its use with naturally occurring groundwater, southern California has engaged in a two-step process. First, all groundwater rights in a particular basin must be adjudicated. Once basins have been adjudicated, special water districts are formed to manage basin-wide development and use of water. Cal. Water Code Ann. § 109–25. Pumping allocations are made among users consistent with adjudicated rights, and pumping assessments are levied to purchase imported water to fulfill the needs that cannot be met by local supplies. *Id.* § 109–315.

Some districts use market mechanisms to adjust uses of groundwater and imported water. The Orange County Water District buys imported water from MWD and then allocates imported water and groundwater by pricing incentives, attempting to achieve an economic solution to conjunctive use problems. A basin-wide goal is set for the proportional use of groundwater and imported MWD water. Users who pump more groundwater than the indicated proportion of their total entitlements are subject to a special pump tax equal to the difference between the cost of pumping an acre-foot of groundwater and the cost of buying an acre-foot of MWD water. Thus, everyone effectively pays the same for an acre-foot of water, whether groundwater or MWD water.

IV. GROUNDWATER RECHARGE AND STORAGE

Storage capacity greatly enhances flexibility in water planning decisions. If erratic seasonal surface flows are collected and stored underground they can be pumped and used as needed throughout the year. Aquifer storage avoids many of the high costs, environmental effects, evaporation losses, and pollution problems of surface reservoirs. As explained above in Section III.B, southern California uses underground storage in conjunction with its importation of waters from the Colorado River and northern California rivers. Similarly, Arizona has adopted a program to enable it to store Central Arizona Project water underground and pump it as needed.

There are several ways to augment the natural recharge of aquifers with imported surface water. Water can be placed directly into the aquifer through injection wells or it can be spread on the overlying lands so that it percolates down in to the aquifer.

Despite its advantages over surface storage, underground storage may be infeasible unless the importer has legal rights in the stored supply. Public agencies and private investors are reluctant to undertake an expensive importation scheme without the right to recapture and to exclude others from taking waters it has captured or imported and stored. Absent comprehensive statewide programs to determine who has rights to use underground storage space, conjunctive use and underground water storage projects have been slow to gain momentum. Yet the cases support the existence of three types of storage rights: (1) the right of a public agency to import and store water without obligation to overlying landowners; (2) the right to protect the stored water against use by others; and (3) the right to recapture the stored water.

Generally speaking, commingling stored and naturally occurring groundwater does not cause the

stored water to lose its separate identity. *See, e.g.,*
Jensen v. Dep't of Ecology, 685 P.2d 1068 (Wash.
1984) (en banc). In California, underground storage
constitutes a beneficial use, Cal. Water Code § 1242,
and a public importer and storer has a right in the
stored supply as long as its use does not harm
existing groundwater rights. In City of Los Angeles
v. City of San Fernando, 537 P.2d 1250 (Cal. 1975),
the court held that Los Angeles had the exclusive
right to recapture imported water it stored in an
groundwater basin. In Niles Sand & Gravel Co. v.
Alameda Cnty. Water Dist., 112 Cal. Rptr. 846 (Ct.
App. 1974), a water district was engaged in a
groundwater storage program. Niles pumped water
out of its sand and gravel pit, which was
hydrologically connected to the storage aquifer. The
dewatering operation drew down the level of the
stored water in the aquifer while the water district
was attempting to recharge it to prevent salt-water
intrusion. The court enjoined pumping, ruling that
the storage plan was within the police power of the
water district and that the district had a "public
duty" to maintain the water level. Consequently, the
gravel company's use was burdened with a "public
servitude" in favor of storage; thus, there was no
compensable taking. *Id.* at 854.

Similarly, the Nebraska Supreme Court held that
a state law recognizing rights to store and recover
water in the aquifers under the lands of others did
not violate the property rights of overlying
landowners. *See* In re Application U-2, 413 N.W.2d
290 (Neb. 1987) (approving an application for
recognition of incidental aquifer storage); Neb. Rev.

Stat. § 46–295 (recognizing that "rights to water intentionally or incidentally stored underground and rights to withdrawal of such water should be formally recognized and quantified").

The New Mexico legislature has encouraged conjunctive use through the Ground Water Storage and Recovery Act, which creates a permit procedure for storage and recovery projects. N.M. Stat. Ann. § 72–5A–1. Prior to issuing a permit, the State Engineer must establish a storage account for each project, and must limit well withdrawals to the "recoverable amount"—the amount that has reached the aquifer, remains in storage, and can be withdrawn without impairing vested rights. *Id.* § 72–5A–9. Absent compliance with this permit scheme, under New Mexico case law, once imported water percolates into an aquifer, it becomes public water subject to appropriation. Kelley v. Carlsbad Irrigation Dist., 415 P.2d 849 (N.M. 1966).

Statutes in several other states facilitate storage by authorizing permits or other types of regulatory programs. *See, e.g.,* Ariz. Rev. Stat. Ann. § 45–801.01 (encouraging a "flexible and effective regulatory program for the underground storage, savings and replenishment of water"); Utah Code Ann. §§ 73–3b–101 through 73–3b–402 (authorizing underground storage permits if the project is hydrologically feasible, will not cause unreasonable harm to land, will not impair existing water rights, and will not adversely affect water quality); Wash. Rev. Code Ann. § 90.44.460 (authorizing issuance of reservoir permits that enable artificial storage and recovery of water in underground formations).

V. CONTROLLING GROUNDWATER CONTAMINATION

Some states have statutes that regulate pumping and/or regulate pollution to prevent groundwater contamination. Federal laws limit, mostly indirectly, the discharge or use of materials that may cause pollutants to enter groundwater. Common law remedies are also available to redress those who are harmed by aquifer pollution.

A. REGULATION OF GROUNDWATER PUMPING

Groundwater extraction can cause pollutants to migrate from a contaminated aquifer into a relatively pure one. Improperly constructed wells and wells that draw out water in large quantities or at high rates can attract contaminated water into the aquifer. Sources of contamination include seawater intrusion, other saline or otherwise naturally contaminated waters, land disposal of pollutants, waste injection wells, and runoff from agriculture, city streets, and industry. The use of extracted groundwater can also cause pollution. If groundwater is already contaminated, its application to land or other uses can affect other aquifers or surface sources. A related problem is the "produced water" pumped incidentally as part of oil or gas extraction. Disposal of polluted produced water has become a major problem. *See, e.g.,* Starrh

& Starrh Cotton Growers v. Aera Energy LLC, 63 Cal. Rptr. 3d 165 (Cal. Ct. App. 2007), *aff'd in part,* 2012 WL 210452 (Cal. Ct. App. 2012) (awarding a farmer $8.5 million in damages against a company that contaminated well water by dumping millions of gallons of produced water). Concerns have mounted with the growth of hydraulic fracturing ("fracking") in recent years, prompting the U.S. Environmental Protection Agency to launch a Study of the Potential Impacts of Hydraulic Fracturing on Drinking Water Resources. U.S. EPA, Progress Report (2012), available at http://www.epa.gov/ hfstudy/pdfs/hf-report20121214.pdf.

A few states deny or condition well permits to prevent groundwater contamination by, for instance, controlling the rate and extent of extraction. In Arizona and Colorado, criteria for imposing permit conditions in certain districts or critical areas include prevention of groundwater contamination. Ariz. Rev. Stat. Ann. § 45–596(I); Colo. Rev. Stat. § 37–91–110. However, critical areas are rarely designated specifically to deal with contamination problems.

State permitting agencies often examine the effects of an application for a new well or for a change in well location to see if it will draw saline or other lower quality water into parts of an aquifer used by existing pumpers. If serious degradation is likely, the agency may deny or condition the permit, but minimal increases in the rate of intrusion or concentrations of pollution may be considered reasonable and the permit granted in the interest of allowing full development of water resources. Stokes v. Morgan, 680 P.2d 335 (N.M. 1984).

Virtually no jurisdictions deny the right to use groundwater because the use, as opposed to the extraction, of water will cause contamination. The Oklahoma Supreme Court has ruled, however, that an agency decision to allow withdrawal of groundwater for use in a waterflood operation (spreading water in old oil fields to help produce secondary recovery of oil) required a finding that it would not cause "waste" by either pollution or depletion. Oklahoma Water Res. Bd. v. Texas Cnty. Irr. and Water Res. Ass'n, Inc., 711 P.2d 38 (Okla. 1984).

B. REGULATION OF POLLUTING ACTIVITIES

1. State Regulation

To prevent pollution, comprehensive groundwater quality laws should regulate land use and other activities, in addition to well construction and use, because land-based activities are the major sources of aquifer contamination. Some laws classify aquifers according to the uses that can be made of them and allow more or less pollution to occur in order to protect those actual or anticipated uses. States that have enacted somewhat comprehensive groundwater protection laws include Arizona, Florida, and Wisconsin. Ariz. Rev. Stat. Ann. § 45–401; Fla. Stat. § 403.061; Wis. Stat § 160.001.

It is rare for the same agency that regulates groundwater allocation to regulate polluting activities. This fragmentation can cause a regulatory vacuum as well as interagency conflicts. *See, e.g.,* Matador Pipelines, Inc. v. Oklahoma Water Res. Bd., 742 P.2d 15 (Okla. 1987) (Corporation Commission has exclusive authority over pollution so Water Board did not have jurisdiction to order clean-up after break in oil pipeline).

The proposed Keystone XL oil pipeline is a prominent example of instances where statutes other than water-related provisions may impact groundwater. The original proposed pipeline route from Alberta, Canada, crossed over large portions of the Ogallala (High Plains) Aquifer. Concerns about groundwater contamination sparked controversy and prompted a special session of the Nebraska legislature in 2011. Nebraska ultimately enacted legislation that gave the governor the power to approve the pipeline route. Neb. Rev. Stat. § 57–1503(4). However, the pipeline remains in legal limbo, in part due to litigation concerning whether the governor or the state Public Service Commission has the power to regulate the route under the Nebraska Constitution. *See, e.g.,* Thompson v. Heineman, No. CI122060, 2014 WL 631609 (Neb. Dist. Ct.), *vacated,* Thompson v. Heineman, 857 N.W.2d 731 (Neb. 2015); Neb. Const. Art. IV, § 20. At the federal level, President Obama vetoed a bill that would have authorized construction, citing a need to follow executive branch procedures for determining whether the pipeline serves the national interest. Veto Message to the Senate: S. 1, Keystone XL Pipeline Approval Act (Feb. 24, 2015).

2. Federal Regulation

The Clean Water Act, described in Chapter 7.VI, *infra,* controls discharges of pollutants from point sources. 33 U.S.C. § 1251 *et seq.* Although the Act has not been applied specifically to protect groundwater, it does regulate industrial and other point sources of pollutants into surface waters, thereby indirectly controlling some sources of groundwater contamination. Non-point source pollution can seep into aquifers and run down wells from irrigation return flows and runoff from farming, construction, city streets, and mine sites. Although the Clean Water Act requires states to develop plans to control these sources, there are no significant sanctions for failing to implement effective programs.

The Safe Drinking Water Act, 42 U.S.C. § 300h, has a wellhead protection program that provides for designation and protection of wells and well fields used to extract drinking water. The Act includes an underground injection control program that requires permits and adherence to certain standards. It also regulates disposal of liquid waste, including some hazardous waste that is injected into deep wells.

Controlling landfills and cleaning up old dump sites are important means of preventing groundwater contamination. The Solid Waste Act, also known as the Resources Conservation and Recovery Act (RCRA), 42 U.S.C. §§ 6901–6991i, controls every aspect of hazardous waste generation, transportation, storage, treatment, and disposal. It also sets guidelines for state regulation of nonhazardous wastes. In addition, RCRA regulates underground storage tanks (such as gasoline tanks) to prevent leaking.

The Comprehensive Environmental Response, Compensation, and Liability Act (CERCLA), 42 U.S.C. § 9601 *et seq.*, also known as "Superfund," establishes a federal program to clean up releases of hazardous substances. CERCLA creates a cause of action against almost anyone connected with past disposal activities, not only for cleanup costs but also for damages to natural resources. The resource most frequently harmed is groundwater. *See* Utah v. Kennecott Corp., 801 F. Supp. 553 (D. Utah 1992) (setting aside CERCLA consent decree as giving inadequate protection to groundwater).

The Surface Mining Control and Reclamation Act (SMCRA), 30 U.S.C. §§ 1201–1328, aims to prevent water pollution by regulating coal-mining activities and reclaiming disturbed mine sites. SMCRA also requires that surface mine operators replace the water supply of any owner whose supply has been damaged by contamination. 30 U.S.C. § 1307(b).

Finally, legislation controlling the production and use of toxic substances provides indirect protection of groundwater. The Federal Insecticide, Fungicide, and Rodenticide Act (FIFRA), 7 U.S.C. §§ 136–136y, requires registration of pesticides and other chemicals regularly applied in farming. It also allows the U.S. EPA to limit the distribution, sale, or use of pesticides in order to protect the environment. The screening and reporting requirements of the Toxic Substances Control Act,

15 U.S.C. §§ 2601–2692, may also play a role in groundwater protection. *See, e.g.,* In re Methyl Tertiary Butyl Ether (MTBE) Products Liability Litigation, 559 F. Supp. 2d 424 (S.D.N.Y. 2008).

C. STATE JUDICIAL REMEDIES

Most state courts entertain liability suits by well owners against persons, including other well owners, whose activities cause groundwater pollution. Common law actions for groundwater contamination include nuisance, trespass, and negligence suits. Mowrer v. Ashland Oil & Refining Co., 518 F.2d 659 (7th Cir. 1975); City of Attica v. Mull Drilling Co., 676 P.2d 769 (Kan. Ct. App. 1984). Some state laws, like Oklahoma's Oil Well Pollution Act, create special rights of action. Okla. Stat. tit. 52, § 296.

Groundwater contamination cases sometimes turn on whether federal statutes expressly or implicitly preempt state programs and actions. The outcome depends on a reading of the federal statutory provision to determine if Congress intended to preempt state laws. If Congress intended, for instance, not to burden interstate commerce with varying state-by-state requirements, the state law may be preempted. On the other hand, if Congress intended to leave state remedial programs and causes of action intact as a way of making pollution control more effective, states laws are not preempted. *See, e.g.,* In re Methyl Tertiary Butyl Ether (MTBE) Products Liab. Litig., 457 F. Supp. 2d 324 (S.D.N.Y. 2006) (the Clean Air Act did not preempt state tort claims), *aff'd,* 725 F.3d 65 (2d Cir. 2013); Attorney General v. Thomas Solvent Co., 380 N.W.2d 53 (Mich. Ct. App. 1985) (CERCLA did not preempt state public nuisance suit).

CHAPTER SIX

DIFFUSED SURFACE WATERS

Much of water law deals with the use and allocation of water between users under riparian law, prior appropriation, and other legal systems. These systems address water that has entered a waterbody regulated by the state allocation system. Diffused surface waters, such as runoff from rainfall or snowmelt, have not yet joined a distinct watercourse or waterbody. The law treats diffused surface water separately from surface water allocated from watercourses.

When dealing with diffuse surface water sources, the law is often focused on how to channel, control, or drain the water in order to make the land more valuable. For example, landowners may direct surface flow toward another's land in order to keep water from collecting and saturating or flooding their property. In wetter climates, most litigation involves conflicts around channeling and drainage. In arid areas, the issue of whether a landowner may take and use surface flows unrestrained by state laws concerning appropriation of water may also arise.

I. DIFFUSED SURFACE WATERS DISTINGUISHED FROM WATERCOURSES

A. DIFFUSED SURFACE WATERS

Surface water not in or connected with a watercourse is considered "diffused surface water."

The Restatement (Second) of Torts § 846 defines this as "water from rain, melting snow, springs or seepage, or detached from subsiding floods, which lies or flows on the surface of the earth but does not form a part of a watercourse or lake." Diffused surface water usually includes water flowing in draws, swales, gullies, ravines, and hollows. It may also include water in puddles, depressions, marshes, and small ponds. A spring maybe treated as a watercourse rather than diffused surface water if the spring runs directly into a stream or has a large enough flow to constitute a stream. Martiny v. Wells, 91 Idaho 215, 419 P.2d 470 (1966). Generally, if water flows with some frequency and historical regularity, and carves a recognizable channel or reaches a lake or pond having some permanency, it is considered to be in a watercourse. Watts v. State, 140 S.W.3d 860, 870 fn. 6 (Tex. App. 2004); Happy v. Kenton, 362 Mo. 1156, 1160, 247 S.W.2d 698, 701 (1952); Hoyt v. City of Hudson, 27 Wis. 656, 661, 9 Am.Rep. 473 (1871). Floodwaters, usually considered to be in a watercourse, become diffused surface waters when they lose their connection with a stream, such as by overflowing the banks and settling elsewhere. Mogle v. Moore, 16 Cal. 2d 1, 104 P.2d 785 (1940).

B. WATERCOURSES

State law defines which waters are within the definition of a "watercourse" for purposes of the allocation system in the states. In general, states exert authority over "natural watercourses." A natural watercourse is usually defined as a body of water flowing in a defined channel with bed and banks. *See, e.g.,* Locklin v. City of Lafayette, 7 Cal. 4th 327, 345, 867 P.2d 724, 734 (1994); State v. Hiber, 48 Wyo. 172, 44 P.2d 1005 (1935). In both Texas and Kansas, a watercourse exists in there is a defined bed and bank, a current or flow of water, and a permanent source of supply. Edwards Aquifer Authority v. Day, 274 S.W.3d 742, 752 (Tex. App. 2008) aff'd, 369 S.W.3d 814 (Tex. 2012); Johnson v. Board of County Com'rs of Pratt County, 259 Kan. 305, 314, 913 P.2d 119, 127 (1996). In Indiana, a watercourse is not defined by whether there are bed and banks, but rather by whether there is a substantial existence, unity, regularity, and dependability of the water's flow along a distinguishable course. Town of Avon v. West Central Conservancy Dist., 957 N.E.2d 598, 602 (Ind. 2011) (including lakes by not requiring that water be flowing). Most states require water to be present for a substantial portion of the year in order to qualify as a natural watercourse, but some states consider dry streams or lakebeds to be "natural watercourses." *See, e.g.,* Bilo v. El Dorado Broadcasting Co., 101 Ark. App. 267, 271, 275 S.W.3d 660, 663–64 (2008); Maddocks v. Giles, 728 A.2d 150, 152–53 (1999); Mogle v. Moore, 16 Cal. 2d 1, 8, 104 P.2d 785, 788 (1940). Water flowing in a surface depression only as the result of rainfall or snowmelt usually is not considered to be in a watercourse (see *supra* Chapter 3.III.D).

Theoretically, almost all waters may be included in the definition of a "watercourse." Most rivers have tributaries which in turn include not only small streams but also the gullies and washes that channel rainwater and snowmelt throughout the watershed. A watercourse may also include underground water that is hydrologically connected with surface water. But there are limits to the confidence with which science can trace water destined for streams and lakes, and to the state's practical and political ability to impose controls on water use. Thus, each state adopts criteria for defining "watercourses" that come under state regulation.

C. OTHER WATERS

Water other than diffused surface water may have to be disposed of or drained from one's land. For instance, a person using water diverted from a stream or lake (*e.g.*, for irrigation or to power a mill) may need to dispose of the unconsumed water, often referred to as "tail water." Tail water is not diffused surface water and it can only be drained across the land of another within a natural stream channel in a manner that does not increase lower landowner's burden. Loosli v. Heseman, 66 Idaho 469, 162 P.2d 393 (1945).

Water impounded on one's land, such as in a reservoir, is treated under special rules. A landowner who builds a dam or otherwise backs up water (whether or not it is diffused surface water) and causes another person's land to be flooded is subject to action for trespass. Bobo v. Young, 258 Ala. 222, 223, 61 So. 2d 814, 815 (1952). However, if the flooding is continuous and satisfies the relevant statute of limitations, the landowner may gain a prescriptive right to flood the land. Stewart v. Shook Hill Rd. Prop. Owners' Ass'n, 726 So. 2d 694, 696 (Ala. Civ. App. 1998). Government entities with the power of eminent domain may be subject to an inverse condemnation suit and be liable for compensation. Arkansas Fish and Game Comm'n v. United States, 133 S. Ct. 511 (2012); Akins v. State, 61 Cal. App. 4th 1, 43, 71 Cal. Rptr. 2d 314, 341 (1998), *as modified on denial of reh'g* (Apr. 23, 1998).

II. PROTECTION FROM DAMAGE BY SURFACE FLOWS

Disputes often arise when diffused surface waters cannot be diverted directly into a watercourse without causing harm to others. For example, an upper landowner may augment natural drainage to make marshy land useful, divert floodwaters to protect land or buildings, or fill, build on, or pave land as part of developing it. In each case, drainage patterns are altered, affecting lower landowners. Lower landowners can raise their land level or construct dikes, buildings, or other obstructions to the flow of surface waters that back water up onto the lands of upper landowners. Historically, states split between two rather extreme and opposite rules to resolve such disputes: the "common enemy doctrine" and the "civil law doctrine." Today, most jurisdictions have adopted a third doctrine, the rule of reasonable use.

A. COMMON ENEMY RULE

The common enemy rule, with its roots in English common law, provides that landowners may take any action necessary in order to avoid diffused surface waters without liability for resulting damage to one's neighbor. Such actions include building a barrier to water flowing down from adjoining land, such as a dike along one's upper boundary, or altering natural drainage patterns by a system of berms, ditches, or pumps to keep it out of a basement or away from a field. The doctrine may also allow development of drainage systems to augment natural drainage. Excavations may be made for drains and channels to collect and divert flows or accumulations of water. Argyelan v. Haviland, 435 N.E.2d 973, 977 (Ind. 1982). The only limitation is that one may not store surface water (as in a dam or reservoir) and then "cast it" upon another.

The common enemy rule is sometimes called the "Massachusetts rule," but it has since been rejected there. Graziano v. Riley, 83 Mass. App. Ct. 280, 983 N.E. 2d 249 (2013); Tucker v. Badoian, 384 N.E.2d 1195 (Mass. 1978) (embracing a reasonable use rule). It is still followed in a few other states, such as Indiana. *See, e.g.,* Romine v. Gagle, 782 N.E.2d 369 (Ind. App. 2003). However, nearly all states that once followed the common enemy rule today have modified it with the familiar tort concept of reasonableness. The deflection or other activity causing surface water to flow onto the lands of another must be in good faith, not be negligent, and not cause substantial harm. The modified rule still allows landowners to divert the flow of diffused surface waters, so long as not done maliciously, unreasonably, or negligently. Millard Farms, Inc. v. Sprock, 829 S.W.2d 1, 2 (Mo. Ct. App. 1991); McCauley v. Phillips, 216 Va. 450, 453, 219 S.E.2d 854, 858 (1975). Some states, Washington for example, have modified the rule so extensively that they effectively apply the reasonable use rule, described below. Currens v. Sleek, 138 Wn. 2d 858, 983 P.2d 626 (Wash. 1999).

B. CIVIL LAW RULE:
NATURAL FLOW THEORY

The civil law rule, traceable to the Code Napoleon, entitles every landowner to have the natural drainage maintained. Each owner has a reciprocal duty to refrain from adversely affecting others by damming, channeling, or diverting diffused surface waters that would change or increase drainage. The rule effectively places a servitude upon adjoining lands for natural drainage. The upper owner cannot modify the natural system of drainage so as to increase the burden on the lower owner and the lower owner must accept the surface water that naturally drains onto his land. If a person interferes with the natural flow of surface waters and that interference results in hindering another's interest in the use and enjoyment of his land, that person is liable to the other.

The civil law rule is unsuited to settled areas because it prevents most development, inhibiting improvement of land. For example, construction of a building or paving a parking area displaces natural runoff. In rural areas, cultivation for agricultural use often depends on altering the natural drainage pattern. These activities would not be permitted under literal application of the doctrine.

As with the common enemy doctrine, the civil law rule has been modified to fit societal needs and values. Several states have incorporated notions of reasonableness into the civil law doctrine to allow for some alteration of natural drainage patterns. Colorado and Iowa allow deviations that do not change the quantity or manner of flows. Hankins v. Borland, 163 Colo. 575, 580, 431 P.2d 1007, 1010 (1967); Ditch v. Hess, 212 N.W.2d 442, 448 (Iowa 1973). Maryland insists that its "reasonableness of use" test is but a qualification of the civil law, though the outcomes are hard to distinguish from a reasonable use rule. Whitman v. Forney, 181 Md. 652, 31 A.2d 630 (1943); Kidwell v. Bay Shore Dev. Corp., 232 Md. 577, 583–84, 194 A.2d 809, 812 (1963). Some states, including Alabama, Florida, Pennsylvania, and South Dakota, have made "reasonable use" exceptions to the civil law rule to accommodate development in urban areas where lots are typically small and close together.

In addition to employing reasonableness concepts, some states have incorporated elements of the common enemy rule for different types of diffuse surface water. For instance, Arizona and California have held that "floodwaters" are subject to the common enemy rule. Southern Pac. Co. v. Proebstel,

61 Ariz. 412, 150 P.2d 81 (1944); Mogle v. Moore, 16 Cal. 2d 1, 104 P.2d 785 (1940).

C. REASONABLE USE DOCTRINE

Allowing landowners reciprocal rights to make reasonable alterations in the natural drainage of their property leads to increased uses of property and enhanced land values. Thus, courts and legislatures have crafted numerous exceptions to temper the effects of the common enemy and civil law rules. Most have adopted some form of the reasonable use doctrine as embodied in the Restatement (Second) of Torts §§ 822–831, 833. The reasonable use doctrine was first invoked to determine rights in cases involving interference with diffused surface waters in New Hampshire. Bassett v. Salisbury Mfg. Co., 43 N.H. 569 (1862). Other states have gradually come to embrace it. *See, e.g.,* McGlashan v. Spade Rockledge Terrace Condo Development Corp., 62 Ohio St. 2d 55 (1980). In the last several decades more than 16 states have modified their rules to apply principles of reasonable use. *See e.g.,* Sanford v. University of Utah, 26 Utah 2d 285, 488 P.2d 741 (1971); Trucker v. Badoian, 376 Mass. 907, 384 N.E.2d 1195 (1978); Getka v. Lader, 71 Wis. 2d 237, 238 N.W.2d 87 (1976).

The reasonable use doctrine takes either of two forms: negligence or nuisance. In jurisdictions that apply a nuisance-like theory, courts generally balance the gravity of harm against the utility of the conduct. To determine the gravity of harm, a court may consider the extent and character of the injury, the social value of the activity harmed, the suitability of the harmed use to the location, and the difficulty that the injured party would have had avoiding the harm. In evaluating the utility of the conduct, courts may consider the social value of the activity for the location, the impact on the activity if compensation for harm were required, and the difficulty to the person harmed of avoiding injury. McGlashan v. Spade Rockledge Terrace Condo Development Corp., 62 Ohio St. 2d 55 (1980) Assessing these relevant factors allows the courts to be flexible and steer away from the harsh results the traditional doctrines produced.

Several other jurisdictions resolve drainage disputes with a negligence-like standard. Liability is imposed on landowners who drain property in an unreasonable manner that proximately cases harm to a neighboring landowner. Hall v. Wood, 443 So. 2d 834 (Miss. 1983).

Regardless of the approach taken, the cases involving diffused surface water tend to be very fact specific. Often "reasonableness" criteria will not point clearly to a particular result. Several jurisdictions refer to the common enemy or civil law rule in deciding what is "reasonable." For example, in California, the reasonable use doctrine is considered to be a modification of the civil law rule previously used. The California Supreme Court, in deciding disputes over diffused surface waters, noted that judicial determinations of reasonableness depend on a case-by-case judgment. Keys v. Romley,

412 P.2d 529 (Cal. 1966). If the conduct and uses of both parties are reasonable and necessary, the burden of any harm will fall on the landowner who changes the natural drainage system, a result that is consistent with the civil law rule.

D. PUBLIC CONTROL OF SURFACE DRAINAGE

1. Public Drainage Projects

In the United States, there are numerous special districts that administer drainage projects. Drainage districts are typically formed under state law after a local election or petition showing consent of a majority of affected landowners. The projects are usually publicly financed, and assessments are made against all property benefited, whether or not all individual landowners have consented. Tex. Water Code Ann. § 56.011; La. Rev. Stat. Ann. § 38:1580; Kan. Stat. Ann. § 24–401; Mo. Ann. Stat. § 242.020. The rules of liability discussed above may be modified as applied to drainage districts to support the overall goals of the district.

Projects undertaken by drainage districts can increase the agricultural capacity of drained lands and provide "new" land for buildings and other improvements. Indeed, many thousands of acres of marshes and swamplands in drainage districts have been reclaimed for development and use. Drainage or flood control districts may also construct and maintain levees in an effort to foster and protect development in floodplains. In the mid to late 1990s, the common practice was to construct concrete-lined channels to divert stormwater runoff away from developed areas; more recently, cities in arid regions have begun to explore opportunities to use stormwater runoff for treatment or aquifer recharge.

2. Public Restrictions on Draining Wetlands

A wetland is an "ecosystem that depends on constant or recurrent, shallow inundation or saturation at or near the surface of the substrate." National Research Council, *Wetlands: Characteristics and Boundaries 3* (1995). Marshy areas and other types of wetlands were considered useless in the past, but they provide important habitat for migratory waterfowl and other birds, fish, and wildlife. Drainage has an adverse effect on habitat and may also diminish recreational opportunities, increase fluctuations in streamflows, create flooding problems, and lower groundwater levels. Consequently, many states and the federal government have passed laws regulating activities that would impair the desirable qualities of swamps, marshes, and other wetlands. *See, e.g.,* R.I. Gen. Laws Ann. § 2–1–21 (prohibiting drainage of freshwater wetlands without the approval of the department of environmental management).

The Clean Water Act (CWA) allows the federal government to control pollution of navigable waters, defining navigable waters as "the waters of the United States, including the territorial seas." CWA § 502(7), 33 U.S.C. § 1362(7). *See supra* Chapter

7.VI. The regulatory definition of navigable includes certain wetlands. Section 404 of the CWA, 33 U.S.C. § 1344, has become the principal statutory means for protecting wetlands in the United States. Anyone who attempts to fill, dredge, drain, or otherwise modify covered wetlands must obtain a Section 404 permit from the U.S. Corps of Engineers.

At the time the CWA was passed, Congress construed its Commerce Power very broadly, and the U.S. Supreme Court extended CWA jurisdiction to non-navigable tributaries and adjacent wetlands. U.S. v. Riverside Bayview Homes, Inc., 474 U.S. 121, 133 (1985). However, in Solid Waste Agency of Northern Cook County v. Corps of Engineers, 531 U.S. 159 (2001) (SWANCC), the Court concluded that the Corps' Migratory Bird Rule, which asserted jurisdiction over isolated, non-navigable wetlands that provide actual or potential bird habitat, exceeded the Corps' statutory authority. The Court emphasized Congress' express use of the term "navigable" in the CWA, and found that clear congressional intent is required "[w]here an administrative interpretation invokes the outer limits of Congress' power," especially where it encroaches on a traditional state power. *Id.* at 171.

In Rapanos v. United States, 547 U.S. 715 (2006), the Court found that "the Corps' had stretched the term 'waters of the United States' beyond parody" in attempting to regulate non-adjacent, modest or intermittent flows of water. Justice Kennedy in his concurring opinion stated that the Corps' jurisdiction depends upon the existence of a "significant nexus" between the wetlands or other waterbodies in question and actually navigable waters. If wetlands significantly affect the chemical, physical, and biological integrity of navigable waters, the Corps has jurisdiction over such waters. *Id.* at 779–80. Kennedy's concurrence is controlling in many courts. In 2011, the U.S. Environmental Protection Agency (EPA) released its draft Guidance defining "water of the United States," relying primarily on the Kennedy nexus test, and the EPA subsequently engaged in notice-and-comment rulemaking to clarify the CWA's jurisdictional reach. The proposed rule, published at 79 Fed. Reg. 22188 (April 21, 2014) (to be codified at 40 C.F.R. 230.2), utilizes the significant nexus test to determine the nature of connectivity and effects of streams and wetlands on navigable waters.

III. USE OF DIFFUSED SURFACE WATERS

The regulation of surface water is often dependent on an individual state's definition of which water is subject to control by the state. Some states follow a rule of capture, and refuse to regulate the use of diffused surface waters. Other states regulate the right to use diffused surface water through the state water law allocation system. In recent years, several states have grappled with the issue of rainwater catchment, with some allowing appropriators to capture it and put it to use and others prohibiting any interference with it.

A. USE OF DIFFUSED SURFACE WATERS

Most states recognize an absolute right of landowners to use any diffused surface waters on their lands, including waters from ravines and gullies, rainfall, snowmelt, and any standing water. This entitles them to dam, store, use, or sell the water and, consequently, to prevent it from flowing to adjoining lands without regulation. However, the application of this rule varies among states, particularly with regard to which waters evade regulation. As noted above in Section I.A, most states limit regulatory control to "natural streams" or "watercourses" as opposed to diffused surface waters. For example, Indiana and South Dakota allow landowners to capture diffused surface waters. Gene B. Glick Co. v. Marion Const. Corp., 165 Ind. App. 72, 79, 331 N.E.2d 26, 31 (1975); Terry v. Heppner, 59 S.D. 317, 239 N.W. 759, 759 (1931). North Dakota expressly excludes diffused surface waters from state control. Burlington N. & Santa Fe Ry. Co. v. Benson Cnty. Water Res. Dist., 2000 ND 182, 618 N.W.2d 155, 160 (2000). In Arizona and New Mexico, the omission of diffused surface waters from the definition of waters subject to appropriation effectively excludes them from state control. Espil Sheep Co. v. Black Bill & Doney Parks Water Users Ass'n, 16 Ariz. App. 201, 203, 492 P.2d 450, 452 (1972); N.M. Stat. Ann. § 72–1–1.

Some riparian states exercise some control over diffused surface waters by subjecting them to the reasonable use doctrine. *See, e.g.,* Dudley v. Beckey, 132 N.H. 568, 570, 567 A.2d 573, 574 (1989);

Enderson v. Kelehan, 226 Minn. 163, 168, 32 N.W.2d 286, 289 (1948). Iowa affirms the right of a landowner to use diffused surface waters, but the right is conditioned on a continuation of minimum flows necessary to protect the rights of lower water users. Iowa Code Ann. § 455B.270.

States seeking broad control of waters are likely to define diffused surface waters narrowly, since watercourses are subject to state regulation. A few western states, including Nevada and Oregon, claim regulatory control over all waters. In re Manse Spring, Nye Cnty., 60 Nev. 280, 108 P.2d 311, 314 (1940); O.R.S. § 537.110. A Texas statute explicitly exerts state control over all "storm water, floodwater, and rainwater of every river, natural stream, canyon, ravine, depression, and watershed in the state" by making it the "property of the state." Tex. Water Code Ann. § 11.021. The Texas Supreme Court limited the effect of this statute by holding that it cannot apply to lands granted (presumably to private owners) prior to the effective date of the law because the right to such water had vested in the landowners. Turner v. Big Lake Oil Co., 96 S.W.2d 221, 228 (Tex. 1936). The provision was further qualified by a decision holding that "[d]iffuse surface water belongs to the owner of the land on which it gathers, so long as it remains on that land prior to its passage into a natural watercourse." City of San Marcos v. Texas Comm'n on Envtl. Quality, 128 S.W.3d 264, 272 (Tex. App. 2004).

Utah and Colorado also extend state control to diffused surface waters. The Utah constitutional provision asserting jurisdiction over all waters in the state precludes the use of diffused surface waters outside the state regulatory scheme. Stubbs v. Ercanbrack, 13 Utah 2d 45, 49, 368 P.2d 461, 463 (1962); *see* Richlands Irrigation Co. v. Westview Irrigation Co., 80 P.2d 458 (Utah 1938) (holding that all water destined for a stream is effectively part of the stream). Similarly, Colorado's Constitution provides that "natural streams" are within the state's power. Colo. Const. Art. 16, § 5. The Colorado courts have construed this provision as reaching diffused surface water, so that a landowner may not capture and use runoff destined for a stream outside of the appropriation system. Empire Lodge Homeowners' Ass'n v. Moyer, 39 P.3d 1139, 1148 (Colo. 2001); Nevius v. Smith, 279 P. 44 (Colo. 1929). The Colorado and Utah approach is based upon the realization that stream flow depends on runoff. Landowners may still acquire water rights in diffused surface waters so long as they comply with state appropriation law.

B. RAINWATER CATCHMENT

Rainwater catchment is a mechanism by which rainwater is collected, either actively or passively, and then made available for various uses. Active rainwater catchment involves an artificial structure that gathers rain and diverts the stored water to gardens, lawns, or indoor uses. Frequently, this form of rainwater catchment method is used to supplement residential uses of water. Passive rainwater catchment usually involves using the contours of the earth to collect the rain for irrigation or groundwater recharge. Troy L. Payne & Janet Neuman, *Remembering Rain,* 37 Envtl. L. 105 (2007); Katherine Cummings, *Adapting to Water Scarcity: A Comparative Analysis of Water Harvesting Regulation in the Four Corner States,* 27 J. Envtl. L. & Litig. 539 (2012).

States that follow the prior appropriation doctrine have struggled with how to handle rainwater harvesting. If water is being collected at the source, there may be less available for downstream appropriators. Some states, like Colorado, have passed statutes that require a permit to harvest rainwater. Col. Rev. Stat. Ann. § 37–90–105(f). Permits limit the amount, use, and location of rainwater that can be appropriated.

Some states adopt a more neutral approach to rainwater catchment. Utah, for example, allows the harvest of rainwater so long as there is no injury to downstream appropriators. Wrathall v. Johnson, 40 P.2d 755, 766 (Utah 1935). Utah does not require a permit to capture and use rainwater, but those who harvest rainwater must register with the state engineer. Utah Code Ann. § 73–3–1.5(5)(a).

Other states encourage, or even mandate, rainwater catchment. Arizona accomplishes this through city-level ordinances for rainwater harvesting to "conserve energy, water, and other natural resources." Tucson, Ariz., Code ch. 23, Land Use Code § 3.7.1.1(A). Arizona also offers tax credits to those who install "water conservation system[s] for the collection of rainwater or residential greywater." Ariz. Rev. Stat. Ann. § 43–1090.01(A). New Mexico similarly encourages rainwater capture, but with the condition that any rainwater catchment should not reduce the amount of runoff that would have occurred from the site in its natural pre-development state. Rainwater/Snowmelt Harvesting Policy, N.M. Office of the State Eng'r (Nov. 24, 2004), http://www.ose.state.nm.us/wucp_policy.html. Some New Mexico cities have also adopted ordinances that require rainwater harvesting for large residential and commercial development. Santa Fe City Code § 14–8.4.

CHAPTER SEVEN
NAVIGABLE WATERS

Use of navigable waterways has played an important role in the exploration, settlement, and economic development of North America. Lewis and Clark's exploration of the Louisiana Purchase lands relied partly on river transport, as did the early westward movement of settlers. Before the advent of the railroads and modern motorized transport, waterways provided the most feasible means of shipping freight. Large cities grew on the banks of the nation's rivers, nourished by these natural arteries of transportation and trade. Accordingly, there is strong federal interest in assuring the free flow of commerce along navigable waterways.

The federal government continues to play a significant role in water resources management through its primacy in matters concerning navigation, its financial support of major water development projects, its programs and policies for the public lands, and its regulation of water quality and endangered species. As the federal role in water resources management has grown, so too have tensions between state and federal sovereignty. Conflicts tend to be especially acute in the western states because of water scarcity and the concentration of federal lands there.

Waters within state boundaries are generally allocated according to state and local laws absent some preemptive exercise of congressional power. In California Oregon Power Co. v. Beaver Portland

Cement Co., 295 U.S. 142 (1935), the Supreme Court held that persons taking title to public lands take only those water rights perfected according to state law because estates in land and water were severed by the 1877 Desert Land Act. Nevertheless, federal authority is paramount when Congress chooses to exercise a constitutionally based power that requires water. The sources of federal authority include the commerce power (and its subsidiary the navigation power), the property power, and the treaty power. Even the defense power has been invoked to uphold the federal government's construction of a hydroelectric dam that provided power to munitions plants. Ashwander v. Tennessee Valley Auth., 297 U.S. 288 (1936). The question is rarely whether power *exists*, but rather whether Congress *intended* to exercise its power to displace state law.

The preemptive federal power to reserve waters from appropriation in order to carry out the purposes designated for public lands is discussed in Chapter Eight. This chapter is concerned with other uses of federal power pertaining to navigable waters.

I. CONTEXT COUNTS IN DETERMINING NAVIGABILITY

Of all the public uses of waterways, navigation has had special commercial importance throughout American history. In dividing sovereign prerogatives between the states and the national government, the Constitution gives commerce power to the U.S. Congress. U.S. Const. art. I § 8, cl. 3. In Gibbons v. Ogden, 22 U.S. 1 (1824), the Supreme Court held that a state grant to Robert Fulton of an exclusive right to operate steamships on New York waterways was repugnant to the commerce clause. Chief Justice Marshall declared, "All America understands, and has uniformly understood, the word 'commerce' to comprehend navigation." *Id.* at 190. *See* Kaiser Aetna v. United States, 444 U.S. 164 (1979) ("It has long been settled that Congress has extensive authority over this Nation's water under the Commerce Clause.").

A congressional determination that the act in question is necessary for navigation is usually conclusive evidence that it is within the commerce power. *See, e.g.,* United States v. Chandler-Dunbar Water Power Co., 229 U.S. 53 (1913); United States v. Twin City Power Co., 350 U.S. 222 (1956). In an early case, the United States sought to enjoin a private irrigation project from diverting water from a non-navigable tributary of a river because the diversions threatened the navigability of the river's mainstem. The Supreme Court held that the navigation power extended to tributaries of navigable rivers, upholding a federal statute prohibiting obstructions to the "navigable capacity" of United States waters. United States v. Rio Grande Dam & Irr. Co., 174 U.S. 690, 708 (1899). Even federal projects that arguably interfere with navigability have been upheld as proper exercises of the commerce power. *See* Arizona v. California I, 283 U.S. 423 (1931) (rejecting Arizona's contention that the recital of navigation as the purpose of the

Boulder Canyon Project Act, which authorized extensive damming and consumption of the Colorado River, was a subterfuge). In addition, flood control projects on non-navigable tributaries have also been upheld as within the purview of the commerce clause. Oklahoma ex rel. Phillips v. Guy F. Atkinson Co., 313 U.S. 508 (1941). However, in United States v. Gerlach Live Stock Co., 339 U.S. 725 (1950), the Court did not accept Congress's declaration in the Flood Control Acts of 1937 and 1940 that the comprehensive, multi-purpose Central Valley Project was "for the purposes of improving navigation. . . ." Nevertheless, the Court found authority for the project under the constitutional power to spend for the general welfare. *Id.* at 738 (citing U.S. Const. art. I, § 8, cl. 1).

Beyond the basic commerce clause power, issues often arise as to which definition of "navigability" applies to a particular situation. It is critical to consider the context of the dispute to determine whether the waterbody in question is "navigable" in fact and in law. These topics are covered in detail in the following sections of this chapter, but a snapshot of the legal landscape is provided here.

The federal test of navigability for admiralty jurisdiction—the body of law that governs maritime disputes—was first articulated by the Supreme Court in The Daniel Ball, 77 U.S. (10 Wall.) 557, 563 (1871): "Those rivers must be regarded as public navigable rivers in law which are navigable in fact. And they are navigable in fact when they are used, or are susceptible of being used, in their ordinary condition, as highways for commerce, over which trade and travel are or may be conducted in the customary modes of trade and travel on water." While the issue in *The Daniel Ball* involved admiralty, the Court subsequently adopted the same test for determining ownership of submerged lands beneath rivers and lakes. *See, e.g.,* United States v. Utah, 283 U.S. 64, 76 (1931); PPL Montana v. Montana, 132 S. Ct. 1215 (2012).

A more narrow test has emerged to determine whether the federal government must compensate a private property owner for taking an interest in a waterbody or submerged lands. This doctrine, known as the navigational servitude, recognizes the public's paramount interest in the flows of "great navigable streams," and makes private rights subordinate on such streams. However, only those waterbodies that are capable "of being used as a continuous highway for the purpose of navigation in interstate commerce" in their natural condition are subject to the non-compensation rule of the navigational servitude. Kaiser-Aetna v. United States, 444 U.S. 164, 178 (1979).

Several modern federal statutes define navigability much more broadly. For example, the CWA defines navigable waters as "waters of the United States, including the territorial seas." 33 U.S.C. § 1362(7). The term "waters of the United States" does not require that the watercourse be navigable in fact by commercial or recreational vessels. U.S. v. Riverside Bayview Homes, 474 U.S. 121 (1985). Although navigability under the CWA even includes wetlands that are adjacent to navigable rivers and lakes, the term excludes most intermittent flows of water. Rapanos v. U.S., 547 U.S. 715 (2006). By contrast, the Federal Power Act limits the definition of navigable waters to those waterbodies covered by Congress's commerce clause authority that are suitable "for use for the transportation of persons or property in interstate or foreign commerce." 16 U.S.C. § 796(8).

In addition to the myriad definitions found at the federal level, states apply their own definitions of navigability for purposes such as the public trust doctrine and public recreational access and use. These topics are covered in Sections II.B–C of this Chapter.

II. NAVIGABILITY FOR TITLE

Determining title to submerged lands is one of the most important uses of the term "navigability." Whether a waterway is navigable for title turns on whether it is "navigable in fact." The Daniel Ball, 77 U.S. 557, 563 (1870). It is not necessary that the waterway is actually used for navigation at a given time; if the stream once was navigable, navigability for title is not defeated by subsequent disuse. Utah v. United States, 403 U.S. 9 (1971); United States v. Appalachian Elec. Power Co., 311 U.S. 377, 407 (1940). If the stream or lake is navigable, title to the submerged lands is held to pass to the state at statehood. From that point forward, states have leeway to adopt a state law definition of "navigability" to determine ownership, public access rights, and the application of the public trust doctrine.

A. FEDERAL DEFINITION OF NAVIGABILITY FOR TITLE

English common law gave all subjects rights to navigate and to make other uses of certain waterways, such as fishing and hunting. Submerged lands that were susceptible to these uses were held by the Crown, subject to public rights. Unlike other lands held by the Crown, these lands could not be used or conveyed by the monarch contrary to the public rights. Because of the nature of the public's uses of the waterways, these restrictions were held to apply to all lands affected by the ebb and flow of the tide. Although tidal influence may have adequately described the waterways that were most important to the public in the island kingdom of England, it fell short in the United States, where large navigable rivers go far inland, well beyond the point where they are affected by the tides. Consequently, the U.S. Supreme Court expanded federal jurisdiction and title beyond the "ebb and flow" test in favor of looking also at the navigable character of the river or lake. The Propeller Genesee Chief v. Fitzhugh, 53 U.S. 443 (1851).

Generally speaking, if a stream or lake was navigable under the federal test (explained in detail below), title to the bed passed to the state upon its admission to the Union. Litigation over title of submerged lands has arisen when both the federal government and a state claim title, or between grantees when both sovereigns have attempted to transfer the same land. *See* Alaska v. U.S., 545 U.S. 75 (2005) (finding that Congress retained title to submerged lands underlying the waters of Glacier Bay National Park in the Alaska Statehood Act). In some cases, disputes arise over oil and other valuable resources found in the submerged lands. *See, e.g.*, Boone v. Kingsbury, 273 P. 797 (Cal. 1928); Phillips Petroleum Co. v. Mississippi, 484 U.S. 469 (1988).

The navigability for title doctrine granted new states title to ribbons of land through large expanses of federal public lands. The original thirteen states took their sovereignty from foreign nations, principally England. Since the Crown held title to the beds and waters in all waters affected by the tide, the Crown's rights passed to the original states as England's successors. Then, upon formation of the United States, the states ceded control of the waters flowing in navigable rivers and agreed to grant the national government the power to regulate interstate and foreign commerce. Because commerce was then primarily waterborne, the commerce clause was understood to establish federal control of navigable waterways. Thus, control of the *flow* was necessarily surrendered to the federal government by the states, but the states retained title to the *beds*, subject to the federal government's "navigation servitude"—or right to keep waterways open to navigation. As such, the state's title to the beds comes by operation of the Constitution and not as a conveyance from

Congress. Idaho v. Coeur d'Alene Tribe, 521 U.S. 261 (1997).

In Pollard v. Hagan, 44 U.S. (3 How.) 212, 216 (1845), the Supreme Court set out the principle that states acquired title to noncoastal tidelands upon admission into the Union. Prior to admission, tidelands were held in trust by the federal government for the people of future states. Later, the Court held that *coastal* tidelands remained in federal ownership. United States v. California, 332 U.S. 19 (1947). Congress responded by passing the Submerged Lands Act, which turned over control of tidelands to the states. 43 U.S.C. § 1311.

The definition and rules for deciding whether a waterway is navigable are matters of federal common law. Hughes v. Washington, 389 U.S. 290 (1967). The federal test of navigability for title is whether the waterbody was "navigable in fact" at the time the state entered the Union. In other words, the waterway must have been susceptible to being used as an "avenue of commerce" in its ordinary condition at the time of statehood. The Daniel Ball, 77 U.S. (10 Wall.) 557 (1870). The Great Salt Lake was found to meet the test based on evidence that a few small boats used the lake for trade at the time Utah became a state. Utah v. United States, 403 U.S. 9 (1971).

In addition to lands beneath navigable waters, the federal government also held in trust and conveyed to new states the beds of non-coastal, non-navigable waters that were influenced by the tides. Phillips Petroleum Co. v. Mississippi, 484 U.S. 469

(1988). These were Crown lands, too, but since they were not navigable, the federal government did not assume admiralty jurisdiction or a navigational servitude over them. *Id.* at 476. They remained, nevertheless, subject to the public trust for non-navigation purposes. Thus, the Supreme Court held that the beds of non-coastal tidelands were held in trust by the United States until a state was formed, at which point they passed to the new state. *Id.* at 484. *See* Section II.C below (The Public Trust Doctrine).

Submerged land extending from the mean high water line beneath the water belongs to the state. (This line is the shoreline as determined by an average of the high water marks over all seasons, *see* 33 C.F.R. § 329.11(a)(1)). Along a navigable waterbody, riparian property ownership extends from the uplands to this line, while the state owns the bed of the river beginning at this line. The mean high water line also delineates the area in which the federal navigation servitude may operate to destroy private property interests that interfere with navigation without paying compensation.

Title to non-navigable beds of waters usually passed from the federal government to riparian landowners. Under the law of a few states, such as Wisconsin and Iowa, the state took title to the lands beneath certain "non-navigable" waters that had not been conveyed to private parties at the time of statehood. The states adopted their own tests of state navigability for this purpose.

B. STATE DEFINITIONS OF
NAVIGABILITY FOR TITLE

The U.S. Supreme Court has recognized that states may "establish for themselves such rules of property as they deem expedient with respect to the navigable waters within their borders and the riparian lands adjacent to them." Arkansas v. Tennessee, 246 U.S. 158, 176 (1918). In other words, with some exceptions, "it is left to the States to determine the rights of riparian owners in the beds of navigable streams which, under federal law, belong to the State." Bonelli Cattle Co. v. Arizona, 414 U.S. 313, 319 (1973), *overruled on other grounds,* Oregon v. Corvallis Sand & Gravel Co., 429 U.S. 363 (1977). Thus, states may adopt restrictions on conveyances of private or state-owned beds of waterways by common law or by statute. These restrictions, and commensurate public use rights, are often based on a state definition of navigability.

States vary considerably in the tests they use to delineate state versus private title to the beds and banks of waterbodies within each state. Robin Kundis Craig, *A Comparative Guide to the Eastern Public Trust Doctrines: Classifications of States, Property Rights, and State Summaries,* 16 Penn St. Envtl. L. Rev. 1, 11 (2007). Some states recognize both the navigable-in-fact test and the tidal test in asserting state title to submerged lands. Others reject definitions of "navigability" and instead use a floatability, or "saw log," definition, asking whether a stream would allow passage of valuables such as logs on their way to the mill. *See, e.g.*, Kamm v. Normand, 91 P. 448, 449 (Or. 1907); State ex rel. Medlock v. South Carolina Coastal Comm'n, 346 S.E.2d 716, 719 (S.C. 1986).

Several states have adopted expansive definitions of navigability that are directly related to the stream's capacity for recreation—the "pleasure boat," People v. Mack, 97 Cal. Rptr. 448 (Ct. App. 1971), or "recreational use" test, Arkansas v. McIlroy, 595 S.W.2d 659 (Ark. 1980); Parks v. Cooper, 676 N.W.2d 823 (S.D. 2004). In these states, a waterway that is useful for rowboats, canoes, rafts, or the like is considered navigable and subject to public use. Property rights of riparians are qualified to the extent necessary to allow such public use rights. A Michigan court, on the other hand, has expressly rejected this approach, though the case dealt with private lakes that the court found to be too small for recreation. Bott v. Natural Res. Comm'n, 327 N.W.2d 838 (Mich. 1982).

Some state legislatures have delineated ownership and public interests in waterways by statute. Mississippi, for example, declared all waterways with at least 100 cubic feet per second mean annual flows to be "public waterways," with the stream and bed subject to "the right of free transport" and open to fishing and water sports. Miss. Code. Ann. § 51–1–4(1). However, small waters and man-made lakes and ponds are susceptible of private ownership, and, where they are privately owned, they cannot be taken without just compensation. Ryals v. Pigott, 580 So.2d 1140

(Miss. 1990), *cert. denied,* 502 U.S. 940 (1991). By comparison, the Arizona legislature has empowered a special commission to determine whether a watercourse is non-navigable; when it does, that determination constitutes a waiver and relinquishment of the state's right, title, or interest in the bed of the watercourse. Ariz. Rev. Stat. Ann. § 37–1130.

C. THE PUBLIC TRUST DOCTRINE

Following the tradition in the English common law and Roman law before that, United States courts recognized that navigable waters and the submerged land under those waters are held for the common benefit. The Daniel Ball, 77 U.S. (10 How.) 557, 563 (1871). Thus, when state governments granted private rights to submerged land, they did so subject to conditions and limitations designed to protect the public's interest in these resources—the so-called public trust doctrine. Arnold v. Mundy, 6 N.J.L. 1, 13 (1821); Commonwealth v. Alger, 61 Mass. 53, 94 (1851).

Under the equal footing doctrine, which places new states on equal footing with the original thirteen colonies, states hold navigable waters and the land underneath them as an attribute of state sovereignty, subject to public purposes. Pollard's Lessee v. Hagan, 44 U.S. (3 How.) 212 (1845); Shively v. Bowlby, 152 U.S. 1, 49–50 (1894). In comparison to ordinary real property, navigable waters and their underlying soils are especially valuable for public purposes, and as such these public trust resources cannot be freely transferred to private ownership. THOMPSON, LESHY, AND ABRAMS, LEGAL CONTROL OF WATER RESOURCES 591 (5th ed. West 2013).

The 1892 case of Illinois Central Railroad v. Illinois, 146 U.S. 387 (1892), is considered the seminal case on the public trust doctrine. The case involved a conflict between a railroad and the state of Illinois over title to a portion of the bed of Lake Michigan. In holding that Illinois did not have the authority to dispose of the bed of Lake Michigan to a private party, the U.S. Supreme Court articulated the contours of this public servitude on private interests:

> The State holds the title to the lands under the navigable waters. . . . But it is a title different in character from that which the State holds in lands intended for sale. It is different from the title which the United States holds in the public lands which are open to preemption and sale. It is a title held in trust for the people of the State that they may enjoy the navigation of the waters, carry on commerce over them, and have liberty of fishing therein freed from the obstruction and interference of private parties.

Id. at 452.

The *Illinois Central* opinion did not make clear whether the public trust doctrine rests primarily on state or federal law. However, the Supreme Court in its 2012 decision in *PPL Montana*, stated that the public trust doctrine "remains a matter of state law." PPL Montana, LLC v. Montana, 132 S. Ct. 1215 (2012). In some jurisdictions, the doctrine has been interpreted very narrowly, with courts limiting its reach to the specific purposes listed in *Illinois Central*—fishing, commerce, and navigation. Bell v. Town of Wells, 557 A.2d 168 (Me. 1989). In other jurisdictions, the public trust doctrine has been expanded to protect the public's interest in the water itself and other ecological values. *See* Marks v. Whitney, 491 P.2d 374 (Cal. 1971) (expanding the doctrine to encompass changing public needs); National Audubon Society v. Superior Court (Mono Lake), 658 P.2d 709 (Cal. 1983) (applying the doctrine to limit diversions from non-navigable tributary streams); In re Water Use Permit Applications (Waiahole), 9 P.3d 409 (Haw. 2000) (applying the doctrine to all water resources, including groundwater); Glass v. Goeckel, 703 N.W.2d 58 (Mich. 2005) (recognizing the public's right to walk along the shoreline of Lake Huron).

As *National Audubon Society (Mono Lake)* and other cases recognize, there may be circumstances in which a state may transfer resources subject to the public trust doctrine, particularly where such transfers further a value within the scope of the trust or where developing trust lands or waters does not substantially impair the public's interest in trust resources. *See* Eldridge v. Cowell, 4 Cal. 80, 87 (1854) (filling of San Francisco Bay upheld because development allowed for a deep water port); Caminiti v. Boyle, 732 P.2d 989 (Wash. 1987) (en banc) (in dicta, stating that private recreational docks constructed on public trust lands were

acceptable because they promoted public trust
objectives). Despite instances where the courts have
held that trust property may be transferred, there is
a strong presumption against such transfers,
requiring that the intent be clearly expressed.
People v. Calif. Fish Co., 138 P. 79, 86, 88 (Cal.
1913); CWC Fisheries, Inc. v. Bunker, 755 P.2d
1115, 1118–21 (Alaska 1988); Coastal Petr. v.
American Cyanamid, 492 So.2d 339, 344 (Fla. 1986).
Moreover, while some states have sought to
legislatively exempt certain bodies of water, or even
the entire state, from the public trust doctrine, a
number of courts have held that states do not have
plenary authority to abolish the public trust
doctrine. *See* Brusco Towboat Co. v. State ex rel.
State Land Bd., 589 P.2d 712,718 (Or. 1978); San
Carlos Apache Tribe v. Superior Court ex rel. Cnty.
of Maricopa, 972 P.2d 179, 215 (Ariz. 1999) (en
banc); Ariz. Center for Law in the Pub. Interest v.
Hassell, 837 P.2d 158, 173 (Ariz. Ct. App. 1991);
Lawrence v. Clark Cnty., 254 P.3d 606, 612 (Nev.
2011). Idaho provides an interesting example where
the state legislature explicitly recognized the public
trust doctrine with regard to the beds of navigable
waterways, but expressly prohibited the application
of the doctrine to the appropriation or use of water
or water rights. Idaho Code Ann. § 58–1203(2)(b).
See supra Chapter 3.V.B.3 (prior appropriation,
beneficial use, and the public trust doctrine).

III. NAVIGATIONAL SERVITUDE

The "navigational servitude" is a concept that
allows the federal government in special

circumstances to affect private property without paying compensation. Although the Fifth Amendment to the Constitution prohibits the taking of private property for a public use without just compensation, when the federal government destroys or removes privately-owned structures in or near navigable waterways, or when federal dams flood land adjoining a waterway or destroy the water power value of a private hydroelectric plant by raising the water level, the government is not required to compensate the owners.

A. BASIS OF THE NAVIGATIONAL SERVITUDE

Historically, navigation was an important public right. In England, any rights that had been granted by the Crown to utilize the beds of certain waters were subordinate to the public right of free and unhindered passage of vessels for navigation; interference with the public right created a nuisance subject to abatement. A similar concept authorizes the United States government to control and protect the navigable capacity of waterways through the commerce clause of the Constitution, in some cases without compensating affected property owners.

Some decisions have attempted to justify the non-compensation rule, known as the navigational servitude, on a "notice" theory. Since investments in navigable waterways are made with knowledge of the paramount importance of navigation, investors can have no reasonable expectation of compensation for removal or destruction of a structure that obstructs travel on a navigable waterway. *See, e.g.,*

Boone v. United States, 944 F.2d 1489, 1495 (9th
Cir. 1991); U.S. v. Kansas City Life Ins. Co., 339
U.S. 799, 808 (1950). Other courts have alluded to
the servitude as a facet of the government's public
trust responsibilities to protect both navigation and
fisheries. Martin v. Lessee of Waddell, 41 U.S. (16
Pet.) 367, 413 (1842); Phillips Petroleum Co. v.
Mississippi, 484 U.S. 469, 483 n.12 (1988); Zabel v.
Tabb, 430 F.2d 199, 215 (5th Cir. 1970).

B. EXTENT OF THE
NAVIGATIONAL SERVITUDE

The application of the navigational servitude
depends on the location of the affected property, the
type of property rights involved, and the purpose of
the government action. Ordinarily, the navigational
servitude applies only to property located on, and
property rights in, navigable streams. Takings of
property on non-navigable tributaries must be
compensated. U.S. v. Kansas City Life Insurance
Co., 339 U.S. 799 (1950). However, the right of
compensation can be defeated if Congress expressly
states that its purpose is the improvement of
navigation and there is a reasonable relation to
navigation.

On a waterway subject to the navigational
servitude, the servitude extends to the ordinary
high water mark of the stream. Non-compensability
applies to the streambed (including all land under
the stream up to the ordinary high water mark) and
structures within the stream.

1. Obstructions to Navigation

The earliest cases applying the navigational servitude concerned removal of obstructions to navigation. The first case to reach the Supreme Court involved the condemnation of a toll-collecting franchise on the Monongahela River. Monongahela Navigation Co. v. United States, 148 U.S. 312 (1893). The government action was compensable because the Court found that the locks and dam had been constructed at the "implied invitation" of Congress. *Id.* at 334. *Monongahela* has been distinguished in later decisions as an estoppel case. *See, e.g.,* United States v. Rands, 389 U.S. 121, 126 (1967).

Subsequent cases dealing with obstructions to navigation held that obstructions are subject to the servitude. For instance, in Union Bridge Co. v. United States, 204 U.S. 364 (1907), the government successfully utilized the 1899 Rivers and Harbors Act, 33 U.S.C. § 403, to force modifications of an obstructing bridge on the Allegheny River. Finding the loss non-compensable, the Court justified the servitude on a notice theory: the bridge company built the bridge with the knowledge that the federal government might someday use its navigation power.

2. Damage to Property in Navigable Waterways

An early case, United States v. Lynah, 188 U.S. 445 (1903), held that flood damage to the land between a stream's low and high water marks caused by a federal dam was compensable. The decision, had it stood, might have given landowners on navigable streams a right to have the water level maintained in its natural or historic condition. *Lynah* was overruled, however, by United States v. Chicago, Milwaukee, St. Paul & Pac. R.R., 312 U.S. 592 (1941), which held that the navigational servitude extends to lands on a navigable stream up to the ordinary high water mark—an average of the high water marks over all seasons.

Everything below the ordinary high water mark within a navigable waterway is subject to the navigational servitude. Thus, compensation has been denied for privately owned oyster beds destroyed by dredging Great South Bay in New York. Lewis Blue Point Oyster Cultivation Co. v. Briggs, 229 U.S. 82 (1913). *See also* Avenal v. United States, 33 Fed. Cl. 778 (1995), *aff'd*, 100 F.3d 933 (Fed. Cir. 1996) (dismissing a takings claim by oyster lessees because they had no compensable interest in the salinity of waters adversely affected by a freshwater diversion project).

3. Projects on Navigable Streams Causing Damage to Property Rights on Non-Navigable Tributaries

When water backs up behind a dam on a navigable stream, causing flooding or other damage to property on a non-navigable tributary, the damage is compensable unless Congress expressly invokes the navigation power to protect the navigable capacity of the mainstem of a river. In

United States v. Cress, 243 U.S. 316 (1917), a government dam on a navigable mainstem raised the water level in tributaries, flooded lands along the tributaries, and destroyed the water power potential of a mill located on a tributary. The Supreme Court held that the injuries were compensable. *Id.* at 327.

The *Cress* rule has been criticized because it makes the compensability of property turn upon its location: taking of property on a non-navigable tributary is compensable, yet an identical injury on a navigable stream is non-compensable. Yet the Court reaffirmed the *Cress* rule, awarding compensation in a case in which farmland became saturated because a dam on the Mississippi River caused an adjacent non-navigable tributary to flood. United States v. Kansas City Life Ins. Co., 339 U.S. 799 (1950).

By contrast, in United States v. Willow River Power Co., 324 U.S. 499 (1945), a dam on a navigable river raised water levels in both the mainstem and a tributary. This destroyed the waterpower value of a diversion through an artificial channel from a tributary into the mainstem. The Court denied compensation, finding that the affected property right was in the mainstem, not in the tributary as in *Cress*. *Id.* at 510.

When flooding on a tributary is caused by a dam on the tributary, Congress can avoid compensation only if it invokes its power to protect the navigable capacity of the mainstem. In United States v. Grand

River Dam Auth., 363 U.S. 229, 230 (1960), the Grand River Dam Authority (GRDA) was tasked by the Oklahoma legislature to develop hydroelectric power on the Grand River, a non-navigable tributary to the Arkansas River. Three dams were planned in pursuit of this goal, with the Fort Gibson site being the furthest downstream. The federal government, as part of a comprehensive management plan for the basin, constructed a dam at the site for flood control purposes. The GRDA asserted a "taking" of its right to develop electric power at the Fort Gibson site. The Court rejected the claim, stating that "[w]hen the United States appropriates the flow either of a navigable or a nonnavigable stream pursuant to its superior power under the Commerce Clause, it is exercising established prerogatives and is beholden to no one." *Id.* at 233. Federal use of the dam, however, did not destroy the state's rights in the dam for purposes of hydropower—the state's interest merely became inferior to federal usage for flood control. *Id. See* Wagoner Cnty. Rural Water Dist. No. 2 v. Grand River Dam Auth., 241 P.3d 1132 (Okla. Civ. App. 2010), *cert denied* 131 S. Ct. 1045 (2011) ("The fact that one interest may be superior to another does not extinguish the inferior interest; it merely establishes the priority of the superior use.").

4. Waters Rendered Navigable by Private Effort

If waters formerly non-navigable are rendered navigable by private activity, the government must pay compensation if it seeks to assure public access

to the newly navigable waterway. In Kaiser Aetna v.
United States, 444 U.S. 164 (1979), a developer
deepened a pond and converted it into a marina by
opening a channel to the ocean. The Army Corps of
Engineers sought a public right of access to the
marina in exchange for the issuance of a federal
permit. The Supreme Court found that the
navigational servitude did not apply to the pond
because, prior to its improvement, the pond was
incapable of being used as a highway for the
purpose of navigation in interstate commerce. Its
maximum depth at high tide was only two feet, it
was separated from the adjacent bay and the ocean
by a natural barrier beach, and its principal
commercial value was limited to fishing. Moreover,
the pond had always been considered private
property under Hawaiian law. Although present
navigability was sufficient to invoke federal
regulatory power (*i.e.,* to prevent activities from
interfering with navigation or to require federal
permits for development), payment of just
compensation was required to obtain public access.
Id. at 179–80. A companion case, Vaughn v.
Vermilion Corp., 444 U.S. 206 (1979), applied *Kaiser
Aetna* to deny the servitude to a system of human-
made canals in Louisiana that connected the Gulf of
Mexico with an inland waterway.

In an interesting twist on the navigational
servitude, Parm v. Shumate, 513 F.3d 135, 143 (5th
Cir. 2007), found that recreational fishermen did not
have a right to hunt and fish over private riparian
lands temporarily flooded by the Mississippi River
both because the servitude does not burden land

that is only submerged when the river floods and because the servitude does not encompass recreational fishing. The court noted that Louisiana law limits public use to navigation and reserves to private property owners the right to refuse consent to fishermen's entry on their land. *Id*. at 145.

C. MEASURE OF DAMAGES
FOR CONDEMNATION

The taking of uplands (lands above the ordinary high-water mark) is compensable even if they are located on a navigable stream. However, private rights that depend on the flow of a navigable stream, such as waterpower value, site value, and consumptive use of water, are subject to the navigational servitude and are non-compensable.

1. Value of Water Power

In United States v. Chandler-Dunbar Water Power Co., 229 U.S. 53 (1913), the United States condemned both a power plant located in St. Mary's River and the adjacent uplands to preserve the river's navigability. Although there was no dispute that compensation must be paid for the uplands, the Supreme Court found the taking of the waterpower value attributable to rapids in the stream non-compensable, both because the servitude allowed removal of structures from the river and also because the claimed water power right turned on unimpeded streamflow. *Id*. at 73–74. The Court dismissed as "inconceivable" the idea that rights to the flow of running water in a navigable stream are capable of private ownership subject to compensation. *Id.* at 69.

2. Site Value

Land adjacent to a waterway may be more valuable because of its usefulness as a hydroelectric power site, a recreational area, or a port or marina. When riparian lands above the ordinary high-water mark are condemned as part of a federal project, the question arises whether the condemnation award should include the site value. United States v. Twin City Power Co., 350 U.S. 222 (1956), involved land along the navigable Savannah River acquired by a power company as a possible reservoir site. The power site value was approximately seven times the agricultural value of the land. The Court held that the increment of value attributable to the land's location on the stream was inherent in the flow of the stream and thus non-compensable. *Id.* at 226 (citing *Chandler-Dunbar*).

The decision in *Twin City Power Co.* does not modify the physical reach of the servitude as including only that part of the streambed below the high-water mark. It does, however, exclude from compensability the portion of the value of uplands attributable to the streamflow. Although uplands are clearly compensable, their value may only include suitability for non-riparian purposes such as agriculture or mining.

United States v. Rands, 389 U.S. 121 (1967), reaffirmed this principle. Rands owned land along the Columbia River in Oregon, and the state held an option to buy the land for use as a port site. The land, which was about five times more valuable as a port site than for the next most valuable uses (sand, gravel, and agriculture), was taken by the United States as part of a comprehensive plan for development of the Columbia River. The Court held that special values, such as port site value arising from access to a navigable waterway, are subject to the navigational servitude, thus denying any compensation attributable to such values. In addition, the Court held that the increased value of the land remaining in Rands' ownership due to its new riparian location was a benefit to be deducted from the amount of any compensable harm. *Id.* at 126.

The rule of *Rands* may have harsh results, as illustrated in an example provided by the late Dean Trelease. Suppose a tract of land is worth $10,000 regardless of proximity to the water, but location on the waterfront adds a value of $5,000 to the portion of land on the water. If the half of the tract on the water is taken and flooded, the condemnation award is limited to the nonriparian value ($5,000), since port site value is not considered. But value is added to the remaining land because it is now on the waterfront ($5,000) and this value will be deducted from the award. Consequently, the owner receives no compensation for the flooding of the lost land.

Because of the effect of the *Rands* rule, pressure was brought to bear on Congress to expand compensability for condemned lands. In 1970, Congress passed § 111 of the Rivers and Harbors

Act, 33 U.S.C. § 595(a), which provides that the compensation for land taken for a navigation improvement project is the fair market value of the property in its highest and best use, which may be based upon access to or utilization of navigable waters. Thus, an owner can recover waterfront value of land taken, but the amount of actual recovery still must be reduced by the enhanced value of uplands now located on the water. In Trelease's hypothetical above, § 111 would give the landowner $10,000 for the flooded land (port site value included), but $5,000 would be deducted for appreciation of the remaining land for a net compensation of $5,000. Section 111 also limits compensability for depreciation of remaining (uncondemned) land that results from loss of access to navigable waters.

The rule that the value added to uplands by proximity to a navigable stream is non-compensable has been judicially limited by allowing compensation if flowage easements are taken. A flowage easement is an interest in land that allows the holder to flood the land of another. In United States v. Virginia Elec. & Power Co., 365 U.S. 624 (1961), a power company planned to construct a reservoir for hydroelectric power purposes and bought a flowage easement to allow it to flood the land of another. The United States then decided to build a federal project on the same site. The power company conceded that potential hydropower value was non-compensable, but argued that the flowage easement had other value not dependent upon streamflow. The Court agreed, reasoning that the holder of a flowage easement has the right to destroy, by flooding, the value of the subservient fee. The fee owner, before sacrificing the use of the land for agriculture, timber, or grazing, would charge the easement holder the value of those uses. Thus, the easement has "a marketability roughly commensurate with the marketability of the subservient fee." *Id.* at 630. The Court limited the award by discounting the easement's value to reflect the possibility of its non-exercise since a fee owner would sell a flowage easement for less if the holder of the easement were unable or unlikely to flood the land. The fact that the federal government had decided to build the project, however, was not to be included in the calculation of the "probability of the easement's exercise." *Id.* at 632, n.5.

In another flowage easement case, Big Oak Farms, Inc. v. United States, 105 Fed. Cl. 48 (2012), landowners who owned parcels situated within the Birds Point-New Madrid Floodway alleged that the Corps of Engineers took their property without just compensation when the Corps activated the Floodway by intentionally breaching the levee that protected their property, thereby causing flood damage to their land and crops, as well as leaving behind detrimental sand and gravel deposits. The Corps had purchased flowage easements for most of the Floodway, but plaintiffs claimed that the damage exceeded the scope of the easements. The court noted that government actions may not, in effect, impose upon a private landowner a flowage easement without compensation. *See* Arkansas Game & Fish Comm'n v. United States, 133 S. Ct.

511 (2012); Quebedeaux v. United States, 112 Fed. Cl. 317 (2013). However, the Floodway landowners in *Big Oak Farms* failed to state a viable takings claim. The court explained that a property loss is compensable as a taking if the government intends to invade a protected property interest, or if the asserted invasion is the direct, natural, or probable result of, and not the incidental injury inflicted by, the government action. To constitute a taking, the government's invasion must appropriate a benefit to the government at the expense of the property owner, or at least preempt the owner's right to enjoy his property for an extended period of time, but the Floodway plaintiffs failed to demonstrate that the Corps' interference with their property rights was substantial and frequent enough to rise to that level. 105 F.3d at 56–59. The court also found that the Flood Control Act immunizes the government from tort liability arising from damages associated with operation of the Floodway. *Id.* at 53.

3. Water Rights Created Under State Law

Federal power may come into conflict with state-created water rights in a number of ways. If a state-sanctioned water right is taken or totally destroyed by federal action, the right to compensation will depend in part on whether the water right was subject to the navigation servitude. (Regulatory takings claims related to water rights but arising in other contexts are covered elsewhere in this book.)

The United States may regulate water use to carry out federal legislative purposes. The primary question for a court is whether Congress intended to override, or preempt, state law. California v. U.S., 438 U.S. 645 (1978). In United States v. Rio Grande Dam & Irrig. Co., 174 U.S. 690 (1899), the Supreme Court sustained the federal government's regulatory power to prevent the exercise of state-created water rights in order to carry out federal legislation protecting the navigable capacity of streams. Congress may also authorize officials to distribute water from a federal project without regard to priorities established under state law. Arizona v. California, 373 U.S. 546 (1963).

When a federal project makes it necessary to appropriate or destroy a state-created water right, compensation must be paid unless the purpose of the project is for navigation, in which case the rights are subject to the navigation servitude. In United States v. Gerlach Live Stock Co., 339 U.S. 725 (1950), farmers in California's Central Valley irrigated their grasslands with the seasonal overflow of the Sacramento River. As part of the massive Central Valley Project, the government constructed Friant Dam, which eliminated the river's seasonal flooding, thus depriving downstream landowners of the overflow. The government contended that the loss was non-compensable since Congress had authorized the Central Valley Project for the control of navigation. The Court found that the project was a reclamation project, not a navigation project, despite a general congressional declaration that the entire project was to improve navigation. *Id.* at 739. Because the 1902 Reclamation Act expressed an intention that the federal government comply with state law in acquiring property for such projects, the water rights were held to be compensable.

IV. HYDROPOWER

Hydroelectric power is a significant source of non-carbon-based, renewable energy. Hydroelectric generation typically uses the energy of a river's flow, plus gravity, to produce electricity. The federal government has been involved in hydroelectric projects for over a century, beginning with the exercise of its authority to prevent obstructions to navigation and evolving into a more comprehensive role through the Federal Power Act of 1920.

A. FEDERAL POWER ACT

The Federal Power Act of 1920 established a comprehensive national policy for hydroelectric power development. 16 U.S.C. §§ 791a *et seq.* The Act was the result of years of effort by conservationists, who had sought federal legislation to ensure comprehensive nationwide waterpower planning. The Act's purposes are to reconcile conflicting uses (e.g., navigation, irrigation, recreation, wildlife preservation, hydropower, and flood control), develop "the long idle water power resources of the nation," and "avoid unconstitutional invasion of the jurisdiction of the states." First Iowa Hydro-Elec. Co-op. v. Fed. Power Comm'n, 328 U.S. 152, 171 (1946).

The Federal Power Commission, now the Federal Energy Regulatory Commission (FERC), was

created as an independent agency to administer the
Act. 16 U.S.C. § 792. FERC has authority to license
private hydropower facilities and to regulate
interstate sale and transmission of electricity. 16
U.S.C. § 797.

In the absence of an existing, pre-1920 right-of-
way, the Act requires that a license be obtained
from FERC for hydroelectric power facilities,
including "dams, water conduits, reservoirs,
powerhouses, or other works incidental thereto,"
that cross, adjoin, or are located in navigable
waters, public lands, or federal reservations. 16
U.S.C. § 817. It also requires that permits be
obtained for use of surplus water or waterpower
from a government dam. 16 U.S.C. § 797(e).

Facilities on non-navigable waters require
licenses if the Commission finds the "interests of
interstate or foreign commerce would be affected" by
the proposed project. 16 U.S.C. § 817. Citing this
language, courts have upheld broad extensions of
the Commission's licensing jurisdiction. In Federal
Power Commission v. Union Elec. Co., 381 U.S. 90
(1965), a power company proposed to build a
"pumped-storage" facility, in which water is pumped
to a high reservoir, stored, and then released to
generate power during periods of peak demand. The
Supreme Court sustained a Commission decision to
require a license for the project because the power
generated would be transmitted across state lines.
Id. at 109–10. The Court added that, if the project
was not properly operated, timing of the flows of the

navigable portion of the river downstream could be affected. *Id.* at 93, n.5.

Despite its wide-ranging authority, the Commission has declined to exercise jurisdiction in certain situations, even where power generation has a substantial effect on navigable waters and interstate commerce. Only if the project produces power by hydroelectric generation will the Commission require a license. The Supreme Court upheld the Commission's refusal to assert jurisdiction over several huge coal-fired power plants that would use large quantities of cooling water from the navigable Colorado River and would transmit power in interstate commerce throughout the Southwest. Chemehuevi Tribe v. Federal Power Comm'n, 420 U.S. 395 (1975). The Court found that the plants were not "project works" requiring a license under the Act, nor did they use "surplus water" from a federal dam. *Id.* at 412–13. The Court reasoned that Congress only intended to license hydroelectric power plants, not plants that burn fossil fuels to make steam for power generation. *Id.* at 405.

Hydroelectric licenses must be renewed every fifty years. 16 U.S.C. § 799. FERC must evaluate existing projects "completely anew" during relicensing procedures to ensure that the projects will continue to meet the requirements of federal law. City of Tacoma v. FERC, 460 F.3d 53, 74 (D.C. Cir. 2006). In *City of Tacoma,* FERC imposed a number of conditions to protect the environment, to restore fish populations, and to mitigate a project's effect on the Skokomish Tribe's reservation. The City claimed that these conditions made license renewal economically infeasible and that it had no choice but to shut its project down; thus, FERC had effectively decommissioned its project. Although the Act directs FERC to grant licenses "upon reasonable terms," the court held that Congress implicitly afforded FERC the power to shut down projects by imposing reasonable and necessary conditions that cause the licensee to reject the license. *Id.* (citing 16 U.S.C. § 808(a)(1)).

B. CONFLICT WITH STATE LAW

Federal dams can dramatically affect the flow of streams, disrupting state water allocation. Although conflicts usually involve state-sanctioned water rights, other state laws for the protection of fish habitat and the environment may also be affected. This is especially evident in states such as Oregon and Washington, where large federal dams obstruct spawning and migration of salmon and other anadromous fish.

The Federal Power Act has two provisions that appear to shield state law from federal encroachment. Section 9(b) requires license applicants to submit satisfactory evidence of compliance with state laws concerning hydropower development. 16 U.S.C. § 802(b). Section 27 provides:

Nothing contained in this chapter shall be construed as affecting or intending to affect or in any way to interfere with the laws of the respective states relating to the control, appropriation, use, or distribution of water used in irrigation or for municipal or other uses, or any vested right acquired therein.

16 U.S.C. § 821. Both sections seem to preserve state law, but judicial interpretation has limited their sweep.

In First Iowa Hydro-Electric Co-op. v. Federal Power Comm'n, 328 U.S. 152 (1946), the Supreme Court held that § 9(b) does not give state governments a veto power over federal projects. The Commission had granted a license to a hydropower co-operative to construct a dam on a tributary of the Iowa River. The Court found that where compliance with both state and federal permit requirements appeared impossible, subjecting the project to state law would frustrate the Act's purpose of comprehensive nationwide planning. *Id.* at 180–81. According to the Court, § 9(b) is merely informational; if the Commission is satisfied with the degree of state law compliance, a state permit need not be obtained. *Id.* at 178.

The *First Iowa* rule was extended in California v. FERC, 495 U.S. 490 (1990), when California attempted to impose higher minimum flow requirements on a hydroelectric project than compelled by the FERC license. Unlike *First Iowa*, where the issue was whether a state could effectively *deny* a permit to the project, the question was whether a state could determine the *conditions* on which water could be used by the project. The Supreme Court found that § 27 added nothing to the

§ 9(b) requirement of state law compliance as
interpreted in *First Iowa*. *Id*. at 498. The Court also
distinguished its contrary interpretation of a
different statutory provision with nearly identical
language, Section 8 of the Reclamation Act, 43
U.S.C. § 383, which authorizes state-imposed
conditions on water use permits for federal Bureau
of Reclamation projects. *Id*. at 504. *See* California v.
United States, 438 U.S. 645 (1978). In *California v.
FERC*, the Court found that the Federal Power Act
"envisioned a considerably broader and more active
federal oversight role in [private] hydropower
development than did the Reclamation Act" in
financing and building major federal water projects.
495 U.S. at 492. Thus, § 27 is a general provision
that cannot override the preemptive effect of specific
provisions or the overall purpose of the Federal
Power Act. It does require compensation to be paid,
however, if state-created rights are taken by
eminent domain. Portland General Elec. Co. v.
Federal Power Comm'n, 328 F.2d 165 (9th Cir.
1964); Scenic Hudson Preservation Conference v.
Federal Power Comm'n, 453 F.2d 463 (2d Cir. 1971).

Where a federal statute delegates responsibility
for environmental protection to a state, however,
FERC's exclusive authority may be qualified. The
Clean Water Act § 401, 33 U.S.C. § 1341, is a key
example. Section 401 requires that, before a federal
permit or license is granted, the federal agency
must obtain a certification that state water quality
standards will not be violated by the permitted
activity. The Supreme Court has upheld a state's
imposition of minimum streamflow requirements

deemed necessary to satisfy state water quality standards as a condition of certification for a FERC license. PUD No. 1 of Jefferson Cnty. v. Washington Dep't of Ecology, 511 U.S. 700 (1994); S.D. Warren Co. v. Maine Bd. of Envtl. Protection, 547 U.S. 370 (2006).

A hydropower license endows the licensee with certain preemptive powers of the federal government. In City of Tacoma v. Taxpayers of Tacoma, 357 U.S. 320 (1958), the city applied for a FERC license to build a dam on a tributary of the Columbia River. The State of Washington opposed the project because the reservoir behind the dam would flood a state fish hatchery and state law forbade municipalities from condemning state property. Nonetheless, the Commission granted the license. The Supreme Court held that the license delegated to the city federal eminent domain power to condemn state property. *Id.* at 340.

C. PROTECTION FOR FISH AND WILDLIFE

Hydroelectric power generating facilities can significantly disrupt fish habitat and migration patterns. Columbia River harvests of salmon are now only a small fraction of their size 100 years ago, in large part because of the construction of hydropower dams and facilities on major rivers and tributaries. Such facilities obstruct upstream spawning migration, alter water temperatures, and change the chemical composition of the water, thereby endangering the fish species.

Under the Federal Power Act, FERC must, prior
to issuing project licenses, find that the proposed
project is "best adapted to a comprehensive plan" for
water development, navigation, water power, "and
for other beneficial public uses, including
recreational purposes." 16 U.S.C. § 803(a). The 1986
amendments to the Act expressly directed FERC to
consider a project's effects on fish and wildlife. *Id.;*
16 U.S.C. § 797(e).

Courts will examine a FERC refusal to develop a
comprehensive plan to determine if FERC's decision
can be supported by the record. *Compare* National
Wildlife Fed'n v. Federal Energy Regulatory
Comm'n, 801 F.2d 1505 (9th Cir. 1986) (finding that
the record supported neither FERC's refusal to
develop a comprehensive plan for the Salmon River
Basin nor FERC's refusal to collect baseline
environmental data before granting preliminary
permits), *with* Brady v. FERC, 416 F.3d 1, 9–10
(D.C. Cir. 2005) (holding that FERC had authority
to approve a marina proposal even though the state
agency had not yet completed a comprehensive
shoreline management plan). FERC orders will be
overturned if they are arbitrary and capricious. In
City of Centralia, Wash. v. FERC, 213 F.3d 742
(D.C. Cir. 2000), the court remanded a FERC order
requiring an applicant to conduct a $300,000 study
to determine if the impacts of its facility on
anadromous fish necessitated the construction of a
$1,000,000 tailrace barrier. The court found that
FERC had failed to balance energy and
environmental values, and had marshaled no
meaningful evidence that the facility was harmful to

fish. Under the circumstances, requiring an expensive and inconclusive study "borders on the absurd." *Id.* at 750.

Several other federal environmental statutes require consideration of fish and wildlife values in projects constructed or licensed by the federal government. The National Environmental Policy Act (NEPA), 42 U.S.C. § 4332, requires preparation of an environmental impact statement (EIS) identifying the environmental consequences of any proposal for a major federal action that may significantly affect the human environment. NEPA assures that decisionmakers are aware of the environmental effects of their actions as well as the existence of any viable, less environmentally destructive alternatives, but it does not require the agency to choose the most environmentally friendly outcome. Robertson v. Methow Valley Citizens Council, 490 U.S. 332, 351 (1989); LaFlamme v. FERC, 852 F.2d 389, 398 (9th Cir. 1988).

The Fish and Wildlife Coordination Act (FWCA), 16 U.S.C. §§ 661–666c, demands "equal consideration" for wildlife conservation in water resource development programs. Washington State Dep't of Fisheries v. FERC, 801 F.2d 1516, 1519 (9th Cir. 1986). In practice, it is extremely difficult to give meaning to a requirement of parity between the values of the multiple purposes of water projects on the one hand and fish and wildlife values on the other. However, if FERC fails to consider fishery issues before issuing a license under the FPA, it fails to give fish "equal consideration" under the

FWCA. Confederated Tribes & Bands of the Yakima Indian Nation v. FERC, 746 F.2d 466 (9th Cir. 1984), *cert. denied,* 471 U.S. 1116 (1985). Also, to help assure protection of state interests in fish and wildlife, the Act requires coordination among the agency undertaking or permitting a project, the U.S. Fish and Wildlife Service, and relevant state fish and wildlife agencies before construction of a project. 16 U.S.C. § 662(a).

Of all of the statutory provisions that protect fish and wildlife, the Endangered Species Act (ESA) is the most powerful. Section 9 of the ESA prohibits the "take" of any listed species, including habitat destruction that harms the species, by any person, including federal, state, and private actors. 16 U.S.C. § 1538. In addition, section 7 of the ESA requires each federal agency to "insure that any action authorized, funded, or carried out by [the] agency . . . is not likely to jeopardize the continued existence of any endangered species or threatened species," 16 U.S.C. § 1536(a)(2). If an agency determines that a proposed action "may affect" a listed anadromous fish species or its critical habitat, the agency must engage in a formal consultation to avoid jeopardy to the species. 50 C.F.R. § 402.14(a). *See* Nat'l Wildlife Fed'n v. Nat'l Marine Fisheries Serv., 839 F. Supp. 2d 1117 (D. Or. 2011) (continuing an injunction on operations of the Columbia River Power System's dams and reservoirs because they jeopardized listed salmonids).

Although not really an environmental statute, the Pacific Northwest Electric Power Planning and Conservation Act, 16 U.S.C. § 839, is a comprehensive act for allocating supplies and mitigating impacts of federally produced hydropower. The Act contains significant requirements for preserving and restoring anadromous fisheries in the Pacific Northwest, the region hardest hit by the impacts of hydropower facilities. Under the Act, a regional council develops a plan for protection, mitigation, and enhancement of fish and wildlife. Furthermore, managers of federal power facilities are required to afford "equitable treatment" to fish and wildlife, insuring that their operations do not subordinate fish and wildlife to other project objectives. 16 U.S.C. § 839b. The Council's plans must be "tak[en] into account at each relevant stage" of FERC proceedings. *Id.*; National Wildlife Fed'n v. Federal Energy Regulatory Comm'n, 801 F.2d 1505 (9th Cir. 1986).

When Indian tribes have treaty fishing rights on a river, interference with instream flows by diversion, impoundment, or pollution that damages fish habitat may reduce the ability of tribes to take a meaningful share of fish. *See* Skokomish Indian Tribe v. United States, 410 F.3d 506 (9th Cir. 2005) (alleging that a federally-licensed power project violated tribal treaty rights), *cert. denied,* 546 U.S. 1090 (2006). The federal government may be liable in damages for failing to protect treaty rights. U.S. v. Mitchell, 463 U.S. 206 (1983). Moreover, section 4(e) of the Federal Power Act requires the U.S. Department of Interior to develop license conditions to protect the purposes and uses of Indian reservations. *See* City of Tacoma v. FERC, 460 F.3d 53 (D.C. Cir. 2006) (citing 16 U.S.C. § 797(e)).

V. FLOOD CONTROL

Historically, the federal interest in water development was closely tied to maintaining commercial navigation. However, federal interests in flood control expanded significantly throughout the twentieth century. Today, there are numerous congressional legislative measures focused squarely on flood control, which comes firmly within the Commerce Clause power. The Army Corps of Engineers is most frequently at the heart of flood control disputes, as it is the entity often tasked with carrying out federal flood control legislation.

A. THE RIVERS AND HARBORS ACT

The Rivers and Harbors Act of 1899 gave the Corps authority to carry out projects to prevent obstructions to navigation and to promote federal navigational interests. 33 U.S.C. §§ 401–418. For years, the Corps focused primarily on navigation and did little under the Act in terms of flood control, in part because Congress stipulated that no federal money could be used to protect land from flooding or for any purpose other than navigation. Even so, the Corps constructed miles of levees along the Mississippi River not only to constrict and improve the navigational channel but also to provide incidental flood control benefits. Today, the Corps has undertaken extensive transportation improvements as well as flood control on mainstems and tributaries of navigable waters. Christine A. Klein & Sandra B. Zellmer, *Mississippi River Stories: Lessons from A Century of Unnatural Disasters,* 60 SMU L. Rev. 1471, 1480 (2007).

B. THE FLOOD CONTROL ACTS

A series of catastrophic floods throughout the early twentieth century prompted Congress to supplement the Rivers and Harbors Act of 1899 with legislation specifically aimed at flood control. The Flood Control Acts, enacted between 1917 and 1965, expanded federal power on navigable rivers for purposes of flood control. For a detailed history and assessment, *see* Christine A. Klein & Sandra B. Zellmer, MISSISSIPPI RIVER TRAGEDIES: A CENTURY OF UNNATURAL DISASTERS (NYU Press 2014).

Although state and local governments often derive extensive economic benefits from federal flood control projects, they have not always embraced the influx of federal infrastructure. For example, the Denison Dam and Reservoir project on the Red River in Texas and Oklahoma inundated both state and private lands. Oklahoma sued, alleging that it would be injured by the project due to the loss of 100,000 acres. Oklahoma ex rel Phillips v. Guy F. Atkinson Co., 313 U.S. 508, 511 (1941). The Supreme Court ruled that the project was a proper exercise of Congress' commerce power. *Id.* at 516. In making this determination, the Court specifically cited the flood control purposes of the project and the history of flooding in the river basin:

"Floods pay no respect to state lines. Their effective control in the Mississippi valley has become increasingly a subject of national concern in recognition of the fact that single states are impotent to cope with them effectively." *Id.* at 521–22. The Court additionally found that the commerce power was by no means limited to maintaining navigability on navigable streams. "There is no constitutional reason why Congress cannot under the commerce clause treat the watersheds as key to flood control on navigable streams and their tributaries." *Id.* at 525.

The Flood Control Act of 1917 was the first federal enactment that explicitly appropriated money for river improvements other than navigation. Pub. L. No. 64–367, 39 Stat. 948 (1917). Congress allocated $45 million for flood control work between the mouth of the Ohio and the mouth of the Mississippi. The project was supervised by the Mississippi River Commission, an entity comprised of Corps officials, a representative of the U.S. Geological Survey, and a few civilian members. Local institutions were required to secure the necessary rights-of-way for levees and to contribute one-half of the cost of levee construction. The 1917 Act also authorized the Corps to implement the Sacramento River Flood Control Project, in partnership with the state of California. Federal-state levees and other projects were aimed at controlling Central Valley and San Joaquin River floods, largely to protect the populated centers of Sacramento and Stockton. Alf W. Brandt & Andrea P. Clark, *Preparing for Extreme Floods: California's*

New Flood Plan, 27 Nat. Res. & Env't (ABA) 45 (Fall 2012). In 1953, the federal government transferred responsibility for the Sacramento River Flood Control Project to the state. *Id.*

In 1928, after a devastating flood killed hundreds of people and caused over $200 million in property damage (about $2 billion in 2000 dollars) in the lower Mississippi River Basin, Congress "passed a veritable deluge of Flood Control Acts." Klein & Zellmer, *Mississippi River Stories,* 60 SMU L. Rev. at 1485. The 1928 Act declared that the federal government would take responsibility for the Mississippi River through the construction of more federal levees, spillways, and reservoirs, but it also immunized the federal government from any liability "of any kind . . . for any damage from or by floods or flood waters at any place." 33 U.S.C. § 702.

Each subsequent enactment added another layer to the complicated assortment of authorities for the construction and maintenance of flood control devices. Importantly, the 1936 Act delegates broad discretion to the Corps to construct any flood control project it chooses (so long as Congress agrees to appropriate the necessary funds) whenever "the benefits to whomsoever they may accrue are in excess of the estimated costs." 33 U.S.C. § 701a.

The Flood Control Act of 1944, ch. 665, 58 Stat. 887 (codified as amended in scattered sections of 16, 33, and 43 U.S.C.), authorized the addition of five huge mainstem dams on the Missouri River. The Corps was given control over dams and reservoirs on the river's mainstem for flood control and navigation purposes, while the Bureau of Reclamation was charged with promoting irrigation through projects primarily on the tributaries. As is the case with other rivers under its management, the Corps must adopt a Master Water Control Manual to outline management strategies and lay out a hierarchy of river management goals. The Missouri River Manual lists flood control as a priority interest, followed by navigation, irrigation, water supply, hydroelectric power, recreation, and wildlife. Sandra Zellmer, *Mudslinging on the Missouri: Can Endangered Species Survive The Clean Water Act?*, 16 Drake J. Agric. L. 89, 94 (2011).

In addition to the Flood Control Acts, periodic Water Resources Development Acts (WRDAs) often include flood control projects and related measures. The WRDA of 1986 authorized the construction or modification of a variety of flood control and navigation projects, along with a number of projects intended to protect coastal concerns, recreation, and fisheries. Pub. L. No. 99–662, 100 Stat. at 4109, 4111. Similarly, the WRDA of 1990 included projects for navigation and flood control as well as storm water management. Pub. L. No. 101–640, 104 Stat. 4604, 4605–11.

Under these statutes and other enactments, the Corps has carried out its flood control duties with a vengeance by constructing dams, reservoirs, and levees to constrain major rivers throughout the nation. In return, population centers and farmers along the river gained a heightened perception of safety and developed ever-more land in floodplain and coastal areas. The federal government is not always able to hold back the flood waters, though, and the extreme weather events and rising sea levels associated with climate change are likely to make floodplain and coastal properties more vulnerable in the future.

While the government may be obligated to pay for a "taking" of land inundated by the construction or operation of federal reservoirs or spillways, where the federal project did not increase the "immemorial danger of unpredictable major floods to which respondent's land had always been subject," compensation will not be required. U.S. v. Sponenbarger, 308 U.S. 256, 265 (1939). However, the Court allowed a takings claim to proceed in Arkansas Game and Fish Comm'n v. U.S., 133 S. Ct. 511, 513 (2012), when the Corps deviated from its Water Control Manual for a dam on the Black River by extending flooding, at the request of local farmers, into a state wildlife management area during the area's peak timber growing season. The Court held that " 'where real estate is actually invaded by superinduced additions of water, earth, sand, or other material . . . so as to effectually destroy or impair its usefulness, it is a taking . . . ,' " where the damage is foreseeable and severe, albeit temporary. *Id.* at 518–19 (citation omitted).

VI. ECOLOGICAL CONCERNS AND ENVIRONMENTAL LEGISLATION

Navigation, hydropower, and flood control measures are often at odds with environmental goals. Dams, reservoirs, levees, and channelization have radically changed the function, processes, and structure of riparian ecosystems throughout the nation. Klein & Zellmer, *Mississippi River Stories,* 60 SMU L. Rev. at 1508–10; Dan Tarlock, *Hydro Law and the Future of Hydroelectric Power Generation in the United States,* 65 Vand. L. Rev. 1723, 1735–38 (2012).

Valuable sediment deposits, which fertilized land during flooding and sustained sandbars, islands, and other natural formations in and beside the rivers, have been trapped behind dams and levees or moved too rapidly through channelized river corridors to serve their ecological purposes or to provide ecosystem services. Sandra Zellmer & Lance Gunderson, *Why Resilience May Not Always Be a Good Thing: Lessons in Ecosystem Restoration from Glen Canyon and the Everglades,* 87 Neb. L. Rev. 893, 906–07, 913–19, 924 (2009).

Additionally, dams interrupt the life cycles of migrating fish. In Marsh v. Oregon Natural Res. Council, 490 U.S. 360 (1989), the Corps sought to construct a dam on Elk Creek in the Rogue River Basin in order to prevent flooding. The Oregon Natural Resources Council (ONRC) argued that the Corps had not taken into consideration possible "worse case scenarios" following an internal departmental report that cited concerns about the fish population of Elk Creek, and had failed to consider the cumulative effect of three dam projects in the basin. *Id.* at 368. The Court rejected ONRC's argument that a supplemental EIS was necessary to account for the new information, and found that the Corps had conducted a "reasoned evaluation" of the impacts to fish. *Id.* at 385.

Several federal environmental statutes address the ecological problems raised by dams and other water development projects. The ESA and several other important enactments, including CWA § 401, are addressed *supra* Sections IV.B–C. The CWA includes several other provisions related to water quality and, by extension, riparian ecology and water-dependent species.

The CWA expresses an overarching goal "to restore and maintain the chemical, physical, and biological integrity of the Nation's waters." 33 U.S.C. § 1251(a). The Act also includes an interim goal of achieving "water quality which provides for the protection and propagation of fish, shellfish, and wildlife." *Id.*

To achieve these goals, the CWA regulates discharges of pollutants, including soil and nutrients like phosphorous and nitrogen, from point sources through various permit programs. 33 U.S.C. §§ 1342, 1344. However, the U.S. Environmental Protection Agency (EPA) and several courts have excluded dams from coverage. *See* 40 C.F.R. § 122.3(i); Nat'l Wildlife Fed'n v. Gorsuch, 693 F.2d 156 (D.C. Cir. 1982); Nat'l Wildlife Fed'n v. Consumers Power Co., 862 F.2d 580 (6th Cir. 1988).

But see Greenfield Mills, Inc. v. Macklin, 361 F.3d
934 (7th Cir. 2004) (holding that a dam was "point
source" when an artificial mechanism was used to
convey pollutants into a river). The EPA's relevant
regulation has been remanded to the agency as
arbitrary and capricious. Catskill Mountains
Chapter of Trout Unlimited, Inc. v. U.S. E.P.A., 8 F.
Supp. 3d 500 (S.D.N.Y. 2014) (invalidating 40
C.F.R. § 122.3(i)).

The CWA also requires states to develop water
quality standards. 33 U.S.C. § 1313(a)–(c). Water
quality standards include designated uses of water
bodies, numeric or narrative criteria as necessary to
protect those uses, and the prevention of
degradation of the current condition of water bodies
within the state. States submit their water quality
standards to EPA for review and approval. Water
bodies that fail to meet approved water quality
standards must be identified as impaired, and total
maximum daily loads and pollutant management
plans must be adopted. 33 U.S.C. § 1313(d). Water
quality standards that fail to promote riparian
ecology or to protect the conservation needs of
water-dependent species may violate the CWA, and
possibly the ESA. Zellmer, *Mudslinging on the
Missouri,* 16 Drake J. Agric. L. at 102.

In addition to the CWA and the ESA, the Wild
and Scenic Rivers Act (WSRA) preserves the
"outstandingly remarkable" values (ORVs) of
designated river segments by protecting the rivers
and their banks from the adverse effects of dams,
hydroelectric projects, roads, and other activities. 16

U.S.C. § 1271. ORVs may include "scenic, recreational, geologic, fish and wildlife, historic, cultural, or other similar values." 16 U.S.C. § 1271. Although the WSRA does not prohibit any and all development, *see* Rivers Unlimited v. U.S. Dep't of Transp., 533 F. Supp. 2d 1 (D.D.C. 2008) (upholding a determination to construct a new bridge over a segment of the Little Miami River), designated river segments are to be preserved in free-flowing conditions and managed to preserve and enhance their ORVs for the benefit and enjoyment of present and future generations. Friends of Yosemite Valley v. Norton, 348 F.3d 789, 793 (9th Cir. 2003), *clarified*, 366 F.3d 731 (9th Cir. 2004) (citing 16 U.S.C. § 1271).

A key provision of the Act forbids FERC from licensing "any dam, water conduit, reservoir, powerhouse, transmission line or other project works under the Federal Power Act on or directly affecting any [designated] river. . . ." 16 U.S.C. § 1278(a). The Act also prohibits all other federal agencies from assisting in the construction of any water resources project that would have a direct and adverse effect on a designated river. 16 U.S.C. § 1278(a). *See* Sierra Club N. Star Chapter v. Pena, 1 F. Supp. 2d 971 (D. Minn. 1998) (upholding Park Service's determination that a proposed bridge would adversely affect the St. Croix River's ORVs and enjoining federal agencies from assisting in the bridge's construction); Sierra Club N. Star Chapter v. LaHood, 693 F. Supp. 2d 958 (D. Minn. 2010) (issuing a permanent injunction against the bridge).

In addition, the Act requires that each wild and scenic river segment be "administered in such manner as to protect and enhance the values which caused it to be included in said system. . . ." 16 U.S.C. § 1281(a). Guidelines issued by the Departments of Interior and Agriculture interpret this mandate "as stating a nondegradation and enhancement policy for all designated river areas, regardless of classification." 47 Fed. Reg. 39,454, 39,458 (1982). The Guidelines also direct the administering agency to manage each river segment so as to protect and enhance its ORVs, "while providing for public recreation and resource uses which do not adversely impact or degrade those values." *Id.*

CHAPTER EIGHT

FEDERAL AND INDIAN RESERVED RIGHTS

I. RESERVED RIGHTS DOCTRINE

The reserved rights doctrine allows the federal government to reserve adequate water for particular federal purposes including uses on Indian and public lands. Although most water rights in the western United States enjoy a priority based on when they were first put to a beneficial use, most rights on federal and Indian lands have priority dating back to the dates the government set the lands aside, even if water use begins long after others have appropriated waters from the stream. Federal reserved rights differ from the power of eminent domain, because under a reserved right the federal government is not taking property for which it must provide compensation. Rather, the government reserves land from the public domain and sets it aside for a particular public purpose, like a National Park or lands for tribal use. If that purpose requires water, the reserved rights doctrine is the legal basis for asserting a water right even if the reservation is silent as to water and a right must be implied. In addition, aboriginal Indian ownership of an area can lead to a determination that the original tribal rights to water continue.

The reserved rights doctrine first emerged in a case involving lands that had been reserved for an Indian Reservation, Winters v. United States, 207

U.S. 564 (1908), but was extended to include other federal lands in Arizona v. California, 373 U.S. 546 (1963). After the Supreme Court's decision in *Arizona v. California*, essentially two lines of case law developed—one dealing with reserved rights on Indian lands and the other addressing reserved rights for other federal purposes. Reserved rights are significant, especially in the arid West, because they exist as a matter of federal law in a system that allocates water rights at the state level. As a result, principles of state law, such as diversion, beneficial use, priority dates, use-or lose, do not apply to reserved rights. Despite their basis in federal law, reserved rights may be quantified in state general stream adjudications under the McCarran Amendment. Some of the most controversial issues arise at the interface of state and federal jurisdiction where quantification, adjudication, and administration of a decree are at stake.

A. ORIGIN OF THE DOCTRINE— *WINTERS V. UNITED STATES*

The Supreme Court announced the reserved rights doctrine in Winters v. United States, 207 U.S. 564 (1908), a case that involved a conflict between Indians of the Fort Belknap Reservation in Montana and nearby non-Indian settlers over waters of the Milk River. In 1888, the Indian tribes agreed to cede territory to the United States that was part of the lands reserved by them in an earlier treaty, and to be confined to a relatively small reservation. The federal government induced settlers to take up homesteads on the ceded lands. The homesteaders began using water from the Milk River for irrigation, perfecting their water rights under Montana state law. A short time later, the Indians began diverting large quantities of water for irrigation. The settlers diverted water upstream from the reservation, preventing the tribes from getting sufficient water. The United States then brought suit against the settlers on behalf of the tribes.

The Supreme Court held that although the settlers had established rights under state law and had begun using water before the Indians, the Indians held a prior water right at least as of the date of the reservation. Because the government's policy, expressed in the 1888 agreement, was to make the Indians a "pastoral and civilized people" and because the reserved lands were arid, the Court found it inconceivable that either the Indians or the government would agree to the vast land cession unless enough water was reserved to make the reservation lands useful. Although the agreement setting forth the reservation was silent on the subject, the court found that water rights existed by "necessary implication" to accomplish the agreement's stated purpose. Without water rights, cultivation of the ceded lands would be impossible. The Court applied the established rule of construction that ambiguities in an Indian agreement or treaty should be resolved in the Indians' favor and as the Indians would have understood the agreement.

Once asserted and more importantly adjudicated, Indian reserved rights can have an important impact on the quantity of water available to non-Indians. Often the priority dates for tribal claims predate many of the state law based claims held under the prior appropriation doctrine. *See* United States v. Adair, 723 F.2d 1394 (9th Cir. 1983) (establishing a priority date for the tribal water rights claims based on aboriginal uses as time immemorial, predating all state law based claims; and 1864 for irrigation uses based on the treaty date). Moreover, Indian reserved rights cannot be extinguished except by express legislation, even after the reservation is terminated and the land sold off, so long as there is a continuing purpose to be served. *Id.* As a result, the presence of unadjudicated, time immemorial water rights has a tremendous impact on water resources management in the arid West. In response to this impact, many tribal water rights claims are addressed through negotiated water rights settlements between the tribe, federal government, and the state, among others.

B. APPLICATION TO FEDERAL NON-INDIAN RESERVATIONS—*ARIZONA v. CALIFORNIA*

Beginning in 1955 with the *Pelton Dam* decision, the Supreme Court began to foreshadow its view that the federal government, through its regulatory function under the Commerce Clause and its proprietary function under the Property clause, retained some authority over water on public domain lands after statehood when those lands were reserved for specific federal purposes. In *Pelton Dam*, the Court held that a *reservation* of federal land for particular purposes (not merely the existence of public land available for homesteading or other dispositions) removed water sources on that land from appropriation pursuant to state law. Federal Power Comm'n v. Oregon, 349 U.S. 435 (1955). In 1963, with its decision in Arizona v. California, 373 U.S. 546, the Court held that the reserved rights doctrine announced in *Winters* applied to federal lands reserved for non-Indian purposes. In this context, Congress, or the Executive, has the power under the property clause to reserve waters from appropriation when it sets aside federal lands. As a result of these cases, the courts will find that a water right exists for reserved federal lands even if the reservation documents are silent as to water rights if water is necessary to carry out the purposes of the reservation.

Following *Arizona v. California*, the Supreme Court has continued to recognize the implied reservation of water for federal lands to the extent those rights are necessary to fulfill the purposes of the land reservation. For example, the Supreme Court upheld the government's claim to the amount of water in a limestone cavern at Devil's Hole National Monument required to preserve the habitat of the pupfish, a prehistoric species mentioned in the proclamation setting aside the monument. Cappaert v. United States, 426 U.S. 128 (1976). The quantity of water reserved, however, is limited to the amount necessary for the reservation's specific purposes. United States v.

New Mexico, 438 U.S. 696 (1978). *See* Section III.D of this Chapter. No Supreme Court decision has questioned the existence of federal power to reserve water from appropriation under state law. Rather, the persistent question has been whether, in the absence of an express reservation, Congress intended to exercise its powers and the quantity reserved.

C. BASIS FOR THE EXERCISE OF FEDERAL AUTHORITY

The reserved water rights doctrine is closely tied to the history and settlement of the western United States. Prior to statehood, the federal government held land pursuant to treaties, purchases, and conquest. From 1866–1877, a series of federal statutes authorized public land to be "patented" into private ownership and ultimately made subject to the jurisdiction of newly formed states. The territorial governments and soon-to-be formed state governments, at around the same time, were recognizing and applying prior appropriation principles among miners and settlers. *See supra* Chapter Three (Prior Appropriation). Through the federal statutes that allowed for land disposition, including the Mining Act of 1866 and the Desert Land Act of 1877 among others, Congress began to recognize these appropriative rights. *See* Basey v. Gallagher, 87 U.S. 670 (1875); California Oregon Power v. Portland Beaver Cement, 295 U.S. 142, 158, 164 (1935). Until the Supreme Court's decision in *California Oregon Power*, however, there were questions about whether federal land patents included some kind of water right for these private patentees. The Court concluded that the 1877 Desert Land Act had "effected a severance of all waters upon the public domain, not theretofore appropriated, from the land itself" and recognized that private water rights were established under state law. 295 U.S. at 158, 164. With this decision, the Court established that the allocation of water rights to private parties was a matter of state law and that a federal patent carried no right to water under federal law. 2 Water and Water Rights § 37.01(a).

While *California Oregon Power* made clear that the federal government was not in the business of allocating private rights, the Court also articulated several important exceptions with regard to public rights where federal law would continue to apply, including securing water needed to carry out purposes on federal land and water needed to protect navigational interests. These two exceptions, as well as other recognized bases for the assertion of federal rights, are rooted in the federal Constitution in the Property Clause, art. IV, § 3, the Commerce Clause, the Indian Commerce Clause, art. I, § 8, cl. 3, the treaty power, art. II, § 2, cl. 2 and the Supremacy Clause, Art. VI, cl. 2.

With regard to the management of federal property, Congress has power to reserve water for use on public lands under the property clause, art. IV, § 3, which authorizes it "to dispose of and make all needful Rules and Regulations respecting the Territory or other Property belonging to the United

States." The navigation power, based in the commerce clause, art. I, § 8, cl. 3, also provides authority for the federal government to protect the public's interest in water under federal law. In United States v. Rio Grande Dam & Irrigation Co., 174 U.S. 690 (1899), the Court upheld the ability of Congress to regulate the flow of a non-navigable stream that affected the navigable capacity of navigable waters. In *Rio Grande*, the Court also stated, in dictum, that a state "cannot by its legislation destroy the right of the United States, as owner of lands bordering on a stream, to the continued flow of its waters; so far at least as may be necessary for the beneficial uses of the government property." *Id.* at 703. However, the property clause, mentioned in dictum in *Rio Grande*, is the most commonly cited source of power for federal reservations of water and the basis for the Supreme Court's decisions in *Winters* and *Arizona v. California*, the two foundational cases establishing the federal reserved water rights doctrine.

Reserved water rights for Indian tribes may also be based on preexisting aboriginal rights reserved in treaties entered into by the United States under its the treaty power, art. II, § 2., or agreements ratified by Congress, or Executive Orders. A leading example can be found in the Northwest through treaties, which guarantee a "right to fish at usual and accustomed grounds." United States v. Adair, 723 F.2d 1394, 1417–1418 (9th Cir. 1983). *See* United States v. Winans, 198 U.S. 371 (1905); Cohen's Handbook of Federal Indian Law 1209–10

(2012); and 2 Water and Water Rights § 37.01(b). Some refer to these rights as "treaty reserved" rights, but the distinction is not all that useful because even in the *Winters* case, an 1851 treaty was signed prior to signing the subsequent agreements between the U.S. and the tribe.

D. RELATIONSHIP TO STATE WATER LAW

1. Prior Appropriation Jurisdictions

Federal reserved water rights remain controversial in the West largely based on the way in which these rights interact with state law regarding the allocation of private rights. As discussed above, the 1877 Desert Land Act was interpreted in California Oregon Power Co. v. Beaver Portland Cement Co., 295 U.S. 142 (1935), as confirming that private rights on federal land are established according to state law. Notwithstanding the role of the states in allocating private rights, the Court also established that the federal government retained the power to reserve water to protect federal property. These federal rights create conflict within the states because they operate under federal law, not state law.

For example, a federal reserved water right is not subject to abandonment or forfeiture under state law for non-use. A federal reserved water right is not required to fall within the state's definition of beneficial use. This beneficial use exception has been controversial where the federal needs for water is primarily for instream or non-consumptive uses that may not be fully protected under state law. *See* Cappaert v. United States, 426 U.S. 128 (1976); United States v. New Mexico, 438 U.S. 700 (1978); High Country Citizens' Alliance v. Norton, 448 F. Supp. 2d 1235 (D. Colo. 2006). Many reserved rights claims are un-quantified and as a result states and the private water users within the state could be impacted when federal claims are quantified and risk upsetting the allocation system that the state has established by a state through its priority system.

While all water rights are exercised based on a priority date, the reserved rights doctrine uses the date of the reservation, not the date of diversion for beneficial use or the date of asserting the right, to establish priority. This raises concerns among state water law administrators and holders of state water rights because federal reserved water rights often remain unused for many years and exist in uncertain quantities. Unquantified or unused federal reserved rights create a cloud on active water users and potentially disrupts a state's water rights system. With regard to tribal rights, especially those based on treaties, a tribe can assert a right with a very senior priority date or even "time immemorial"—a time in prehistory. Water rights for these reservations hold priority dates before most state-based rights were established. U.S. v. Adair, 723 F.2d 1394 (9th Cir. 1983).

Lastly, state law cannot interfere with federal property rights or defeat federal purposes and programs. Only Congress can relinquish water interests held by the United States. High Country Citizens' Alliance v. Norton, 448 F. Supp. 2d 1235, 1248 (D. Colo. 2006). Because the doctrine is based on federal, not state law, under the Supremacy Clause, any inconsistent state law is preempted. *See* U.S. Const. art. VI, cl. 2; California v. United States, 438 U.S. 645 (1978).

2. Riparian Jurisdictions

Winters and other reserved rights cases arose in jurisdictions that generally follow the doctrine of prior appropriation, which uses priority to allocate private water rights. But under riparian water law, no special significance attaches to the order in which people began using water. *See supra* Chapter Two. Generally, every landowner bordering a stream has a right to use a reasonable quantity of water. In times of shortage, available supplies are shared by all riparians. If the federal government must share the burden of shortage equally with other users, no assurance exists that federal purposes can be carried out.

The courts have not decided how the concept of reserved water rights applies in a riparian jurisdiction. 2 Water Rights § 37.01(c)(2). However, a Virginia state court judge gave it careful consideration in 2007 and questioned whether reserved rights would be necessary in a riparian jurisdiction where all reasonable uses of riparian owners are protected. Mattaponi Indian Tribe v. Commonwealth, 72 Va. Cir. 444 (2007). The court recognized, though, that "riparian law does not guarantee a riparian owner sufficient water for a particular purpose" as the reserved water rights doctrine does. *Id*. at 457–58. Reserved rights were asserted by the Seminole Tribe in Florida, but the issue was resolved in a settlement agreement. *See* 25 U.S.C. §§ 1772–1772(g). In any event, riparian rights, like prior appropriation rights, are premised on state law, while reserved rights depend on the implied intent of Congress (and the tribes in the case of Indian reserved rights). If there is evidence of implied intent to reserve water for a federal purpose, it should trump any state law to the contrary. Judith V. Royster, Winters in the East: Tribal Reserved Rights to Water in Riparian States, 25 W. & Mary Envtl. L. and Pol'y Rev. 168 (2000).

II. FEDERAL WATER RIGHTS FOR INDIAN LANDS AND PURPOSES

Federal law recognizes three categories of aboriginal or Indian water rights—(1) those based on the reservation of land, referred to as "Winters" or reserved rights; (2) those based on treaty, referred to as "Winans" rights; and (3) those based on Pueblo title to lands from the Treaty of Guadalupe Hildago and the Gadsden Purchase.

A. DETERMINING PURPOSE FOR WATER RIGHTS—DISTINGUISHING *WINTERS, WINANS,* AND PUEBLO WATER RIGHTS

Indian reserved rights arise under federal law through treaties, statutes, agreements, and executive orders. Like all federal rights, the

Supremacy Clause protects Indian reserved rights from interference by inconsistent state law. Moreover, consistent with its trust responsibility to tribes, the federal government has an obligation to assert and defend Indian water rights. Robert T. Anderson, *Indian Water Rights and the Federal Trust Responsibility,* 46 Nat. Resources J. 399 (2006). While each type of reserved right shares these basic attributes, each differs primarily when courts begin to determine the purpose of the water right. The purpose associated with the water right can have a tremendous impact on the quantity of water needed to accomplish that purpose.

Reserved water rights to support aboriginal practices are referred to as *Winans* rights, and are most often associated with treaty reservations, although they can be part of an Executive Order reservation. Typically, in these treaties tribes ceded vast portions of land to the United States in exchange for recognition of certain pre-existing, aboriginal, subsistence activities that usually involve non-consumptive use of water. U.S. v. Adair, 723 F.2d 1394, 1411 (9th Cir. 1983); State ex rel. Greely v. Confederated Salish and Kootenai Tribes of the Flathead Reservation, 712 P.2d 754, 764 (Mont. 1985). *Winans* rights are dependent on water over an extended period of time rather than underlying land title. 2 Water and Water Rights § 37.02(a)(2). For Pacific Northwest tribes included in the Stevens' treaties, the ability to fish at usual and accustomed fishing grounds represents the basis for a reserved water right to accomplish this purpose. United States v. Winans, 198 U.S. 371, 384

(1905);   Washington   v.   Washington   State
Commercial Passenger Fishing Vessel Ass'n, 443
U.S. 658, 661 (1979). *Winans* rights can include
water sufficient to support hunting, fishing, and
trapping rights, as well as water sufficient to
support productive habitat. U.S. v. Adair (Adair II),
187 F. Supp. 2d 1273, 1275 (D. Or. 2002).

Reserved water rights established through the
reservation of land for uses not associated with
aboriginal practices are known as "Winters" rights.
These rights are based upon the federal government
agreeing through treaty, executive order, statute, or
other agreement to reserve land from the public
domain as homelands for tribal communities. The
federal government's purpose in setting aside this
land was typically to transform Indian people into
farmers who would need water to accomplish this
purpose. Arizona v. California, 373 U.S. 546 (1963);
In re General Adjudication of the Gila River System,
35 P.3d 68, 78–79 (Ariz. 2001).

Pueblo rights differ from *Winans* and *Winters*
rights primarily because Pueblo communities own
the underlying land and the water rights derive
from Spanish and Mexican law. Water and Water
Rights § 37.05. When the United States signed the
Treaty of Guadalupe Hildago to obtain much of the
Southwest, it expressly recognized pre-existing
property titles, including water rights. *See* Treaty of
Guadalupe Hildago, Art. VIII, 9 Stat. 922 (1848);
State ex rel. Reynolds v. Aamodt, 618 F. Supp. 993
(D.N.M. 1985); State ex rel. Martinez v. Kerr
McGee, 898 P.2d 1256, 1264–65 (N.M. App. 1995).

See supra Chapter Four. Pueblo rights are unique in terms of purpose because the courts have recognized that they include surface and groundwater sufficient to meet the community's present and future needs, with consideration given adverse effects on third parties. *Reynolds,* 618 F. Supp. 993, 998–99.

B. QUANTIFYING RESERVED WATER RIGHTS

1. *Winters* Rights—Practicably Irrigable Acreage (PIA Standard)

Winters rights are associated with the reservation of land for Indian people for the purpose of transforming nomadic tribes into settled agrarians. In Arizona v. California, 373 U.S. 546, 600 (1963), the Supreme Court established the "PIA standard" as the measure of the *Winters* reserved right. The PIA standard grants an amount of water needed to irrigate all of the Indians' practicably irrigable acreage. It was adopted by the Court over the objection of the Colorado Basin states who urged a standard based on the tribes' reasonably foreseeable needs or a standard based on equitable apportionment of available water. *Arizona v. California*, 373 U.S. at 600–01.

The Wyoming courts applied the PIA standard to quantify water rights for the tribes of the Wind River Reservation. In re General Adjudication of All Rights to Use Water in the Big Horn System, 753 P.2d 76 (Wyo. 1988) (*Big Horn*). The Wyoming Supreme Court limited the scope of the PIA

standard by establishing a two-part test for lands
subject to the PIA standard—(1) the land must be
capable of sustained irrigation and (2) irrigable at a
reasonable cost. *Id.* at 101–05. The U.S. Supreme
Court granted certiorari in the *Big Horn* case and
the PIA test was affirmed, without opinion, by an
evenly divided court. Wyoming v. United States, 492
U.S. 406 (1989). *See* Andrew C. Mergen and Sylvia
F. Liu, *A Misplaced Sensitivity: The Draft Opinion
in Wyoming v. United States,* 68 U. Colo. L. Rev. 683
(1997) (describing a draft opinion by Justice
O'Connor that would have established a new test
based on sensitivity to the impact on state and
private appropriators). In *Big Horn,* the Wyoming
court also limited the purpose of the reservation to
purely agricultural needs, notwithstanding several
references to a "permanent homeland" in the treaty
in question. Thus, it refused to recognize reserved
rights for fisheries, mining, industrial, or wildlife
purposes. The U.S. Supreme Court did not review
this portion of the decision.

After the *Big Horn* decision, state courts
exercising jurisdiction under the McCarran
Amendment have taken different approaches to
quantifying *Winters* rights. The Arizona Supreme
Court rejected the use of the PIA method as the sole
method for determining the amount of water
necessary for a tribe and established a "feasibility
test" plus a non-exclusive list of factors to be
considered when evaluating tribal claims. In re
General Adjudication of the Gila River System, 35
P.3d 68, 780–79 (Ariz. 2001). The Arizona court's
test addresses a broader range of factors, including

a tribe's culture, history, natural resources, and present and future population. In New Mexico, limitations on a tribal right were affirmed based on a reasonable cost and feasibility analysis. State ex rel. Martinez v. Lewis, 861 P.2d 235, 246–51 (N.M. App. 1993). For an exhaustive description of the cases, *see* Cohen's Handbook of Federal Indian Law at 1220–1224 (2012).

2. *Winans* Rights—Needs-Based Standards for Non-Irrigation Rights

Winans reserved rights are not predicated on the reservation of land or the purpose of creating an agrarian lifestyle for tribal people. Rather, *Winans* rights are based on particular and existing, often non-consumptive, uses of water that are protected through treaties or reservation documents. For example, a treaty right to take fish in common with non-Indians has been interpreted to entitle the tribes to a maximum of 50 percent of the harvest of salmon each year. *See* Washington v. Washington State Commercial Passenger Fishing Vessel Ass'n, 443 U.S. 658, 686 (1979) (providing that "the central principle here must be that Indian treaty rights to a natural resource that once was thoroughly and exclusively exploited by the Indians secures so much as, but not more than, is necessary to provide the Indians with a livelihood—that is to say a moderate living"). The Klamath Tribe's treaty rights ensure a quantity of water sufficient to support hunting and fishing, including as currently exercised. U.S. v. Adair, 723 F.2d 1374, 1410–12 (9th Cir. 1983), *cert. denied*, 467 U.S. 1252 (1984). The Ninth Circuit has

also recognized the Colville Tribe's right to re-
establish a fishery to replace the one lost to dam
construction. Colville Confederated Tribes v. Walton
(Colville I), 647 F.2d 42, 48 (9th Cir. 1981).

3. Pueblo Rights—Looking to Historic Uses

Pueblo rights are a unique feature of New Mexico
water law. For New Mexico pueblo tribes whose
water rights are not federally reserved, adjudicating
courts have looked at "historically irrigable acreage"
or an estimated average of the water used to
irrigate between the signing of the 1848 Treaty of
Guadalupe Hidalgo and the 1923 Pueblo Lands Act.
State ex rel. Reynolds v. Aamodt, 618 F. Supp. 993,
996 (D.N.M 1985); *accord* State ex rel. Martinez v.
Kerr McGee, 898 P.2d 1256, 1264–65 (N.M. App.
1995). The *Winters* standard does not apply to
Pueblo rights because the purpose was to protect
historic rights not create new rights based on a
reservation, U.S. v. Abouseleman, Civ. No. 83 cv
10141 MV-ACE at 26 (D. N.M. Oct. 4, 2004),
although lands set aside by the United States for
Pueblo use after 1848 may have Winters rights.
Cohen, supra at 321–324.

C. PRIMARY V. SECONDARY PURPOSES
FOR INDIAN WATER RIGHTS

For non-Indian reserved rights, *see* Section III of
this Chapter, the courts have limited the scope of
the reserved right to an amount of water needed to
achieve the primary purposes of the reservation.
Cappaert v. United States, 426 U.S. 128 (1976);

United States v. New Mexico, 438 U.S. 696, 700 (1978). The federal courts have not addressed whether this primary v. secondary purpose distinction applies in the context of Indian reserved rights. *See* Felix Cohen, Handbook of Federal Indian Law 1217–1220 (2012 ed.). The Arizona court, however, held that the distinction does not apply in the context of Indian reserved rights because "the essential purpose of Indian reservations is to provide Native American people with a 'permanent home and abiding place,' that is a 'livable' environment." In re General Adjudication of the Gila River System, 201 Ariz. 307, 313, 35 P.3d 68, 74 (Ariz. 2001).

D. CHANGE IN USE ON-RESERVATION

Once Indian reserved water rights have been quantified, they may be put to uses other than those for which they were quantified. For example, the Indian reservations along the Colorado River are entitled to certain quantities of water based upon their irrigable acreage. But the tribes may apply the water allocated to them to non-agricultural purposes. *See* Arizona v. California (Arizona II), 439 U.S. 419, 422 (1979) (affirming the Special Master's Report that stated once rights were established they could be utilized or disposed of for the benefit of the Indians as relevant law would allow); *See also*, United States v. Washington, 375 F. Supp.2d 1050, 1070 (W.D. Wash. 2005) ("Once the water rights of the Lummi have been quantified, the water may be used for any purpose, including domestic, commercial and industrial purposes.")

However, a divided decision of the Wyoming court in a later phase of the *Big Horn* case held that water rights quantified based on practicably irrigable acreage could not be changed to instream flow uses for fish without complying with Wyoming state law procedures for change of use. In re General Adjudication of All Rights to Use Water in the Big Horn River System (Big Horn III), 835 P.2d 273, 279–80 (Wyo. 1992). The decision was not appealed and there was no majority opinion for the court explaining the rationale.

E. USES OUTSIDE THE RESERVATION— TRANSFER OF INDIAN WATER RIGHTS

Federal reserved rights are considered to be interests in real property and are held subject to the restraints on alienation established by federal Indian Law, namely the Indian Non-Intercourse Act. 25 U.S.C § 177. Absent federal legislative permission, tribes probably cannot sell, lease, or exchange their water rights. 2 Water and Water Rights § 37.02(f). While Congress has not yet given any blanket approval to Indian water leasing or other marketing arrangements, several water rights settlement approved by Congress have given specific authorization for transfer or lease of water rights off-reservation. Public Law 109–410, 120 Stat. 2762 (2006) (authorizing tribes to enter into leases of water rights); Public Law 106–382; 114 Stat. 1454 (implementing provisions of the Fort Peck/Montana Compact of 1985 that allow leasing of Indian water rights). Recent reserved water rights settlements anticipate off-reservation leasing and other arrangements for non-Indian water use. The 1973 report of the National Water Commission recommended that leases of Indian reserved water rights be allowed to enable non-Indians to make efficient use of water resources not immediately needed by Indians. National Water Commission, Water Policies for the Future—Final Report to the President and to the Congress of the United States, 51–61 (1973).

In addition to the limitations imposed by the Indian Non-Intercourse Act, at least one state Supreme Court has rejected a proposal to sell reserved water rights off of the reservation. In re General Adjudication of the Big Horn Sys., 753 P.2d 76, 100 (Wyo. 1998).

F. WATER RIGHTS FOR INDIVIDUAL INDIAN ALLOTMENTS

The General Allotment Act of 1887, known as the "Dawes Act," fostered a policy of dividing up tribal lands into individual holdings. Act of Feb.8, 1887, 24 Stat. 388, ch. 119. The purpose was to convert Indians from their nomadic ways to agricultural pursuits; it was thought that the most efficacious way to do this was to give each Indian a parcel to farm. This failed policy continued for nearly 50 years until the passage of the Indian Reorganization Act of 1934. 25 U.S.C. § 461. Nothing in the General Allotment Act partitions a tribe's water rights as it did with tribal lands conveyed in severalty to individual Indians. Grey v. United States, 21 Cl.Ct. 285 (1990). In fact, Section 7 of the Act empowered the Secretary to promulgate regulations to "secure a just and equal distribution" of irrigation water among reservation Indians. 25 U.S.C. § 381. This provision merely confirmed that allottees have a right to use some share of tribal water rights, not that they would hold reserved rights. United States v. Powers, 305 U.S. 527, 533 (1939).

Many of the lands that were distributed through allotment were then conveyed to non-Indian owners. This raised questions of whether a non-Indian owner of allotted land could also claim a share of the tribal water right. In Colville Confederated Tribes v. Walton (*Colville I*), the Ninth Circuit Court of Appeals interpreted the Allotment Act as giving individual allottees a right to use a share of the tribe's reserved water rights. 647 F.2d 42, 50–51 (9th Cir. 1981). A non-Indian purchaser of an allotment can take the right to use a share of the tribe's reserved water with a priority date as of the creation of the reservation provided there has been reasonable diligence in putting the water to use. These *Walton* rights have been criticized as giving allotment purchasers an advantage over their neighbors whose lands were homesteaded; they obtain rights superior to most other private water users. This disrupts state law water allocation schemes, provides an incentive to transfer Indian lands to non-Indians, and divests tribes of their reserved water rights in a piecemeal fashion without congressional authorization. *See*, David H. Getches, Water Rights on Indian Allotments, 26 S.D. L. Rev. 405 (1981); Richard B. Collins, Indian Allotment Water Rights, 20 Land and Water L. Rev.

421 (1985). The Wyoming Supreme Court followed the Ninth Circuit's rule in Walton in considering claims from non-Indian allotees holding water rights. In re General Adjudication of All Rights to Use Water in the Big Horn River System, 899 P.2d 848 (Wyo. 1995).

If tribes reacquire former reservation lands the water rights associated with those lands are maintained, including a priority date at the time of the reservation, unless the land were ceded "surplus" lands. 2 Water and Water Rights § 37.02(f)(3). If tribes reacquire lands that were deemed "surplus" under the General Allotment Act, those lands have reserved rights, but courts have split on the priority date that will attach at reacquisition. The Ninth Circuit has held that the priority date is the date of reacquisition. United States v. Anderson, 736 F.2d 1358, 1363 (9th Cir. 1984). The Wyoming Supreme Court has held that the water rights maintain the original reservation priority date. In re Big Horn (Big Horn II), 753 P.2d 76, 113–14 (Wyo. 1988).

G. WATERS SUBJECT TO RESERVATION

Reserved water rights can be established for any water that is unappropriated at the time of the federal reservation. Winters v. United States, 207 U.S. 564, 577 (1908); Arizona v. California, 373 U.S. 546 (1963). In addition to having unappropriated water, there are questions involving whether the water sources must be within the boundaries of the reservation for a reserved right to exist. 2 Water

and Water Rights § 37.02(d). The courts have yet to
address precisely which water maybe claimed and
under what circumstances, but existing case law
gives a sense that reserved rights can be established
in off-reservation waters. Today, one of the most
important resolutions of this issue involves whether
groundwater can be reserved. *See* Section III.G of
this Chapter.

In cases like *Winters* where a stream borders an
Indian reservation or runs through a reservation,
selection of the particular land probably was
influenced by proximity to water, implying a
reservation of water from that source. But, a
reservation is not necessarily deprived of the benefit
of reserved water rights simply because there are no
water sources within its boundaries or because
those located there are inadequate for reservation
purposes. Thus, in Arizona v. California, 373 U.S.
546 (1963), the Supreme Court upheld an allocation
of water from the Colorado River to the Cocopah
Reservation some two miles away; water from the
river had been delivered to the reservation by an
irrigation canal for several years before the decision.
Id. at 596–98. In addition, the Ninth Circuit has
recognized a *Winans* reserved right that affected
waters outside the reservation even when that
original reservation had been terminated. U.S. v.
Adair, 723 F.2d 1394, 1411–12 (9th Cir. 1983).
Reservations of water-short tracts may have
occurred for many reasons. For example, Indians
may have chosen to retain an area where most of
them lived, ceding lands between their residential
community and water sources. Or, a reservation of

public land such as a national monument may have been created on a small tract dependent on a water source elsewhere.

Almost all states (except the original thirteen, Texas, and Hawaii) were created largely out of the public domain, where the government had control of virtually all waters. At the sufferance of the United States, private rights in those waters were created pursuant to state or territorial law. The reserved rights doctrine holds that the government impliedly withdrew its consent to creation of private rights each time it earmarked public lands for a specific federal purpose to the extent necessary to fulfill that purpose. Thus, the fact that a reservation was detached from water sources does not prove an absence of intent to reserve waters some distance away. Judicial references to such rights being "appurtenant" to reserved lands apparently refer not to some physical attachment of water to land, but to the legal doctrine that attaches water rights to land to the extent necessary to fulfill reservation purposes. Katie John v. United States, 720 F.3d 1214 (9th Cir. 2013) (reserved water rights are not limited to water within the borders of a federal reservation). The question whether a non-adjacent source may be used if on-reservation water is available may be influenced by practical considerations (such as ease of delivery or water quality) that make a distant source more practicable. If the government or a tribe elects one source from among several, a court is likely to defer to its exercise of discretion in making such a choice;

but if the choice is unreasonable, a court can be expected to intervene.

The Department of the Interior has taken the position that the doctrine applies to groundwater on Indian reservations, and the Arizona Supreme Court agreed that federal reserved rights extended to groundwater of an Indian reservation and the tribe was entitled to protection from groundwater pumping. In re the General Adjudication of All Rights to Use Water in the Gila River System & Source (Gila III), 989 P.2d 739, 797 (Ariz. 1999). The only instance in which a court has held to the contrary was in Wyoming's *Big Horn* adjudication. In re General Adjudication of the Big Horn Sys., 753 P.2d 76, 99–100 (Wyo. 1988).

III. FEDERAL RIGHTS FOR OTHER (NON-INDIAN) RESERVATIONS OF LAND

With the Supreme Court's decision in the *Pelton Dam* case in 1955 and then its decision in *Arizona v. California* in 1963, the reserved water rights doctrine, thought by some to be a principle of Indian law, was recognized as establishing water rights for non-Indian federal reserved lands. Federal Power Comm'n v. Oregon (Pelton Dam), 349 U.S. 435, 448 (1955); Arizona v. California, 373 U.S. 546, 601 (1963). In *Pelton Dam,* the Court upheld an implied reserved water rights for a power site withdrawal. In *Arizona v. California,* the Court upheld the extension of the reserved rights doctrine to a national recreation area, a national forest, and two wildlife refuges. The reserved water rights doctrine provides that when the federal government sets aside land for particular purposes, it also reserves sufficient unappropriated water to accomplish those purposes regardless of limitations that might otherwise be imposed on the use of that water under applicable state law.

Because many federal reservations were established before many state-based private rights were recognized, reserved water rights have been controversial and the subject of considerable litigation. Despite attempts to invalidate the extension of the doctrine to non-Indian federal lands, the doctrine has been upheld. The Supreme Court has, however, placed some limitations on the scope of federal reserved rights in terms of the purposes that can be protected and the quantities of water that can be reserved. Cappaert v. United States, 426 U.S. 128, 141 (1976); United States v. New Mexico, 438 U.S. 696, 700 (1978).

A. EXPRESS V. IMPLIED RIGHTS

The reserved water rights doctrine provides that a water right can be *implied* even if the reservation document is silent as to water. Winters v. United States, 207 U.S. 564, 576–77 (1908); United States v. Powers, 305 U.S. 527, 532 (1939); Arizona v. California, 373 U.S. 546, 600 (1963); Cappaert v. United States, 426 U.S. 128, 138 (1976); United States v. New Mexico, 438 U.S. 696, 698 (1978). When Congress or the Executive does not expressly reserve a water rights, the Court has found the creation of an implied federal reserved water rights based on an examination of the intent in reserving the federal land. In *Cappaert*, the Court stated that "the issue is whether the Government intended to reserve unappropriated and thus available water. Intent is inferred if the previously unappropriated waters are necessary to accomplish the purposes for which the reservation was created." 426 U.S. at 139.

Federal reserved water rights can also be expressly created in statutes, treaties or executive orders. *See, e.g.,* Calif. Desert Protection Act of 1994, Pub. L. No, 103–433, 108 Stat. 4471; Great Sand Dunes National Park and Preserve Act of 2000, Pub. L. 106–530, 114 Stat. 2527; Agua Fria Proclamation No. 7263 65 Fed. Reg. 2817, 2818 (January 11, 2000); Cascade Siskiyou Proclamation No. 7318, 65 Fed. Reg. 37247, 37250 (June 9, 2000). In fact, given the uncertainty, time, controversy, and cost associated with litigating reserved rights, Congress and the Executive have increasingly been explicit about reserved rights in new public land reserves. *See* John D. Leshy, *Water Rights for New Federal Land Conservation Programs: A Turn-Of-The-Century Evaluation*, 4 U. Denv. Water L. Rev. 271, 278 (2001) (citing specific examples of Congressional and Executive Branch reservations where water was expressly addressed).

B. RESERVATION CAN BE MADE THROUGH STATUTE, TREATY OR EXECUTIVE ORDER

Congress exercises its power to reserve waters whenever it sets aside land for purposes that require water. The land can be set aside by an act of

Congress, a treaty, or an executive order made
pursuant to a delegation of authority to the
President by Congress. Arizona v. California, 373
U.S. 546, 598 (1963); Parravano v. Babbitt, 70 F.3d
539, 547 (9th Cir. 1995).

C. PRIORITY DATE

Reserved water rights have a priority date based
on the date of the reservation. Cappaert v. United
States, 426 U.S. 128, 138 (1976). Reservations that
have lands added at a later date for similar or
additional purposes may have more than one
priority date. *See* United States v. Denver, 656 P.2d
1, 30 (1982) (recognizing that Rocky Mountain
National Park has multiple priority dates—1897,
when the area was set aside as a national forest,
and 1915 and 1930, when the area was established
as a national park). In Arizona v. California, 373
U.S. 546, 600 (1963), the Supreme Court followed
the relation back doctrine with regard to reserved
water rights by setting the priority date based on
when the lands were withdrawn rather than when
the final decision to designate these lands for
particular purposes was made.

D. DETERMINING THE PURPOSE
OF THE RESERVATION

1. Quantity

The quantity of water subject to federal or Indian
reserved rights is limited to the quantity necessary
to fulfill the purposes of the reservation. The
amount may change over time as needs change so

long as they are within the original purposes for
establishing a reservation. The Supreme Court held
that the government impliedly reserved "only that
amount of water necessary to fulfill the purpose of
the reservation, no more." Cappaert v. United
States, 426 U.S. 128, 141 (1976). In United States v.
New Mexico, 438 U.S. 696, 700 (1978), the Court
further limited the quantity of water that could be
reserved to water that fulfilled the the specific
purposes for which the land was reserved, not
secondary purposes. 438 U.S. at 700.

2. Primary Purposes

In *New Mexico*, the Court examined the language
and   legislative   history   of   the   Organic
Administration Act and its predecessor bills to reach
its conclusions regarding primary versus secondary
purposes. The Court found that, at the time of the
Organic Act, Congress had two primary purposes for
establishing national forests: timber production and
watershed protection. 438 U.S. at 714–715 (citing 16
U.S.C. § 473). The Act did not refer to fish and
wildlife or stock watering purposes for which the
U.S. had asserted rights. The Court contrasted the
Organic Act with legislation expressing concern for
wildlife as a primary purpose (such as the National
Park Service Act of 1916). It concluded that only
primary purposes trigger implied reserved rights.
Subsequent legislation such as the 1960 Multiple-
Use   Sustained-Yield   Act   broadened   the
administrative mandates for national forests to
include wildlife, recreation, and range, but did not
change the primary purpose of the national forest

reservations and therefore did not reserve any additional water for existing forests. *Id.* at 714–15. *See* United States v. City and County of Denver, 656 P.2d 1, 25–28 (Colo. 1982); United States v. Challis, 988 P.2d 1199, 1203–1207 (Idaho 1998).

3. Securing Water for Secondary Purposes Under State Law

In *U.S. v. New Mexico,* 438 U.S. at 702, the Supreme Court stated that the federal government must turn to state law to fulfill "secondary purposes" that were outside or beyond the primary purposes of the reservation. Even outside the context of the Court's decision in *New Mexico,* the federal government can and does hold rights under state law. *See, e.g.,* 60 Fed. Reg. 9894, 9937 (1995) (stating that BLM will assert rights under state law for livestock grazing on public land). In some instances, Congress may direct the federal government to acquire rights under state law. Great Sand Dunes National Park and Preserve Act of 2000, Pub. Law 106–530, 114 Stat. 2527, 16 U.S.C. § 410hhh.

States, however, cannot restrict the federal government's ability to secure state-based water rights or regulate those rights if those restrictions frustrate a federal purpose. In California v. United States, 438 U.S. 645, 677–78 (1978), the Supreme Court held that the state could condition use of state water rights acquired by the United States for a federal reclamation project, but any conditions that conflicted with congressional directives on how the

project was to operate would not be valid. A careful
examination of the relevant statutes is required to
determine congressional intent to allow the land
manager to appropriate and use water
inconsistently with state law.

Applications by the federal government to
appropriate water are considered on an equal basis
with applications by private parties. State v.
Morros, 766 P.2d 263, 269 (Nev. 1988). However,
difficult issues arise if state law fails to recognize
the kind of right that the federal government needs
to protect federal purposes. Frequently this tension
emerges in the context of instream flow rights.
Several western state courts have recognized federal
rights for instream flow. *See, e.g., id.;* DeKay v. U.S.
Fish and Wildlife Serv., 524 N.W.2d 855, 858 (S.D.
1994); McClellan v. Jantzen, 26 Ariz. App. 223, 225,
547 P.2d 494, 496 (1976). In Nevada and Arizona,
the state legislature has amended the water codes
in an attempt to overturn the results in these cases.
Nev. Rev. Stat. § 533.503; Ariz. Rev. Stat. § 45–
152(b). Often, questions of ownership, control,
subordination, and enforcement of federal rights
established under state law makes state-based
water rights much less attractive for the federal
government. Adell L. Amos, *The Use of State
Instream Flow Laws for Federal Lands: Respecting
State Control While Meeting Federal Purposes,* 36
Envtl. L. 1287, 1249 (2006). Courts have determined
that the federal government owns rights secured
under state law in the context of federal
Reclamation Projects. Strawberry Water Users
Ass'n. v. U.S., 2006 U.S. Dist. LEXIS 19767 (D.

Utah), *aff'd*, 576 F.3d 1133 (10th Cir. 2009); Klamath Basin General Stream Adjudication, Lead Case no. 003, Interim Order at 21, 29 (Jan. 12, 2006).

In states where riparian rights are recognized, the federal government, as a riparian landowner, may have water rights under state law. After the Supreme Court's decision in *U.S. v. New Mexico*, the Forest Service sought and secured recognition of riparian rights under California law to protect wildlife resources in the Plumas National Forest. In re Water of the Hallett Creek Stream System, 749 P.2d 324, *cert. denied sub nom.* California v. United States, 488 U.S. 824 (1988). The court noted, however, that these riparian rights were subject to state administrative control and could be restricted, like any other riparian right, where a conflict arose. *Id.* at 337; 2 Water and Water Rights § 37.06(c).

4. Other Regulatory Authority to Secure Water—Federal Regulatory Rights

Another outgrowth of the Supreme Court's decision in *U.S. v. New Mexico* was the emergence of efforts to utilize various federal regulatory and management authorities to protect water resources on federal reservations. Three categories of these "federal regulatory rights" exist. 2 Water and Water Rights § 37.06(c).

The first category of federal regulatory rights emerges from the federal government's authority to own, manage, and protect federal public lands and carry out congressionally-mandated purposes. The federal government possesses the authority to assert non-reserved federal rights to carry out congressional purposes on federal lands. 6 Op. Off. Legal Counsel 328 (1982); *see* Great San Dunes National Park and Preserve Act of 2000, Pub. L. No. 106–530, § 9(b)(2)(B) (directing the federal government to secure a federal water right to protect the Dunes ecosystem using the state process).

The second category of federal regulatory rights involves using general regulatory authority to manage public lands, particularly when permitting uses, in a manner that protects various environmental values. For example, the Forest Service and the Bureau of Land Management have broad authority to regulate activities on federal land, including placing conditions on rights-of-ways to protect resources. 43 U.S.C. §§ 1761(a)(1), 1765(a). Asserting rights on this basis, so-called "bypass flows" has been extremely controversial. The Ninth Circuit has upheld Forest Service's authority to impose bypass flows restrictions as a condition for a right-of-way permit. County of Okanogan v. National Marine Fisheries Service, 347 F. 3d 1081 (9th Cir. 2003). *See also* Trout Unlimited v. U.S. Dept. of Agriculture, 320 F. Supp. 2d 1090, 1106–10 (D. Colo. 2004) (upholding Forest Service's authority to impose bypass flows), *appeal dismissed,* 441 F.3d 1214 (10th Cir. 2006).

The third category of federal regulatory rights involves the assertion of water rights to carry out particular commands of specific regulatory statutes that do not involve the management of underlying federal lands, such as the Clean Water Act, the Endangered Species Act, and the Federal Power Act. 33 U.S.C. § 1251–1387; 16 U.S.C. § 1531–43; 16 U.S.C. § 792–825. To satisfy the requirements of these statutes—achieving water quality standards, protecting endangered species, or complying with terms of a hydropower license—water may be needed. The courts have upheld the exercise of this type of authority and its implications on water rights. Riverside Irrig. Dist. v. Andrews, 758 F.2d 508 (10th Cir. 1985); United States v. Glenn-Colusa Irrig. Dist., 788 F. Supp. 1126 (E.D. Cal. 1992); Public Interest Research Group of New Jersey v. Yates Indus., 757 F. Supp. 438 (D.N.J. 1991).

E. APPLICATION TO SPECIFIC CATEGORIES OF FEDERAL LAND

After the Supreme Court's decisions in *Cappaert v. United States* and *U.S. v. New Mexico*, the careful consideration of primary purposes became the central feature in trying to establish federal reserved water rights and the quantities in which they could be protected. These purposes are quite varied for different types of federal land reservations.

1. National Forests

In *United States v. New Mexico*, 438 U.S. 696 (1978), the Supreme Court rejected the government's claims of reserved rights for instream flows for a national forest established in 1899. The

instream flows, the government argued, were
needed for wildlife, recreation, aesthetics, and stock
watering. *Id.* at 705. However, the purposes stated
in the 1897 Organic Act only included "securing
favorable conditions of water flows, and furnish[ing]
a continuous supply of timber." *Id.* at 706. The
Court noted that the Multiple-Use Sustained-Yield
Act of 1960 expanded the purposes of national
forests to protect outdoor recreation, range, and fish
and wildlife. *Id.* at 714. Ultimately, the Court held
the new purposes to be secondary, and therefore not
within the scope of the reserved rights doctrine. *Id.*
at 715. The *New Mexico* court held that the United
States could secure rights for so-called "secondary
uses" under state law.

2. National Parks and National Monuments

Reserved water rights for National Parks derive
from the 1916 Organic Act which specifically
mentions the protection of water. 16 U.S.C. § 1c(a).
United States v. New Mexico contrasts the broad
coverage of this Act with the narrower coverage of
the Forest Service's original enabling act. 438 U.S.
696, 703 (1978). Compared to the Forest Service, the
National Park Service has had little difficulty
securing water for park purposes. Cappaert v.
United States, 426 U.S. 128 (1976); High Country
Citizens' Alliance v. Norton, 448 F. Supp. 2d 1235
(D. Colo. 2006). *Cf.* United States v. Denver, 656
P.2d 1, 27 (Colo. 1982) (narrowly construing the
purposes at Dinosaur National Monument, but
broadly construing Rocky Mountain National Park
purposes).

In addition to National Park units, the Park Service also manages numerous National Monuments. National Monuments are generally created by the Executive pursuant to the Antiquities Act of 1906. 113 P.L. 287, 128 Stat. 3094, 320301 2014 Enacted H.R. 1068. Reserved water rights may be asserted for the purposes of protecting a monument's historic or scientific significance. *See Cappaert*, 426 U.S. 128 (affirming reserved rights for Devil's Hole Monument); *U.S. v. Denver*, 656 P.2d at 28–29 (finding no reserved rights for recreation at Dinosaur Monument, but recognizing that there may be reserved rights for preserving fish habitats of historic and scientific interest). Many more recently created National Monuments have express federal reserved water rights or have statements that disclaim any reserved rights. *See e.g.* Rio Grande Del Norte National Monument, 2013 WL 1192324, at *4 (explicitly disclaiming any reserved rights to water).

3. National Wildlife Refuges

Wildlife refuges are managed by the Fish and Wildlife Service and are typically established though Executive Order. 16 U.S.C. § 668dd. The particular language of the various Orders has been used to establish the existence of a federal reserved water right. *See* Arizona v. California, 373 U.S. 546, 601 (1963) (recognizing a federal reserved water right for Havasu Lake National Wildlife Refuge); United States v. Alaska, 423 F2d 764, 767 (9th Cir. 1970) (recognizing a federal reserved water right for Kenai National Moose Range). The National

Wildlife Refuge System has not fared as well in
state court, with perhaps its most devastating loss
in United States v. State, 135 Idaho 655, 664, 23
P.3d 117, 126 (2001), as amended (May 1, 2001),
where the court rejected a federal reserved water
rights claim to protect the islands of the Deer Flat
National Wildlife Refuge. *Cf.* United States v.
Alpine Reservoir Co., 341 F.3d 1172, 1180–83 (9th
Cir. 2003) (upholding the Nevada State Engineers
transfer of irrigation rights to the Stillwater
National Wildlife Refuge for wetland restoration).

4. Wild and Scenic Rivers

Reserved waters for Wild and Scenic rivers,
unlike other federal designations, are not tied to
federal lands. The Wild and Scenic Rivers Act
explicitly calls for a quantity of free flowing water
necessary to sustain the "outstandingly remarkable
scenic, recreational, geologic, fish and wildlife,
historic, cultural, or other similar values" for which
a Wild and Scenic section is designated. 16 U.S.C.
§ 1271. *See* Potlatch Corp. v. United States, 12 P.3d
1256, 1258–59 (Idaho 2000) (upholding Wild and
Scenic reserved right but limiting it to the minimum
amount necessary to accomplish the purposes);
Oregon Natural Desert Assoc. v. Green, 953 F.
Supp. 1133, 1145–46 (D. Or. 1997) (upholding Wild
and Scenic reserved rights).

5. National Recreational Areas

National Recreation areas are managed by
various agencies and are typically areas that are

subject to heavy recreational use. Federal reserved water rights were recognized for the Lake Mead National Recreation Area in *Arizona v. California*. 373 U.S. 546, 601 (1963). *See* Potlatch Corp. v. United States, 134 Idaho 916, 925, 12 P.3d 1260, 1268–69 (2000) (recognizing a reserved right for Hells Canyon National Recreational Area as an express reservation of water); Idaho v. United States, 12 P.3d 1284, 1289–90 (Idaho 2000) (rejecting reserved rights for the Sawtooth National Recreation Area, finding that its purposes did not require water).

6. Wilderness Areas

Wilderness Areas are established under the Wilderness Act and can be managed by various agencies. The Wilderness Act provides that its purpose is to preserve areas in their natural condition for recreational, scenic, scientific, educational, conservation and historic uses. 16 U.S. C. §§ 1131(a), 1133(b).

The issue of implied reserved water rights in federally designated wilderness remains largely unsettled and quite controversial. The first court to confront the question held that reserved water rights are created when a wilderness area is established. Sierra Club v. Block, 622 F. Supp. 842, 859–60, 862 (D. Colo. 1985). However, the decision was vacated on appeal because the issue was not "ripe." It was not clear that harm to the wilderness character of the area would be so great and immediate as to violate the preservation mandate of

the statute. Sierra Club v. Yeutter, 911 F.2d 1405,
1414 (10th Cir. 1990). In a subsequent case, the
Colorado District Court confirmed that primary
purposes of the Wilderness Act include water
necessary for the preservation of wildlife, fish, and
other preservation-oriented uses. *High Country
Citizens' Alliance v. Norton*, 448 F. Supp. 2d at
1247. Although *Yuetter* and *High Country*
recognized that there was a reserved water right for
wilderness, the Idaho Supreme Court has gone back
and forth on this issue, eventually reversing a
politically unpopular decision that had reserved all
unappropriated waters instream within the bounds
of wilderness areas. Potlatch Corp. v. United States,
12 P.3d 1260 (Idaho 2000). For analysis, *see* Sandra
Zellmer, *Wilderness, Water, and Climate Change*, 42
Envtl. L. 313, 357–60 (2012).

In some instances, Congress has expressly
reserved water rights for wilderness areas. *See*
California Desert Protection Act, 108 Stat. 4471,
4498 (1994); Washington Park Wilderness Act, PL
100–668 102 Stat. 3961 (1998); Arizona Desert
Wilderness Act, Pub. L. No. 101–628, 104 Stat. 4469
(1990). In other cases, Congress has disclaimed
reserved rights for wilderness areas, usually to
alleviate irrigators' concerns and facilitate passage.
Colorado Canyons National Conservation Area and
Black Ridge Canyons Wilderness Act, Pub. L. No.
106–353, 114 Stat. 1374, 1378, § 6(l)(2) (2000).

7. Bureau of Land Management (BLM): Specified and Unspecified Public Lands

Unlike other federal lands, BLM lands are generally not reserved for particular purposes to which water rights attach. Even the Federal Land Policy and Management Act of 1976, which outlines specific purposes for BLM lands, was held to reserve no express or implied water rights on its own. Sierra Club v. Watt, 659 F.2d 203, 206 (D.C. Cir. 1981). However, the BLM administers a handful of National Monuments for which water may be reserved to protect specific historic or scientific purposes of the Monuments. Additionally, the National Landscape Conservation System Act included in the 2009 Omnibus Public Lands Act names the BLM as a key administrator over newly named conservation areas, wilderness study areas, Wild and Scenic rivers, and a National Monument. Pub. L. No. 111–11, § 2002(a); 123 Stat. 991.

8. Military Bases

Water is essential to run a military base, whether for consumption, power generation, or other military purposes. Unlike other federally reserved lands very little litigation has been brought involving military bases, although a few federal cases have addressed the issue in tangential ways. In Nevada, the federal court found that state law did not govern groundwater pumping on a naval base. Nevada ex rel. Shamberger v. United States, 165 F. Supp. 600 (D. Nev. 1958). *See* United States v. District Ct. in & for Water Dist. No. 5, 401 U.S. 527, 529 (1971) (implying reserved right for petroleum and shale oil reserves). The State of Nevada recognized groundwater rights for Nellis Air Force Base necessary for national defense purposes—a right that has been coined National Defense Water Rights. *See* Michael J. Cianci Jr. et al, *The New National Defense Water Right—An Alternative to Federal Reserved Water Rights for Military Installations*, 48 A.F. L Rev. 159 (2000). By contrast, the State of Idaho rejected a reserved water rights claim for the Mountain Home Air Force base. In re Snake River Basin Adjudication, Case No. 39576, Subcases 61–11783 (Idaho Dist. Ct. April 6, 2001).

F. TRANSFER OF FEDERAL RESERVED RIGHTS

By their nature, reserved water rights exist for the fulfillment of reservation purposes. In some situations, this may dictate that waters be used by private parties on the reserved public lands or Indian lands, such as a concessionaire operating a lodge in a national park or a lessee of irrigated tribal land. At least one state court has recognized the authority of the federal government to use its reserved rights in this way. United States v. Denver, 656 P.2d 1, 34 (Colo. 1982). Some states have asserted that reserved rights transfer to them when they became the trustees of school lands granted to the state by the federal government. But each court that has considered this issue has either avoided the question or ruled against the state. *See* Department of State Lands v. Pettibone, 702 P.2d 948 (Mont. 1985) (avoiding the question); State ex rel. State Engineer v. Comm'r of Public Lands, 200 P.3d 86, 95–99 (N.M. App. 2008) (concluding that state school lands have no reserved rights); In re Gila River System, Contested Case No. W1–104, Report of the Special Master (2007) (holding that state school lands have no associated reserved rights).

G. WATER SUBJECT TO RESERVATION

The courts have not provided a definitive answer on whether reserved rights may be claimed for water outside the boundaries of the reservation. 2 Water and Water Rights § 37.03(d). However, in *United States v. Cappaert*, the Supreme Court recognized a reserved right that impacted shared groundwater resources some of which occurred outside the reservation boundary. 426 U.S. 128, 143 (1976). The Supreme Court upheld an injunction against groundwater pumping by a private water user who had perfected water rights under state law after establishment of a nearby national monument. The purpose of the monument—preservation of the desert pupfish—would have been jeopardized by continued groundwater pumping. The Supreme Court in *Cappaert* said, "we hold that the United States can protect its water from subsequent diversion, whether the diversion is of surface or groundwater." *Id.* Another federal district court has held that the "same implications which led the Supreme Court to hold that surface waters had been reserved would apply to underground waters as well." Tweedy v. Texas Co., 286 F. Supp. 383, 385 (D.Mont. 1968). A state water court in Colorado ruled that reserved rights are limited to those waters "on, under, or touching the reserved lands," but on appeal the Colorado Supreme Court declined to address this issue, asserting that it was merely hypothetical. United States v. Denver, 656 P.2d 1, 31–33 (Colo. 1982).

IV. ADJUDICATION AND ENFORCEMENT OF RESERVED RIGHTS

In the prior appropriation system, ideally the priority dates and quantities of everyone's rights are known so that the system can be efficiently and effectively administered. This information, together with information on annual and seasonal flows, enables water rights holders to predict how much water may ordinarily be diverted. However, incorporating reserved water rights into state water law schemes presents difficulties. First, the quantities of rights impliedly reserved are without an easily definable limit. Second, historically, holders of reserved rights, the United States and Indian tribes, are immune from suit by virtue of their sovereign status, frustrating state efforts to adjudicate their rights or to regulate their water use. Third, if the reserved rights claims are substantial and hold an early priority but are not quantified, there is a degree of uncertainty for all junior water rights holders.

Several developments address these complexities. First, with the McCarran Amendment in 1952, Congress waived sovereign immunity such that the United States must assert reserved rights claim in a state general stream adjudication. Second, the U.S. continues to have the option of asserting reserved rights claims in federal court, particularly if there is no general stream adjudication pending in the state. However, the Colorado River abstention doctrine, discussed below, urges federal courts to abstain from deciding the quantity if the state has a pending proceeding. Finally, the trend toward negotiated settlements that are often enacted as congressional legislation provides a non-litigation mechanism for quantifying federal reserved water right claims for Indian and non-Indian land.

A. QUANTIFICATION BY ADJUDICATION

The most common method of quantification is by adjudication in federal or state court, although negotiated settlements are increasingly utilized to address unadjudicated reserved rights claims. With the passage of the McCarran Amendment in 1952, Congress waived sovereignty immunity and consented to be joined in state suits determining the water rights of all users on a system. Dugan v. Rank, 372 U.S. 609, 618 (1963). While the McCarran Amendment allowed federal water rights to be determined in state court, it did not remove jurisdiction over those claims from federal courts. Rather, Congress created a system of concurrent state and federal jurisdiction. The Supreme Court eventually articulated an abstention doctrine, known as Colorado River abstention, to address the appropriate relationship between state and federal courts when exercising this concurrent jurisdiction.

Colorado River Water Conservation District v.
United States, 424 U.S. 800, 818–20 (1976).

1. Joinder of the United States in State Court Actions—McCarran Amendment

Because the United States may not be sued
without its consent, Congress must waive
governmental immunity for a particular action or a
general class of cases. The United States has waived
its sovereign immunity for certain water rights
cases through the McCarran Amendment, 43 U.S.C.
§ 666. The statute specifically consents to joinder of:

> the United States as a defendant in any suit (1)
> for the adjudication of rights to the use of water
> of a river system or other source, or (2) for the
> administration of such rights, where it appears
> that the United States is the owner of or is in
> the process of acquiring water rights by
> appropriation under State law, by purchase, by
> exchange, or otherwise, and the United States
> is a necessary party to such suit.

Thus, when the state initiates a proceeding,
typically a general stream adjudication, to
determine the relative rights of private parties
throughout a stream system, the United States has
consented to jurisdiction over reserved rights
claims. United States v. District Ct. in & for Cty. of
Eagle, 401 U.S. 520, 524 (1971). The Amendment's
language refers only to federal "rights by
appropriation under State law, by purchase, by
exchange, or otherwise," but the court in *Eagle
County* found that the word "otherwise" included

reserved rights. *See* Justin Huber & Sandra Zellmer, The Shallows Where Federal Reserved Water Rights Founder: State Court Derogation of the Winters Doctrine, 16 U. Denv. Water L. Rev. 261, 289 (2013) (critiquing state court adjudication of federally reserved rights under the McCarran Act).

This language has been interpreted to include tribal reserved water rights claims as well. Colorado River Water Conservation District v. United States (Akin decision), 424 U.S. 800, 809–12 (1976); Arizona v. San Carlos Apache Tribe, 463 U.S. 545, 567 (1983). The water rights of Indian tribes are not federal property, but are rather private rights held by the United States as a fiduciary for the tribes. Consequently, it has been argued that they do not come within the consent to be sued under the McCarran Amendment, which applies only to rights of which "the United States is the owner." But in the *Akin* case, the Supreme Court ruled that Indian reserved rights are also covered by the Amendment because, "bearing in mind the ubiquitous nature of Indian water rights in the Southwest, it is clear that a construction of the Amendment excluding those rights from its coverage would enervate the Amendment's objective." 424 U.S. at 811. The Court has recognized that the McCarran Amendment does not waive the immunity of a tribe and that tribes may bring their own suits to adjudicate water rights. But concurrent federal court proceedings initiated by the tribe are subject to dismissal under *Akin* if the same rights are at stake in state proceedings.

The McCarran Amendment authorizes joinder of the United States only in a comprehensive adjudication of water rights in a stream system. This includes ongoing proceedings in Colorado's water courts, United States v. District Court In and For the County of Eagle, 401 U.S. 520, 524 (1971), and even state agency proceedings that are adjudicative in nature and are overseen by the courts. United States v. Oregon, 44 F.3d 758, 767 (9th Cir. 1994). It does not subject the government to state court jurisdiction in private suits to decide priorities between the United States and particular claimant. Dugan v. Rank, 372 U.S. 609 (1963).

Once the government is joined, it must adhere to state procedural requirements. *See* United States v. Bell, 724 P.2d 631, 642 (Colo. 1986) (failure to claim water source specifically precludes later filing for priority dates as of date of reservation). But the Supreme Court has made clear that McCarran's reach is jurisdictional only. It does not change the federal substantive law of reserved rights. Arizona v. San Carlos Apache Tribe, 463 U.S. 545, 566–68 (1983). The Supreme Court has also established that the McCarran Amendment's waiver of sovereign immunity does not allow a state court to collect statutorily required filing fees from the United States. United States v. Idaho, 508 U.S. 1, 8–9 (1993). Once the issues have been litigated, the doctrine of res judicata, or claim preclusion, bars the parties and those in privity with them from re-litigating issues that were conclusively determined. Nevada v. United States, 463 U.S. 110, 143–44

(1983); Montana v. United States, 440 U.S. 147, 153 (1979);

2. Reserved Rights Claims in Federal Court

Federal court jurisdiction does exist if the United States initiates suit. *See* 28 U.S.C. § 1345 (setting forth original jurisdiction in federal district courts for all civil actions, suits, or proceedings commenced by the United States). Although there is concurrent jurisdiction after the McCarran Amendment, the Supreme Court has upheld district court dismissal of a federally initiated action filed before the United States had been joined in a parallel state court proceeding. Colorado River Water Conservation District v. United States, 424 U.S. 800 (1976) (*Akin* case). However that case may be distinguishable because it involved exceptional circumstances. Although the federal suit was filed six weeks before the United States was served in the state court action, the state proceedings concerning the stream system in question had been ongoing and some 1000 other parties, though not the United States, were already before the state court. In the short time involved, nothing had occurred in federal court. The state court proceedings were comprehensive; the federal court action was piecemeal.

In 1983, the Supreme Court provided additional guidance on the relationship between state and federal courts with competing cases involving federal claims. Arizona v. San Carlos Apache, 463 U.S. 545 (1983). While the Court recognized that concurrent proceedings would be duplicative and wasteful, and could spawn an "unseemly and destructive race to see which forum can resolve the same issue first," the Court also emphasized that federal courts possessed concurrent jurisdiction. 463 U.S. at 367. After *San Carlos*, the lower courts have been divided on when the federal court should abstain in light of an ongoing state proceeding. 2 Water and Water Rights § 37.04(a)(2). *See* United States v. Adair, 723 F.2d 1394, 1405–06 (9th Cir. 1983), *cert. denied*, 467 U.S. 1252 (1984) (upholding the federal court's decision to proceed on existence of tribal claims in Oregon but deferring to the state proceedings for quantification); *cf.* Salt River Pima-Maricopa Indian Community v. United States, 12 Indian L. Rep. 3009 (D. Ari. 1985) (refusing to retain jurisdiction in federal court except with regard to certain exclusion of Indian lands); United States v. Bluewater-Toltec Irrig. Dist., 580 F. Supp. 1434, 1446–47 (D. N.M. 1984) (recognizing concurrent jurisdiction but abstaining to state court jurisdiction).

3. Duty to Assert Reserved Rights Claims

Often non-governmental entities, or sovereign tribes in the case of Indian reserved rights, have significant interests in the federal government robustly defending and prosecuting its reserved rights claims. With regard to Indian reserved rights, the United States is the trustee for those rights, but the U.S. Attorney General has the discretion, as the entity that represents the U.S. on tribal interests, to determine when to assert these rights. 25 U.S.C. §§ 2, 9; Pyramid Lake Paiute Tribe v. Morton, 499

F.2d 1095, 1097 (D.C. Cir. 1974). Both the Ninth and Tenth Circuits, however, have affirmed the trust duty, but have not held that it requires the federal government to assert tribal claims. Rather, the federal government must provide procedural regularity with regard to managing the trust. United States v. Eberhardt, 789 F.2d 1354, 1360–61 (9th Cir. 1986); Northern Arapahoe Tribe v. Hodel, 808 F.2d 741, 750 (10th Cir. 1987).

With regard to non-Indian federal reserved rights, there is no definitive answer. 2 Water and Water Rights § 37.04(b)(2). Concerned that the United States was not effectively protecting and prosecuting its reserved water rights claims in Utah, the Sierra Club filed suit urging that the United States had a public trust obligation to assert its rights. The D.C. Circuit dismissed the case on ripeness grounds, but did announce in dicta that, "in the event of a real and immediate water supply threat to the scenic, natural, historic or biotic resource values ... the Secretary must take appropriate action." Sierra Club v. Andres, 487 F. Supp. 443, 448 (D.C. Cir. 1980). Attempts to get a court to order the government to claim reserved rights when officials have exercised their prosecutorial discretion not to do so have been largely unsuccessful. Sierra Club v. Yeutter, 911 F.2d 1405, 1414 (10th Cir. 1990). In Shoshone-Bannock Tribes v. Reno, 56 F.3d 1476, 1481 (D.C. Cir. 1995), the tribes failed to show a legal limitation on the Attorney General's discretion. However, in Pyramid Lake Paiute Tribe v. Morton, 354 F. Supp. 252, 256–57 (D.D.C. 1972)

supplemented, 360 F. Supp. 669 (D.D.C. 1973) rev'd,
499 F.2d 1095 (D.C.Cir. 1974), the court found an
abuse of discretion in failing to claim and protect an
Indian tribe's reserved rights.

B. NEGOTIATED SETTLEMENTS

Another means of quantifying reserved rights is
by negotiated agreement. In the face of long and
costly adjudication proceedings and the potential
impact of un-quantified time-immemorial (or early
priority date) rights, negotiated settlements began
to emerge as an option to addressing reserved water
rights claims. These settlements can be costly and
time consuming because regardless of the format—
adjudication or settlement—the complexities of
bringing all the appropriate parties and
determining the quantity of water rights are still
present.

There is considerable variation in the form of
these negotiated agreements—from the Reserved
Water Rights Compact Commission in Montana, to
stipulated settlement agreements as part of an
ongoing McCarran adjudication, to settlement
facilitated through the Secretary's Indian Water
Rights Office at the Department of Interior. 2 Water
and Water Rights § 37.04(c)(1). In 1990, the federal
government published guidance for conducting
Indian water rights settlements. 55 Fed. Reg. 9223
(1990). Settlements typically not only quantify
Indian rights, but also provide funds (federal plus
state cost sharing) or water sources (often from a
new or existing federal project) to enable tribes to

use water without infringing on established non-Indian uses. Many settlements allow for limited marketing of Indian water on and off the reservation. Some provide "development funds" to the tribes. In addition, a settlement may deal with matters like efficient use, conservation, environmental concerns, and interstate compact obligations.

Once the terms are agreed upon, most of these agreements are ratified, and often funded, by Congress. Well over thirty Indian water rights settlements in one form or another have been negotiated. 2 Water and Water Rights § 37.04(c)(1). *See* Robert T. Anderson, Indian Water Rights, Practical Reasoning, and Negotiated Settlements, 98 Cal. L. Rev. 1133, 1160–63 (2010) (providing a comprehensive list to date).

CHAPTER NINE

INTERSTATE AND INTERNATIONAL ALLOCATION

Because state and international political boundaries generally do not correspond to the boundaries of river basins or aquifers, unique approaches are often needed to manage water and to settle disputes. Traditional exercises of state police power or national sovereignty may be inadequate to undertake desirable planning concerning transboundary waters or to resolve disputes. As the demands for water within shared basins intensify, the need for both interstate and international management and planning increases, as does the need for a reliable method of resolving disputes over the allocation, depletion, and pollution of transboundary waters.

The first three sections of this chapter illustrate how interstate disputes have been resolved by judicial allocation (interstate litigation), compacts (interstate agreements), and legislative allocation (congressional apportionment). Section IV addresses constitutional constraints on state efforts to prevent water exports. Finally, Section V turns to international waters. International treaties or conventions governing international water disputes typically reflect the doctrines of limited territorial sovereignty and equitable apportionment. Treaties often contain a dispute resolution mechanism or defer to the International Court of Justice (ICJ) for interpretation when conflicts arise.

I. INTERSTATE ADJUDICATION

A. LITIGATION BETWEEN PRIVATE PARTIES

A typical interstate suit between private parties involves a downstream plaintiff alleging harm from diversions of an upstream defendant in another state. Some cases involve upstream pollution. The court in which the suit is brought must have jurisdiction over both parties and subject matter.

1. Personal Jurisdiction

Personal jurisdiction is usually obtained by personal service upon the defendant within the defendant's state of residence. Long-arm statutes, however, have removed the necessity of bringing suit in the defendant's state. 4 Wright and Miller, Fed. Prac. & Proc. Civ. § 1068 (3d ed. 2014 update).

2. Subject Matter Jurisdiction

Private parties generally bring suit in the state courts of defendant's or plaintiff's state. Action may be brought in federal court if the suit meets the requirements of subject matter jurisdiction (*i.e.*, diversity of citizenship and amount in controversy, or a federal question).

The ability of a court in one state to adjudicate water use in another state was not always well settled. An early view held that an action to establish water rights was in the nature of a quiet title action over real property; thus, the suit must be brought in the state where the real property is situated. Conant v. Deep Creek & Curlew Valley Irr.

Co., 66 P. 188 (Utah 1901). Subsequent opinions adopted the more liberal view of jurisdiction that once a court obtains personal jurisdiction over a nonresident *party*, the decree need not operate directly upon the *property*; the court can enforce its decree by using the coercive effect of its contempt power. The Ninth Circuit employed this personal jurisdiction-coercion theory in Brooks v. United States, 119 F.2d 636 (9th Cir. 1941). *Brooks* involved the water rights of Arizona and New Mexico users on the Gila River. Defendants had submitted to jurisdiction in Arizona and the court was held to have exclusive jurisdiction to adjudicate the matter, although the rights of water users in the adjoining state had to be considered.

Problems of jurisdiction are magnified in a general stream adjudication, where all affected users on a stream must be joined. If the United States has water rights on the stream, it too must be joined. A federal statute, the McCarran Amendment, waives sovereign immunity and consents to state court jurisdiction to adjudicate federal water rights in general stream adjudications for this purpose. 43 U.S.C. § 666. In order to invoke the McCarran Amendment, plaintiffs must demonstrate that the contested matter is "a comprehensive adjudication of all water rights" of the involved basin in that particular state. Frenchman Cambridge Irr. Dist. v. Heineman, 974 F. Supp. 2d 1264, 1280 (D. Neb. 2013).

3. Applicable Law

Where individual water users in one state attempt to prevent interference with interstate waters by individual water users in another state, substantial differences in the respective state laws can make it difficult to determine rights. For instance, if a downstream state follows riparian law and an upstream state follows appropriation law, can an individual in the downstream state insist on unimpeded flows, thereby defeating the established uses of upstream appropriators? It is theoretically simpler, however, to integrate priorities of water users on a stream that crosses state lines when both are appropriation states. In an early case, the Supreme Court presumed that disputes among such users would be resolved by priority, as if no state boundary existed. Bean v. Morris, 221 U.S. 485 (1911). However, the decision did not limit either state in how it defines or regulates rights to waters within its boundaries (absent federal legislation or an interstate adjudication). The idea that Congress conveyed public lands into private hands upon the condition that waters would be allocated by prior appropriation without regard to state lines has been argued, but not widely accepted. *E.g.*, Howell v. Johnson, 89 F. 556 (C.C.Mont. 1898).

Basic differences in state water laws as well as jurisdictional and enforcement problems have led states to pursue litigation in which they represent their citizens collectively in their *parens patriae* capacity to protect the health, safety, and welfare of the citizenry. *See, e.g.*, Kansas v. Colorado, 206 U.S.

46, 117 (1907). As described below, this type of litigation allows for more comprehensive solutions, but it has been limited to major interstate rivers where there is a multiplicity of parties rather than litigation among individuals on a small stream with few competing users, as in Bean v. Morris, 221 U.S. 485 (1911).

4. *Parens Patriae* Suits

When one state sues private parties in another state in its role as *parens patriae* to prevent harm to its own citizens, the Supreme Court has original, but not exclusive, jurisdiction; there is concurrent federal district court jurisdiction. 28 U.S.C. § 1251(b)(3).

States have standing to sue in their *parens patriae* capacity under certain limited conditions. The state must have an interest independent of its individual citizens so the suit is not merely an attempt to act on behalf of individuals, and a substantial portion of the state's inhabitants must be adversely affected. Massachusetts v. EPA, 549 U.S. 497, 519 (2007); Georgia v. Tenn. Copper Co., 206 U.S. 230 (1907). In disputes over water, this usually requires that the downstream state be substantially affected by actions in an upstream state. Kansas v. Colorado, 206 U.S. 46 (1907).

A state suing in *parens patriae* is deemed to represent all its citizens, and each citizen is bound by the decree. Thus, private suits are often foreclosed once the state's rights are adjudicated. *Parens patriae* actions are further limited by the

Eleventh Amendment to the U.S. Constitution, which states that the judicial power of the United States shall not be construed to extend to any suit brought by citizens of one state against another state. This prevents a state from invoking the Supreme Court's original jurisdiction in a suit against another state if the plaintiff state is seeking a remedy for individual citizens (*e.g.,* money damages) that would be prohibited in a suit brought directly by the individuals. *See id.;* New Hampshire v. Louisiana, 108 U.S. 76, 91 (1883); North Dakota v. Minnesota, 263 U.S. 365, 374–75 (1923).

5. Enforcement

Decrees in private interstate suits can raise difficult enforcement problems, particularly when continuing supervision is required. For instance, in Lindsey v. McClure, 136 F.2d 65 (10th Cir. 1943), the court invalidated the New Mexico State Engineer's attempt to forbid a water company from taking water from a New Mexico dam for use in Colorado. The court stated that the proper enforcement mechanism was by judicial procedure, not by order of the state engineer. In Bean v. Morris, 221 U.S. 485 (1911), however, the Supreme Court did not hesitate to uphold a federal court's enforcement of priorities across state lines where both states followed the prior appropriation doctrine.

B. LITIGATION BETWEEN STATES

1. Original Jurisdiction of the Supreme Court

The Supreme Court has original jurisdiction in all cases in which a state is a party. U.S Const. art. 3, § 2, cl. 2; 28 U.S.C. § 1251(a)(1). In suits between states, the Supreme Court serves as a trial court. Procedurally, the action begins when a state files a complaint and typically moves to hearings on motions to dismiss on jurisdictional or other grounds. If the complaint survives the motions, the respondent state files an answer. The Court often appoints a special master to hear and evaluate evidence, prepare findings of fact and conclusions of law, and recommend a decree, which the Court is free to follow or disregard.

The decree in an adjudication between states is binding on all claimants to the water in question, whether or not they were parties to the suit, because private users have no rights in excess of the state's share of the stream under the doctrine of *parens patriae*. Kansas v. Colorado, 206 U.S. 46 (1907). A decree in such a suit has *res judicata* (claim preclusion) effect. Alaska Sport Fishing Ass'n v. Exxon Corp., 34 F.3d 769, 773 (9th Cir. 1994). Private intervenors are not permitted unless the intervenor can show a compelling interest apart from that of a citizen of the state. South Carolina v. North Carolina, 558 U.S. 256, 266 (2010).

The Supreme Court has been reluctant to hear water allocation disputes for a number of reasons, including: (1) the vagueness of standards of apportionment; (2) the need for continuing supervision and the Court's disinclination to play the role of referee; (3) the daunting nature of technical data involved and the Court's lack of special expertise; and (4) the expense of litigation. Even when it has taken jurisdiction, the Court has suggested that interstate compacts can lead to superior solutions. Sporhase v. Nebraska ex rel. Douglas, 458 U.S. 941, 960 n.20 (1982) (citing Colorado v. Kansas, 320 U.S. 383, 392 (1943)).

2. Justiciability

Article III of the U.S. Constitution confines federal court jurisdiction to "cases or controversies." Even if a court has both personal and subject matter jurisdiction, it may decline to adjudicate cases that are not "justiciable"—that is, in a form suited to judicial resolution. Nebraska v. Wyoming, 325 U.S. 589, 610–11 (1945). A suit may be rendered non-justiciable if it is moot, collusive, not ripe, or a "political question" (i.e., would usurp executive or legislative authority).

The issue of justiciability usually arises in water cases as a ripeness problem (e.g., there is no present "harm" to a downstream state claiming excessive use upstream, leading courts to find no case or controversy). In such cases, the allocation of water rights for future development cannot be adjudicated. Further, the Supreme Court has refused to issue declaratory decrees in interstate water disputes. Arizona v. California, 283 U.S. 423, 464 (1931). This stance can perpetuate inequitable or uneven development on interstate streams because the lack of secure water rights may hinder investment financing or congressional authorization of water development projects.

3. Sources of Law: The Doctrine of Equitable Apportionment

The Supreme Court has developed a body of federal common law to resolve disputes over the allocation of interstate rivers. Federal common law is applied in a narrow class of cases where there is a significant federal policy or interest that will not be effectuated by the application of state law or by federal statutes. As such, the federal courts play a unique role in fashioning the rules of decision in cases involving state boundaries or shared resources like interstate rivers.

If Congress has spoken directly to the issue, the courts will decline to apply common law and instead defer to statutory law. When the Supreme Court took jurisdiction over a nuisance suit by two states charging Milwaukee with polluting Lake Michigan with sewage, it found that federal common law had been displaced by the intervening enactment of the Clean Water Act. Milwaukee v. Illinois, 451 U.S. 304 (1981).

In the rare instances where Congress has entered the realm of interstate water allocation, it has displaced the federal common law. *See, e.g.,* Arizona v. California, 373 U.S. 546 (1963). For the majority of disputes between states over interstate allocations, however, the Supreme Court has

developed a comprehensive federal common law
doctrine known as "equitable apportionment." The
doctrine was announced in 1907 in Kansas v.
Colorado, 206 U.S. 46 (1907). A basic tenet of the
doctrine is that "equality of right," not equality of
amounts apportioned, should govern. "Equality of
right" simply means that the states stand "on the
same level," or "on an equal plane . . . in point of
power and right, under our constitutional system."
Wyoming v. Colorado, 259 U.S. 419, 465 (1922).

The Court is not bound by the laws of the
individual states. Thus, where strict application of
riparian law would have prevented New York, an
upstream state, from diverting water for use in New
York City, the Court denied downstream New
Jersey's request for an injunction. Instead, it sought
to balance equities to "achieve an equitable
apportionment, without quibbling over formulas."
New Jersey v. New York, 283 U.S. 336 (1931).

In a dispute between two prior appropriation
states, the Court has applied the prior appropriation
doctrine as the method of equitable apportionment.
Wyoming v. Colorado, 259 U.S. 419 (1922).
Application of the prior appropriation doctrine is
qualified, however, in that the allocation must be
equitable. Factors that inform equitable
apportionment (and that might justify deviation
from strict priority) include:

   (1) Physical and climatic conditions;

   (2) Consumptive use of water in the several
        sections of the river;

(3) Character and rate of return flows;

(4) Extent of established uses and economies built on them;

(5) Availability of storage water;

(6) Practical effect of wasteful uses on downstream areas; and

(7) Damage to upstream areas compared to the benefits to downstream areas if upstream uses are curtailed.

Nebraska v. Wyoming, 325 U.S. 589, 618 (1945).

In Colorado v. New Mexico, 459 U.S. 176 (1982), the Court refused to apply strict priorities between two prior appropriation states where the effect would have been to protect wasteful and inefficient downstream uses in New Mexico at the expense of newer, more efficient uses in Colorado. But in Colorado v. New Mexico II, 467 U.S. 310 (1984), the Court declined to allocate water to junior users in Colorado to the detriment of the inefficient appropriators in New Mexico because Colorado lacked a concrete, long-term plan for future water use.

Environmental considerations may be taken into account when determining whether to follow strict priorities in an interstate apportionment. In Nebraska v. Wyoming, 515 U.S. 1, 12 (1995), the Court allowed Nebraska to amend its pleadings to include damages to downstream wildlife habitat in addition to downstream irrigators.

The Supreme Court occasionally deviates from strict priority among appropriators in prior appropriation states by use of the "mass allocation" approach. *See* Wyoming v. Colorado, 259 U.S. 419 (1922), *modified*, 260 U.S. 1 (1922), *vacated*, 353 U.S. 953 (1957). Since the Court is reluctant to interject itself into intrastate allocations, it awards to each state a quantity of water to be distributed by the state's appropriation system. The Court may hold that certain specific diversions are within one state's share of the allocation, that a state may have a stated quantity of water, or that a state may have a given percentage of the flow, regardless of the mix of individual priorities within the state.

II. INTERSTATE COMPACTS

Interstate compacts are used to effectuate a variety of objectives by mutual agreement of two or more states. Compacts relating to interstate waters have been formed to allocate water between the states, but also to address issues involving storage, flood control, pollution control, and comprehensive basin planning (principally by joint federal-state compacts). Although the first interstate water allocation compact was enacted in the arid West in response to a dispute over the Colorado River, compacts have been used to settle conflicts in the East and the South as well (the Delaware, the Potomac, and the Susquehanna River Compacts are notable examples). Compacts have an advantage over adjudication in that compacts avoid the justiciability problems encountered when the stream system in question is not yet over-appropriated. A compact allows parties to allocate unappropriated water, thus making a "present appropriation for future use." The ability to make such determinations in advance is crucial to long range water planning.

A. CONSTITUTIONAL AUTHORITY

The basis for negotiating interstate compacts is found in article I, § 10, clause 3 of the Constitution, which states:

> No state shall, without the consent of Congress . . . enter into any agreement or compact with another state, or with a foreign power. . . .

The compact clause impliedly recognizes state power to negotiate and enter into agreements subject to congressional consent. Compacts "adapt[ ] to our Union of sovereign States the age-old treaty making power of independent sovereign nations." Hinderlider v. La Plata River & Cherry Creek Ditch Co., 304 U.S. 92 (1938).

Typically, compact formation involves four steps. First, Congress authorizes negotiation of the compact, usually providing for a federal representative at the negotiations. Then, the compact is negotiated and the affected state legislatures approve the compact. Finally, Congress must consent to the compact.

Congress's consent determines whether the compact is a permissible agreement or a constitutionally prohibited "treaty, alliance, or confederation." Exactly what kind of interstate agreement requires congressional consent is the subject of considerable debate. One view is that consent is required only for agreements that alter the political power of states, potentially upsetting the political balance of the union. Virginia v. Tennessee, 148 U.S. 503 (1893). Others contend that consent is required for all interstate compacts, based on an implication in State ex rel. Dyer v. Sims, 341 U.S. 22, 27 (1951), stating that congressional consent was required for a water sanitation compact, "as for all compacts." Nevertheless, there is general agreement that compacts allocating interstate waters require congressional consent.

B. ADMINISTRATION AND ENFORCEMENT OF COMPACTS

Compacts often call for the creation of an administrative agency, typically a "compact commission," to make rules to implement the compact and to collect information on physical circumstances (*e.g.,* rate of river flow) for determining whether and to what extent certain provisions of the compact are applicable. Compact commissions are usually comprised of members appointed by the governors of the party states and a federal member with no vote or only a tie-breaking vote. States have been hesitant to vest substantial powers or prerogatives in a compact agency.

A state found to have violated a compact may be required to pay damages in cash rather than increased future water deliveries. Texas v. New

Mexico, 482 U.S. 124 (1987); Kansas v. Colorado, 533 U.S. 1 (2001). Monetary damages may be limited to reimbursement for damages actually suffered by the injured state, rather than the economic advantage or enrichment gained by the party in breach. Arbitrator's Final Decision in Kansas v. Nebraska, 538 U.S. 720, p.7 (2009) (No. 126), available at http://dnr.ne.gov/Legal/Rep_ River_Final_Decision_92009.pdf. Disgorgement may also be considered an appropriate remedy. In Kansas v. Nebraska, 135 S. Ct. 1042 (2015), the Court required Nebraska to pay $1.8 million in disgorgement, in addition to $3.7 million in damages to Kansas, under the Republican River Compact. The Court found disgorgement to be an appropriate remedy because it would "remind[ ] Nebraska of its legal obligations, deter[ ] future violations, and promote[ ] the Compact's successful administration." *Id.* at 1057.

The Court in *Kansas v. Nebraska* also adopted the Special Master's recommendation that the accounting procedures of the Compact be reformulated to more accurately account for imported water finding its way to the river. *Id.* at 1063. According to the Court, the contentious history of the states over the Republican River necessitated this rare grant of reformation and that it may not be available as a remedy in other cases. "In another case, with another history, we might prefer to instruct the parties to figure out for themselves how to bring the Accounting Procedures in line with the Compact. But we doubt that further

discussions about this issue will be productive." *Id.*
(internal citations omitted).

C. LEGAL EFFECT OF COMPACTS

1. Limitations on Private Water Users

As is the case with equitable apportionments by
the Supreme Court, apportionments by compact are
binding upon the citizens of the compacting states
whether or not individual citizens were parties to
the negotiations. In Hinderlider v. La Plata River &
Cherry Creek Ditch Co., 304 U.S. 92 (1938), New
Mexico and Colorado had agreed to divide the flow
of the La Plata River equally so each state would get
the full flow of the river every other day. The
plaintiff, a senior appropriator, sought to enjoin the
rotation scheme as a violation of rights established
under state law. The Court denied relief, stating
that a water rights decree under state law cannot
confer water rights in excess of the state's share of
the waters. It also held that there had been no
compensable taking of vested property rights or
violation of due process because the plaintiff had
ample opportunity to object during the negotiations,
and there was no evidence of inequity or bad faith in
the negotiations nor of a defect in the compact's
formation.

2. Effect of Congressional Ratification

State legislation that conflicts with terms of an
interstate compact cannot prevent enforcement of
the compact. State ex rel. Dyer v. Sims, 341 U.S. 22
(1951). But there is some uncertainty over the

extent to which Congress is bound by its ratification of compact terms. Although it cannot modify the terms of an agreement between states, Congress might condition its ratification upon agreement of the states to modify the compact. Congress also retains power to override a compact provision by explicit legislation.

Unilateral state actions that interfere with interstate commerce violate the Dormant Commerce Clause. Sporhase v. Nebraska ex rel. Douglas, 458 U.S. 941 (1982). But Congress has power to authorize states to regulate and impose burdens on commerce that would otherwise be unconstitutional. Thus, congressional consent to a compact may have the effect of immunizing state legislation from attack as an interference with interstate commerce. Tarrant Reg'l Water Dist. v. Herrmann, 133 S. Ct. 2120 (2013); Intake Water Co. v. Yellowstone River Compact Comm'n, 769 F.2d 568 (9th Cir. 1985). Once ratified, a compact has the effect of a federal law and thus may preempt inconsistent state laws. Hinderlider v. La Plata River & Cherry Creek Ditch Co., 304 U.S. 92 (1938).

D. INTERPRETATION OF COMPACTS

The Supreme Court is the final arbiter of the meaning of compacts. Although one guidepost is the Court's own standard of equitable apportionment, the Court's ultimate mission is to determine the intent of the parties. Montana v. Wyoming, 131 S. Ct. 1765, 1771 (2011). In Oklahoma v. New Mexico, 501 U.S. 221 (1991), the Court probed into extrinsic evidence of the history of negotiations of the Canadian River Compact to interpret ambiguous terms consistently with the probable intent of the parties.

The Pecos River Compact provided that New Mexico would deliver water to Texas based on "the 1947 conditions" of the river, with those conditions being defined in a document that used incorrect data. The compact commission (with even representation from the two states) deadlocked on whether to follow the document or to base the allocation on actual river conditions. The special master recommended that the commission be restructured so it could resolve the matter, but the Court found that doing so would change the compact's terms. Instead, it ordered the special master to resolve the matter using accurate data, which the Court apparently believed to be the intention of the parties. Texas v. New Mexico, 462 U.S. 554 (1983).

Whether lower federal courts have jurisdiction to interpret compacts turns on whether the dispute is a federal question (*i.e.*, "arises under the Constitution, laws, or treaties of the United States"). Although courts have found federal question jurisdiction to interpret interstate compact provisions (*see* League to Save Lake Tahoe v. Tahoe Reg'l Planning Agency, 507 F.2d 517 (9th Cir. 1974)), the suit may be barred by other jurisdictional impediments, such as sovereign immunity or lack of standing. Frenchman

Cambridge Irr. Dist. v. Heineman, 974 F. Supp. 2d 1264 (D. Neb. 2013).

III. LEGISLATIVE ALLOCATION

The lone example of a legislative allocation of interstate waters concerns the Colorado River. In Arizona v. California, 373 U.S. 546 (1963), the Supreme Court held that Congress, in passing the Boulder Canyon Project Act of 1928, intended to divide the waters of the river among the lower basin states. In so holding, the Court recognized that Congress has authority to act when the other apportionment mechanisms of compacts and judicial allocation have failed, are unavailable, or are not used.

What made the situation so compelling that Congress ultimately stepped in? Of the lower basin states, California experienced early rapid economic growth and a large population influx. Water was used extensively for irrigation, especially in the Imperial Valley. Arizona had experienced relatively gradual expansion, but it anticipated future growth. Most of Arizona's historic uses had been satisfied by pumping groundwater because geographical obstacles and lack of diversion facilities limited its access to Colorado River water. Declining water tables as a result of groundwater mining, however, indicated that preserving Arizona's economy would eventually require resort to the waters of the Colorado. An elaborate diversion and transportation project was proposed, and the Central Arizona

Project was developed to bring Colorado River water to the most populated parts of the state.

A compact commission in 1922 agreed to allocate the Colorado's annual flow approximately equally between the upper basin states (Colorado, New Mexico, Utah, and Wyoming) and the lower basin states (Arizona, California, and Nevada). At the time, the annual flow was assumed to be over 15 million acre-feet (MAF); we now know that it varies dramatically, from a low of 4.4 MAF to a high of about 24 MAF per year, which makes compact implementation all the more challenging.

Ratification of the compact was stalled by a long-standing dispute between Arizona and California over their respective shares in the 7.5 MAF allocated to the lower basin. Arizona feared the compact would solidify California's claim to most of the water and refused to ratify it. Weary of the impasse, Congress enacted the Boulder Canyon Project Act in 1928, authorizing construction of Hoover Dam and a series of other storage reservoirs on the Colorado. It was opposed by Arizona. The Act was conditioned on acceptance of the compact arrangement by at least six of the seven states. California also had to agree to limit its allocation to 4.4 MAF plus half of any lower-basin surplus. The legislation further authorized a separate lower basin compact that would give Arizona 2.8 MAF and Nevada 300,000 AF. No such compact was negotiated. After several attempts to stop construction of the Hoover Dam failed in the Supreme Court, Arizona brought suit for an equitable apportionment of the waters of the lower Colorado. The suit was dismissed because the United States, an indispensable party, refused to be joined. Arizona v. California, 298 U.S. 558 (1936). The U.S. later consented to suit, and after a three-year trial before a special master, the Supreme Court, approving most aspects of the master's report, held:

(1) Congress may, under its navigation and general welfare powers, apportion interstate streams by legislation.

(2) By enacting the Boulder Canyon Project Act, Congress exercised this power by "apportioning" 4.4 MAF to California and by specifying Arizona's and Nevada's shares through the authorization of a lower basin compact. Furthermore, Congress delegated to the Secretary of the Interior the power to contract for storage and delivery of project waters, and the Secretary then executed contracts reflecting the authorized shares.

(3) Federal law controls both the interstate and intrastate distribution of project waters, preempting state water law. (Note the contrast to the mass allocation approach, which leaves intrastate allocation to state law.) Therefore, the Secretary is empowered to allocate waters in times of shortage by any reasonable method, although "present perfected rights" must be satisfied.

(4) Water from Arizona's tributaries (1.75 MAF) is not part of the allocation to be shared with California, but is available to Arizona in addition to its allocation of 2.8 MAF of mainstem water.

Arizona v. California, 373 U.S. 546 (1963). The Court's inclination to find that federal power to allocate water between states existed and had been exercised in the Boulder Canyon Project Act likely reflects the Court's preference for congressional allocations of interstate waters over judicial allocations that require complex litigation.

A series of large dams and reservoirs were built under the authority of the Boulder Canyon Project Act and subsequent legislation. After many years, the Central Arizona Project was built, placating Arizona's concerns, but as a condition of the authorizing legislation it was necessary for Arizona to agree to subordinate its share of Colorado River to California's entitlement. In the following years, California's demands outstripped its legal entitlement. The Secretary of the Interior deferred to the basin states to negotiate rules for operating the facilities and dealing with shortages and surpluses, particularly as it became apparent that historical flows and cyclical shortage frustrated fulfillment of the expectations of water users in the several states. With rare exceptions, the Secretary then adopted rules reflecting the agreements. These agreements have sought to optimize use of the river's water with provisions for conservation, sharing shortages, redefining "surplus", and allowing water marketing. In 2003, California began implementing a complicated Quantification Settlement Agreement that is intended to bring its usage of Colorado River water within limits of the Compact. In re Quantification Settlement Agreement Cases, 134 Cal. Rptr. 3d 274 (2011), *cert. denied*, 133 S. Ct. 312 (2012).

Meanwhile, Arizona created a "water bank" to store its currently unneeded allocation of Colorado River water in aquifers around the state for future use. In 2004, Arizona agreed to store 1.25 MAF of its share for Nevada to use in times of shortage. Nevada agreed to pay $400 million to cover storage and delivery costs, and the two states agreed to a maximum recovery rate of 40,000 acre-feet per year until the bank reserves are fully exhausted. Nevada will take Colorado River water from Lake Mead, while Arizona will take less water from the Central Arizona Project. Robert Glennon and Jacob Kavkewitz, *A "Smashing Victory": Was Arizona v. California a Victory for the State of Arizona?*, 4 Ariz. J. Envtl. L. & Pol'y 1, 35 (2013).

IV. STATE RESTRICTIONS ON WATER EXPORT

The commerce clause of the U.S. Constitution, art. I, § 8, cl. 3, empowers Congress to regulate commerce with foreign nations, with Indian tribes, and among the states. The Constitution does not explicitly limit the ability of states to burden commerce, but courts have found "negative implications" from the grant of commerce power to

Congress. This doctrine, known as the Dormant Commerce Clause, forbids states to discriminate against or unreasonably burden interstate commerce, even if Congress has not legislated in the affected area. The doctrine is aimed at preventing protectionism and promoting free trade.

In evaluating state legislation for a potential conflict with the commerce clause, courts consider first whether the statute facially discriminates against nonresidents. "Discriminatory" in this context means differential treatment of in-state and out-of-state economic interests. Discriminatory provisions motivated by economic protectionism are subject to a "virtually *per se* rule of invalidity," which can only be overcome by a showing that there is no other means to advance an important local purpose. United Haulers Ass'n, Inc. v. Oneida-Herkimer Solid Waste Mgmt. Auth., 550 U.S. 330, 337 (2007). If the statute is not discriminatory but has incidental burdens on interstate commerce, it will be upheld unless "the burden imposed on such commerce is clearly excessive in relation to the putative local benefits." Pike v. Bruce Church, Inc., 397 U.S. 137, 142 (1970). This is a balancing test that considers (1) whether a legitimate state interest is present; (2) if so, whether the state interest outweighs any competing national interest; and (3) whether less burdensome alternatives are available to accomplish the state's purpose.

In Sporhase v. Nebraska ex rel. Douglas, 458 U.S. 941 (1982), the Supreme Court invalidated a Nebraska statute that restricted groundwater exports to only those states that allowed reciprocal privileges to Nebraska, finding it unconstitutional on its face. The *Sporhase* opinion reviewed two earlier decisions: Hudson Cnty. Water Co. v. McCarter, 209 U.S. 349 (1908), which held that New Jersey could prohibit the interstate transfer of publicly owned water, and City of Altus v. Carr, 255 F. Supp. 828 (W.D. Tex. 1966), which struck down a Texas law that prohibited the export of groundwater which, under state law, was treated as an article of commerce. The *Sporhase* Court rejected the public ownership theory of *Hudson County*, and concluded that groundwater is an article of commerce subject to the Commerce Clause. It recognized, however, that a state may have a legitimate interest in granting "in times of severe shortage . . . a limited preference for its own citizens" in the utilization of water; thus "[a] demonstrably arid State conceivably might be able to marshal evidence to establish a close means-end relationship between even a total ban on the exportation of water and a purpose to conserve and preserve water." *Id.* at 958. In the years since *Sporhase,* states have had no luck in utilizing this caveat. *See* El Paso v. Reynolds, 597 F. Supp. 694 (D.N.M. 1984) (finding that provisions that gave priority to New Mexico citizens during severe water shortages unlawfully discriminated against interstate commerce).

A unique issue was raised in Tarrant Reg'l Water Dist. v. Herrmann, 133 S. Ct. 2120 (2013). Texas claimed that the Red River Compact allowed it to cross state lines and divert a portion of Oklahoma's allocation of water, and that Oklahoma's attempt to stop Texas violated the Dormant Commerce Clause. Oklahoma law requires out of state diversions to be approved by the Oklahoma Water Resources Board, and prohibits permit issuance when the proposed diversion would prevent Oklahoma from meeting its interstate compact obligations. Oklahoma law also requires that water be "developed to the maximum extend feasible for the benefit of Oklahoma so that out-of-state downstream users will not acquire vested rights therein to the detriment of the citizens of [Oklahoma]." *Id.* at 2129. The Supreme Court found that the Compact did not create cross-border rights as Texas had claimed, and that Congress, by giving its consent to the compact, insulated the state parties from Dormant Commerce Clause challenges for decisions within the purview of the compact. *Id.* at 2137.

V. INTERNATIONAL ALLOCATIONS

Transboundary surface waters and aquifers are of vital importance to the countries and people who share them. Throughout time, upstream nations have sought to control waters originating in their territory. The historic doctrine of "absolute territorial sovereignty," however, has given way to the practical necessity of dealing amicably with neighboring nations. Today, more flexible doctrines of limited territorial sovereignty and equitable apportionment generally govern the resolution of international water disputes, most often by means of treaties.

The United States is party to several water treaties with Canada, including the 1909 Boundary Waters Treaty, the Niagara River Water Diversion Treaty, the Saint Lawrence Treaty, and the Columbia River Treaty. Treaties with Mexico include the 1906 Irrigation Convention and the 1944 Treaty concerning the Colorado and other rivers. Once the federal government enters into a treaty with another nation, it is the "Supreme Law of the Land" under the Constitution; any inconsistent state laws are preempted. Thus, treaties affect the manner and extent to which state-defined rights may be exercised.

A. NOTABLE INTERNATIONAL TREATIES

1. Mexico

The 1944 Treaty for the "Utilization of Waters of the Colorado and Tijuana Rivers and of the Rio Grande," 59 Stat. 1219, was an effort to end years of disagreement between the United States and Mexico over the waters of rivers shared by the two countries. Among other things, it established the U.S.-Mexico International Boundary and Water Commission to administer the treaty and to resolve disputes. The commission deals with allocations of water and projects related to flood control, hydroelectric power, and water quality. The Commission's decisions are recorded in the form of Minutes. Once approved by both governments, Minutes enter into force as binding obligations. For a comprehensive list of Minutes and their text, *see* IBWC, http://www.ibwc.gov/Files/Min180_311.pdf.

Management of the Colorado River proved to be the most troublesome issue addressed by the treaty. The United States, as the upstream nation, initially relied on the "Harmon Doctrine," which is based on a theory of absolute territorial sovereignty. However, pressures from Mexico to receive a share of water from the river grew as uses in Mexico increased.

The 1922 Colorado River Compact among the seven states touching the river required the upper and lower basin states to contribute equally to any future obligation to deliver water to Mexico. The 1944 treaty between the two countries allocated to Mexico a guaranteed annual flow of 1.5 MAF of Colorado River water, to be reduced in the event of a serious drought in the U.S. Negotiations were concluded in haste, and several troublesome ambiguities were glossed over. Most notably, the treaty said nothing about water quality. Later, upstream development caused the river's salinity to increase as more water was consumed and large dams and storage reservoirs were created; less water in the river also meant greater evaporation from storage reservoirs and greater concentrations of salinity. Irrigators added to the problem by returning waters with high concentrations of dissolved solids.

In 1961, the Wellton-Mohawk Irrigation District in Arizona began pumping drainage water from beneath its lands, releasing the saline water into the Colorado River just north of Mexico. Mexico protested, and the U.S. and Mexico reached a series of interim agreements under which the U.S. consented to undertake salinity abatement measures. The final agreement, Minute 242 of the International Boundary Waters Commission, places a ceiling on the increase in the River's salinity below Imperial Dam. The U.S. has since implemented several salinity abatement projects, such as bypassing the Wellton-Mohawk return flows, building projects that intercept other natural and human-made sources of salt, and constructing a huge desalination plant. These federal projects are, in effect, an "insurance policy" against development constraints being imposed on the Colorado River basin states by the salinity control obligation.

However, many water problems with Mexico remain unsettled. For instance, there is currently no system for dividing transboundary groundwater. As unregulated pumping continues, border cities such as El Paso and Juarez find themselves competing for dwindling supplies. The two countries have developed cooperative plans to share scientific information and study the shared aquifers. In addition, the International Boundary Waters Commission was given increased authority over water quality in the border region in Minute 261.

Environmental concerns recently come to the forefront of U.S.-Mexico relations. The once flourishing Colorado River Delta is now only a fraction of its historic size. In 2012, Minute 319 recognized the benefits of providing water for the delta ecosystem, and allocated thousands of acre-feet for a seasonal pulse flow. The U.S. will also contribute $21 million to Mexico for infrastructure and environmental projects.

2. Canada

The Boundary Waters Treaty of 1909, 36 Stat. 2448, revolutionized international relations between the United States and Canada. The treaty established the International Joint Commission, which has the power to resolve water disputes over shared resources between the two countries. Additionally, the Commission serves as a permitting body, which must approve any new projects that would raise the water levels on either side of the international boundary.

One issue concerned storage responsibilities of the two nations and Canada's right to share the benefits obtained by the U.S. from storage in Canada. Large-scale storage was most feasible in Canada, but Canada had no incentive to build it. Initially, the U.S. offered to pay Canada compensation for any damages caused by the flooding of Canadian lands behind the U.S. dams. Canada instead sought a share of the far more valuable downstream benefits to the U.S. from storage, including increased hydroelectric power and protection from floods. After much debate over downstream benefit sharing, in 1964 the two nations agreed to an equal sharing of economic benefits in the Columbia River Treaty. The treaty specifies that Canada will provide 15.5 MAF of storage, the U.S. will operate dams to obtain maximum benefits from the Canadian storage, and the U.S. may (for a price) demand storage releases in emergencies despite Canadian hydropower needs. In addition, Canada agreed not to proceed with its plans to divert water from the Columbia River away from the U.S. and into the Fraser River for power production in Canada. Either country may terminate the Treaty in 2024. This provision may trigger negotiations between the U.S. and Canada to update the Treaty to address future needs for flood control, power generation, and improving ecosystem integrity for salmon and other species.

The boundary waters of the Great Lakes have also been subject to ongoing negotiations over water quality and quantity. In 2005, the eight Great Lakes states signed the Great Lakes-St. Lawrence River Basin Water Resources Compact, which was subsequently ratified by the state legislatures and given congressional consent. As a compact, and not a treaty, it does not bind Canada, but the Provinces of Ontario and Quebec have agreed to participate. The Compact covers surface and groundwater and provides decision-making standards for both withdrawals and consumptive uses. Importantly, it provides that withdrawals and consumptive uses may not cause "significant individual or cumulative adverse impacts to the quantity or quality of the Waters and Water Dependent Natural Resources and the applicable Source Watershed," and must comply with all applicable laws and international agreements. Pub. L. No. 110–342 § 4.11, 122 Stat. 3740.

3. The 1997 Watercourses Convention

In May 2014, Vietnam became the 35th state to ratify the 1997 Watercourses Convention, leading to the convention's entry into force on August 17, 2014. G.A. Res. 229, U.N. Doc. A/51/869 (1997), reprinted in 36 I.L.M. 700 (1997). The Convention, which includes groundwater resources in its definition of "watercourse," embodies several customary water law traditions. Most notably, Article 5 includes the principles of equitable and reasonable utilization, Article 7 requires prevention of significant harm, and Article 12 requires prior notification of planned measures. The Convention also places watercourse states under an obligation to "protect and preserve the ecosystems of international watercourses," and imposes a duty to take appropriate measures to prevent or mitigate conditions that might be harmful to other watercourse states, whether those conditions are man-made or natural. *Id.* arts. 20, 27.

4. International Court of Justice and International Treaties

The International Court of Justice (ICJ) has jurisdiction over international water disputes and has the authority to employ general principles of international law to interpret treaties. This jurisdiction has rarely been invoked, as the ICJ only has jurisdiction in cases where states consent or submit to jurisdiction. ICJ Statute, art. 36, June 26, 1945, 59 Stat. 1055, 1060, 33 U.N.T.S. 993. The decision of the ICJ has no binding force except between the parties and in respect to the particular case brought before it. *Id.* art. 59. The United States rejected the ICJ's compulsory jurisdiction in 1985 and now only recognizes its jurisdiction on a case-by-case basis. *See* Medellin v. Texas, 552 U.S. 491, 500 (2008) (citing Letter from U.S. Dept. of State (Oct. 7, 1985), *reprinted in* 24 I.L.M. 1742 (1985)).

In 1997, the ICJ handed down a decision regarding a treaty between Hungary and Slovakia concerning the construction of the Gabcikovo-Nagymaros dam on the Danube River. Gabcikovo-Nagymaros Project (Hung. v. Slovk.), Judgment, 1993 I.C.J. (Sept. 7, 1997), available at http://www.icj-cij.org/docket. It determined that Hungary's environmental concerns were no excuse for unilaterally terminating the treaty and stopping the project in Slovakia, both because the perceived perils of the project were not sufficiently established when Hungary attempted to terminate the treaty and because terminating the treaty was not the only means Hungary had to safeguard its interests.

In 2010, the ICJ decided a case concerning a treaty between Argentina and Uruguay over use of the Uruguay River. Pulp Mills on the River Uruguay (Arg. v. Uru.), Judgment (Apr. 10, 2010), available at http://www.icj-cij.org/docket/files/135/15877.pdf. It held that Uruguay had breached the treaty by failing to notify and consult with Argentina before constructing a series of pulp mills on the river. Despite the violation, the ICJ found that its declaration of the breach was a sufficient remedy, and that ordering the removal of the mills would be unreasonable. Argentina was unable to prove that Uruguay acted without the due diligence required under the treaty, or that the mills negatively impacted living resources, water quality, or the ecological balance of the river.

B. SUPREMACY OF TREATIES
OVER STATE WATER LAW

Article I, Section 8 of the U.S. Constitution gives Congress the power to regulate foreign commerce. In addition, Article II, Section 2 gives the President power to enter into treaties with the advice and consent of the Senate. Article VI, Section 2 provides for the supremacy of treaties and other federal laws. State law is thus subservient to international treaties. Zschernig v. Miller, 389 U.S. 429, 441 (1968). For example, in Sanitary Dist. of Chicago v. United States, 266 U.S. 405 (1925), the Supreme Court enjoined the City of Chicago from diverting water out of Lake Michigan because the diversions lowered the lake level and were in excess of amounts allowed under the 1909 Boundary Waters Treaty with Canada.

CHAPTER TEN

WATER SERVICE AND SUPPLY ORGANIZATIONS

While much of the study of water law involves the water rights of individual appropriators who obtain their water directly from surface or groundwater appropriations, the majority of domestic and commercial water users, as well as a significant number of agricultural users, receive their water through a public or private water organization. These water organizations come in many different forms and are established under state and federal law.

In the western United States, these organizations historically included the distribution of water through small acequia communities that developed over centuries between indigenous Pueblo communities and Spanish-colonial settlements, some of which are still operational today. From the mid-1800s to the mid-1900s, water organizations were primarily developed in the West to supply the agricultural sector. Today, about 50% of water used for irrigation in the western United States today is controlled and delivered by one form of water organizations or another. In the early 1900s, major federal and state governments began constructing major projects were developed to store and move large quantities of water, sometimes thousands of miles to develop the agricultural sector and provide municipal and industrial water for building cities in the arid West. Such projects include the massive

Central Valley Project in California operated by the U.S. Bureau of Reclamation and the California State Water Project, which is managed by the state's Department of Water Resources.

Today, the majority of water used for municipal, industrial and agricultural purposes is provided by a public, quasi-public, or private water institution ranging in size from small, local water delivery companies to large federal agencies. Examples of such organizations include the Metropolitan Water District in Los Angeles, California, the Southern Nevada Water Authority headquartered in Las Vegas, Nevada and the for-profit American Water headquartered in New Jersey with offices in 15 states. Unless created under federal law, state law governs the creation and operation of these organizations. One or more agencies may be involved in the process of getting water from its source to the end user's tap. That process can include water collection or extraction, transportation, storage, treatment, and distribution.

Water organizations come in many different shapes and forms, and much of the private practice of water law involves representing these entities. Understanding their legal authorities, which can include the authority to condemn land and water, tax local property, and issue tax-exempt bonds to fund operations and infrastructure, is essential. These organizations play a tremendous role in the allocation and management of water across the nation in both riparian and prior appropriation jurisdictions. Moreover, when an individual is part

of a water organization, the individual typically
does not hold the water right. Rather the water
entity holds and manages the water right on behalf
of, or in service to, those that are part of the
organization.

Water organizations reduce the cost and risk of
water development by eliminating the need for
users to develop their own water access and delivery
systems. Organizations can consolidate supplies of
water from multiple sources or water rights, thus
reducing the risk associated with relying solely on a
single supply. Organizations are also able to take
advantage of special legal powers associated with
their formation under state or federal laws.

Private water companies outnumber public water
companies, but public systems are much larger in
terms of the volume of water delivered and the
number of people serviced, especially when public
municipal water suppliers for cities, towns, and
metropolitan areas are included. Most private water
companies are investor owned; a few are "mutuals,"
owned by the water users. Many water companies
are considered public utilities, and are regulated as
such by a state agency. Historically, many private
companies or districts came under criticism for
overcharging, favoring some users over others, and
failing to re-invest or deal with public health crises
through waterborne disease. Recent trends,
however, may be moving back toward private
suppliers as municipalities and local governments
are struggling to afford the cost of maintaining
public facilities. *See* Craig Anthony (Tony) Arnold,

*Privatization of Public Water Services: The States'
Role in Ensuring Public Accountability,* 32 Pepp. L.
Rev. 561 (2005) (noting the growing trend toward
privatization and examining implications of state
laws authorizing public entities to contract with
private firms to provide water services).

The scarcity of available water was a barrier to
settlement of the arid West. Early settlers utilizing
federal public lands settled near streams where
water was readily accessible for use in mining and
agriculture. But as development expanded, the
construction and maintenance costs to deliver water
to lands that did not have readily available and
reliable water supplies posed a substantial obstacle.
Water users first began building ditches to
distribute irrigation water, but the growing number
of farmers soon exhausted the supply of easily
irrigable lands. Those users unable to pay the cost of
building their own ditches formed cooperative
efforts to carry water over considerable distances.
Often they would construct a main canal with
lateral ditches to distribute water to several
farmers. They also built storage facilities to assure
water availability during times of limited supply
and high demand.

The early acequia communities of the Southwest
used communal ditches to irrigate their lands,
providing models for cooperative irrigation efforts.
Some of these ancient acequia community ditches
still operate today in New Mexico. The earliest
settlers to accept and use cooperative methods were
the Mormon pioneers in Utah; their strong social

organization facilitated successful irrigated agriculture in the dry, inhospitable Utah Territory. The early settlers' enterprises evolved into a variety of public and private organizations created to deliver water.

All of these various water organizations are constituted either under state or federal law. In the eastern states, where riparian rights prevailed, it was necessary to pass special laws granting authority to companies and even municipalities selling water to their residents to take water for use on non-riparian lands. In the western United States, the federal government initially, and then the newly constituted state governments adopted laws that facilitated the creation of water organizations to deliver water to users and reduce the risk associated with development.

Under state law, there are five broad categories of water organizations: (1) regulatory bodies; (2) municipal water suppliers; (3) private suppliers; (4) irrigation districts; and (5) state-owned and operated water projects. Under federal law, there are two significant agencies: (1) the Army Corps of Engineers and (2) the Bureau of Reclamation. Each of these is discussed below.

I. STATE WATER ORGANIZATIONS

A. REGULATORY STRUCTURE AT THE STATE LEVEL

State regulatory bodies engage in the administration of water laws, including permitting requirements for water withdrawals, rate-setting, water supply planning, maintenance of water quality and conservation initiatives. These regulatory bodies include state natural resources districts, state engineer offices, water resources departments and local groundwater management districts. It is common for the water allocation function and the water quality function to be separated into different agencies, which can create challenges for managing these two fundamental aspects of water resources. In each state the exact names of the various agencies may differ and the jurisdictional scope of each agency will be defined under state law. The key to understanding the dynamics of water allocation and management within an individual state often lies in first mapping the jurisdiction and inter-relationships of the state agencies. A few examples are provided below, but each state has its own unique structure so it is important to check the details for the accurate terminology and jurisdictional reach of a particular agency.

In Colorado, the Colorado Water Quality Control Commission promulgates water quality standards under the Colorado Water Quality Control Act and assists in administering pollution control measures. The Colorado Division of Water Resources (DWR), also known as the Office of the State Engineer, administers water rights, represents Colorado in interstate water compact proceedings, monitors stream flows and water use, approves construction and repair of dams, and maintains numerous databases of Colorado water information. By

comparison, the Colorado Water Conservation
Board engages in joint federal-state water project
and water use planning and is involved in financing
public and private irrigation projects, while the
Ground Water Commission determines rights and
regulates water use in designated groundwater
basins. For details, *see* Gregory J. Hobbs, Jr.,
Colorado Water Law: An Historical Overview, 1 U.
Denv. Water L. Rev. 1 (1997).

Nebraska has a unique system that splits
governance responsibilities between the state
Department of Natural Resources, which oversees
appropriation permits for surface water uses, the
state Department of Environmental Quality, which
handles water pollution issues, and local natural
resources districts (NRDs), which are responsible for
groundwater management. Neb. Rev. St. § 46–703.
NRDs are authorized to levy certain types of taxes
and to issue bonds to carry out their functions, but
the state constitution prohibits them from levying
property taxes for state-wide purposes. Kiplinger v.
Nebraska Dept. of Natural Resources, 282 Neb. 237,
803 N.W.2d 28 (2011); Garey v. Nebraska Dept. of
Natural Resources, 277 Neb. 149, 759 N.W.2d 919
(2009).

In Oregon, the Oregon Department of
Environmental Quality regulates water quality
through a number of state programs and carries out
the State's obligation under the Clean Water Act.
The Water Resources Commission, appointed by the
Governor, regulates water quantity by setting
policies, adopting rules, and delegating authority to

the Water Resources Department. The Commission develops "basin programs"—place-specific strategies for managing the water resources of the state in a given river basin. In each basin program, the Commission may "classify" allowable beneficial uses, detail preferences for future water use, and even withdraw streams and aquifers from appropriation if the action is necessary to conserve the state's water resources. Or. Rev. Stat § 536.340(1), Or. Rev. Stat. § 536.410(1). With its delegated authorities, the Water Resources Department directly administers and enforces surface and ground water rights.

B. MUNICIPAL WATER COMPANIES/ PUBLIC UTILITIES

Water utilities can be private companies or public organizations who have the right to divert, store, and distribute water to customers by means of constructed infrastructure and facilities. Nearly every state statutorily defines private and public water companies as "public utilities," authorizing them to provide a public service, by statute in nearly every state. Private companies may be corporations, partnerships, or sole proprietorships.

While water itself may be sold as a commodity to the end user, the water organization itself typically holds the water rights. Many western states consider the water to be the property of the state and the company's fees to be for the treatment and delivery of water as well as the maintenance of the facilities. In exchange for an exclusive franchise or monopoly to serve an area, these utilities are subjected to regulation by a state commission or board. Typical regulations require delivery of water to all consumers within a defined service area, non-discrimination among consumers, and submission of major transactions (*e.g.,* sale of assets, mergers, dissolutions, or acquisitions) for approval to the relevant commission or board. The most significant form of control is rate regulation. As with other types of utilities (*e.g.,* electric, telephone, gas), rates are fixed to allow a reasonable profit. A consumer owns no water right as such, but has rights defined under state public utility law.

Unlike other utilities, including electricity, natural gas, and telephone services, municipal water supply continues to be run primarily by public agencies, usually a city or municipality. Laws of most states recognize the authority of cities to distribute water to their residents. A municipality that serves its citizens may be considered a public utility subject to regulation, however, under many state laws, municipal water suppliers are exempt from public utility regulation. *See* West's F.S.A. § 367.022(2) (2002) (exempting water systems owned, operated, managed, or controlled by governmental authorities from utility regulation by the Public Service Commission); Board of County Comm'rs of Arapahoe County v. Denver Bd. of Water Comm'rs, 718 P.2d 235 (Colo. 1986) (a city is a public utility, but is statutorily exempt from Public Utilities Commission regulation); Moongate Water Co., Inc. v. City of Las Cruces, 302 P.3d 405

(N.M. 2013) (small municipalities are not subject to the Public Utilities Act).

Additionally, state statutes or constitutions often authorize municipalities to sidestep certain restraints in water law to carry out their water service responsibilities. For example, in prior appropriation jurisdictions, municipalities may be able to appropriate water in ways and for purposes not available to other users. Thornton v. Farmers Reservoir & Irrigation Co., 194 Colo. 526, 575 P.2d 382 (Colo. 1978) (state legislation could not limit city's constitutional powers by restricting condemnation of water rights to those needed for 15 years in the future). Also in prior appropriation states, cities can secure a water right to meet reasonably anticipated future needs, even if they cannot yet demonstrate a beneficial use for it, despite otherwise applicable laws against speculative uses. Pagosa Area Water & Sanitation Dist. v. Trout Unlimited (Pagosa I), 170 P.3d 307 (Colo. 2007) (explaining the non-speculation doctrine as it applies to governmental water supply agencies in Colorado, and how this differs from private appropriators); Reynolds v. City of Roswell, 99 N.M. 84, 654 P.2d 537 (1982). Likewise, riparian states may allow municipalities (which are not riparians) to obtain and use rights to water on non-riparian lands. To obtain these rights, however, the municipalities will likely have to use their power of condemnation and compensate the affected riparians. See Schroeder v. City of New York, 371 U.S. 208 (1962) (noting that New York law gave the city power to condemn riparian rights, but finding that the posting of notices on trees in the general vicinity of plaintiff's property and the publication of notice in small county newspapers many miles away did not constitute adequate notice required by due process clause). Most states allow cities to use their eminent domain power outside city borders in order to acquire needed water. *See* Matter of Vill. of Poland, 224 A.D.2d 933, 637 N.Y.S.2d 575 (App. Div. 1996) (finding that the village had express statutory authority to condemn a parcel required for water supply even though the parcel was located mostly outside the village's boundaries).

A city can deny or withhold water service on grounds reasonably related to public health and safety. Dateline Builders, Inc. v. City of Santa Rosa, 194 Cal.Rptr. 258 (Ct. App. 1983) (city's denial of sewage service to a developer because development exceeded general growth plan was lawful); Swanson v. Marin Mun. Water Dist., 128 Cal.Rptr. 485, 493 (Ct. App. 1976) (water district properly exercised its discretion to deny services to a new customer in anticipation of a future water shortage, but it may not limit the number of new customers solely to limit development). Refusal to serve must not be arbitrary or malicious.

Municipalities do not have a duty to serve consumers outside their boundaries, even if they have available water to do so. Fulghum v. Town of Selma, 238 N.C. 100, 76 S.E.2d 368 (N.C. 1953). But if they regularly do so, the majority rule provides that serving outsiders must be done on reasonable and nondiscriminatory terms. City of Texarkana v.

Wiggins, 151 Tex. 100, 246 S.W.2d 622 (1952); Platt
v. Town of Torre, 949 P.2d 325 (Utah 1997). This
does not mean that the same rates must be charged
if, for example, the municipality incurs higher costs
in delivering services to the area in question.
Charging differential rates based solely on the fact
that the water users' location is outside of the
municipal boundary is not a reasonable motive.

Courts have split when the municipality's
primary goal in denying service is to limit local
development. In some cases, development moratoria
pending the municipality's good faith efforts to
expand service capacity have been upheld. *See, e.g.,*
Swanson, 128 Cal.Rptr. at 493; Kaplan v. Clear
Lake City Water Auth., 794 F.2d 1059 (5th Cir.
1986). However, other courts have ruled that
communities may not use water connection
moratoria simply to slow growth. *See, e.g.,* In re
Centex Homes, LLC, 411 N.J. Super. 244, 985 A.2d
649 (App. Div. 2009); Robinson v. City of Boulder,
190 Colo. 357, 547 P.2d 228 (1976), *overruled on*
other grounds, Board of County Com'rs of Arapahoe
County v. Denver Bd. of Water Com'rs, 718 P.2d 235
(Colo. 1986). For discussion, *see infra* Section VI.

Landowners have sometimes argued that the
denial of service that leaves land with no economic
value has resulted in a regulatory taking of property
that is compensable under the Fifth Amendment.
See, e.g., Lockary v. Kayfetz, 917 F.2d 1150 (9th Cir.
1990). Such a finding would depend on rather
difficult proof that the plaintiff's land had no
economically viable use without the water service,

not that there was a mere reduction in property value. *Id.* at 1155. However, *Lockary* was a test case, and the plaintiffs ultimately dropped the suit. By the same token, the denial of a service provider's abstract right to serve a community (not actual service) is not compensable as a taking. Moongate Water Co., Inc. v. City of Las Cruces, 302 P.3d 405, 412 (N.M. 2013).

Some states authorize the creation of special districts, variously named, to deal with problems of procuring water supply outside the scope of irrigation. They are akin to "irrigation districts" that develop and transport water, and then distribute it to a number of water companies, municipalities, and large consumers. Colorado uses "water and sanitation districts" extensively as vehicles for providing water and sewage infrastructure for housing developments. The developer forms the district and then turns over future responsibility for operating it to the homeowners. California has passed enabling legislation for the creation of special districts, known as municipal water districts and replenishment districts. These districts manage imported surface waters and local groundwater resources by administering rights determined in basin-wide adjudications, limiting pumping to safe annual yield rates, importing supplies, and preventing salt water intrusion.

II. PRIVATE WATER SUPPLIERS AUTHORIZED BY STATE LAW

A. CARRIER DITCH COMPANIES

Private, for-profit companies, known as carrier ditch companies, achieved early popularity during settlement of the West. As people settled farther from water sources, profit-seeking investors allowed carrier ditch companies to finance construction of irrigation works to deliver water to individual users. The relationship between the water user and the carrier ditch company is contractual. The company typically holds the legal interest in the appropriation, and in turn carries the water for sale to consumers who have contracted with the company. As with other types of appropriators, if the company fails to ensure continued beneficial use of the water, the company could lose its appropriation. City of Westminster v. Broomfield, 769 P.2d 490, 493 (Colo. 1989).

Nearly all carrier ditch companies failed because of infeasibility due to bad financial planning, engineering errors, or because projected uses did not materialize. Farmers opted for "free" groundwater, chose to dry-land farm rather than pay for water delivery, or were too fearful that these companies would take advantage of their natural monopoly and charge excessive fees. Although a few carrier ditch companies still operate in Texas, California, and Colorado, many investors recouped some of their money by selling their interests to other entities that transformed these failing companies, reorganizing them as irrigation districts or non-profit mutual ditch companies.

B. MUTUAL DITCH/WATER COMPANIES

Mutual ditches are distinct from carrier ditches in that the shareholders of mutual ditch companies are the sole owners of both the ditch and the diversion works, and they share the costs of operation without profit. In contrast, carrier ditches are entitled to reasonable returns on their investments over and above their costs. Left Hand Ditch Co. v. Hill, 933 P.2d 1, 3 (Colo. 1997).

Mutual water companies exist to serve their shareholders, essentially acting as a cooperative water venture. Some states regulate them as public utilities, but most do not because they are nonprofit corporations or associations owned by the water users themselves, in theory making regulation less necessary.

Typically, irrigators who want to jointly construct ditches to deliver water to their fields organize a non-profit company if allowed under state law. These non-profit water companies are not usually permitted to sell water to anyone but their own shareholders, nor may they be compelled to do so. Water rights of a mutual company are generally held by the shareholders themselves, the quantity of rights being evidenced by shares of stock as opposed to contracts as with a carrier ditch company. *See* East Jordan Irr. Co. v. Morgan, 860 P.2d 310, 311 (Utah 1993); Jacobucci v. District Court, 189 Colo. 380, 541 P.2d 667, 670–72 (1975). Bylaws usually restrict the shareholders to asserting and changing their water rights through the company. *East Jordan Irrig. Co.*, 860 P.2d at 321–322.

The greatest growth of mutual ditch companies occurred after western state constitutions (Arizona, Colorado, New Mexico, Utah, and Wyoming) exempted ditches, canals, and the associated works owned by mutuals from state property taxation. In addition, some mutual ditch companies were formed to contract with the federal government for reclamation project water.

C. IRRIGATION COMPANIES

As early as the 1860s, state laws authorized the formation of irrigation companies. These companies were formed in several ways, including: by holders of water rights who transferred their rights to the newly formed companies in exchange for stock; by joint owners of a ditch who traded their interests for stock, expanded the facilities, and sold stock to others; by land developers who conveyed a share of stock along with each acre sold; and by local water users after bankruptcy of for-profit companies serving the area.

A number of these quasi-private companies were formed under the 1894 Carey Act, 43 U.S.C.A. § 641, which awarded one million acres of arid federal lands to any western state that would cause the land to be irrigated and settled. Often this goal could be accomplished by encouraging the formation of companies to build irrigation works. The lands were then sold by the state to individuals who bought shares in a mutual ditch or irrigation company formed to operate the irrigation works. Like carrier companies, many Carey Act corporations failed because they could not repay capital costs; some reorganized as irrigation districts. For an assessment of Carey Act corporations in Idaho, *see* John A. Rosholt, *The Carey Act,* 53 Advocate (Idaho) 24, 26 (2010).

1. Financing

Irrigation and mutual ditch companies secure revenue almost exclusively from water users (*i.e.,* by user fees and stock assessments), but some issue bonds secured by irrigation works or shareholders' lands. Assessments of stock (to pay operating costs and bond amortization) may be enforced by withholding water for non-payment. Henderson v. Kirby Ditch Co., 373 P.2d 591 (Wyo. 1962). Shares may not be subject to securities laws because the shares represent a contractual arrangement among shareholders for distribution and use of jointly owned water rather than a medium of investment in an entity organized for profit. *See* Salt Lake City Corp. v. Cahoon Irrigation Co., 879 P.2d 248, 252 (Utah 1994).

2. Ownership of Rights

Companies typically issue shares of stock that represent the quantum of the shareholder's right to receive water. There is no obligation to serve members of the public in the service area who are not shareholders in the company. Thayer v.

California Development Co., 164 Cal. 117, 128 P. 21
(Cal. 1912). The company holds the water rights and
represents its users against other appropriators, but
each shareholder is a beneficial owner of the
individual water rights. High Plains A & M, LLC v.
S. Colorado Water Conservancy Dist., 189 Colo. 380,
120 P.3d 710, 723 (Colo. 2005). *See* Jacobucci v.
District Court, 541 P.2d 667 (Colo. 1975)
(shareholders in a mutual ditch company are real
parties in interest and should be joined in an action
to condemn water rights of the company).

3. Transfers

Holding water rights as shares of ditch company
stock facilitates transfers among shareholders of the
company. Transfers of the right to the delivery of
water may be accomplished by a transfer of the
stock certificate and recordation on the books of the
company. John D. Musick, Jr., *Reweave the Gordian
Knot: Water Futures, Water Marketing, and Western
Water Mythology*, 35 RMMLF-INST 22 (1989).
Moreover, stock in mutual companies is commonly
considered appurtenant to (and thus passes with)
land that is described on the face of the stock
certificate. *See, e.g.,* Locke v. Yorba Irr. Co., 35 Cal.
2d 205, 217 P.2d 425 (1950). In fact, no paper shares
exist in some small companies because rights simply
pass with the land. However, contrary presumptions
may be imposed by statute. For example, a Utah
statute provides that irrigation company stock does
not pass with the land without an express
declaration by the transferor that the stock is

appurtenant. Abbott v. Christensen, 660 P.2d 254, 256 (Utah 1983) (citing U.C.A., 1953, § 73–1–10).

To protect the company against having to make uneconomical water deliveries to distant users, shares may be made inseverably appurtenant to land or transfers may be subject to approval under provisions in the articles of incorporation or bylaws. The company itself may restrict transferability, *e.g.*, by requiring the company's consent. Riverside Land Co. v. Jarvis, 174 Cal. 316, 163 P. 54 (Cal. 1917). California has recognized the right of companies to prohibit transfers to another ditch or to lands not served by an irrigation district. Consolidated People's Ditch Co. v. Foothill Ditch Co., 205 Cal. 54, 269 P. 915 (Cal. 1928); Jenison v. Redfield, 149 Cal. 500, 87 P. 62 (Cal. 1906). Although Colorado has allowed transfers if the transferor continues to bear a proper share of maintenance costs, Wadsworth Ditch Co. v. Brown, 39 Colo. 57, 88 P. 1060 (Colo. 1907), a bylaw limitation on changing the place of use to lands within a single county has been upheld. Fort Lyon Canal Co. v. Catlin Canal Co., 642 P.2d 501 (Colo. 1982). If a change in the place or type of use results in harm to others, the transfer may be restricted. City of Boulder v. Boulder and Left Hand Ditch Co., 192 Colo. 219, 557 P.2d 1182 (Colo. 1976). Transfers from agricultural shareholders to urban interests have also been restricted. *See* Mark Squillace, *Water Transfers for a Changing Climate,* 53 Nat. Resources J. 55, 108 (2013) (noting that "most ditch companies' water rights were granted strictly for agricultural use over a relatively small geographic area that may not include significant

urban centers," and advocating reform to allow
excess distribution capacity to be made available to
third parties to promote efficient transfers).

4. Priorities

As a rule, no priorities exist among shareholders
in the same water supply, so each gets a
proportionate share when supplies are insufficient
for all users. In other words, the rights of mutual
ditch company shareholders are conditioned by the
amount of water available and by the number of
shareholders entitled to use the water. Great
Western Sugar Co. v. Jackson Lake Reservoir &
Irrigation Co., 681 P.2d 484, 491–492 (Colo. 1984).
This is true among shareholders of the same class.
But if users convey water rights to a mutual
company with different priority dates, the company
can issue different classes of stock related to the
priorities and with different burdens and privileges,
including priority in a water distribution schedule.
Thus, a holder of shares evidencing a high priority
may be assessed at a higher rate because the high
priority confers greater benefits. Robinson v. Booth-
Orchard Grove Ditch Co., 31 P.2d 487 (Colo. 1934).

5. Regulation

A mutual ditch or irrigation company may be, but
is not always, treated as a public utility subject to
regulation. If incorporated, mutual ditch and water
companies are subject to general state statutes
applicable to private business corporations. Colo.
Rev. Stat. Ann. § 7–42–101; N.D. Cent. Code § 61–

13–02; and Wyo. Stat. Ann. § 17–12–101. Some states incorporate mutual ditch companies under special statutes relating to nonprofit corporations. Utah Code Ann. § 16–6–1 (repealed); and Wyo. Stat. Ann. § 17–6–101 (repealed); Okla. Stat. Ann. 18 § 863. Public utility status usually results if water service is provided to users other than shareholders. *See, e.g.,* Yucaipa Water Co. No. 1 v. Public Utilities Comm'n, 54 Cal.2d 823, 357 P.2d 295 (Cal. 1960).

III. QUASI-PUBLIC IRRIGATION DISTRICTS

Irrigation districts are formed under special provisions of state law and enjoy a governmental or quasi-governmental status, yet most have a certain degree of legal autonomy that exempts them from taxation and public accountability. They are somewhat akin to local government entities, but are governed by a board of directors elected by local residents that distribute water within a geographical boundary. Some also perform functions such as electric power generation, drainage, and flood control. Together with mutual companies, irrigation districts distribute about half of all water used in the West, giving them significant economic power and political influence. Squillace, *Water Transfers, supra,* at 65.

Irrigation districts exist under several names, including conservancy district, conservation district, reclamation district, water control district, and fresh water supply district. Although they have many different organizational forms and powers, the distribution of irrigation water is common to each. As John Leshy has stated, the form of these districts is "rather like snowflakes, each with its own unique form designed to meet the needs and interests of each region and its water users." Special Water Districts—The Historical Background in Special Water Districts; Challenges for the Future, 11, 23 (James Corbridge ed., 1983).

A. FORMATION OF DISTRICTS

Beginning with California's Wright Act in 1887, all western states passed laws authorizing formation of irrigation districts. The statutes define the organizational form, powers, and purposes of the districts. Typically, they provide for formation upon petition of local landowners or electors. Sometimes, a state court can act upon the petition after a hearing; often, an election is required. Some types of districts may be formed by an act of the legislature without voter or landowner consent.

Reluctant property owners can be forced to participate in a district project for the benefit of an area when the project is feasible only with full participation. Once enough voters have elected to form a district, everyone within the district's jurisdiction is subject to its authority, including its powers of taxation and eminent domain. In Fallbrook Irrigation Dist. v. Bradley, 164 U.S. 112 (1896), the Supreme Court concluded that irrigation was a "public use" and thus the state could use its powers of taxation and eminent domain to bring water to the land. Since this decision, objecting landowners have been uniformly unsuccessful in challenging formation of districts. *See*, e.g., People ex rel. Rogers v. Letford, 102 Colo. 284, 79 P.2d 274 (Colo. 1938) (inclusion and taxation of non-irrigable lands with an adequate water supply and within incorporated cities did not violate due process clause).

B. BENEFITS OF DISTRICTS

Possessing power to levy assessments against all property within their boundaries, irrigation districts historically provided an effective way to finance irrigation works. They helped solve problems of capital formation that had beset agriculture in much of the arid West. Benefits of being a governmental entity, such as tax exemption and the ability to raise capital by selling tax exempt bonds, motivated people to form districts. Irrigation districts may also enjoy governmental immunity from suit. *See* Love v. Harlem Irr. Dist., 245 Mont. 443, 802 P.2d 611 (1990); Krenning v. Heart Mountain Irr. Dist., 200 P.3d 774, 781 (Wyo. 2009). However, where a district is formed for a governmental purpose, such as irrigation supply, and then engages in other economic activities, it may lose status. 26 U.S.C. §§ 115, 501(c)(12). *Cf.* Hohokam Irr. & Drainage Dist. v. Arizona Pub. Serv. Co., 204 Ariz. 394, 64 P.3d 836 (2003) (irrigation district had the power to sell electricity purchased on wholesale market because revenues were committed to reducing the cost of providing irrigation water to the district's member-farmers).

The most powerful motive behind the creation of most irrigation districts was to provide a vehicle for participation in federal reclamation projects. The federal reclamation program began around the turn of the century. It subsidizes water projects benefiting much of the irrigated agriculture of the western United States. *See infra* Section V.B. At first, the government intended to operate the projects directly, but a 1922 statute authorized contracts with irrigation districts to manage, operate, and maintain federal projects upon their completion and to distribute the water from them. The districts usually must agree to repay project costs directly attributable to irrigation benefits, which is accomplished by imposing assessments and user charges.

C. OWNERSHIP OF WATER RIGHTS

Irrigation districts, not their constituents, own the water rights they exercise. The users' rights are essentially contractual. Fort Vannoy Irr. Dist. v. Water Res. Comm'n, 345 Or. 56, 93, 188 P.3d 277, 299 (2008). *But see* Bryant v. Yellen, 447 U.S. 352 (1980) (Boulder Canyon Project Act requiring satisfaction of "present perfected rights" preserved individual users' rights under state law).

D. ELECTION OF BOARDS

Board members of irrigation districts are usually elected, though some states have different types of districts that provide for appointment of members (*e.g.,* "conservancy districts"). The right to vote in a

district election may be in each elector, each
landowner, or weighted according to the amount of
acreage owned. The Supreme Court held that
irrigation district voting is not subject to the one-
person, one-vote principle established under the
Equal Protection Clause of the Fourteenth
amendment to the Constitution. Ball v. James, 451
U.S. 355 (1981).

In *Ball*, a multipurpose district limited voting
privileges to landowners and allowed one vote per
acre of owned land. The plaintiffs, who each owned
less than one acre of land, alleged that the district's
broad powers (to condemn property and sell tax-
exempt bonds) and non-irrigation purposes
(providing hydroelectric power to metropolitan
Phoenix) affected non-landowning voters sufficiently
to require that they be given voting rights. The
Court disagreed, following the rule of Salyer Land
Co. v. Tulare Lake Basin Water Storage District,
410 U.S. 719 (1973), that certain districts may limit
the voting franchise to landowners. The Court in
Ball decided the voting scheme was constitutional
because it had a "reasonable relationship" to its
statutory objective; the district could rationally limit
the vote to landowners and weigh the votes
depending on acreage because it reflected the risks
each landowner could incur. As a result, a few large
landowners can control decision-making in some
districts.

Ball and *Salyer* have been distinguished in cases
where the particular nature of a water district is not
directly linked with landownership. Where the

decisions of a district can substantially affect non-landowner residents, laws disenfranchising the non-landowner residents by denying them a vote in district elections may be constitutionally suspect. *See* Bjornestad v. Hulse, 281 Cal.Rptr. 548, 229 Cal.App.3d 1568 (Ct. App. 1991) (examining constitutional concerns raised by non-landowner residents who were concerned with and paid for a district's provision of water and sanitation services).

E. FINANCIAL ASPECTS

Irrigation districts may be empowered to raise revenue by assessing property, imposing taxes, charging users for water, and marketing other services. *See* Hohokam Irr. & Drainage Dist., 64 P.3d 842 (Ariz. 2003) (irrigation district may sell electricity in order to raise revenues and defray costs of providing water). The state law that authorizes the district's creation specifies which of these powers the district can utilize. For instance, in Colorado "conservancy districts" may tax all lands in their boundaries, but "irrigation districts" are limited to taxing irrigable lands. It is not necessary that taxes be in proportion to the benefits received. Millis v. Board of County Comm'rs of Larimer County, 626 P.2d 652 (Colo. 1981).

State laws may allow assessments to be levied upon all land in a district based upon the value of the land or upon land classifications (*e.g.*, tract size or type of soil). Some districts impose a flat assessment for each acre of land. In addition to taxes and assessments, user fees are sometimes charged for water actually used.

Bonds may be issued by virtually all irrigation districts for purposes authorized by statute, including securing indebtedness and financing district operations. Judith Basin Land Co. v. Fergus Cnty., Mont., 50 F.2d 792 (9th Cir. 1931); Sullivan v. Blakesley, 350 Wyo. 73, 246 P. 918 (Wyo. 1926). In fact, this governmental authority stimulated the formation of most early districts.

F. FUNCTIONS

Irrigation districts began as rather simple organizations whose sole purpose was to deliver irrigation water, but today many districts are involved in other activities such as hydroelectric power generation, operation of recreation facilities, drainage, flood control, sanitation, and municipal and industrial water supply. An example is the Salt River Project Agricultural Improvement and Power District, serving metropolitan Phoenix, Arizona. *Ball,* 451 U.S. 355; City of Mesa v. Salt River Project Agr. Imp. & Power Dist., 92 Ariz. 91, 373 P.2d 722 (1962). This district derives ninety-eight percent of its total revenue from power sales. Naturally, multiple purposes complicate administration of irrigation districts and may lead to conflicts among different constituencies. Irrigation users may feel, with some justification, that their interests are subordinated in disregard of the original legislative purpose for creating irrigation districts.

Although irrigation districts are commonly spoken of as "political subdivisions of state government," they have both public and private attributes, enjoying many benefits of both. Their public character gives them tax-exempt status, the power to tax, and freedom from regulatory agency interference, yet their private character allows them entrepreneurial flexibility and a degree of independence from electors. In *Ball, supra,* the Supreme Court recognized that the Salt River Project Agricultural Improvement and Power District was a "governmental entity," but also was a "business enterprise" in its dealings with power consumers. As the federal government's willingness to finance costly reclamation projects declines and the functions of irrigation districts move farther from their original purposes, many state legislatures may reappraise the place of the districts in political and economic life.

IV. STATE OWNED AND OPERATED WATER PROJECTS

Though playing a much smaller role than the federal government, a few states play a part in acquiring and distributing water supplies. The California State Water Project (SWP), in particular, plays a significant role in providing Californians with water for municipal, industrial, and agricultural uses. After being approved in 1959, the SWP has developed extensive pumping and power plants, reservoirs, lakes, storage tanks, canals, tunnels, and pipelines to deliver water to 29 water suppliers and over 23 million people. To deliver water to southern California, the SWP pumps water 2,000 feet and moves it through the California Aqueduct over the Tehachapi Mountains, making it the highest single water lift in the world. Today, the SWP bills itself as the nation's largest publicly built and operated water and power development and delivery system. California Dept. of Water Resources, *California State Water Project Today* (2014), http://www.water.ca.gov/swp/swptoday.cfm. *See* Marc Reisner, Cadillac Desert: The American West and Its Disappearing Water (Penguin 1993).

Unlike the subsidies and tax revenues required by most federal projects, state projects are mostly financed by water payments and revenue bonds. Close coordination between a state and federal project is sometimes necessary. The SWP shares some facilities with the federal Central Valley Project (CVP), and water can be interchanged between SWP and CVP canals to meet peak demands. *See, e.g.,* San Luis & Delta-Mendota Water Auth. v. Jewell, 747 F.3d 581 (9th Cir. 2014) (upholding the U.S. Fish and Wildlife Service's biological opinion on CVP's and SWP's impacts to federally listed smelt); United States v. State Water Res. Control Bd., 182 Cal. App. 3d 82, 97, 227 Cal. Rptr. 161, 165 (Cal. Ct. App. 1986) (assessing water quality implications of appropriation permits for various units of CVP and SWP).

V. FEDERAL ORGANIZATIONS

Two agencies dominate the playing field of federal institutional water law: the U.S. Army Corps of

Engineers (USACE) and the Department of Interior's Bureau of Reclamation. As federal actors, the decision making processes of both agencies must satisfy all applicable law, including, most notably, the National Environmental Policy At (NEPA), 42 U.S.C. § 4332 and the Endangered Species Act (ESA) 16 U.S.C. §§ 1536, 1538. These environmental provisions play an increasingly important role in the procedures and outcomes of both agencies. This section, however, focuses on provisions directly related to the authorizing legislation for these federal organizations and the allocation of water resources within the projects managed by these agencies.

A. ARMY CORPS OF ENGINEERS

The USACE has broad Congressional authority to investigate, construct, and operate water projects as part of its mission to strengthen the Nation's security by maintaining America's infrastructure in and around navigable waters. An array of federal statutes provides the USACE with significant operational discretion regarding navigational concerns and flood control. *See, e.g.,* Rivers and Harbors Act of 1899, 33 U.S.C. §§ 401, 403, 540; Water Resources Development Act, 42 U.S.C. § 1962, 2309a; Flood Control Act, 33 U.S.C. § 701a. Each individual USACE project also has numerous specific authorizations that provide further details on the purposes and scope of that particular project. *See, e.g.,* the Willamette Basin Project in Oregon: Flood Control Act of 1936 § 5 (authorizing bank protection works); Flood Control Act of 1938 § 2, 33

U.S.C. § 701–1(b) (approving the general comprehensive plan for flood control and navigation); Flood Control Act of 1944 § 7, 33 U.S.C. § 709 (assigning the Secretary of War the duty to prescribe regulations for the project's operations).

The USACE is accountable for employing both engineering and economics to promote navigation, control floods, providing recreational opportunities, protect water quality, and store water supplies. *See* 33 U.S.C. 701a (stating the "Federal Government should improve or participate in the improvement of navigable waters or their tributaries, including watersheds thereof, for flood-control purposes if the benefits to whomsoever they may accrue are in excess of the estimated costs"). The USACE also plays a large part in providing hydroelectric power and numerous other water development activities. Additionally, the USACE conducts a research and development program dedicated to water resources. USACE Institute for Water Resources, *Mission*, http://www.iwr.usace.army.mil/About/Missionand Vision.aspx (visited Aug. 18, 2014).

In fulfilling its duty to regulate and protect the Nation's water resources, balanced with the need for sustainable development, the USACE evaluates Clean Water Act § 404 permits and determines whether to allow activities that result in dredging or placement of fill materials in the nation's waters and wetlands. Permits may be denied if the project is not water-dependent, and they may be vetoed by the U.S. Environmental Protection Agency if they "will have an unacceptable adverse effect on

municipal water supplies, shellfish beds and fishery
areas (including spawning and breeding areas),
wildlife, or recreational areas." 33 U.S.C. § 1344(c).
Once a valid permit has been issued, it is the
USACE's duty to enforce the terms of the permit
and impose penalties to those who are not in
compliance. 33 U.S.C. §§ 1319, 1344(n).

B. BUREAU OF RECLAMATION

To facilitate westward expansion, Congress
passed the Reclamation Act of 1902, 43 U.S.C.
§§ 371 *et seq.*, authorizing the federal government to
construct irrigation projects to provide a more
reliable source of water. Farmers who utilized the
irrigated land were expected to pay off the
government's debt, interest-free, over a period of
years. 43 U.S.C. §§ 461, 485h(e). Subsidized by
general tax revenues, the Bureau of Reclamation
embarked on an ambitious program of water
development throughout the 17 western states,
constructing hundreds of dams and power plants
and miles of canals. Its mission today "is to manage,
develop, and protect water and related resources in
an environmentally and economically sound manner
in the interest of the American public." Bureau of
Reclamation, *Mission Statement* (2009), http://www.
usbr.gov/main/about/mission.html. Like the
USACE, each individual Reclamation Project has
specific authorizing legislation that builds upon the
basic foundation of the Reclamation Act of 1902 and
sets forth specific direction with regard to that
particular project. See, e.g. Boulder Canyon Project
Act of 1928, 43 U.S.C. § 617 et seq.; Central Valley

Project Improvement Act, 106 Stat. 4706 (1992). In many of the specific legislative enactments in the mid-to late 1900s, Congress specifically mandated purposes beyond simply the storage and delivery of irrigation water. For example, the 1992 Central Valley Improvement Act (CVPIA) mandates changes in management practices of California's Central Valley Project to protect, restore, and enhance fish and wildlife habitat.

Except when state law is directly in conflict with a provision of the federal reclamation law, the Reclamation Act requires federal compliance with state water law. California v. United States, 438 U.S. 645 (1978). State law generally governs disputes between federal reclamation interests and state-sanctioned water rights, provided there is no conflict with federal law. Wild Fish Conservancy v. Jewell, 730 F.3d 791, 799 (9th Cir. 2013); In re Application of Denver By Board of Water Comm'rs, 935 F.2d 1143, 1151 (10th Cir. 1991). Questions involving conflict between state water law and federal law in Reclamation projects have often arisen in the context of application of the Endangered Species Act to Reclamation projects. See, e.g., Natural Res. Def. Council v. Houston, 146 F.3d 1118 (9th Cir. 1998); Klamath Water Users Protective Ass'n v. Patterson, 204 F.3d 1206 (9th Cir. 1999); Rio Grande Silvery Minnow v. Keys, 333 F.3d 1109 (10th Cir. 2003). Another example of this dynamic between state and federal law comes from the Central Valley Project in California where Reclamation is required to operate their facilities in conformity with California water law, based on

Section 8 of the Reclamation Act. Whether
Reclamation can renew certain water supply
contracts under federal law when the delivery of the
water is alleged to threaten the existence of the
delta smelt and thus violate the ESA is the subject
of ongoing litigation. Natural Resource Defense
Council v. Salazar, 686 F.3d 1092 (2012).

Although it was successful in fostering westward
expansion, the reclamation program, in most areas,
has not recovered the full cost of development. *See*
San Luis Unit Food Producers v. United States, 772
F. Supp. 2d 1210, 1251 (E.D. Cal. 2011) (rejecting
argument that the Bureau violated its statutory
duties by failing to collect water revenues because
statutes did not instruct it to recoup costs in any
particular time sequence or amount per annum, let
alone the maximum possible speed), *aff'd*, 709 F.3d
798 (9th Cir. 2013). Water users within Bureau
projects continue to repay the capital investments,
but often at subsidized or reduced rates. For
example, the Bureau contracts with local water
districts, and charges operating and maintenance
costs that go towards the initial costs of its original
water development, but these contracts often don't
generate funds sufficient to cover the up-front costs
of project development. 43 U.S.C. §§ 390aa et seq.

A great deal of controversy surrounds the
environmental degradation caused by reclamation
projects, such as reducing water levels in lakes,
jeopardizing fish and other aquatic and riparian
species, increasing salinity, and allowing
contaminants to enter waterbodies. The Bureau

tries to address these concerns, as well as limited water supplies and increasing demands, through water conservation, water recycling and reuse initiatives, and operational changes. *See* Reed D. Benson, *Environmental Issues in the Allocation and Management of Western Interstate Rivers,* 24 Ind. Int'l & Comp. L. Rev. 183 (2014).

VI. THE INTERFACE OF WATER ORGANIZATIONS AND LAND USE PLANNING ORGANIZATIONS

Historically, land use planners did not consider water scarcity as a barrier to urban growth. As a practical matter, however, access to clean, reliable water supplies is a limiting factor, not just in the arid West but also in the more populous areas of the East. Developers have traditionally incorporated the cost of new roads, utilities, schools, and other infrastructure into their decisions; it only makes sense that water supplies should be factored into those decisions as well. Some states have started to incorporate the reality of water scarcity into their development plans. Several have started to enact "assured water supply" laws, essentially requiring developers to show that an adequate water supply exists for new communities before being granted approval for such expansion.

Arizona's program mandates that in areas where water is being over-drafted, developers must obtain a certificate of assured water supply from the Director of Water Resources. The Arizona legislature defined "assured water supply" as "sufficient ground water, surface water, or effluent that will be continuously available to satisfy the water needs of a proposed use for at least one hundred years." Ariz. Rev. Stat. § 45–576.07(A).

In the 1990's, California passed a law requiring developers to show sufficient water supply for their development projects. Developers were able to find ways around the legislation, so in 2001 the law was strengthened. The stricter law required a Water Supply Assessment for developments of over 500 or more residential units (or the equivalent) to prove that the project would have sufficient water for a minimum of twenty years. The stricter law also restricted local cities and counties from allowing developers access to construction permits unless sufficient water was available.

Some states require land use planners and water agencies to assess the expected water demand and supply as a condition of approval for municipal water permits or permit extension in an attempt to better integrate water and land-use planning. This encourages local land-use entities to update their plans with new development and population increases, and connect that data to available water supplies. *See, e.g.,* Or. Admin. R. 690–086–0010 et seq. (Water Management and Conservation Plans in Oregon). *See also Guidelines for the Preparation of Planning Documents for Developing Community Water System Projects* (2001), http://www.oregon. gov/owrd/docs/guidelines_2001.pdf (visited Oct. 29, 2014). Oregon Dept. of Land Conservation and Dev., *Oregon's Statewide Planning Goals and Guidelines*

(2010), http://www.oregon.gov/owrd/docs/guidelines_
2001.pdf (describing Oregon's Statewide Planning
Goals including Goal 5—assessing natural
resources, which include groundwater resources—
and Goal 11 Public Facilities, which include water
systems).

Some water districts have adopted moratoria,
stopping the supply of water for new development
altogether. These districts have broad authority to
do so when water is limited. *See* Bldg. Indus. Ass'n
v. Marin Mun. Water Dist., 235 Cal. App. 3d 1641, 1
Cal. Rptr. 2d 625 (Cal. App. 1st Dist. 1991); *Cf.*
Swanson v. Marin Municipal Water District, 56
Cal.App.3d 512, 128 Cal. Rptr. 485 (Ct. App. 1976)
(holding that the water district had a continuing
obligation to use all reasonable efforts to augment
its available water supply in order to meet
increasing demands, not intending for the moratoria
to continue indefinitely.

INDEX

References are to Pages

RESTATEMENT (SECOND) OF TORTS